Sex, Nation and Dissent in Irish Writing

Sex, Nation and Dissent in Irish Writing

edited by

ÉIBHEAR WALSHE

CORK UNIVERSITY PRESS

First published in 1997 by
Cork University Press
University College
Cork
Ireland

British Library Cataloguing in Publication Data
A CIP catalogue record for this book is available from
the British Library.

ISBN 1 85918 013 2 hardcover
1 85918 014 0 paperback

Typeset by Tower Books of Ballincollig, Co. Cork
Printed by ColourBooks, Baldoyle, Co. Dublin

Contents

Acknowledgements

In researching and commissioning this essay collection, I was helped and supported in many ways and I wish to thank those involved. The Department of English, UCC and the Arts Faculty aided my research with a travel grant and an Arts Faculty Research Fund grant and I wish to thank them.

Emma Donoghue first gave me the impetus for this collection and I thank her for her stimulating conversations and for her friendship. Lance Pettitt was also a very important source of constructive advice and insight, as was Barra O Seaghdha and I am very grateful to both of them. I would also like to express my gratitude to the RTÉ archives, the staff of the National Library of Ireland, The British Library, Colin Smythe, David Alderson, Anne Fogarty, Roz Cowman, Pat Coughlan and Mary Breen, all of whom gave me much needed practical help and advice with the essays. Thank you also to my friends Donald O'Driscoll, Ciaran Wallace, Sheila Quinn, Brian Doherty, Barry Stokes, and John Calnan, for hospitality during my study leave and I am also indebted to Kieran Rose for his useful work on the history of law reform in Ireland. Finally I would like to thank David Norris, firstly for his help and support with this collection, and secondly for making almost everything possible for the rest of us.

List of Contributors

David Alderson has taught at the Universities of Northumbria and Newcastle. He is currently lecturer in literature at Staffordshire University.

Mary Breen teaches in the Department of English at University College, Cork. Her research interests include gender and Irish writing and the work of James Stephens, George Moore and Kate O'Brien. She is co-ordinator of women's studies in UCC.

Patricia Coughlan lectures in the Department of English at University College, Cork. She has edited a collection of essays, *Spenser and Ireland* (1989), and published articles on seventeenth-century English writings about Ireland and many aspects of Anglo-Irish literature, including Mangan, Maturin, Le Fanu, representations of femininity in modern Irish writers, and narrative in Beckett.

Roz Cowman lecures in creative writing, literature and women's studies in the Department of Adult and Continuing Education at University College, Cork. She is also a poet. Her first collection, *The Goose Herd*, was published in 1989. She won the Patrick Kavanagh award in 1985.

Colin Cruise was born in Bangor, Co. Down and was educated in Belfast. He teaches art history at Staffordshire University and has recently contributed to two books on art and culture: *The Gendered Object* (Manchester University Press, 1995) and *Reframing Pre-Raphaelitism* (Scolar Press, 1995).

Emma Donoghue playwright, novelist and broadcaster, recently completed a PhD on eighteenth-century writers' friendships. Her play, *I Know My Own Heart*, was produced in 1993 and her novels *Stir-Fry* and *Hood* appeared in 1994 and 1995. A history, *Passions Between Women: British Lesbian Culture 1668-1801*, was published in 1993.

Anne Fogarty lectures in the Department of English, University College, Dublin. She has published articles on Renaissance literature and women's writing. She is currently working on a study of sixteenth-century colonial writing on Ireland, entitled *Colonial Plots: Reading History in Edmund Spenser's the Faerie Queene*.

David Grant was born in Dublin in 1959 and educated in Belfast and at Cambridge. He has been publicity manager of the Belfast Festival, managing editor of *Theatre Ireland* and programme director of the Dublin Theatre Festival. He is currently associate director of the Lyric Theatre, Belfast.

Declan Kiberd lectures in English at University College, Dublin. He is the author of *Anglo-Irish Attitudes* and *Men and Feminism in Modern Literature*. He has edited *An Crann faoi Bhláth — The Flowering Tree: Irish Poetry with Verse Translations* and *The Students' Annotated Ulysses*. His most recent publication is the highly acclaimed *Inventing Ireland*.

Lillis Ó Laoire lectures in Irish at the University of Limerick. He is an award-winning singer in the traditional Irish style and a critic. He wrote the introduction to Cathal Ó Searcaigh's poetry collection *Home Coming*, published in 1993.

Lance Pettitt is senior lecturer in Irish-studies at St Mary's University College, London. He has published articles in *Irish Studies Review*, *The Sunday Tribune* and *South Atlantic Quarterly* and an essay on the TV film, 'The Treaty' in *Ireland and Cultural Theory* (Macmillan, forthcoming 1997). He is editor of the *BAIS Newsletter*.

Éibhear Walshe lectures in the Department of English at University College, Cork. His doctoral research is in contemporary Irish drama and his published work includes examinations of the Irish novel, gender and writing, and dissidence in Irish literture. He edited *Ordinary People Dancing: Essays on Kate O'Brien*, which appeared in 1993.

Introduction
Sex, Nation and Dissent

ÉIBHEAR WALSHE

There remained in the minds of many people until recently a doubt as
to whether the terms 'Irish' and 'Homosexual' were not mutually exclusive.

DAVID NORRIS[1]

This collection of essays is, primarily, an exploration of the homoerotic
as an imaginative element in Irish writing, and for the first time situates
the lesbian and gay perspective in Irish critical studies. The interest of
this study lies in its identification of those Irish writers whose imaginative
concerns centre around the homoerotic and in its consideration of the
ways in which they represent alternate sexual identities. In this connection, I believe that, as Jonathan Dollimore argues,

> homosexuality provides a history remarkably illuminating for the issues
> of marginality and power upon which contemporary debates, cultural,
> psychoanalytical and literary, have been converging.[2]

In no sense is this a comprehensive survey of Irish lesbian and gay writing,
and neither does it claim that such writing constitutes a coherent tradition.
Therefore the title *Sex, Nation and Dissent* operates as a set of questions
and interrogations into these texts rather than as direct assertions. In the
case of each writer discussed here, 'sex' is always homoerotic or same-sex
desire, but 'nation' varies from Irish to Anglo-Irish to Ulster unionist to
English masquerading as Irish, and 'dissent' is never automatic for the sexually 'other' Irish writer. It is tempting but inaccurate to reconstruct O'Brien,

1

Somerville and Ross, MacLiammoir, etc. in the light of late twentieth-century lesbian and gay identity — rebel desire is no guarantee of political radicalism. Rather I see the simple act of identifying such a perspective as important in itself because, as Elaine Showalter argues in the context of women's writing, 'When women are studied as a group, their history and experience reveal patterns which are almost impossible to perceive if they are studied only in relation to male writers.'[3]

The parallel experience of feminism in the academy is illuminating within this context. Much of the distrust of lesbian and gay studies as a valid academic pursuit is a distrust also experienced by feminism over the past ten years or so in Ireland. Indeed, the critic Gayle Rubin links feminism and lesbian and gay studies explicitly when she asserts: 'The suppression of the homosexual component of human sexuality is a product of the same system whose rules and relations oppress women.'[4] (Significantly, in Irish universities, lesbian and gay studies began in women's studies courses.) A further drawback in lesbian and gay literary studies is that many critical readings of the texts have been misleading and unclear. Eve Kosofsky Sedgwick perceptively describes this lack of clear engagement: 'As each individual story begins in the isolation of queer childhood, we compulsorily and excruciatingly misrecognise ourselves.'[5] The aim in this collection is to explore this critical position within the context of Irish studies and to present a number of perspectives on Irish texts, engaging directly with issues of same-sex desire and lesbian and gay identity.

This collection takes as its starting-point two moments in Irish history: the criminalisation of same-sex desire in Britain and Ireland by means of the Labouchere Amendment (1885), and the construction of the political and cultural project of the Celtic Revival with Yeats's first collection of poetry (1889). Literary production became an arena for the assertion of national difference and the play, and the poem and the pamphlet were all deployed as part of a widespread and continuing resistance to the colonial. Irish writers like Yeats, seeking to free Ireland from the control of the colonising power, sought an autonomous self-image in opposition to the imperial culture.

However, a lesbian and gay presence within any national literature troubles privileged formations of what traditionally constituted 'woman' and 'man'. Specifically, it troubled and complicated what could be termed 'masculinist nationalism' in both British and Irish cultural discourse. In his essay 'Momentary Pleasures: Wilde and English Virtue' David Alderson examines Wilde's deployment of Celticism as part of a wider programme of aesthetic subversion. Alderson contends that 'the racial character of the Celt became another means of legitimating his hostility to English moralism', and focuses on Wilde's disruption of English Protestant puritanism. He interprets Wilde's aesthetic as 'an affront to the dominant sense of an English national character, one which prided itself on its own uprightness'. Thus, in writings like Wilde's, the homosexual identity could unsettle and make problematic established notions of 'manliness', 'womanliness' and 'national identity'. (Wilde is an important source of inspiration for Irish representations of the homoerotic, as my essay on Michael MacLiammoir, and Declan Kiberd's essay on Elizabeth Bowen's *The Last September* demonstrate.)

In particular, the primacy of a particular form of masculinist nationalism in Irish writing led, inevitably, to the suppression of a number of counter-discourses (i.e. feminism, radical socialism, lesbianism, the homoerotic). In Ireland, where religious and judicial codes refused legitimacy and public space for same-sex desire, any lesbian or gay sensibility could only have existed in contradistinction to mainstream cultural discourse. That it *did* exist is one of the arguments presented in this volume, and the purpose of this study is to present investigations into the effect of unlicensed and divergent sexual identity on certain Irish creative imaginations.

As with any cultural discourse, Irish nationalism had a distinct lesbian and gay presence. Irish lesbian and gay writing, in common with most other Irish writing, evinces a connection and a preoccupation with politicised Irish nationalism. One could argue that Irish lesbians and gay men were not exactly excluded from the formulation of cultural revolu- tion — quite the opposite, in fact. Quite close to the source of national pride and identity — the creation of an Irish republic — there also existed traces of lesbian and gay writing.

For example, Roger Casement, knighted for his services to the British Foreign Office, was converted to Irish republicanism after his experiences of Belgian atrocities in the Congo. His involvement with the Easter Rising of 1916 led to his arrest and treason trial, during which, his diaries, the so-called 'Black Diaries', were circulated by the British government. These diaries were a frank and, in many ways, disarmingly honest account of Casement's daily life, with daily expenditure and sexual encounters all accounted for in a businesslike manner. The strategy was to ensure his conviction and execution by exposing the 'black' and unwholesome nature of his sexuality. Casement was subsequently executed, and since then con- troversy has raged over the authenticity of these diaries, some Irish republicans feeling unhappy with the notion that one of the leading figures of the 1916 Rising might also have preferred and enjoyed (as the diaries tell us) sex with other men.

Eva Gore-Booth, sister of revolutionary and government minister, Con- stance Gore-Booth, was another voice from these revolutionary circles. (As with any study of Irish writing, Ascendancy literature is a key interest in this collection, with essays on Gore-Booth, Bowen, Somerville and Ross, and

Molly Keane.) Eva Gore-Booth found expression for a lesbian sensibility through the dominant tropes of the Celtic Revival. Emma Donoghue, in her essay 'How could I fear and hold thee by the hand?', argues persuasively that 'without ever casting herself as a political or sexual dissident, this woman quietly subverted her whole heritage'. Donoghue sees this subversion as a 'feminising and a lesbianising' of the poetry of Gore-Booth's friend and admirer Yeats in poems such as her 1905 work, 'The Perilous Light':

> The Eternal Beauty Smiled at me
> From the long lily's curve'd form,
> She laughed in the wave of the sea,
> She flashed on white wings through the storm.
> In the bulb of a daffodil
> She made a joyful little stir,
> And the white cabin on the hill
> Was my heart's home because of her.[6]

Crucially, others of these revolutionaries were just as capable of expressing same-sex desire, as is shown by the following poem, 'Little Lad of the Tricks' by Pádraic Pearse:

> There is a fragrance in your kiss
> that I have not found yet
> in the kisses of women
> or in the honey of their bodies.
>
> Lad of the grey eyes,
> that flush in thy cheek
> would be white with dread of me
> could you read my secrets.
>
> He who has my secrets
> is not fit to touch you:
> is that not a pitiful thing,
> little lad of the tricks.[7]

This poem, first published in Irish in 1909 without controversy, was then published in English in 1914 and caused great consternation amongst Pearse's friends, alarmed at his explicit articulation of homoerotic desire. Since then many efforts have been made to explain away and make safe this frank and unequivocally sexual poem. Quite clearly the text reflects a moment of striking honesty for the poet, where his disturbing 'secret', his homoerotic attraction to male beauty, is being confronted. Yet Ruth Dudley Edwards, in her biography of Pearse, writes:

> He knew nothing of homosexuality. When he wrote of beauty, he was inspired by the descriptions, so frequent and so elaborate, of characters

in the old Irish sagas . . . . Pearse was an innocent . . . his lifetime quest for innocence, purity, chastity and perfection had blinded him to the instincts reflected in his poetry.[8]

It seems to me that Pearse was anything but blind to the instincts reflected in his poetry; yet his biographer, however sympathetic and thorough in other ways, feels impelled to contain the explosive nature of this particular poem.

It is useful to compare this kind of biographical revisionism with Ulick O'Connor's forthright assessment of another, later, republican writer, Brendan Behan:

He was also known to have bisexual tastes. John Ryan remembers he was quite open about this, defining the type he liked best: 'clean-skinned, fresh lads'. And Desmond MacNamara remembers that he would usually add to the statement 'preferably working-class'. Brendan used to boast about it almost as if it was a new discovery he had made at borstal. He would refer to it mockingly as his 'Hellenism'. 'Brendan would get up on anything in those years', an IRA man put it to me. Another IRA officer remembers the shock he got when walking down Fleet Street after an IRA meeting in Jury's Hotel in the centre of Dublin and came across Brendan in an alley kissing a man they both knew well, a composer with left-wing sympathies, though he was not a member of the IRA.[9]

After independence there was something of a difference. Post-colonial countries like Ireland have particular difficulty with the real presence of the homoerotic. Colonialism itself generates a gendered power relationship and, inevitably, casts the colonising power as masculine and dominant and the colonised as feminine and passive. One of the consequences of this resistance to the imperial was an increased unease with the shifting and 'unstable' nature of sexual difference, and so a narrowing of gender hierarchies ensues. In Irish cultural discourse, silencing sexual difference became imperative because of a supposed link between homosexuality and enfeebled, 'feminised' masculinity. The post-colonial struggle to escape the influence of the colonising power became a struggle to escape the gendered relation of male coloniser to female colonised. Therefore the post-colonial culture could not permit any public, ideological acknowledgement of the actuality of the sexually 'other'. The post-colonial theorist Ashis Nandy, in his study *The Intimate Enemy*,[10] argues convincingly that the colonial relation is inevitably and profoundly gendered. In this particular context, his thesis could be extended in this manner: the homosexual is assumed to be a transgendered 'pretend' woman and the lesbian to be an unsexed 'pretend' man, and thus lesbian and gay identity is acutely threatening and unsettling within any post-colonial culture. For a nation 'coming of age', the lesbian and gay sensibilty must be edited out, shut up.

Ireland provides a striking example of this kind of post-colonial censorship. (For a full historical account of gay law reform in Ireland see Kieran Rose's excellent *Diverse Communities: The Evolution of Lesbian and Gay Politics in Ireland*.[11]) In his study, 'Homosexual People and the Christian Churches in Ireland'[12] David Norris argues persuasively that the history of prosecution of same-sex desire in Ireland is intertwined with the history of colonisation. The moment when homosexuality stopped being a sin and became a crime took place in 1540 under Henry VIII, as part of a repressive Tudor policy of centralisation and colonisation. British law was responsible for the continued criminalisation of Irish gay men, but, ironically, it was de Valera's pro-family, pro-Catholic Irish constitution of 1937 that allowed a court case to be taken by David Norris against the Irish government for discrimination on the grounds of sexual orientation.

A distrust of the 'unmanly' homosexual resulted in a complete obliteration of the homoerotic from within nationalist discourse. In much the same way, Connolly's socialism and the Gore-Booths' feminism became subaltern in the Irish Free State. The tenuous nature of national identity necessitated a denial of difference, with its incipient threat of dissidence, and thus same-sex desire continued to be criminalised in Ireland long after Britain had decriminalised homosexual acts between consenting adults. The notion of criminality is central here, as Joe Bristow recounts, in calling into existence a modernist perception of same-sex desire between men:

> The homosexual was only a homosexual by the last decade of the nineteenth century . . . . The Labouchere amendment arose largely in reponse to the numerous homosexual scandals of the early 1880s. Its aim was not so much to prohibit same-sex relations between adult males but more to deter the corruption of youth — both young men and young women. Again, the law sought to obscure sexuality — of any kind — from public view . . . . By the time of the Wilde trials, it was clear that the Labouchere amendment had diverted attention from the prime objectives of protecting girls to focus instead on the private world of male sexuality — a sexuality which, if at one time seemed as natural in its lustfulness, was now particularly intriguing because of its (potential) wrong choice of subject. In 1885 what was most familiar about men and sex (they were bestial) had become, ten years later, most strange (they were perverse).[13]

For Irish lesbians, the issue of identity was more complicated because of the lack of a public identity, even a criminalised one. There was more than one attempt (1895 and 1922) to make lesbianism a crime, but this never reached the statute books, and so Irish lesbians were both outside the law and at the same time rendered invisible by lack of official recognition or even condemnation. It is significant that the only Irish lesbian writer directy banned by the Irish government (a banning that led to a parliamentary debate) was Kate O'Brien, and this was because her censored novel referred to male homoerotic desire rather than female desire. This lack of an official identity for Irish lesbians can be seen as something of a mixed blessing, with very little cultural visibility but a greater freedom from prosecution and a consequent imaginative freedom and openness. In relation to this, Anne Fogarty argues, in her essay 'The Ear of the Other: Dissident Voices in Kate O'Brien and Mary Dorcey' that these two Irish lesbian writers 'find themselves in a position to critique those aspects of modern Irish identity which they find confining and anti-democratic'.

Considering lesbian and gay writing in Irish literature, I am not merely highlighting a forgotten and marginal formation. Rather I would argue, as does Jonathan Dollimore in his book *Sexual Dissidence*, that the real threat in homoerotic desire is not difference but sameness. At the core of masculinist panic at the spectre of homosexual desire is the sense of reciprocity, the fear that, as Dollimore puts it, 'civilisation actually depends upon that which it is usually thought to be incompatible with'.[14] Thus, to locate the presence of a homosexual sensibility in Irish writing is also to locate crucial areas of concern and anxiety within so-called mainstream writing. As Ed Cohen argues, what distinguished the emergence of 'the Homosexual' during the second half of the nineteenth century is the fact that at this time it became inseparable and literally incomprehensible from its 'normal' twin, 'the Heterosexual'.[15]

Each of these essays explores a particular writer's representation of sexual identity or the presence of the homoerotic within a genre. At this point, I wish to address the crucial area of biography/autobiography. Public visibility is revealing within this context, as biographers grapple to explain away and make safe the presence of sexual otherness in the lives and writings of their subjects.

Wilde said that it was Judas who always writes the biography, but if Judas was the betrayer of truths, then many of the biographers of Irish writers lack Judas's frankness. An unease with the homoerotic, a need to absolve their subject from such a charge, indeed an essentialist notion that sexuality is only expressed through sexual acts — all of these seem to place the biographer under an obligation to explain away all subversive desires. Actual proof of same-sex acts seems to be required before a biographer will allow for a lesbian or gay sensibility. A plea of physical and emotional innocence, unnecessary if the writer were dealing with a heterosexual subject, is heard again and again in these otherwise perceptive and scholarly biographies. The biographer's anxiety to defend the subject against the charge of active same-sex relationships is undermined by the fact that so many of these writers were perfectly capable of articulating such attachments eloquently and unambiguously. Perhaps this need to defend reflects more on the culture that the biographer is writing for than on any personal reservation on the part of the biographer.

I want to deal here with two biographers who defend their subjects against the charge of sexual 'abnormality' even when these very subjects had been unequivocal in their representation of same-sex relationships. In her essay, 'Lost Time: The Smell and Taste of Castle T', Roz Cowman analyses the 'unique bond of love' between the two Ascendancy writers, Edith Somerville and Martin Ross (Violet Martin), a relationship much debated by various biographers. For example, one biographer, Gifford Lewis, in her excellent social history, *Somerville and Ross: The World of the Irish RM*, rightly attacks another, Maurice Collis, for his attempts to stigmatise Edith Somerville as a pathological invert. 'In his biography of Somerville and Ross, Maurice Collis stated that Edith was a man-hater who was incapable of normal sexual love',[16] Lewis observes, and she goes on to expose the misogyny and homophobia of Collis's view of Somerville. Lewis correctly stressed Somerville's close and loving relations with brothers, cousins and male friends, as well as her balanced and healthy female friendships. In defending Somerville from antagonistic misrepresentation by normalising her, Lewis also sanitises and makes acceptable Somerville's lifelong partnership with Violet Martin. Lewis makes the point that 'it was Ethel Smyth who forced Edith to state that this *best of friendships* had not expressed itself in sensual affection' [my emphasis].[17] This phrase, 'the best of friendships' falls far short of Somerville's own description of her first summer with Martin, written after Martin's death and almost forty years after their first meeting:

> It [was] . . . the beginning of a new era. For most boys and girls, the varying, yet invariable, flirtations and emotional episodes of youth are resolved and composed by marriage. To Martin and to me was opened another way and the flowering of both our lives was when we met each other.[18]

Edith Somerville has no difficulty in naming her relationship with Martin clearly, a lifelong partnership and a union; yet her biographer, however clear-sighted and committed, finds herself unable to do the same. In her essay in this collection Roz Cowman analyses their construction of class and race in the Irish RM novels and concludes that all potential threat of sexual 'difference' in their own relationship is contained and neutralised. Throughout their fiction the erotic is profoundly absent from all human relations, displaced onto the landscape and fleetingly glimpsed in their Dionysian portrayal of the hunt.

This creation of an idealised landscape to offset a displaced eroticism also occurs in the fiction of the Ulster novelist, Forrest Reid. In his essay

'Error and Eros: The Fiction of Forrest Reid as a Defence of Homosexuality'
Colin Cruise comments: 'It must always be difficult to label him as a dissident; indeed, one might more easily see him as trying to harmonise
elements in himself and in society. . . . Rather than taking issue with the
status quo, Reid might seem to be conservative, involving himself in a re-
Edenising of society.' For writers of this period, the homoerotic was often
made safe through such strategies of idealisation.

Another example of a difficulty with lesbian or bisexual experience in
the life of a writer can be seen in Victoria Glendinning's excellent study,
Elizabeth Bowen: Portrait of a Writer.[19] Written in 1977, there is a clear
sense of reticence in this perceptive and sympathetic biography, a feeling
that the biographer is being restrained by the societal mores of her time.
Glendinning considers Bowen's attitude towards lesbianism, linking it with
Bowen's own troubled sense of gender identity: 'If, as a few of her friends
thought, she ever worried about herself as a woman, it was very much
because she wanted to be one. She was a man's woman, not from fellow-
feeling but because she was very fond of men.'[20] However, as Glendinning
expands on Bowen's attitudes towards sexual difference, a more direct sense
of connection emerges, more direct than initially allowed by Glendinning. 'She [Bowen] put these relationships into her books, from the first
novel on. . . . In the Twenties and Thirties lesbianism and homosexuality
were novelist's topics. "If I write a story about two women called 'Barren
Love,'" she wrote to A. E. Coppard in 1932, "shall I bring the G. Cockerel
Press in for the tail end of the homosexuality ramp?"'[21]

As Patricia Coughlan argues in her essay 'Women and Desire in the Work
of Elizabeth Bowen', Bowen's representation of the homoerotic is clear, direct
and wide-ranging, based on her own observations of same-sex relationships; but in the following passage it is difficult to separate Glendinning's
voice from Bowen's:

> There were always women who loved Elizabeth, or pairs of women to
> whom she was an accepting, unquestioning friend. What irked her most
> about lesbian relationships, as in any relationships, was their characteristic-
> ally 'claggy' quality — 'claggy' was her expression for anything over-
> analytical, sentimental, sublimated, mawkish, maudlin. She would discuss
> the troubles of lesbian lovers with a bracing, matter-of-fact, kindly exaspera-
> tion, deploring 'muffishness' and 'squashishness'. Once, in Kerry, she heard
> the young girls of the house announce that they were having such trouble
> with their boyfriends that they had decided to be 'toms'. Elizabeth and
> Eddy Sackville-West told them that on no account must they be toms:
> 'Always', said Elizabeth, 'having terrible rows about bracelets.'[22]

It is unclear whether Bowen herself used this word 'claggy' when speaking of lesbian relationships, or whether Glendinning borrows it from

elsewhere and applies it to this particular topic. As it eventually emerges, Bowen's own experience of same-sex relations was as follows: 'Back in 1936, when May Sarton was very young, May had fallen in love with Elizabeth. From their confidential talks, May understood (as she told in her autobiography) that earlier in her life [Elizabeth] had loved at least one woman, but I gathered that this period was over. Now her love affairs were with men.'[23]

Mary Breen, in her essay on another Ascendancy novelist, Molly Keane, argues that the homoerotic is also presented directly, unequivocally, and on equal terms with heterosexual desire, in what Breen terms a 'democracy of desire'. Thus, novels like *Devoted Ladies* (1934) and *Good Behaviour* (1981) are radical in their frank presentation of lesbian and gay protagonists. However, these protagonists, threatening in the strength and confidence of their homoerotic desires, are eventually removed through death and self-destruction, reflecting a deep-seated cultural fear of same-sex desire.

The culture that felt itself threatened and destabilised by the homoerotic made any public visibility a dangerous thing, and the contrast between the careers of Kate O'Brien and Michael MacLiammoir provides us with a telling example of constricting societal mores in twentieth-century Ireland. Already in *Ordinary People Dancing*[24] I have described the unease and discomfort provoked by O'Brien's writing. As Ailbhe Smyth comments, 'I think of Kate O'Brien's work as an island surrounded by a monochromatic sea of sexless hetero-reality.'[25] Yet this island was buffeted by many tempests of censorship and marginalisation. In this context, her very public punishment for giving voice to the homoerotic is worth recounting, as she was the most visible sexually dissident writer of her society.

O'Brien's fictive representation of sexual dissidence found an imaginative locus in Spain and she chose a Spanish setting for her first banned novel, *Mary Lavelle* (1936). Therefore when the Spanish Civil War broke out, O'Brien had little difficulty in recognising Franco and his Nationalists for what they were, enemies of personal liberty and of all she loved of Spain's courageous, solitary heart. Her attack on Franco took the from of a travelogue, *Farewell Spain* (1937), an imaginative journey, returning to all her best-loved places, historical figures, paintings and music, and wresting them from the appropriating clutches of Franco. She fought him with the only weapons available to her, memory, evocation and proud, possessive love. For her pains, she was barred from entering Spain by Franco when he emerged victorious at the end of the civil war. *Farewell Spain* was censored there and in Ireland, and O'Brien was now silenced in two Catholic, paternalistic cultures.

However, her novel *That Lady* (1946), perhaps her most accomplished novel, can be seen as an ultimate repudiation of all of these attempts to marginalise and silence her. An historical novel set in sixteenth-century Spain, *That Lady* takes the real historical personage Ana de Mendoza as protagonist and sets her up in opposition to her authoritarian ruler, Philip II. Philip, in accord with his belief in the absolute power of the monarch, interferes in a matter of private morality concerning Ana, an influential noblewoman and his lifelong friend. The central scene in the novel contains Ana's countering of Philip's authoritarianism and her counter-assertion of personal liberty:

> There have been, Philip, as long as I can remember, thoughts and even acts in that private life, which, presented to the world, would seem to injure this or that. If I do wrong in it, that wrong is between me and heaven. But here below, so long as I don't try to change it into public life, I insist that I own it.[26]

O'Brien, with her highly controversial profile as censored writer, was perfectly aware that she was articulating a notion of sexual self-determination that would profoundly disturb Irish state control of morality. Consequently the state sought to isolate her. Her later life, the loss of earnings from her writing, her loss of critical and popular interest, her novels, one by one, going out of print, the lack of interest in her last, most openly lesbian novel *As Music and Splendour* (1958, *still* out of print!) — all of these facts connect to a state desire to silence her fiction.

In sharp contrast, her friend Michael MacLiammoir found a place of cultural centrality in Ireland — from the 1930s until the late 1970s. A leading figure in Irish theatre for over forty years, an actor, dramatist, writer and stage designer, Michael MacLiammoir was also, with his partner, Hilton Edwards, Ireland's only publicly acknowledged homosexual. A strikingly beautiful man in his youth, MacLiammoir kept his beauty alive (Dorian-like) with paint and powder, and his face was a familiar, exotic sight on the streets of Dublin, the avenues of St Stephen's Green, and in the drawing-rooms of the Shelbourne and Gresham hotels. As he grew older, his ever more persistent attempts to remain glamorous and star-like were remarkably successful and helped him to achieve the status of a public figure. When MacLiammoir died in 1978, the President of Ireland attended his funeral and offered his condolences to Hilton Edwards, as chief mourner — and this in a state which criminalised homosexuality and continued to do so for another fifteen years. So successful was MacLiammoir in his creation of a (fictitious) Cork childhood that he now forms part of a parade of famous Cork sons and daughters pictured in the lobby of a popular Cork hotel.

As I have recounted in my essay, MacLiammoir and Edwards founded the Dublin Gate Theatre, a theatre dedicated to the presentation of

European experimental drama to an Abbey Theatre-dominated city. Among other innovations, they presented the first Irish production of Wilde's *Salome*. (Wilde was to be an emblematic figure in MacLiammoir's creative life.) But, as I argue in my essay, MacLiammoir accommodated himself within Irish culture by being less direct and more circumspect than O'Brien, never actually naming his own sexuality. Theatre was the domain that MacLiammoir inhabited, and because of its high public visibility, there was a high degree of screening and self-editing.

*   *   *

> It's well to remember that there is little that is unique about the Irish [gay] experience in this area, apart from the unusually homogeneous nature of our society and the tacit assumption that to be Irish is to be white, heterosexual and Roman Catholic.
>
> DAVID NORRIS [27]

Contemporary Irish lesbian and gay culture has been experiencing a distinct sense of empowerment with the recent decriminalisation of homosexual relations in Ireland, and this collection of essays seeks to reclaim and identify this vital lesbian and gay imagination. It is the movement away from criminality and towards self-assertion that this collection charts, the movement from the (apparently) necessary association of the homoerotic with disease, violence and death, towards the legitimisation of same-sex desire. Political change is often paralleled by the emergence of a confident literary presence, and in Ireland one can observe an appropriation of Irish literary, linguistic and dramatic forms to express a particular Irish lesbian and gay identity. This living presence of a gay sensibility within contemporary Irish culture is found in dramas like Frank McGuinness's *Observe the Sons of Ulster Marching towards the Somme*, collections like Mary Dorcey's *A Noise from the Woodshed*, David Marcus's *Alternate Loves*, Kieran Rose's *Diverse Communities*, Emma Donoghue's novels and plays, and the 'Out-to Play' lesbian and gay theatre project. All of these creative projects reflect a new confidence, a claiming of space and of expression for the contemporary Irish lesbian and gay imagination. In particular, in his essay 'Tangles' David Grant recounts the process of devising a contemporary drama on the subject of gay identity with Wet Paint, the Dublin-based Theatre-in-Education company.

Above all, it is in the poetry of the Irish-language writer Cathal Ó Searcaigh that we find a striking reflection of the imaginative idiom of the contemporary Irish gay imagination. In his essay on Ó Searcaigh, 'The Indelible Mark of Cain', Lillis Ó Laoire discusses 'Ó Searcaigh's openly gay stance and his world's ambivalance to it' and explores his deployment of the poetic resources of the Irish language, often the whipping-post of reproachful cultural nationalism.

Contemporary republican thinking has begun to acknowledge vital links between sex, nation and dissent. In an article entitled 'Invisible Comrades: Gays and Lesbians in the Struggle' in the magazine *The Captive Voice*, Brendi McClenaghan, an openly gay republican prisoner in Long Kesh, makes the following call:

> It is now time, indeed long past time, to open up debate among republicans on the issue of gays and lesbians, our oppression and its causes and on our right to be visible equal partners. I believe that national liberation by its very nature incorporates gay/lesbian liberation as an integral part and it is only through open debate leading to an understanding of gay/lesbian experience that our equality in struggle can be a reality.[28]

In this connection, Lance Pettitt, in his examination of Neil Jordan's *The Crying Game* in his essay on contemporary Irish lesbian and gay film-making in the present volume, makes the point that 'If the republican movement represents a repressed "other" within the political establishment's official version of Irish history and culture, then gay republicanism offers an image of a double oppression.'

In putting this collection together, a distinct difference between lesbian and gay writing has emerged. Men writing from or about a sexually dissident perspective have occupied a more public space, especially in theatre, and have therefore tended to be more circumspect in their representation of sexual otherness. Women, on the other hand, have occupied a different literary space, using letters and diaries, and then novels and short stories, to develop a lesbian sensibility, often more radical and subversive but less widely known. Ailbhe Smyth makes the point

> It would be hard to overestimate either the difficulty or the importance of Mary Dorcey's writing against the heterosexual grain when, for all practical purposes, during the 1980s she was a lone voice. 'It was not in the light we lived but in the spaces in between — in the darkness.'[29]

Compare Dorcey's lone voice, 'writing against the heterosexual grain' in the 1980s, with dramas like Frank McGuinness's *Innocence*, Aodhan Madden's *Sea Urchins*, and the Abbey Theatre productions of plays like *The Gentle Island* and *The Death and Resurrection of Mr Roche*, all dramas where the homoerotic inevitably leads to death, mutilation and disempowerment.

In arranging this collection of essays, I follow a chronological order and confine the scope of the essays from the late nineteenth century to the present. My aim is to open up a context for further research and, in addition, to celebrate the establishment of lesbian and gay studies within Irish writing.

Notes and References

1   David Norris, 'Homosexual People and the Christian Churches in Ireland', *The Crane Bag*, v, no. 2 (1981), p. 31.

2   Dollimore, *Sexual Dissidence: Augustine to Wilde, Freud to Foucault*, Oxford University Press, p. 32.

3   Quoted in Anne Weekes Owen, *Irish Women: An Uncharted Tradition*, Lexington: University of Kentucky Press, 1990, p. 9.

4   Gayle Rubin, 'The Traffic in Women' in *Towards an Anthology of Women*, New York: Monthly Review Press, 1975, pp. 157-210.

5   Eve Kosofsky Sedgwick, *Between Men: English Literature and Male Homosocial Desire*, New York: Colombia University Press, 1985, p. lx.

6   Eva Gore-Booth, *Collected Poems*, London: Longmans, 1929, p. 214.

7   Pádraic Pearse, *Plays, Stories, Poems*, Dublin & London: Maunsel, 1917, pp. 316-7.

8   Ruth Dudley Edwards, *Patrick Pearse: The Triumph of Failure*, London: Faber, 1977, pp. 126-8.

9   Ulick O'Connor, *Brendan Behan*, London: Coronet, 1972, p. 96.

10   Ashis Nandy, *The Intimate Enemy*, New Delhi: Oxford University Press, 1984.

11   Kieran Rose, *Diverse Communities*, Cork University Press, 1994.

12   Norris, op. cit.

13   Joseph Bristow, 'Dorian Gray and Gross Indecency' in idem (ed.), *Sexual Sameness*, London: Routledge, 1992, pp. 49-50.

14   Jonathan Dollimore, 'The Cultural Politics of Perversion' in Bristow (ed.), *Sexual Sameness*, p. 9.

15   Ed Cohen, *Talk on the Wilde Side*, London: Routledge, 1993.

16   Gifford Lewis, *Somerville and Ross: The World of the Irish RM*, London: Penguin, 1985, p. 233.

17   Ibid., p. 238.

18   Edith Œ Somerville and Martin Ross, *Irish Memories*, London: Longmans, 1925, p. 128.

19   Victoria Glendinning, *Elizabeth Bowen: Portrait of a Writer*, London: Phoenix, 1977.

20   Ibid., p. 190.

21   Ibid.

22   Ibid., p. 192.

23   Ibid.

24   Eibhear Walshe (ed.), *Ordinary People Dancing: Essays on Kate O'Brien*, Cork University Press, 1993.

25   Ailbhe Smyth, Foreword to *Alternative Loves*, ed. David Marcus, Dublin: Martello, 1994, p. 5.

26   Kate O'Brien, *That Lady*, London: Heinneman, 1946, p. 236.

27   Norris, op. cit., p. 31.

28 Brendi McClenaghan, 'Invisible Comrades: Gays and Lesbians in the Struggle' in *The Captive Voice* (*An Glór Gafa*), iii, no. 3 (winter 1991).

29 Smyth, op. cit., p. 6.

Some of the material in this essay was previously published in 'Sexing the Shamrock' in *Critical Survey* (1996) and is reproduced here by permission of Oxford University Press.

1 'How could I fear and hold thee by the hand?'

The Poetry of Eva Gore-Booth

EMMA DONOGHUE

A couple of years ago all I knew of Eva Gore-Booth (1870–1926) was that she was one of the two sisters in the W. B. Yeats poem my mother used to quote:

> The light of evening, Lissadell,
> Great windows open to the south,
> Two girls in silk kimonos, both
> Beautiful, one a gazelle.[1]

Eva, it turned out, was the gazelle. The other sister, Countess Constance Markievicz, needed no animal emblem, being famous for doing such public things as setting her Citizen Army to dig trenches in Stephen's Green in 1916, and becoming the first woman to be elected an MP. But all most people know about Eva is that Yeats thought she and her sister made a pretty picture.

I spent my teenage years murmuring over the early work of W. B. Yeats; his Maud Gonne poems were a special consolation in my unspoken passion for a girl in my school. If I had come across Eva Gore-Booth's collected poems, they would have suited me much better than his, by adding to the Celtic cocktail two crucial elements: religious faith, and love between women. But I never knew of Eva as a poet, let alone a lesbian poet, till I came across Gifford Lewis's 1988 biography of her and her longtime companion Esther Roper,[2] which led me back to the poetry, long out of print and available only in research libraries.

16

It was not a matter of luck; it was because she was not included in the heritage of Irish and English literature I grew up on. In 1935 Richard Fox commented that Eva Gore-Booth had an 'assured place' in modern anthologies, ranking next to Yeats.[3] But her reputation must have died quickly, because she was not featured in a single one of the anthologies available to me when I was growing up, and I still cannot account for this except by patriarchal bias. Although some of her poems are conventional, others are quite remarkable, and always they are interesting.

Let me say at the outset that Eva Gore-Booth does not sit easily alongside the men in this anthology. I cannot consider her a 'trans-gendered other' or a marginalised 'sexual dissident', because the society she lived in at the turn of the century still allowed for passionate love between the right sort of women. Gore-Booth comes at the tail-end of the tradition of 'romantic friendship' which has caused so many arguments among historians of sexuality. So as a lesbian historian, the questions I must ask about Eva are not those that can be asked about a man in the same era, for instance Oscar Wilde. Nobody would ever have sent Miss Gore-Booth to jail.

Just about every text that mentions Eva Gore-Booth was written soon after her death and sings her praises. In Sylvia Pankhurst's history of suffragism, for instance, Eva is cast as consumptive martyr and golden-haired saviour of working girls.[4] Letters from other friends about her, excerpted by Esther Roper in the biographical sketch she affixed to Eva's posthumous *Collected Poems*, reinforce this impression of her saintliness and charm. There seems no way to acquire an objective view of Eva Gore-Booth, since, even if anyone had said anything bad of her, loyal Esther would have been unlikely to repeat it.

But it is possible to cut through the haze of nostalgia by a close reading of her poems, and unearth some of Gore-Booth's contradictions. For instance, her polarised images of masculinity and femininity seem to show an essentialist view of gender, yet she founded a magazine to help men and women escape from the prison of sex roles. Gore-Booth was a fervent pacifist, yet many of her poems award heroine status to military leaders, including her own sister Con. A baronet's daughter playing Lady Bountiful to working-class women in the slums of Manchester, Gore-Booth idealised the comradeship of equals. The final piece in the puzzle is that Gore-Booth spent her life with the woman she loved, yet left not a single recorded comment on what we now call sexual orientation.

Out of all these contradictions comes a body of poetry, plays and prose which is too extensive to cover in one essay. My main interest in this essay is how Gore-Booth appropriated linguistic and poetic conventions, as well as Celtic mythology, to feminise and lesbianise the stories handed down to her. Without ever (as far as I can tell) casting herself as a political or sexual dissident, this woman quietly subverted her whole heritage.

What I want to offer here is a consideration of Gore-Booth's life and work through four images she kept circling back to: My Lady of the Spring; The City; Heroines; and Comrades. They can be combined in what I see as Gore-Booth's central image, that of one woman coming to rescue another from an urban prison, and leading her by the hand into a pastoral paradise.

MY LADY OF THE SPRING

Eva's upbringing on a large estate in Sligo was the base from which all her work sprang. Not only was Lissadell beautiful, but it seems to have been rather matriarchal. It is hard to remember her father the baronet, when all we hear of in memoirs is her devotion to her grandmother, her telepathic bond with her nurse, her close friendship with her governesses (particularly 'Squidge'), and her fondness for her sisters Mabel and Con.[5]

When Gore-Booth came to write about nature, she was inheriting traditions of gender polarity. For centuries male poets had cast themselves as suitors in relation to a feminine personification of nature. Simply fitting herself into this tradition, Eva lesbianised the couple.

She casts herself as a poetic suitor of the Sirens and the Muse in early poems from the 1890s such as 'Disillusion' and 'From a Far Country', and portrays herself worshipping such goddess as 'Drudgery', 'Beauty' (in 'The Revolt Against Art') and 'Mercy' (*CP*, pp. 109-12, 219, 557). If a male poet is usually a 'swain' in the world of pastoral poetry, Eva wanders (with no specified role) through a landscape of nymphs, dryads and naiads ('A Spirit in Prison', 'A Song', 'The Fall' and 'The Inner Egeria'(*CP*, pp. 114-15, 121-2, 284-5, 480-8)). This is a countryside which seems entirely female in population except for the odd reference to the god Pan. Poems to named goddesses include 'Andromeda' and 'Athene', as well as several about Psyche (*CP*, pp. 286-7, 471, 269-71, 407-8, 289-90). But more than any abstract representation of womanhood, Eva Gore-Booth seems to want a goddess who represents the fertile nature so pervasive in Sligo. Several poems celebrate Proserpine as a nature goddess, and in 'The Goddess of this World' (*CP*, pp. 252-4) Proserpine is valued more highly than Pallas or Aphrodite, since, as well as rivalling them in beauty, she has a direct impact on the poet's daily life:

> Because of her I keep my door ajar
> For every thought or dream that comes my way. (*CP*, p. 285)

There is a hint here that Gore-Booth is casting herself as Paris, adjudicating between goddesses.

Mostly Gore-Booth's nature goddess is not given any Greek or Latin name, but is simply Eva's personification of the beauties of nature, particularly in spring. Some of these poems are gushy and conventional, such as the early 'Love Song' addressed to 'my Lady of the Spring'. This kind was rather common among Gore-Booth's Irish contemporaries; Alice Furlong's poem 'To Spring', personifies the season as universally seductive,[6] as does Ella Young's description of 'My Lady of Dreams'.[7] Katherine Tynan produces one in which spring has died because her male lover has rejected her in favour of summer;[8] Gore-Booth, by contrast, avoids using such a heterosexual storyline.

One of Gore-Booth's better nature poems is 'February at Adare' (*CP*, pp. 105-6), in which she offers a precise and erotic description of coming across Spring in the form of a woman of a somewhat Pre-Raphaelite appearance dozing beside a river:

> She seemed as one about to wake, who lingers
> Yet on the blessed borderland of consciousness
> Her hair streamed down between her claspèd fingers,
> And fell upon the stream like a caress,
> To make a little passing stir and shiver
> In the cool surface of the lazy river. (*CP*, p. 140)[9]

Eva was particularly fond of the month she was born, May, and personified it as a walking goddess. The oddly melancholic poem 'To May' concentrates on minute bodily gestures, describing the hands and feet of the goddess, a sweet but remote object of desire (*CP*, p. 148). Gore-Booth puts the emphasis on the youth, beauty and purity of her nature goddesses, rather than on their fertility; the title 'lady' fits better than 'mother'.

Such poems can be read as simple hymns to nature, or (considering their physical sensuousness) as covert love poems to women. I think the truth is somewhere in the middle; they are 'about' nature, but it is clear that their imagery is informed by Gore-Booth's aesthetic and erotic appreciation for the beauties of particular women. In one interesting poem written in 1905, 'The Perilous Light', the goddess appears as both nature and the writer's muse. Rather than sleeping or wandering by, she is shown here to focus her seductive attention on the poet:

> The Eternal Beauty smiled at me
> From the long lily's curvèd form,
> She laughed in a wave of the sea,
> She flashed on white wings through the storm.

The coquette becomes more like a wife in the next verse:

> In the bulb of a daffodil
> She made a joyful little stir,

And the white cabin on the hill
Was my heart's home because of her.

The move towards the domestic world of the 'heart's home' reduces the chasm between goddess and poet, so the Eternal Beauty can be described almost as an equal by the end of the poem: 'the Lover of the Brave,/The comrade of the perilous quest' (*CP*, pp. 276-7). Increasingly over the years Gore-Booth is drawn to images of female comradeship, rather than worship, to express her love both for ideals and for real women.

But even this early it is noteworthy tht Eva shows no awkwardness or self-consciousness about casting herself as a female lover of goddesses in these poems; she does not seem to feel any need to hide behind a masculine poetic persona. In the poems where she speaks as a man, it seems to be because she has something specific to say about a man's life, not that she is trying to veil the lesbian couple.

THE CITY

By staying in Sligo and writing poems about nature, Eva Gore-Booth was doing the acceptable feminine thing. In a letter to Olivia Shakespear of 1895 W. B. Yeats wrote that although his new friend Eva Gore-Booth had 'talent' and 'ambition', she knew no 'literary people' and like all Irish writers needed 'a proper respect for craftsmanship & that she must get in England'.[10] What he probably had in mind was a few years spent moving in London literary circles. He could not have anticipated that in the following summer in Italy her meeting with Esther Roper, a BA working to unionise the women of Manchester, would have had such a life-changing impact. Later that year Eva and Con spoke at a women's suffrage rally in Sligo, and by 1897 Eva had settled in Manchester with Esther and her brother Reginald, in a terraced house smaller than the outbuilding of Lissadell that was used to house a visiting carriage.

The move can be understood as a sort of class rebellion. Although her upbringing might have seemed idyllic, at the age of nine Eva had seen famine decimate the local peasantry, and had helped with her father's soup kitchen. Esther Roper claimed that the Gore-Booth girls had often visited the local cottages, growing up on terms of 'natural friendliness with workers everywhere and a complete unconsciousness of class distinctions',[11] but the sight of starving peasants must have given the young aristocrats at least some awareness of class distinctions. Both sisters seem to have been left with a sense of outrage, anger and (no doubt) guilt. So each turned into a political fighter, though for different causes.

Yeats was evidently disgusted at their choice to reject the calm of Sligo.

He saw Con as having been coarsened by revolution, and when he told Eva that he had sent an appeal for clemency to the Secretary of State on Con's behalf after the Rising of 1916, his letter went on to wax lyrical about the girls in the woods of Lissadell.[12] In his poem in memory of the sisters, written in 1927, he described both of them as wasting their beauty and their lives. 'I know not what the younger dreams,' he wrote crossly,

> Some vague Utopia — and she seems,
> When withered old and skeleton-gaunt,
> An image of such politics.[13]

His implication seems to be that Eva's body would not have grown thin and ill if she had stayed apolitical. He goes on to point out the 'folly' of fighting political enemies, since 'youth and innocence' have no enemy but 'time'. Yeats seems irritated that the sisters have not stayed within the frame of the poem, posing as lovely mute swans to be the stuff of his nostalgic poetry, but instead have fled the nest.

Although the 'Utopia' Eva worked for was often mystical, it was not particularly 'vague'; perhaps it was vague to Yeats because he had not followed her political work in any detail. Where he advocted listening to the peasants' stories and turning them into poems for the literate and leisured to read, Eva had a much more direct relation to the poor. Rather than writing about the working-class girls for whom she was campaigning in Manchester, she opened the world of literature to them by running classes on poetry and plays at the Labour Union. Eva's charm seemed to have crossed class barriers, as all the pupils and fellow-workers quoted in Roper's memoir sound besotted with her. She also used her own writing in a political way, for example by giving poems free to small pacifist journals. As well as being a writer, she was a full-time campaigner; she fought alongside Esther for employment rights for barmaids, circus gymnasts and flower-sellers. At one point she had a go at working in a mine to see what it was like. The couple moved from Manchester to London in 1910 for health reasons; there they helped war victims, and the English and German wives of interned prisoners. Eva spent most of her income on donations such as 300 oranges for Christmas at an Eastend girls' club.[14]

What all this adds up to is that the nature-worshipping poet spent her adult life in smoky cities. Gore-Booth never felt exiled from home; although her family can be presumed to have been rather shocked at what they would have seen as her rapid downward mobility and exhausting lifestyle, she remained on good terms with them. Each summer she and Esther went to stay with Con in Dublin, then on to Lissadell for friendly chats with her father the baronet, so it was not that Eva had no home to return to.[15] It was her choice to live far from her pastoral paradise, presumably because her political work and her bond with Esther kept her in England.

The real importance of the move to the city, in Gore-Booth's poetry, is how she turned it into a symbolic domain of oppression. Her nostalgia for Sligo made her tap into the traditional contrast between the evil, imprisoning city and the free 'green world' — even though, paradoxically, it was in the city that she found happiness with Esther.

In many poems written over several decades Gore-Booth contrasts 'the city's din' with the world of nature and Ireland. (This was a fairly common motif during the Literary Revival, for example the poem Yeats grew to loathe, 'The Lake Isle of Innisfree' (1893), which is presented as a sense memory stealing upon a man who must walk on 'pavements grey'.[16]) Gore-Booth does little with the motif in an early poem like 'Rest', simply expressing a longing for the countryside. 'Spring in Manchester' and 'The Elm Boughs' look at the phenomenon of those poor plants that do manage to grow up in the smoke, ignored by 'Nature' their neglectful mother. (*CP*, pp. 110, 153-5, 287). Sometimes the urban/rural polarity seems entirely symbolic, as in a poem like 'Survival' (1905), which is not about plants at all, but about the poet's own spiritual claustrophobia:

> There is nothing good, there is nothing fair,
> Grows in the darkness thick and blind —
> Pull down your high walls everywhere,
> Let in the sun, let in the wind.

Increasingly we get a sense of the countryside not as a literal place, but as a spiritual domain that can be visited at any time if need is great. Similarly, 'Peace' starts by protesting: 'I am sad with the city's sadness, sick of toil', moving on to the final declaration: 'I will fling down my soul to rest in this green glade' (*CP*, p. 305).[17]

Where Gore-Booth parts company with Yeats is in her tendency to draw links between men and the evil city on the one hand, and women and the good countryside on the other. She begins to hint at this connection in 'The Queen's Flight', when the queen discovers that she wants to be a wandering beggarmaid again. Alternate lines highlight the contrasting worlds:

> The castle ramparts are stately and high,
> No fort defends the free dome of the sky;
> The King's hall is guarded by bolt and bar —
> Behold, I am free as the wild things are. (*CP*, p. 200)[18]

Here the contrast is between court and beggary, but is no coincidence that the queen is a woman leaving a court of male authority.

The male pronoun used as generic, a linguistic convention that still lingers today to sexist effect, can be cleverly used by Gore-Booth as a sort of pun, a way of suggesting that the worst things about human society are male. For instance, in the poem 'Symbols' the word 'men' may mean human beings, but there is a definite hint of maleness too. The (presumed female) 'I' persona sees a mystical light,

> But the words and the deeds of men are as smoke that darkens the
>   wind —
> Black smoke from the mills of the world blown across the
>   unfaltering blue. (*CP*, p. 210)

Gore-Booth's horrifying vision of the industrial oppression her unions were combating comes to its climax in a poem called 'The City' (1904). The grass is 'entombed' under paving stones, and one of Gore-Booth's female personifications, 'The buried Spirit of the Wise and Fair', is imprisoned under 'giant Labour-houses'. The poem ends with a surge of apocalyptic hope:

> Then does the Spirit of the Wise and Fair
> Break from her sepulchre and walk the town,
> The iron bounds are loosened everywhere —
> No pavement gray can crush the green grass down.

The same 'Spirit of the Wise and Fair' crops up in a later poem 'A Symbol', this time ripping the blindfold off Justice. (*CP*, pp. 221-2, 257). Gore-Booth does not make it clear whether these ideas just happen to be personified in feminine form, or whether they can actually be associated with real women.

Similarly, 'The Land to a Landlord' suggests but never clarifies a gender polarity, by dramatising the conflict between a (male) landowner and the (feminine) world of nature. This, one of Eva's best pieces, is an extraordinary protest poem for the daughter of a landlord to write:

> Though you are king of the rose and the wheat,
> Not for you, not for you is the bog-myrtle sweet,
> Though you are lord of the long grass,
> The hemlock bows not her head as you pass. (*CP*, p. 238)

Although she never directly accuses men of being primarily responsible for the rape of the earth, Gore-Booth makes her point by setting the impotent patriarch of this poem against a world of feminised plants. She makes the drama even clearer in a later poem, 'Dreams':

> Men drench the green earth and defile her streams
> With blood, and blast her very fields and hills
> With the mechanic iron of their wills,
> Yet in her sad heart still the spirit dreams. (*CP*, p. 516)

Even though 'men' can be read as the generic pronoun for the human race, the contrast between masculine industrial work and mother earth in this poem makes it clear at whose door Gore-Booth is laying the blame.

Other poems are set in a very specific city, the London through which Gore-Booth marched in the early years of the twentieth century with crowds of working women, demanding better conditions and suffrage. The poem 'Women's Trades on the Embankment' finds no sweet resolution in the image of a goddess, but denounces (male) politicians, particularly the Prime Minister who has just recommended 'patience'. In Gore-Booth's next poem, 'The Good Samaritan', the male victim of the Gospel story is feminised as 'Justice' who has fallen among thieves. The rich and the politically power-ful pass right by, while workers of all kinds stop to help her (*CP*, pp. 404-6). So Gore-Booth's contrast is not always between men and women, but sometimes between the rich and the poor. In both cases, though, the enemy is the rich male politician.

In a triumphantly powerful poem of 1906 entitled 'Women's Rights' all the hints of gender difference come together in the nearest thing Eva ever wrote to a separatist manifesto. The poem begins deceptively as a simple pastoral vision of Glencar waterfall in spring, then turns political.

> But where men in office sit
> Winter holds the human wit . . .
>
> Oh, whatever men may say
> Ours is the wide and open way.
>
> Oh, whatever men may dream
> We have the blue air and the stream.
>
> Men have got their towers and walls,
> We have cliffs and waterfalls.
>
> Oh, whatever men may do
> Ours is the gold air and the blue.
>
> Men have got their pomp and pride —
> All the green world is on our side. (*CP*, p. 409)

As if she knows that the struggle for female suffrage is not nearly over — it was to take another twelve years before women over thirty would be granted the vote in Britain — in this poem Gore-Booth is shifting her battleground to the realm of the symbolic. Suffragism was a movement of streets and railings, urban rallies and prisons, but Gore-Booth manages here to invest it with all the charm of the open countryside. Even at her most feminist, Gore-Booth's focus is never on hating men, but on enjoy-ing the company of women. The males in 'Women's Rights' are not dramatic villains but sad bureaucrats in dusty offices, watching the women canter off to the waterfalls together.

This image of leaving the enclosure, of risking life outside the town, crops up a lot in Gore-Booth's work. An effective short poem entitled 'The Anti-Suffragist' describes the woman who resists political rights as a princess carried out of her imprisoning tower in old age, blinking and protesting at the light; the female rescuer has come too late for this Rapunzel (*CP*, p. 497).

Gore-Booth manages, then, to draw a convincing contrast between the oppressive world of the enclosed city that men have built and the free space of the 'green world'. The latter is not exclusively female — Pan dances among the nymphs — but is certainly feminine in values. So when in her late poems Gore-Booth's religious loyalty turns back from Eastern mysticism to Jesus, she manages to feminise him by showing the plants bowing down to him as if to a nature goddess (and never a landlord):

> O Christ, a burden of gloom
> May haunt the wallèd room,
> But the blue shining out of doors
> Is yours, is yours. (*CP*, p. 588)

The contrast between walled rooms and blue air recalls the earlier poem 'Women's Rights'. So rather than disrupting the gender polarity that Gore-Booth has set up, the introduction of her unpatriarchal Christ brings him over to the side of the women.

The problem with this kind of nature imagery is that it reinforces essentialist distinctions between man and culture on the one hand, and woman and nature on the other, which tend to limit what men and women can be. In the privately circulated journal *Urania* that Eva Gore-Booth edited from 1916, with the motto 'Sex is an Accident', a London-based group of women and men put forward their suggestions for wriggling out of what they saw as the theatrical roles of masculinity and femininity, into a new and freer life as human beings. So although she harnessed traditional woman–nature links in her poetry, and used them to feminist effect, ultimately Gore-Booth seems to have tired of gender roles, preferring to imagine some escape from them.

HEROINES

We have already seen how in her poetry Gore-Booth likes to either praise a feminised ideal, or use such a personification to bring resolution to a poem of conflict. But all these goddesses, whether unnamed, or particular ones like Psyche or Persephone, tend to act as simple symbols. In this section I want to look at Gore-Booth's human heroines who, though they may occasionally overlap with the divine ones, are generally shown as glamorous figures full of complexity and conflict.

Apart from Joan of Arc, who inspires two Gore-Booth poems (*CP*, pp. 112, 532),[19] all the heroines are Celtic. Ireland itself shows up as a female personification twice: in 'Clouds' as a passive weeping woman, roused by a female Justice, and in 'The Thriftless Dreamer' as an equally vague female protected by angels. (*CP*, pp. 127-8, 407-8). But mostly Gore-Booth prefers to write about the individualised Irish women described in legends.

It has often been supposed that it was W. B. Yeats who got Gore-Booth started on Irish mythology, but according to her governess, quoted by Esther Roper, Eva had spent her youth in a sort of communal female project of peopling the Sligo landscape in imagination. 'How her writings bring back memories of days spent by the Atlantic,' wrote her governess, 'and the happy times when we tramped about wild places, and imagined all that had happened there in the old stormy days.'[20]

Yeats visited Lissadell in November 1894 and told the Gore-Booth family old Irish stories. Thinking that Eva's poems showed 'promise', and being charmed with her to the point where he considered proposing marriage, he focused his storytelling on her.[21] It is clear what he expected; as he had told Katharine Tynan six years before on publication of his book of fairy tales, 'You and I will have to begin to turn some of these stories into poems.' He set to work on Eva, and by April 1895 had sent her books of Irish legends; his letter to Olivia Shakespear crowed: 'I am always ransacking Ireland for people to get writing at Irish things. She [Eva] does not know that she is the last victim.'[22] But Gore-Booth did not join wholeheartedly in this project of cultural translation; instead of 'turning stories into poems', as he would have liked, she used details from the legends for poems about other things — generally, love between women.

Other Irish women poets involved in the Celtic revival tended to make a feature of retelling the great heterosexual love stories. Katherine Tynan dealt thus with Diarmaid and Gráinne, Oisín and Niamh, Aibhric and Fionnuala. Ella Young wrote a poem about Maeve's daughter as a lost virgin, and one about Niamh which focused on the story of her seducing Oisín. By contrast, what seems to have appealed to Gore-Booth about the women of Celtic legend was their independence and their focus on other women. 'Lament of the Daughters of Ireland' is a hymn of discontent with the feminine role and nostalgia for the heroic past:

> We are the daughters of crownèd Queens, the children of the sword,
> Our mothers went forth to the battle strong-armed and eager to dare,

Their souls were fierce with freedom, they loved, and they called no
                                                                    man lord,
Freely the winds of Eirinn could tangle their loose-flowing hair.
                                                     (*CP*, pp. 197-8)

We do not know exactly what was in the collections of legends that Yeats
sent Gore-Booth in 1895, but we do know that the late nineteenth-century
versions tended to make Cuchulain central. By contrast, Eva Gore-Booth's
poems and poetic dramas put tiny movements between women at the centre.

For example, the standard version of the Cuchulain story, as seen in
T. W. Rolleston's *Myths and Legends of the Celtic Race* (1911), explained that
Maeve sent the monstrous children of the druid Calatin abroad to learn
magic so they would be better able to revenge themselves on Cuchulain
for having killed their father. When Cuchulain was being tended in his
depression in a secluded glen by Niamh, the wife of his faithful friend
Conaill (and, in some versions, Cuchulain's lover), Calatin's daughter Badb,
'taking the form of a handmaid of Niam [*sic*], beckoned her away . . . and
put a spell of staying on her', and then in the form of Niamh persuaded
Cuchulain to go to the war which would be his downfall.[23]

In *Unseen Kings,* an early play which seems to represent her first attempt
at reviving the Celtic myths, Eva Gore-Booth makes this tiny incident central. The main character becomes, not our rather sullen hero, but Niamh,
glossed in the *dramatis personae* as a 'prophetess' and described in Gore-
Booth's note as 'a wise woman who, in the old myths, stood for the Spiritual
Beauty'. (Whether deliberately or by mistake, Gore-Booth is here conflating
Niamh, the wife of Conaill, with Niamh of the Golden Hair, queen of Tír
na nÓg.) In the play's striking central episode, Niamh is approached by
a dishevelled female Stranger, who, rather than pretending to be Niamh's
maid as in the legend, offers as her credentials the fact that she is 'knit
by love unto the heart' of the goddess Fand. The Stranger explains how
far she has travelled to talk to Niamh:

> O I have greatly dared — and wandered far —
> And trusted in strange dreams and faery fires;
> For well I know thy star is as my star
> And thy desire the soul of my desires. (*CP*, p. 205)

Their mysterious sense of identification gives weight to the Stranger's attempt to lure Niamh out into the night, where they can talk more freely
than in the enclosure. Her speeches are seductive, out of all proportion
to the occasion:

> Ah, Lady Niamh, leave the drowsy fort,
> Come forth with me into the clear starlight,

> Feel the cool wind, see how the flashing dew
> Has woven a starlit crown for thy long hair . . .
>   (*CP*, pp. 179-80)

Once again we find the image of one woman leading another out into the freedom of the green world. When Niamh agrees, it is made to seem like a life-changing decision, a symbolic choice of risk and the love of a stranger:

> NIAMH: I will go forth with thee into the night. (*She takes the Stranger's hand.*)
> STRANGER: Does thou not fear?
> NIAMH: Nay, then, why should I fear?
>   My soul is luminous with a strange light
>   As of deep waters cool and green and clear
>   Or sunlight in a green-hung forest glade.
>   How could I fear and hold thee by the hand?
>   Shall not all evil things shrink back afraid
>   From Niamh and the messenger of Fand? (*They go out together.*)
>   (*CP*, p. 181)

This image of the two women, walking hand in hand through unimaginable danger, is central to Gore-Booth's work.

Whereas Niamh in the legend is a fool who gets tricked, in Gore-Booth's version she is a heroine accepting a risky invitation. Even when the Stranger returns, having magically 'taken on herself the outward form of Niamh' (*CP*, p. 183), and rejects Cuchulain's love in order to send him off to war against Maeve's armies, the luring of Niamh into the night is not made to seem evil, but merely the working of fate. When Niamh returns, she is not so much horrified as dazed (*CP*, p. 186). Basically, Gore-Booth has taken the story of a man going to war and made it into a lesbian seduction.

The story that came to really preoccupy Gore-Booth was that of Maeve, the High Queen of Connacht, said to be buried above Lissadell under the great cairn on the mountain of Knocknarea. First introduced in *Unseen Kings* as Cuchulain's glamorous enemy, Maeve shows up elsewhere in the poems published with this play. 'A Hermit's Lament for Maeve' is a sad poem of failed service, spoken in a hermit persona that is probably male, though made ambiguous by comparison to a nun. The next poem, 'To Maeve', defends the dead queen's reputation against all those who assume that female heroes must be immoral:

> They have buried thy golden deeds under the cairn on the hill,
> And no one shall sing of thy hero soul in the days to come.
>   (*CP*, pp. 194-5)

But of course, that is exactly what Eva is doing; she casts herself as the lone, faithful harper, engaged in a feminist re-evaluation of Maeve that is motivated by erotic devotion. In her next play, *The Triumph of Maeve* (written 1902, published 1905), Gore-Booth opens with a poem that expresses how her 'dream at twilight' is disrupted by a wind from the 'haunted hill' of Knocknarea:

> There is no rest for the soul that has seen the wild eyes of Maeve;
> No rest for the heart once caught in the net of her yellow hair —
> $\qquad\qquad\qquad\qquad\qquad$ (*CP*, pp. 312-13)

The orthodox version of the Maeve story is that she fought with the men of Ulster to win their great Brown Bull so that her possessions would match those of her husband. But Eva Gore-Booth recasts it as a story of women at both ends. Maeve goes to war, in the play *The Triumph of Maeve*, to avenge her fellow-heroine Deirdre of the Sorrows, who was betrayed by the King of Ulster. The main love of Gore-Booth's Maeve is her daughter Fionavar, and there is no mention of her husband. (In traditional versions of the legend, Maeve uses her daughter as bait, offering her to Ferdia as his wife if he will fight Cuchulain.[24]) Maeve also has a company of comrades, warriors both male and female, who follow her into war, declaring:

> Yea, we will follow thee unto the end,
> Seeking thy smile as flowers seek the sun. (*CP*, p. 342)

Maeve would like to offer a more egalitarian model:

> Ye shall go with me as friend goes with friend,
> Thus in all freedom shall this deed be done. (*CP*, p. 333)

But she is very much the queen, so this does not ring true. It may show Eva Gore-Booth's ambivalence about being a well-born feminist leader who believed in equality but had difficulty living it. (Uneasy feelings about our need for heroines are no less common in the lesbian and feminist movements today.)

The mother–daughter dyad is central to *The Triumphs of Maeve*. At sixteen, Fionavar wants to go to war as her mother's intimate and comrade:

> I would go with thee, I would have my share
> Of thy great deeds, and when the songs are sung
> My name shall be with thine as our hearts beat
> Together . . . (*CP*, p. 334)

When the battle is won, and Fionavar has died of grief from looking at the battlefield, Maeve withdraws from court society — 'Once she had many lovers, now no man / May please her' (*CP*, pp. 380, 382) — and finally casts off her crown and robes. In Rolleston's book of legends, Maeve next appears in retirement on an island, where she bathes every morning in a pool until a revenge killing ends her life with a slingshot.[25] But Gore-Booth provides a much more romantic and spiritual ending: Maeve sets out to find Tír na nÓg, on a journey less physical than spiritual, described as 'the way to my own soul' via nature (*CP*, p. 393). There is a hint that, rather than rushing to join Fionavar and Deirdre in death, Maeve will find some consolation in her retirement.

And sure enough, she is healed by a vision of Niamh, the fairy queen of Tír na nÓg. In a later poem, 'The Vision of Niamh', the relationship between Maeve and Niamh, both semi-human, semi-divine figures from legend, is seen by the poet's persona in a cheering 'vision' of her own. Maeve is described in her 'high mountain camp' at the moment of confrontation with absolute beauty:

> And leaning from the shadow of a star
> With hands outstretched to hold the hands of clay,
> One looked into her spirit fairer far
> Than sun or moon of any mortal day.

This is not just another hymn to a nature goddess; it is a story of one woman curing her sorrows by romantic devotion to another:

> For thee Maeve left her kingdom and her throne,
> And all the gilded wisdom of the wise,
> And dwelt among the hazel trees alone
> So that she might look into Niamh's eyes.

Maeve's search for peace is personalised as a search for Niamh, which makes her forget battles, and even the death of her daughter Fionavar. Just as Maeve is comforted, so the poet seems uplifted by this glimpse of the legendary lesbian past:

> Ah, Niamh, still the starry lamp burns bright,
> I can see through the darkness of the grave,
> How long ago thy soul of starry light
> Was very dear to the brave soul of Maeve. (*CP*, p. 498)

Just when Eva had taken the Maeve story as far is it could go, along came a real-life example of a woman whose martial spirit this pacifist poet could not help but glorify. Her sister Constance was a minor leader in the 1916 Rising in Dublin and was sentenced to death, then (being a woman) jailed instead. Eva's poem 'To Constance — In Prison' uses the now familiar contrast between imprisonment (in her own case metaphorical, but in Con's case all too literal) and the green world to which the imagination always has access: 'Yours is that inner Ireland beyond green fields and brown', she writes encouragingly to her sister, and 'there are woods and primroses in the country of your mind'. But mythology is an even more potent source of comfort for a sister steeped in the rhetoric of nationalism. In Eva's poem 'Christmas Eve in Prison' she urges Con not to feel deserted:

> Is it so vain a thing
> That your heart's harper, Dark Roseen,
> A wandering singer, yet a queen,
> Crownèd with all her seventeen stars,
> Outside your prison bars
> Stands carolling? (*CP*, p. 510)

On first reading, the harper is Ireland, proud of her warrior Constance. Gore-Booth has inverted the usual story of Dark Roseen as a passive victim being sung to by (male) poets, and, I think, added a hint of the homoerotic story of Blondel outside Richard Lionheart's prison window. On second reading, the harper in the poem is not Ireland, but Eva herself, sending in poems to keep Con's spirits up. Either way, in Gore-Booth's renderings of Celtic mythology, the female couple is central.

COMRADES

Gore-Booth's next poem addressed to Constance, 'Comrades', offers a vision not of consolation but of escape. In a scene rather like the story of St Paul being released from prison by an angel, this poem offers Con the night and the wind to break down her doors:

> Free through the world your spirit goes,
> Forbidden hands are clasping yours. (*CP*, pp. 509-11)

Bodies, in Gore-Booth's work, rarely do anything more earthy than holding hands. Yet this life-saving handclasp carries quite an erotic charge when the hands are 'forbidden' ones.

Passionate bonds between women were common throughout the eighteenth and nineteenth centuries, but particularly among educated women at the end of the nineteenth. It seems that for the first time large numbers of women had jobs, which meant that they could afford to live together in pairs or groups instead of marrying men. Feminists had developed a language to celebrate such love: for example, Frances Power Cobbe, coming from an Irish gentry background similar to Gore-Booth's and living in an equally happy partnership with a woman, wrote in an essay of 1863 that the spinster had no reason to fear solitude, having 'inherited the blessed power of a woman to make true and tender friendships, such as not one man's heart in a hundred can even imagine'.[26]

'Comrades' is one of those useful words that strengthens the idea of friendship by reinforcing it with something else — in this case, bonds among those fighting for a common goal. Edward Carpenter used the phrase 'comrade love' as a euphemism for the finer sort of male homosexuality, but for Gore-Booth it seems to have been a term that packed together political solidarity and personal affection, rather like the way 'sisterhood' would come to be used in the 1970s. Gore-Booth's form of feminism was always less a matter of theories than of individual women uplifting and upholding each other. Significantly, the first editorial she wrote for the *Women's Labour News* described the paper's aim as being 'to light a few street lamps here and there in the darkest ways, to let us at all events see one another's faces and recognize our comrades'.

The concept of comradeship implies equality, but Gore-Booth was doomed to remain the Lady Bountiful in many ways. She may have been trying to light metaphorical 'street lamps' of mutual understanding, but the limelight was usually on her. Esther Roper tells a suggestive anecdote of Eva giving an inspiring speech 'one dark and stormy night . . . in a poor and rather squalid street. When her speech was over a woman suddenly rushed out of the darkness, seized her hand and kissed it, vanishing again without a word'.[27] Not much face-to-face mutual recognition there! No more than her heroine Maeve, Eva Gore-Booth's theories of equality never quite matched her practice.

Considering how much her daily life was organised around bonds of friendship, primarily with other feminists, it is surprising how rarely Gore-Booth presented the relationship between women friends as the central theme of a poem. There are several poems that praise the physical and spiritual beauty of particular friends ('To C.A', about Clare Annesley, and 'A Garden Grave' and 'To a Lady — Now Dead', about Lady Mount-Temple), but without highlighting the friendship (*CP*, pp. 516-17, 578). Gore-Booth seems to have generally preferred to leave this cherished ideal of hers in the private realm, where it could avoid both the vulgarising glare of publicity and all the suspicions being cast on it by followers of Havelock Ellis and Sigmund Freud.

On the rare occasions when she does deal with such a relationship explicitly, Eva tends to keep the discussion abstract and gender-neutral, though still impassioned. One wartime poem, 'Utopia', is about the search for a positive ideal to oppose the horrors of the era:

> Is there a force that can end
> The woe of the world's war?
> Yea, when a friend meets a friend
> There shall be peace once more.

She makes friendship into a sort of humanist religion, explaining that this form of 'love' is the only 'God' she can pray to:

> For love at the heart of the storm
> Breaks the waves of wild air,
> And God in our human form
> Is life's answer to prayer. (*CP*, p. 512)

In a witty early poem, 'Triolet', Gore-Booth again keeps the argument very general. She takes the French saying that friendship is only love without wings, and counters with a tribute to its greater constancy: 'If love has lost a wing/He shall not fly away' (*CP*, p. 113).

In the few poems that give any glimpse of the kind of partnership she had with Esther Roper, and that so many of her feminist colleagues enjoyed too, Eva keeps returning to the image of two friends, hand in hand, keeping watch together.[28] One obvious association is with Christ asking his friends to stay awake with him in the garden of Gethsemane. Her second poem with the title 'Comrades' harnesses passion between friends to the idea of their common work:

> We who have followed the same star and fought for the same dream,
> Are bound together for ever by the wild deed's bond and power.
> Behold we have cast our nets into the same dark stream,
> We have climbed the same sheer cliff to seek the same blue flower.
>
> (*CP*, pp. 410-11)

The overflowing rhythm of these lines can only be called erotic, but notice that Gore-Booth is always careful to keep the gaze of the two friends focused on something in addition to each other. The 'blue flower' can be read as a potent symbol for their love, the thing the searchers find when they meet at the top of the cliff.

From the time they settled in Manchester together in 1897 to Eva's death in 1926, when her will left everything 'unto my friend Esther Gertrude Roper', there seems to have been no gap in this relationship.[29] Their backgrounds were very different — Roper was a university graduate from a half-Irish, working-class family, and campaigned for working women's rights in the same area of Lancashire where the Gore-Booths owned land — but somehow their values seem to have coincided. We know very little about the relationship, because there were almost no letters except those printed in her *Collected Poems* (*CP*, p. 65). One of the ironies familiar to any historian of sexuality is that happy domestic partnership leaves none of the rich evidence that frustrated long-distance love does.

They seem to have been a side-to-side pair, rather than face-to-face, according to C. S. Lewis's distinction: 'Lovers are always talking to one another about their love; Friends hardly ever about their Friendship. Lovers are

normally face to face, absorbed in each other; Friends, side by side, absorbed in some common interest.[30] In this sense, Eva and Esther were
Friends (the most serious word for same-sex love that C. S. Lewis's
homophobia could allow), but that capital letter should alert us to the
fact that their partnership was more like a marriage than a friendship.

The tone of the relationship, if we can judge from the occasional glimpse
of it we get in Gore-Booth's letters, was easy-going and undramatic. 'I squat
beside streams and write nonsense', Eva wrote to a friend while travelling
in Italy in 1920, 'and E— somehow makes the world go round in a general
sort of way.' (*CP,* p. 91). The image we get is of Eva as the creator and Esther
as the supportive wife in the background; however, we must remember
that they had moved to Manchester originally to suit Esther's work, and
we have no evidence that one of their careers took priority over the other
in a traditional husband–wife way.

Out of her hundreds of poems, Eva published only three that can be
reliably identified as being about Esther. In a collection of 1904 she included 'The Travellers', subtitled 'To E.G.R.'. She begins by marvelling at
the good luck of the two of them finding each other in the summer of
1895, where 'under olive boughs we found our peace,/ And all the world's
great song in Italy'. In the second verse she explains that the idyllic peace
soon gave way to a difficult shared life, but the problems never touched
the core of the relationship, which she represents as a song:

> Is it not strange though Peace herself has wings
> And long ago has gone her separate ways,
> On through the tumult of our fretful days
> From Life to Death the great song chimes and rings?

The third verse speculates about whether death will end the 'song' of their
shared life:

> And in the darkness friend be lost to friend,
> And all our love and dreams of no avail?

Gore-Booth ends confidently by predicting, in a direct address to Esther,
that the song will outlive them:

> You whose Love's melody makes glad the gloom
> Of a long labour and a patient strife,
> Is not that music greater than our life? (*CP,* p. 247)

As in the poem about the 'blue flower', the focus is never explicitly on
the love between the two women, but on some external symbol, in this
case the 'song', that includes not only their love but their common mission.

The next poem about Esther is simply titled 'To E.G.R.'. It presents Eva, depressed by illness and the foggy atmosphere of the city, inviting Esther to join her in the consolations of a seventeenth-century mystic's imagery:

> Ah, come with me and breathe the sunny air
> In Jacob Boehme's Garden of roses fair.

At the end of its spiritual journey the poem dips back to the pair of women:

> The River of Life is running strong and free,
> White is the May, and all the hyaline sea
> Shines suddenly with Christ's mysterious smile . . .
> Sit by this window, let us watch awhile. (*CP*, pp. 605-6)

In this poem their relationship seems to be slipping away from everyday life. Eva's awareness of her worsening health made her dramatise the friendship as a matter of holding hands on the threshold between life and death.

The first of 'Three Consolations in Illness' is undoubtedly about Esther, though she is not named. In a time of misery and spiritual blindness, Gore-Booth explains,

> A human hand outstretched reached down into the dark,
> I knew a friend was watching by my side
> Holding in her strong heart through the long night
> As in a lamp that dark and hidden light
> Just visible to tired eyes and dim. (*CP*, pp. 641-2)

The disembodied friends in Gore-Booth's love poems have only eyes, hearts and, above all, hands. Put in the context of some other lesbian poetry of the time, Eva's poems to Esther come across as rather stifled; she is always anxious to generalise from the particular of her feelings for Esther towards a greater, more spiritual value.

Eva lived at a particularly interesting point in lesbian history, on the cusp between the placid confidence of 'romantic friends' and the new shamefaced self-assertion of the 'inverts'. Gore-Booth's generation, as described by Lillian Faderman, grew up among Victorian concepts of romantic female friendship, which began to fall under suspicion in Britain around the turn of the century. Some of these women began to denounce the very relationships they had held dear. Others ignored the new theories, but their writings betray a hint of defensiveness; Gore-Booth, with her love poems that tend always towards the abstract and spiritual, fits into this latter category. It was not yet necessary for them to tackle the innuendo head-on as Vera Brittain felt obliged to in her *Testament of Friendship* (1940).

It is tantalising to speculate on how much Gore-Booth had heard about current thinking on sexuality. In 1921 the attempt to extend the Criminal Law Amendment Act to criminalise lesbianism had got through the House

of Commons, but failed in the House of Lords, because the Lords were reluctant to publicise the possibility of lesbian sex to women they assumed would
never have heard of it. It seems symbolic that Eva Gore-Booth died after
the publication in 1924 of Radclyffe Hall's *The Unlit Lamp* (with whose
'romantic friend' heroine she would no doubt have empathised), but before
the same author's notorious 1928 publication of *The Well of Loneliness* (with
whose androgynous, self-aware queer protagonist Eva could have felt little
in common). Probably she would not have read either of the books anyway,
since in the 1920s her preferred reading was St John's Gospel.

In a slightly earlier age Gore-Booth would probably have felt free to express herself less self-consciously. Writing in 1873, for example, before
the sexologists had cast suspicion on such sentiments, Frances Power Cobbe
ended every verse of her ode to her 'Playmate, Friend, Companion, Love'
Mary Lloyd with the line 'I want you — Mary.'[31] Gore-Booth's coolness is
not just a matter of her era, however, but of the emotional tone of the
partnership. The aunt and niece who wrote together as 'Michael Field'
published in the same uneasy times as Eva Gore-Booth, but did not let
anything stop them from putting their fervent lifelong relationship in the
spotlight of their poetry. One of their poems of 1912 is called not 'Friends'
or 'Comrades', but 'Lovers':

> Lovers, fresh plighting lovers in our age,
> Lovers in Christ — so tender at the heart
> The pull about the strings as they engage —
> One thing is plain: — that we can never part.[32]

Whether because of her era's suspicion of the 'inversion' hidden in romantic
friendships, or because of her own taste for privacy, or simply because
of the calm nature of her love for Esther, Eva Gore-Booth would never
have written a poem like that. (Esther wrote no poetry, but chose a quotation from Sappho for their joint gravestone in St John's, Hampstead: 'Life
that is Love is God'.)

The poems Eva Gore-Booth did write, however — not just those about
Esther, but taking her corpus as a whole, with its goddesses, its exaltation
of women, its praise of friendship, and its reworking of Celtic myths into
encounters between women — make her a crucial part of the newly
recovered lesbian heritage.

READING EVA AND ESTHER

As a sort of postscript to my analysis of Eva Gore-Booth's poetry, I want
to look at the way her partnership with Esther Roper has been characterised

by other writers. The question of the definition of sexuality — so succinctly put by Sheila Jeffreys in the title of her essay on lesbian history,
'Does It Matter If They Did It?' — can be illuminated by looking at how
several different texts describe the same relationship.

Esther Roper herself gives the partnership a minimal gloss in her
biographical note on Eva: 'Each was attracted to the work and thoughts
of the other, and we became friends and companions for life.' She describes
Eva as 'a perfect friend', full of 'adventure and gaiety'; she will not admit
to any problems in their relationship through 'years of difficult and trying work, through periods of terrible strain and grief, through ever-recurring
times of intense pain'. As well as their common work, Esther emphasises
nature as a bond, specifically their country walks in Italy and Switzerland:
'Even simple everyday pleasures when shared with her became touched
with magic.' But like Eva, Esther promptly moves on to generalise about
affection, explaining that Eva 'had friends and comrades everywhere'.[33]

These other friends tended to canonise Eva: after her death they swapped
anecdotes about her mysticism and saintliness, which Esther collected
and printed. One who caught sight of Eva on a bus described her as 'more
like a being from another world. She was so etherealized that she gave
you no impression of flesh at all.'[34] This spiritualising vision seems to
have been a common way to justify love between women in this era. The
Irish writer of feminist novels Sarah Grand, living in Bath as its mayoress
in her old age, became an object of worship to young Gladys Singers-Bigger,
who presented Sarah with a diary full of meticulous descriptions of their
meetings and Gladys's feelings on each occasion. Sarah's response in May
1932 was gentle but firm:

> We must escape from our physical prison and rise to the higher plane
> to love truly, and leave it at that. To do otherwise makes confusion worse.
> . . . For the present I have locked the Diary up safely. We must have some
> big talks about it as soon as we can.[35]

To admit that Sarah and Gladys, or Eva and Esther, or any other pair of
women in this era, did inhabit their own bodies was to open the doors
to a kind of dangerous 'confusion' that their friends were not willing to face.

Con Markievicz went farther than most in trying to understand Eva and
Esther's partnership. She seems to have taken it as seriously as a marriage: when she was sneaking some letters out of prison, she wrote to Eva
'let not your right hand know what your left hand doeth (Esther of course
excepted)'. She tended to use the language of blood relation to make it
sound natural and respectable, and also to include herself in the triangle,
by describing Esther as 'a sort of adopted sister, Eva's twin' and their 'spiritual
sister'.[36] But on the occasion of Eva's death Con stepped back and

acknowledged the other two's unique partnership: she wrote to a friend: 'I feel so glad Eva and [Esther] were together and so thankful that her love was with Eva to the end.' To Esther, Con wrote interestingly that she knew Esther must miss Eva even more than she did, because Esther had been 'so much nearer her body than I'. However Con quickly backed out of these muddy waters by disembodying her sister again, adding that 'with her the spirit dominated every bit of her and her body was just the human instrument it shone through'.[37]

Whatever about their loyal friends, other contemporaries seem to have had no thought of a sexual side to the Eva–Esther partnership. As in previous centuries, being educated, religious, committed to one friend, and living a quiet life, seem to have been factors that warded off suspicion. (By contrast, the Irish singers Augusta Holmes and May Belfort in 1890s Paris, being seen as public, scandalous figures, were both rumoured to be having affairs with women — Sarah Bernhardt and Jane Avril respectively.)[38] As Lillian Faderman points out, appearance was also a factor in this transitional era; those women who looked masculine might be spotted as 'inverts' by people who had heard of the sexologists' theories,[39] whereas the beauty and aristocratic refinement of a woman like Eva would shield her from suspicion. By contrast, the poet Charlotte Mew slipped up on two counts, appearance and indiscreet behaviour: since she was already known for wearing a suit and tie, the comic story of her chasing the fifty-one-year-old novelist May Sinclair round a bedroom in 1914 was easily believed.[40]

Partnerships among women like Esther and Eva, who avoided having the 'lesbian' label flung at them, and would probably not have liked the word's associations, continued to be common well into the middle of the century.[41] Such unions became more and more private and unspoken. The few writings on Eva after her death tend to refer to Esther, with little interest, as her 'best friend'.

In writing a joint biography of the pair in 1982, and in placing them in the context of a long list of devoted partnerships among feminists of the time (such as the other Irish writing pair, Somerville and Ross), Gifford Lewis was the first commentator to give Esther the place she deserves in any consideration of Gore-Booth's career. Where I diverge from Lewis is in her insistence that these partnerships must have been as non-sexual as they were presumed to be at the time. She bases most of her argument about Eva's and Esther's platonic relations on a passage in Eva's *Psychological and Poetic Approach to the Study of Christ in the Fourth Gospel*. Here Gore-Booth argues that sex is one of the 'vampire' instincts (along with ego and the herd instinct) which should be transcended in favour of the spiritual life, because giving in to them brings no lasting satisfaction: 'In dealing with the evils of "repressed" sex, the psychologists often seem to forget that the logical results of unrestrained sex instinct are disease and death.'[42]

The simplest way of reading this passage is that Eva disapproved of sex and never engaged in it. This is an attitude that has never quite died out in lesbian feminist communities: a letter in the North American magazine *Lesbian Connection* warns that sex can lead to many diseases (the list includes 'tooth decay') and is probably not necessary or good for women: 'To all you dykes who don't like sex', the letter ends, 'be proud of yourselves for not having accepted the programming of women into sex objects, body parts and sex-crazed fembots!'[43]

Another reading would see Gore-Booth's diatribe against the 'vampire instincts' as the view of a woman in her ailing fifties, who might have been sexually active all her life before turning back to orthodox religion as she neared death.

I would like to suggest a third option. It is not clear to me that transcending the sex instinct, for Eva Gore-Booth, meant never doing anything sexual — any more than ignoring the 'ego' meant giving up a sense of self, or transcending the 'herd' meant forgetting the rest of society. Halfway between the 'repression' the psychiatrists deplore and the 'unrestrained' sexuality Eva rejects there is room for a third concept: a restrained, managed sexual life, always subordinated to the life of the spirit, which need not be punished by 'disease and death'. My argument is necessarily tentative here, because sex was not something Gore-Booth often discussed; any compromises she and Esther may have arrived at would have been kept in the private sphere and not regarded as material for publication.

Another throwaway remark that Gifford Lewis uses to prove that Eva thought sex 'had to be given up' to attain freedom is a line from a review in *Urania*, pitying those whose lives were 'ruled by their pelvic regions'.[44] But again, all this actually shows is Gore-Booth's unwillingness to let lust 'rule' or dominate her life — not a complete denial of desire. Mary Casal, writing in her autobiography of 1930 about a turn-of-the-century relationship, made a distinction between the sexual 'overindulgence' of the 'real inverts' on the one hand, and, on the other, the 'higher plane' of her own relationship with a woman, which included 'sexual intercourse' as an expression of love rather than lust; for her, being a lesbian was a matter of how often, rather than whether, you did it.[45] So it seems that one way women of Casal's and Gore-Booth's generation reacted to the pathologising of lesbianism was to insist that, though their relationships may have been to some extent sexual, they were not entirely, or even primarily, so. Since doctors told them they were freaks 'ruled by their pelvic regions', these women spared no pains to prove that they were in fact living and loving on (that well-loved phrase) 'a higher plane'.

This is an interesting tangent, but not one to which we are ever likely to find a conclusion. Gifford Lewis claims that Eva and Esther never entered each other's rooms except when they were ill;[46] but I do not see this as something that is possible, or even important, to prove. Surely we have moved beyond the double standard of proof, as described by Sheila Jeffreys in an essay of 1984:

> Women who have lived in the same house and slept in the same bed
> for thirty years have had their lesbianism strongly denied by historians.
> But men and women who simple take walks together are assumed to
> be involved in some sort of heterosexual relationship.[47]

If our ongoing debates on the meaning of sexuality are to make any sense, it is crucial that historians stop conflating the sexually active / celibate distinction with the lesbian / heterosexual one. Whether Eva and Esther were celibate and calm in their feelings, celibate but impassioned, occasionally sexual, sexual early on and then 'transcending' it, or discreetly sexual right through their relationship, the fact of their lifelong lesbian partnership remains.

At this turning-point in the history of Irish lesbians, we can learn from Eva and Esther's dedication to love and understanding across barriers of class, religion, and other ideologies; one friend, reminiscing about Eva, said that she tended to start sentences not with 'I think . . .' but with 'Don't you think . . .?'[48] We could also do with a shot in the arm of Eva's blazing energy and gratitude: in a poem written in 1926 during a respite in the bowel cancer that was killing her, she crowed: 'I am alive, alive, alive!'

Notes and References

1   W. B. Yeats, 'In Memory of Eva Gore-Booth and Con Markiewicz [sic]' (written November 1927) in *Collected Poems*, ed. Augustine Martin, London: Arena, 1990, p. 241.

2   Gifford Lewis, *Eva Gore-Booth and Esther Roper: A Biography*, London: Pandora, 1988.

3   Richard M. Fox, 'Eva Gore-Booth' in *Rebel Irishwomen*, Dublin & Cork: Talbot Press, 1935, pp. 47, 49.

4   Sylvia Pankhurst, *The Suffragette Movement: An Intimate Account of Persons and Ideals*, London: Virago, 1977, p. 164.

5   Eva Gore-Booth, 'The Inner Life of a Child' and Esther Roper, 'Biographical Sketch' in *CP*. On Squidge see Lewis, op. cit., p. 23. On Mabel see 'Sweet Peas' in *CP*, p. 142. The Irish activist Frances Power Cobbe seems to have had a similar childhood, relying on nurses and governesses for friendship in her lonely Dublin stately home; see *Life of Frances Power Cobbe, as told by herself* [1894], London: Swan Sonnenschein, 1904, pp. 31-7.

6   Alice Furlong, 'To Spring' in *Roses and Rue*, London: Elkin Mathews, 1899, p. 38.

7   Ella Young, 'My Lady of Dreams' in *Poems*, Dublin: Maunsel, 1906, p. 9.

8   Katherine Tynan (later Hinkson), 'The Dead Spring' in *Louise de la Vallière and other poems*, London: Kegan Paul, 1885, pp. 13-20.

9   For a similar scene see 'Mystery', *CP*, p. 214.

10 W. B. Yeats to Olivia Shakespear, in *Collected Letters*, i: *1865-1895*, ed. John Kelly, Oxford: Clarendon, 1986, p. 463.

11 Roper, 'Biographical Sketch' in *CP*, p. 3.

12 W. B. Yeats to Eva Gore-Booth, in *A Review of English Literature*, iv, 3 (July 1963).

13 W. B. Yeats, 'In Memory of Eva Gore-Booth . . ', op. cit.

14 Fox, op. cit., pp. 45-6.

15 Lewis, op. cit., p. 135.

16 W. B. Yeats, 'The Lake Isle of Innisfree' in *Collected Poems*, p. 35.

17 See also 'In Oxford Street', *CP*, p. 569.

18 Contrast Katherine Tynan's 'King Cophetua's Queen', which celebrates the beggarmaid's elevation to queen status and romantic heterosexual love, in *Louise de la Vallière*, pp. 45-54.

19 Conrast Gore-Booth's fiercely pure Joan with Katherine Tynan's heroine who suffers from heterosexual jealousy: see 'Joan of Arc' in *Louise de la Vallière*, pp. 25-35.

20 *CP*, 'Biographical Sketch', p. 7.

21 W. B. Yeats, *Memoirs*, ed. Denis Donohgue, London: Macmillan, 1972, p. 78.

22 Yeats, *Collected Letters*, pp. 413, 80, 463.

23 T. W. Rolleston, *Myths and Legends of the Celtic Race* (1911), London: Constable, 1992, pp. 228-30.

24 Rolleston, op. cit., p. 216.

25 Rolleston, op. cit., p. 245.

26 Frances Power Cobbe, 'Celibacy vrs Marriage' in *Essays on the Pursuits of Women*, London: 1863, p. 52.

27 Roper, 'Biographical Sketch' in *CP*, pp. 12, 15.

28 The two friends seem to be men in 'An Epitaph', ibid., pp. 130-32.

29 Gore-Booth's will, quoted in Lewis, op. cit., p. 69.

30 C.S. Lewis, *The Four Loves* (1960), Glasgow: Collins, 1977, p. 58.

31 Cobbe, *Life*, p. 710.

32 Michael Field, 'Lovers' in *The Wattlefold: Unpublished Poems*, ed. Emily C. Fortey, Oxford: Blackwell, 1930, p. 193.

33 Roper, 'Biographical Sketch' in *CP*, pp. 9, 35.

34 Anonymous friend, quoted ibid., p. 38.

35 Quoted in Gillian Kersley (ed.), *Darling Madame: Sarah Grand & Devoted Friend*, London: Virago, 1983, p. 194.

36 Constance Markievicz, *Prison Letters*, ed. Esther Roper, London: Longmans, 1934, pp. 144, 312, 315.

37 Ibid, pp. 315, 314.

38 Catherine van Casselaer, *Lot's Wife: Lesbian Paris, 1890-1914*, Liverpool: Janus Press, 1986, pp. 46-7, 58.

39 Lillian Faderman, *Odd Girls and Twilight Lovers: A History of Lesbian Life in Twentieth-Century America* (1991), Harmondsworth: Penguin, 1992, p. 52.

40 See Penelope Fitzgerald, *Charlotte Mew and her Friends*, London: Collins, 1984.

41 See Leila J. Rupp, '"Imagine My Surprise": Women's Relationships in

Mid-Twentieth-Century America', Martin Duberman, Martha Vicinus and George Chauncey, jr (eds), in *Hidden From History: Reclaiming the Gay and Lesbian Past*, London, Penguin, 1991, pp. 395-410.

42   Eva Gore-Booth, *A Psychological and Poetic Approach to the Study of Christ in the Fourth Gospel*, London: Longmans, 1923, pp. 7-8.

43   *Lesbian Connection* (fall 1993).

44   Lewis, op. cit., pp. 6, 103.

45   Mary Casal, *The Stone Wall: An Autobiography* (Chicago: Eyncourt Press, 1930), pp. 165, 185, quoted in Faderman, op. cit., p. 54.

46   Lewis, op. cit., p. 8.

47   Sheila Jeffreys, 'Does It Matter If They Did It?' in *Not a Passing Phase: Reclaiming Lesbians in History, 1840-1985*, ed. Lesbian History Group, London: The Women's Press, 1990, pp. 19-28 (22-3).

48   Roper, 'Biographical Sketch' in *CP*, p. 43.

2 Momentary Pleasures
Wilde and English Virtue

DAVID ALDERSON

CELTICISM AND AESTHETICISM

On vacation from Oxford in 1876 Wilde wrote to his friend William Ward
from Ireland:

> I ride sometimes after six, but don't do much but bathe, and although
> always feeling slightly immortal when in the sea, feel sometimes slight-
> ly heretical when good Roman Catholic boys enter the water with little
> amulets and crosses round their necks and arms that the good S.
> Christopher may hold them up.[1]

Wilde's eroticised view of these Catholic Irish boys — with its pun on
'immortal' — is as indicative of his attitude to the religion which appealed most to him as it is of his early (and conscious) homoerotic desires.
His relationship to the boys is in every way mediated by distance. Wilde
— from a Protestant, Anglo-Irish background, and a student from Oxford
who suppressed the signs of his Irishness — finds the alterior appeal of
these boys in their apparent freedom and naïve faith (the only role attributed to their religion being one of protection, not repression). Moreover,
the religion and the desire are conflated — Wilde feels 'sometimes slightly heretical' in the boys' presence — so that the attractions of sexual and
religious 'perversion' are collapsed. In this way the sexual desirability of
these boys is clearly bound up with their cultural otherness; indeed, this
very fact seems to enable the desire.

At this stage of his life Wilde was flirting with the idea of conversion, like so many Oxonians before and after. The Catholicism which appealed to him, then, was largely of an English pedigree,[2] but the attraction did not lie in the kind of consistency which those such as Newman claimed for the religion. As some testimony to Wilde's seriousness about the faith, it is true that he wrote that the Incarnation helped him 'grasp at the skirts of the Infinite', but typically went on to add that grasping the Atonement was more difficult.[3] Equally demonstrative of Catholicism's real appeal, in this respect, was his flight from it. In 1878 the Rev. Sebastien Bowden wrote earnestly to Wilde from the Brompton Oratory exhorting him to confess his sins and enter the Catholic faith: 'You would put from you all that is affected and unreal and a thing unworthy of your better self and live full of the deepest interests as a man who feels he has a soul to save and but a few fleeting hours in which to save it.' Those emphases on the renunciation of the frivolous and the moral imperative contained in the passing of time decided him; his reply took the form of a bunch of lilies.[4] Wilde was attracted to Catholicism only for so long as it seemed to offer the possibility of an alternative to the supposedly rational and unmistakably unaesthetic, deeply conscientious world of Protestantism (features which, it has been argued, contributed to the development of a male homosexual subculture in Anglo-Catholic circles).[5] Primarily, Catholicism and, by extension, Catholic subjects were symbolically opposed to the constraining world of English puritanism,[6] however wide of the mark this might seem to us. To this extent, then, the attractions of the Catholic Irish boys derived from perceptions Wilde developed in an environment rather different from the one they inhabited, and Wilde seems to endorse the popular Protestant view of Catholicism as sanctioning moral license.

Another anecdote demonstrates the absurd, almost self-parodic quality of the Protestantism which repulsed Wilde. According to Ellmann, Wilde's famous comment about his crockery while at Oxford was the cause of admonishment by the Dean of St Mary's: 'When a young man says not in polished banter, but in sober earnestness, that he finds it difficult to live up to the level of his blue china, there has crept into these cloistered shades a form of heathenism which it is our bounden duty to fight against and to crush out if possible.'[7] The comment clearly undercuts itself, but what is interesting is its demotic appeal to the Pauline discourse of 'fighting'. But fighting what exactly? Not levity, since this is the opposite of the spirit in which the comment was made — or taken at any rate. What appalled the Dean is that here was a man who was setting an aesthetic standard for himself, taking the *form* of a moral exhortation about imitation and subverting it by emptying it of the possibility of transmitting virtue to the imitator. This shockingly sincere statement is then associated with the alien, the 'heathen'.

The case of the blue crockery may seem relatively trivial, but it clearly wasn't to the Dean of St Mary's, whom we might reasonably expect to have been a respected figure. The significance of the incident lies in the way it demonstrates the characteristic English perception of aestheticism, a phenomenon Wilde came to epitomise in popular consciousness (a position he sought to occupy): aestheticism seemed to represent an amoral self-indulgence which was an affront to the dominant sense of the English national character, one which prided itself on its own uprightness. This sense of Englishness as consisting in moral rectitude was pervasive, and it was not only its hostility to aestheticism which Wilde reacted against, since such chauvinistic attitudes were also evident in relation to sexual morality. The resurgence of moral purity campaigns in the later part of the nineteenth century — of which Wilde was explicitly critical, as I argue below — frequently expressed Protestant-xenophobic attitudes towards degenerate Catholic France[8] — and this was a well-established cultural impulse in the definition of English identity.[9] Moreover, such English perceptions of their moral superiority — deriving ultimately, I would argue, from the nation's Protestant history — were also a central component of imperial ideology in ways that significantly influenced Wilde's self-image.

France was not the only predominantly Catholic country to bear negative comparisons with the English. Take this passage from Walter Walshe's alarmist *Secret History of the Oxford Movement*:

> *Popery is an enemy to National Prosperity.* Looking abroad throughout the whole world, we find that Popery degrades the nations instead of raising them to a higher level. . . . Every part of Ireland is under the same government. Why, then, is it that the Roman Catholic portions of that unhappy land are those in which more poverty, dirt, disloyalty, and ignorance are to be found, than in the Protestant portions? The answer to this question must be that the religion of Popery is at the bottom of this marked difference. . . . Has not the word of God taught us that true 'Godliness is profitable unto all things, having promise of the life that now is, and of that which is to come' (1 Timothy iv. 8)?[10]

A less providential view of history may have taught Walshe other reasons for this distinction (where it is not simply the product of bigotry). Central to the claim, though, is the sense (still important to so much imperial ideology) that England is God's favoured nation. This is a status England has *earned*, the redemptive value of work — among other virtues — being fundamental to this definition of 'Godliness' and lending to the English nation a historical purposiveness supposedly lacking in other countries.

Nor was Walshe's anti-Catholicism in this respect an aberration. In the early 1890s, for example, the *Birmingham Evening Gazette* sent a 'special commissioner' to Ireland to report on conditions there and to produce anti-Home Rule propaganda. The reports were pervasively anti-Catholic. In Tuam, for example, the commissioner found 'a depressing kind of place, and but for the enterprise of a few Protestants, the place would be a phantasmagoria of pigs, priests, peasants, poverty and "peelers"'.[11]

Such perceptions of Irish degeneracy were also — and with increasing frequency — attributed to racial difference in the second half of the nineteenth century. As early as 1847, in his tour of Ireland during the Famine, we find William Somerville commenting that 'We once used to hear that it was the Catholic religion which disqualified the Irish for industrial enterprise. . . . But we now hear of the inferiority of the Celtic race to the Saxon'.[12] The stereotypical backwardness, laziness and irrationalism of the Irish, then, came to be underwritten by accounts of racial difference, perceptions which were advanced or legitimated by ethnologists[13] (though, as we have seen, anti-Catholicism did not disappear from colonial attitudes).

Such racial theories increasingly informed cultural debate. Despite his declared sympathies with Celticism, Matthew Arnold believed that English virtue was indicative of a specifically racial superiority. In all of his writings Arnold's project was to reform English culture, and his influential essay on Celtic literature — explicitly informed by contemporary ethnology — was a part of this agenda, arguing that the English were a composite of different racial groups who should draw on their largely neglected Celtic reserves of sensuousness and sentimentality. Arnold held to the stereotype of the incapacity of the Celts/Irish for self-government at the same time as he hoped that the rediscovery of the Celtic racial heritage of the English would humanise their culture and consequently alleviate Irish hostility to the Union.[14] This emphasis in Arnold is a modified form of Renan's thesis: 'that great law by which the primitive race of an invaded country always ends by getting the upper hand, [according to which] England is becoming every day more Celtic and less Germanic'. Such unrestrained 'Hellenism' — and this term is itself significant — could not be countenanced by Arnold, however, as he adhered to the view that 'moral conscience, self-control, seriousness, steadfastness, are not the whole of human life certainly, but they are by far the greatest part of it; without them . . . nations cannot stand'.[15] Race therefore did not justify nationhood, and it was precisely the highly developed aesthetic sense of the Celts — their readiness 'to react against the despotism of fact'[16] — which disqualified them from self-rule. Arnold was convinced that the admission of too much Celticism could lead to the degeneration of Britain.

Nonetheless, more radical versions of this thesis developed, including

Wilde's speech on the 'Celtic Revival' in San Francisco in 1882: 'The Saxon took our lands from us and left us desolate. We took their language and added new beauties to it.'[17] Another, later example was that of Grant Allen, who gave an account of differences in 'racial tastes'. He argued that the proponents of a Celtic cultural revival in England were also political radicals — democrats, Home Rulers and socialists. Allen also maintained the Renanian association of the Celt with aestheticism, as well as the (implicit) gendering of the attributes of imperial rule and of poeticism: 'In our complex nationality the Teuton has contributed in large part the muscle, the thews, the hard-headed organization, the law, the stability, the iron hand; but the Celt has added the lightness, airiness, imagination, wonder, the sense of beauty and of mystery, the sadness, the sweetness.'[18] In the context of such racial tastes, Allen claimed, Wilde was 'an Irishman to the core',[19] and Wilde was enthusiastic about this piece, writing Allen a complimentary letter about it.[20]

Just as Catholicism had seemed to Wilde to be a religion far removed from the conscientiousness of Protestantism, then, accounts of the racial character of the Celt became another means of legitimating his hostility to English moralism. Wilde was even to give a positive gloss to those often denounced Celtic vices of mendacity and idleness. Ironically, though, it may also have been precisely Wilde's Celtic identifications which led him to be critical of the kind of republicanism his mother had celebrated. In his early 'Sonnet on Liberty', for example, he asserts that revolutionary activities appeal to him only insofar as they give form to his own feelings (they 'mirror my wildest passions like the sea'), though he also betrays an ambivalent sympathy with these 'Christs that die upon the barricades'.[21] This valorisation of individual experience is, of course, entirely typical of Wilde, but his rejection of self-sacrifice was not simply a response to the puritanism of English society (though it was mostly expressed in relation to this); it actually lay in his rejection of practical interventions in the course of history and his belief in a different kind of freedom.

ART AND FREEDOM

Wilde's hostility to practical action is a consistent feature of his writings. In his Oxford commonplace book, following a quotation from Pater, he writes:

> We are indeed compassed by the high unver [never?] leaped mountains of necessity, but for him who knows his limitations this dark horizon *becomes the sunlit circle of duty*[.] The cross of Christ will cast no shadow when the sun of Truth is high in the heaven.[22]

The sense of determinism here is consistent with other jottings in this manuscript, but the importance of this passage lies in its demonstration that early in his life Wilde had come to a conviction that the realm of freedom was severely circumscribed and that the culture of self-sacrifice was both deluded and ineffective in terms of its purchase on the future. It is not until 'The Critic as Artist', though, that Wilde fully expounded his understanding of the relationship between history, art and the sinner. In this piece Wilde invokes an utterly deterministic view of history at the same time as he represents art as being the way in which we can exert some freedom from the iron laws of necessity. Gilbert's assertion that speech is superior to action introduces this issue, since action is represented as being impotent, unable to affect the future. Action is counterposed to the imagination which requires inactivity, or 'doing nothing'. Hence it is more difficult to write history than to make it, and

> The one duty we owe to history is to re-write it. . . . When we have fully discovered the scientific laws that govern life, we shall realise that the one person who has more illusions than the dreamer is the man of action. He, indeed, knows neither the origin of his deeds nor their results. ('Critic', p. 359)

The crucial word of the first sentence is not 're-write', but 'duty', since this is a denial of the view that we should draw moral lessons about conduct from the past, or that we can know how our actions will affect the future; it is essentially a denial of that purposiveness so integral to English self-definition. For this reason, the sinner is valorised over the ascetic saint. Sin 'through its intensified individualism . . . saves us from the monotony of type', whereas the prioritisation of conscience and self-denial

> is simply a method by which man arrests his progress. . . . It is well for our vanity that we slay the criminal, for if we suffered him to live he might show us what we had gained from his crime. It is well for his peace that the saint goes to his martyrdom. He is spared the night of the horror of his harvest. ('Critic', pp 360-1)

Wilde therefore takes individualism to its conclusion, seeing the claims of the individual as ultimately disintegrative of the claims of society: 'the security of society lies in its custom and unconscious instinct, and the basis of the stability of society, as a healthy organism, is the complete absence of any intelligence amongst its members' ('Critic', p. 388). Instead instinct should become self-conscious, and the only way in which this is possible is through an awareness of the individual's *modernity* (an important term for Wilde) — that is, an awareness that all other ages are secreted in him through his racial inheritance, his soul. It is also in this that the temptation to evil is to be found, not least through art, which is the record of the soul in other ages: the scientific principle of heredity may have denied the possibility of freedom in the practical sphere, but

> in the subjective sphere, where the soul is at work, it comes to us, this terrible shadow, with many gifts in its hands, gifts of strange temperaments and subtle susceptibilities, gifts of wild ardours and chill moods of indifference, complex multiform gifts of thoughts that are at variance with each other, and passions that war against themselves. And so it is not our own life that we live, but the lives of the dead, and the soul that dwells within us is no single spiritual entity, making us personal and individual, created for our own service, and entering in us for joy. It is something that has dwelt in fearful places. . . . It fills us with impossible desires, and makes us follow what we know we cannot gain. ('Critic', p. 383)

Temptation is the legacy of racial development, then, and art comes to represent the realm of freedom, the means by which this temptation can be given *formal* expression. Imagination 'is simply concentrated life-experience' ('Critic', p. 384). The critical spirit — one of judicious selection — permits the perfection of that culture made available through the soul's inheritance, hence Wilde's emphasis on self-culture, the rejection of sincerity, the adoption of masks and the multiplication of personalities. These are not the product of some proleptic postmodernist theory of the self, but of Wilde's conviction that the self is the culmination of racial development.[23]

All of this connects him with a Hegelian strand of thought in aestheticism which is present, for example, in Pater's important essay on Winckelman.[24] Here Pater argues that Greek culture was of an aesthetic nature, preceding the myth of the Fall and the sense of guilt which accompanied this.[25] Possibly more significant to Wilde is Symonds's version of this thesis, since Symonds's work on the Greeks becomes an explicit defence of same-sex desire. In his *Studies of the Greek Poets* he wrote:

> Like a young man newly come from the wrestling-ground, anointed, chapleted, and very calm, the Genius of the Greeks appears before us. Upon his soul there is no burden of the world's pain; the creation that groaneth and travaileth together has touched him with no sense of anguish; nor has he yet felt sin.[26]

Such a culture preceded any division between body and spirit and consequently based its ethics on the harmony of the two. It was the Greeks' sense of beauty which guided them rather than an abstracted 'Mosaic' conscience. The triumph of the Romans, though, led to a degeneration of this

Greek ideal in moral matters, and the result was the intrusion of a reproachful spiritual regime in the form of Christianity which counter-posed flesh and spirit. Symonds places his faith in science as 'our redeemer'[27] having the capacity dialectically to reconcile the body/spirit duality, uniting conscience with the physical laws which govern our existence.

Here, then, we have the artist personified by Greek culture, insensible of the dictates of conscience and guided by the pursuit of beauty. Symonds is more explicit about precisely what he is defending in *A Problem in Greek Ethics*. Written in 1873, but not published until ten years later — and then privately — the book seems principally an apologia for Greek pederasty as being manly, possibly even originating in the military camaraderie the Dorians introduced into Greek society after the Homeric era.[28] That the real ethical issue of *Greek Poets* is that of male same-sex love is made clear by the analogous passages in *Greek Ethics* which describe the transition from pagan to Christian ethics through the degeneration of the original aesthetic morality of the Greeks once the Roman Empire had overtaken them:

> While the paiderastia of the Greeks was sinking into grossness, ef-feminacy, and aesthetic prettiness, the moral instincts of humanity began to assert themselves in earnest. It became part of the higher doctrine of the Roman Stoics to suppress this form of passion. The Christians, from St Paul onwards, instituted an uncompromising crusade against it.[29]

Symonds's work is crucial to an understanding of the cultural connec-tions between male same-sex desire and aestheticism. In attempting to aestheticise English culture, Wilde must have been conscious all along of the connections Symonds had drawn with such desires (*Dorian Gray* in its very title invokes Symonds's theory about the origins of pederasty in Greek culture). Even so, Wilde was less anxious than Symonds about the correlation between aestheticism, same-sex desire and effeminacy.

While constantly looking back to the Hellenic ideal, though, Wilde is insistent throughout his work that the route to a new aestheticism is through the influence of the Celt. In 'The Critic as Artist' he emphasises that 'it is the Celt who leads in art' ('Critic', p. 396). More significantly, 'Pen, Pen-cil and Poison' is subtitled 'A Study in Green', and to demonstrate that this is not simply a parody of Whistler, Wilde claims that Wainewright

> had that curious love of green, which in individuals is always the sign of a subtle artistic temperament, and in nations is said to denote a laxi-ty, if not a decadence of morals. Like Baudelaire he was extremely fond of cats, and with Gautier, he was fascinated by that 'sweet marble monster' of both sexes that we can still see at Florence and in the Louvre.[30]

Aestheticism, race, amorality and an ambiguous sexuality here dovetail with each other in Wilde's defence of the artist–criminal, the figure of progress who is a calculated affront to English moral self-definition.

BUGGERING GERALD: *A WOMAN OF NO IMPORTANCE*

> Art comes to you proposing frankly to give nothing but the highest quality to your moments as they pass, and simply for those moments' sake.
>
> WALTER PATER[31]

> MRS ALLONBY: Aren't you coming?
> LORD ILLINGWORTH: In a few moments.
>
> OSCAR WILDE, *A Woman of No Importance*, p. 109

The conflict between the 'modern' sensibility as outlined in 'The Critic as Artist' and the conventional view of duty is represented in Wilde's work as that between the dandy and the puritan, and in at least one of his plays it is the puritan who seems to win. In *A Woman of No Importance* it is Mrs Arbuthnot who triumphs over the machinations of Lord Illingworth. The play's debates about morality and marriage have as their context the moral purity debates of the 1880s and 1890s in which women moral purity campaigners frequently established themselves in the role of the country's moral guardians, using rhetoric clearly indebted to evangelical Christianity. These campaigners aimed to reform public and private life by the extension of women's influence and, by this means, to abolish the double standard and improve the morality of public servants. Their intention was to influence public life by the extension of domestic standards, making the family the touchstone of morality — public and private — and setting up the woman as symbol of pristine virtue tainted only by the depravity of men.[32] As the MP Kelvil comments in Wilde's play, 'Woman is the intellectual helpmeet of man in public as in private life. Without her we should forget the true ideals' (*WNI*, p. 89). In this context, it should also be noted that purity movements played an important role in the successful passage of the 1885 Criminal Law Amendment Act into which Labouchere inserted his own amendment outlawing sexual acts between men.[33] The tone of this movement was distinctly indebted to Old Testament morality, and its class composition was also significant, as, according to Mort, 'purity usually worked by forging allegiances between sections of the evangelical middle class, the petty-bourgeoisie and the respectable working class against the aristocracy.'[34] Wilde's adoption of the persona of the aristocratic libertine and his alignment with French culture must be seen in this light as repudiations of dominant English values. Moreover, Wilde polemicised against marriage and the family as a limitation on personality in 'The Soul of Man Under Socialism'.[35]

The thematic concerns of *A Woman of No Importance* are also closely related to Wilde's concerns with the moralisation of time and racial determinism. Mrs Arbuthnot is the woman with a past who initially accepts — and has lived her life accepting — the absolutist judgement (articulated by Hester Worsley) that 'if a man and woman have sinned, let them both go forth into the desert to love or loathe each other there . . . but don't punish the one and let the other go free. Don't have one law for men and another for women' (*WNI*, p. 103). This plea for equal contempt is essentially the problem of the play, in which Mrs Arbuthnot has abjectly accepted the consequences of her sinful past while that of Lord Illingworth has yet to catch up with him. The reason for this is partly that Illingworth philosophically rejects the claims of puritanism in his repudiation of the moral lessons of the past. The central battle becomes one over the possession of Gerald, over his future and, implicitly therefore, that of the race:

> MRS ARBUTHNOT: . . . You don't realise what my past has been in suffering and shame.
> LORD ILLINGWORTH: My dear Rachel, I must candidly say that I think Gerald's future considerably more important than your past.
> MRS ARBUTHNOT: Gerald cannot separate his future from my past.
> LORD ILLINGWORTH: That is exactly what he should do. That is exactly what you should help him to do. What a typical woman you are! You talk sentimentally, and you are thoroughly selfish the whole time. . . .
> MRS ARBUTHNOT: He was not discontented until he met you. You have made him so.
> LORD ILLINGWORTH: Of course, I made him so. Discontent is the first step in the progress of a man or a nation. But I did not leave him with a mere longing for things he could not get. No, I made him a charming offer. He jumped at it, I need hardly say. Any young man would. And now, simply because it turns out that I am the boy's own father and he my own son, you propose practically to ruin his career. (*WNI*, pp 111-12)

Illingworth's position here is the opposite of Old Testament morality about the sins of the parents being visited on the children (*WNI*, p. 124). He refuses such hereditary principles by projecting them onto the selfishness of women, and in this is clearly alluding to purity campaigners. In contrast, Illingworth stimulates Gerald's 'discontent', or temptation — that disintegrative, racially inherited individualism — and promises to satisfy the desires this provokes. Illingworth's claim that this is the route to national as well as individual progress also demonstrates the threat that his philosophy poses to the restrictive English puritan mentality. The opposing attitudes of the play are emphasised by being gendered — though only in the context of the family, since Mrs Allonby's scepticism towards marriage is complemented by an individualism as intense as Illingworth's — and through the class division between middle-class moralist and aristocratic libertine.

That marriage and the institution of the family are related specifically to English virtue is argued by Kelvil: 'It [home life] is the mainstay of our moral system in England, Lady Stutfield. Without it *we would become like our neighbours*' (*WNI*, p. 89, my emphasis). In such a context, of course, the unmarried man is rendered immediately suspicious, not least because of his unrepresentativeness of the English: Lady Caroline, for example, claims that representation of England abroad by an unmarried man such as Lord Illingworth 'might lead to complications' (*WNI*, p. 81). For Illingworth, on the other hand, 'the happiness of a married man . . . depends on the people he has not married' (*WNI*, p. 117).

All of this goes some way to legitimate Lytton Strachey's description of the play following a 1907 revival of it. For Strachey, Lord Illingworth 'has made up his mind to bugger one of the other guests — a handsome young man of twenty', Gerald, and when Mrs Arbuthnot objects on the grounds that Gerald is his son, Illingworth responds 'that it is additional reason for doing it (oh! he's a very *wicked Lord*)'.[36] In opening this section I suggested a trivial joke which might be noticed by those especially cognisant of the intensity of sensory experience implied by the word 'moment'. If this is correct, this in-joke reinforces Strachey's decoding of the play at the point at which Mrs Arbuthnot tells Gerald pointedly: 'Lord Illingworth is very good, I am sure, to interest himself in you for the moment.' Illingworth responds — hand on Gerald's shoulder — 'Gerald and I are great friends already' (*WNI*, p. 108).

The problem for Illingworth, though, is his former momentary interest in Mrs Arbuthnot herself. Unlike his interest in Gerald, *this* moment has implications: it led to pregnancy and to the demand for marriage — carrying the implication, for the dandy, that he must renounce his individualism. Illingworth's initial refusal leads to the uncompromising rejection of the possibility of any atonement on his part through his later offer of marriage: instead Mrs Arbuthnot has become too attached to her sin in the form of Gerald. In fact Gerald — as both perpetual reminder of her transgression and object of her love — embodies the paradox of her situation: 'It is my dishonour that has bound you so closely to me. It is the price I paid for you — the price of body and soul — that makes me love you as I do' (*WNI*, p. 136). The 'price of body and soul' is clearly a reference to the ideal unity of aesthetic experience symbolised for Wilde and others by Greek culture. It is this unity that Mrs Arbuthnot is renouncing, and she demands a similar renunciation on the part of Gerald. In this same lengthy speech she laments the way that the world draws children from the influence of women into a more cosmopolitan environment from which Mrs Arbuthnot excludes herself because of her own sense of shame, relegating her own activities to charity work under the aegis of the church (the church being 'the only house where sinners are made welcome'). Moreover, there is a strong hint that Mrs Arbuthnot's love for Gerald is a suppressed sexual desire — and therefore the counterpart of Lord Ill-ingworth's coded attempt at seduction: at the point at which she tells Gerald that Hester, as his wife, must come first, she begs: 'When you are away, Gerald . . . with . . . her — oh, think of me sometimes' (WNI, p. 138).

The woman puritan, attached to her own shame, is the force which ultimately triumphs in the play. Moreover, Mrs Arbuthnot passes on her mantle of moral guardian to Hester Worsley by sanctioning Gerald's mar-riage to her and at the same time referring to the coded theme of sexual object choice through a pointed substitution: 'Gerald, I cannot give you a father, but I have brought you a wife' (WNI, p. 138).

Wilde's appropriation in A Woman of No Importance of the crucial term 'moment' from aestheticism's manifesto reflects on the relations of both aestheticism and male same-sex acts to English culture. Aestheticism, in developing an élitist aura for itself and in voiding its relations to art objects of any moral significance, rejected the profoundly moralised rela-tions which English philistines wanted to prescribe between art and its audiences.[37] Hence the emphases on the 'uselessness' of art and on the intensity of the individual's experience were at one level a dissident response (though only negatively so). A Woman of No Importance draws an analogy with this: male same-sex acts are coded as preserving the pristine intensity of the moment divorced from any moral implications. On the other hand, normative prescriptions on sexuality lead to familial claims and the consequent limitations on subjective experience and racial diversity which Wilde believed this entailed. If, as Kelvil suggests, marriage is the basis of the English moral order, 'buggery' is its negation, the ultimate out-sider's threat to its integrity. The figure of the dissolute aristocrat — whose association with England's 'neighbours' (the Celts) is inimical to the puritanism of its dominant classes — threatens precisely this domestic order at a time when it was being presented as a model for the political integrity of the state.

THE REVENGE OF THE PHILISTINE

Lord Illingworth's ignominious exclusion at the end of A Woman of No Importance is one of those passages which apparently demonstrate Wilde's

often alleged prescience about his own fate. In fact, of course, it is rather
a recognition of the historical position of the aesthete as Wilde sees him
in Victorian society, a recognition which is maintained in the letter 'De
Profundis'. After his prison sentence Wilde did profess a purely formal
penitence, but he still claimed to be a 'born antinomian'. In particular, he
regretted that aspect which entailed living for the moment, famously relating
it to his prose style: 'What the paradox was to me in the sphere of thought,
perversity became to me in the sphere of passion. . . . I took pleasure where
it pleased me and passed on.'[38]

This letter's strongly determinist, anti-ethical argument (notably in its
repeated claim that everything that is realised is right) is bound up with
Wilde's own sense of himself as the tragic victim of familial relations. But
Wilde also sees this tragedy in specifically racial terms. His prosecution
— which did, of course, try his artistic views as part of its prosecution
of his love — becomes a struggle between the qualities Wilde attached
to competing races. In this context, the Oedipal relations between Alfred
Douglas and Queensberry which ruin Wilde are finally made to connect
with Anglo-Irish relations.

The Douglases are a family whose racial predisposition is to self-ruin
and the ruin of others; Alfred is only the latest incarnation:

> You had yourself told me how many of your race there had been who
> had stained their hands in their own blood; your uncle certainly, your
> grandfather possibly; many others in the mad, bad line from which you
> come.[39]

> Through your father you come of a race, marriage with whom is hor-
> rible, friendship fatal, and that lays violent hands either on its own life
> or on the lives of others.[40]

Significantly, in this context, Wilde represents Queensberry as atavistic,
an unaesthetic racial throwback — precisely Anglo-Saxon and therefore
pre-modern (in Wilde's sense), in an insult which brilliantly inverts English
racist representations of the Irish as simian and prognathous.[41] The court
itself takes on this very persona in its prosecution of Wilde as it vindicates
the rule and continuing racial dominance of the philistine:

> I used to see your father bustling in and out [of the police court] in the
> hopes of attracting public attention, as if anyone could fail to note or
> remember the stableman's gait and dress, the bowed legs, the twitching
> hands, the hanging lower lip, the bestial and half-witted grin. . . . I used
> to feel conscious of his presence, and the blank dreary walls of the great
> Court-room, the very air itself, seemed to me at times to be hung with
> multitudinous masks of that apelike face.[42]

Naturally Wilde presents himself as racially antithetical to the Douglases. Hence his explanation of his indulgent extravagance towards Alfred Douglas: 'the virtues of prudence and thrift were not in 'my own nature or my own race'; Wilde's tolerance was at least partly attributable to 'my own proverbial good-nature and Celtic laziness'.[43] And when Wilde admonishes Douglas's mother, it is with a sense of the bitterness of a more historic conflict and in full conformity with his sense of the racial nature of the philistine/aesthete dichotomy:

> I confess that it pains me when I hear of your mother's remarks about me, and I am sure that on reflection you will agree with me that if she has no word of regret or sorrow for the ruin your race has brought on mine it would be better if she remained silent.[44]

In this way Wilde formally completes his own version of his symbolic relations to his age by insisting on its integration into a larger narrative of British colonial repression — a narrative which, for him, was significant predominantly because of its moralistic denial of the aestheticism which Wilde considered the solvent of restrictive social relations.

*   *   *

'The ages live in history through their anachronisms.'[45] Wilde consciously exploited an ensemble of identifications which, in the context of English culture, were conspicuously anti-bourgeois and amoral — Catholic, dandy and Celt; criminal, sinner and idle artist — and his theorisation of them as related enabled him to make explicit — indeed, visible — his dissident relations to the dominant culture. These personae were all deployed against English piety and the hegemony of the family, of which he was a radical (if sexist) critic. They were also, of course, mystifications of his actual relations to that dominant culture, symptomatic through their disempowering archaisms and underdog connotations (however transgressive) of the power and integrity of the British imperial state and the moral relations it enforced. Unfortunately these identifications — along with the sense of determinism which he imported into his speculations on art and history — also contribute to the accounts of Wilde's life and work which see his criminal conviction as the fulfilment of his own masochistic desire.[46] Wilde courted hostility not because he secretly wanted to be punished, but because he provocatively challenged the moralism of the society in which he made his living. Not least, he opposed its sexual morality. This is not to say that sexual tolerance was generally understood beyond a certain coterie to be a part of his desire for an aestheticised society.[47] Rather, his reification of the aesthete/philistine dichotomy as a dialectical racial conflict was the source of his hope for an aesthetic individualism, one whose anti-puritanism was definitive of its modernity.

Abbreviations

'Critic'   'The Critic as Artist' in *The Artist as Critic: Critical Writings of Oscar Wilde*, ed. Richard Ellmann, London: W. H. Allen, 1970

WNI   *A Woman of No Importance* in Oscar Wilde, *Plays*, Harmondsworth: Penguin, 1954

Notes and References

1   *The Letters of Oscar Wilde*, ed. Rupert Hart-Davis, London: Hart-Davis, 1962, p. 21.

2   Perhaps not wholly, given Speranza's sympathy for Catholicism and her apparent baptism of her sons into it. See Richard Ellmann, *Oscar Wilde*, Harmondsworth: Penguin, 1988, pp 18-19; also Davis Coakley, *The Importance of Being Irish*, Dublin: Town House, 1994, pp 112-14.

3   Wilde, *Letters*, p. 20.

4   Letter and full anecdote are given in Ellmann, op. cit., pp 90-1. Gary Paterson reviews Wilde's Catholicism somewhat moralistically in 'Oscar Wilde and the Scarlet Woman', *Antigonish Review*, lxxxv (1991), pp 241-54, concluding that it was initially an aspect of his aestheticism and, later, of his decadence.

5   See David Hilliard's 'UnEnglish and Unmanly: Anglo-Catholicism and Homosexuality', *Victorian Studies*, xxv (1983) pp 181-200; also Eve Kosofsky Sedgwick's witty comments on gay men's identifications with Catholicism in *Epistemology of the Closet*, Hemel Hempstead: Harvester Wheatsheaf, 1991, p. 140.

6   For further reflections on this English/Irish dichotomy see Éibhear Walshe's Introduction above.

7   Ellmann, op. cit., p. 44.

8   See Frank Mort, *Dangerous Medico-Moral Politics in England Since 1830*, London: Routledge, 1987, p. 113.

9   Linda Colley in *Britons: Forging the Nation, 1707-1837*, New Haven: Yale University Press, 1992, argues that a Protestant British identity is forged throughout the eighteenth and early nineteenth centuries in conscious opposition to Catholic France.

10   Walter Walshe, *The Secret History of the Oxford Movement*, London: Swann Sonnenschein, 1898, pp 362-3.

11   *Ireland As It Is and As It Would Be Under Home Rule*, Birmingham Daily Gazette, 1893, p. 134.

12   William Somerville, *Letters from Ireland During the Famine of 1847*, ed. K. D. M. Snell, Dublin: Irish Academic Press, 1994, p. 177.

13   On the influence of racial theories on anti-Irish feeling see L. P. Curtis jr, *Anglo-Saxon and Celts: A Study of Anti-Irish Prejudice in Victorian England*, Connecticut: University of Bridgeport, 1968. Sheridan Gilley has attacked Curtis's arguments in his 'English Attitudes to the Irish in England, 1780-1900' in Colin Holmes (ed.),

Immigrants and Minorities in British Society, London: Allen & Unwin, 1978, pp 81-110. Gilley clearly overstates his case.

14   Matthew Arnold, 'On the Study of Celtic Literature' in *Complete Prose Works*, iii: *Lectures and Essays in Criticism*, ed. R. H. Super, University of Michigan Press, 1962. Frederic E. Faverty has acknowledged Arnold's indebtedness to racial theory in *Matthew Arnold the Ethnologist*, Illinois: Northwestern University Press, 1951. A more recent and detailed account is provided by Robert J. C. Young in *Colonial Desire: Hybridity in Theory, Culture and Race,* London & New York: Routledge, 1995, ch. 3. Young argues that Arnold was influenced by theories of race which rejected the possibility of permanent hybridity between races, and goes on to suggest that a racial dialectic also permeates Arnold's *Culture and Anarchy*, though here the Celtic influence is transformed into the Hellenic.

15   Matthew Arnold, 'La réforme intellectuelle et morale de la France' in *Complete Prose Works*, vii: *God and the Bible*, ed. R. H. Super, University of Michigan Press, 1970, p. 45.

16   Arnold, 'Celtic Literature', p. 344.

17   Oscar Wilde, 'The Poets of '48' in *The Annotated Oscar Wilde*, ed. H. Montgomery Hyde, New York: Orbis, 1982, p. 374.

18   Grant Allen, 'The Celt in English Art', *Fortnightly Review*, lv (1891), p. 268.

19   Ibid., p. 273

20   Wilde, *Letters*, pp 286-7.

21   Oscar Wilde, *Complete Works*, London: Collins, 1966, p. 709.

22   *Oscar Wilde's Oxford Notebooks: A Portrait of Mind in the Making*, ed. Philip E. Smith II and Michael S. Helfand, Oxford University Press, 1989, p. 141.

23   Terry Eagleton discusses Wilde's determinism and his affinities with postmodernist aesthetics with rather different conclusions from mine in the essay on 'Oscar and George' in *Heathcliff and the Great Hunger: Studies in Irish Culture*, London: Verso, 1995, pp 320-41.

24   On this see the commentary by Smith and Helfand in *Oscar Wilde's Oxford Notebooks*, pp 22-7.

25   Walter Pater, 'Winckelman' (1867) in *The Renaissance*, ed. Donald L. Hill, Berkeley: University of California Press, 1980, esp. pp 176-7.

26   J. A. Symonds, *Studies of the Greek Poets* (1873), 3rd edn, London: A. & C. Black, 1920, p. 554.

27   Ibid., p. 571.

28   J. A. Symonds, *A Problem in Greek Ethics*, London: privately printed, 1908, p. 17. It is not known for certain that Wilde was acquainted with this text, but given his interest in Symonds and the circles he mixed in, the probability is high.

29   Ibid., p. 59.

30   Wilde, 'Pen, Pencil and Poison' in *The Artist as Critic*, p. 324.

31   Walter Pater, 'Conclusion' (1868) in *The Renaissance*, p. 190.

32   Here I am indebted to Kerry Powell's discussion of these movements and their influence on the theatre in his chapter on *The Ideal Husband* in *Oscar Wilde and the Theatre of the 1890s*, Cambridge University Press, 1990, ch. 6.

33   Mort, op. cit., pp 126-30.

34   Ibid., p. 113.

35   Wilde, 'The Soul of Man Under Socialism' in *The Artist as Critic*, pp 265-6.

36   Quoted in Ellmann, op. cit., p. 357n.

37 See Josephine M. Guy, *The British Avant-Garde: The Theory and Politics of Tradition*, Hemel Hempstead: Harvester Wheatsheaf, 1991, pp 88-93.

38 Wilde, *Letters*, p. 466.

39 Ibid., p. 435.

40 Ibid., p. 440.

41 See L. P. Curtis jr's account of the stereotyping of the Irish as apes in his *Apes and Angels*, Newton Abbot: David & Charles, 1971; also R. F. Foster in the title essay from his collection *Paddy and Mr Punch: Connections in Irish and English History*, Harmondsworth: Allen Lane, 1993, pp 171-94.

42 Wilde, *Letters*, p. 492.

43 Ibid., pp 427, 429.

44 Ibid., p. 501.

45 Wilde, 'Phrases and Philosophies for the Use of the Young' in *The Artist as Critic*, p. 434.

46 Examples hardly need mentioning. More recent ones range from the crudely moralistic to the otherwise valuable, e.g. from Christopher Nassar's *Into the Demon Universe: A Literary Exploration of Oscar Wilde* (New Haven: Yale University Press, 1974) to Ellmann's biography. Melissa Knox, still obsessed with Freudian etiologies of homosexuality, argues that 'It almost seems as if Wilde were determined to prove Freud's idea of the death drive. He wanted to destroy the English, he wanted to destroy conventional wisdom and conventional principles, and, to crown it all, he wanted to destroy himself' (*Oscar Wilde: A Long and Lovely Suicide*, New Haven & London: Yale University Press, 1994, p. 37).

47 Alan Sinfield in '"Effeminacy" and "Femininity": Sexual Politics in Wilde's Comedies', *Modern Drama*, xxxvii (1994), pp 34-52, warns against seeing homosexuality as the 'truth' of Wilde's dandy figures, since this would not have been perceived by Victorian audiences and results from reading the plays in the light of the trials. See also Sinfield's *The Wilde Century: Effeminacy, Oscar Wilde and the Queer Moment* (London: Cassell, 1994), which brilliantly discusses historical perceptions of effeminacy and further elaborates on Wilde's significance in this respect. Ed Cohen also suggests that 'the story of the Wilde trials played no small part in crystallizing the concept of "male homosexuality" in the Victorian imagination' (*Talk on the Wilde Side: Towards a Genealogy of a Discourse on Male Sexualities*, New York & London: Routledge, 1993, p. 99).

3 Error and Eros
The Fiction of Forrest Reid as
a Defence of Homosexuality

COLIN CRUISE

The lack of critical writing on Forrest Reid is both notable and revealing. His novels have not been widely distributed or acclaimed since his death in 1947 and are now, in the main, out of print. Reid has not been received into the fold of important or formative Irish writers of the early and mid-twentieth century. Although there was an admirably full critical biography by Brian Taylor in 1980, there ensued no great resurgence of interest in Reid except as a kind of cult novelist, first editions of whose works fetch high prices at auction. This very cult status — as a gay writer with an audience of connoisseurs — raises interesting questions. While one might see him as working within a tradition of pastoral and autobiographical writing in Ireland, lyric and evocative, his general reputation is affected by his stubborn placing of a boy within the dreamy landscape he describes. This *staffage*, to use a term employed in art history — the distribution of this figure in the landscape — challenges rather than supports the sexual mores and religious beliefs of Reid's homeland. The boy, whose feelings are so delicately recorded, whose inner life unfolds throughout the trilogy which sometimes bears his name,[1] might be seen (and indeed was seen by Reid's contemporaries) as a brilliant creation. But his presence reveals to the modern reader an essential feature of the novels: that they are about a particular sexuality. The boy subverts the Christian ideal of manliness and reinvents for himself the manly 'pagan' ideals of classical culture. I discuss the origins of this tendency for Reid below, but I should note here that by the time he came to publish *Uncle Stephen* (1931) the tendency would have been seen as dated and backward-looking, showing an interest in unfashionable (as well as compromising) writers of the 1880s and 1890s. The great Hellenist revival which had begun in the mid-nineteenth century had lingered on into the twentieth century despite the trial of Oscar Wilde and the subsequent villification of Hellenism.[2] Here, some forty years later, Reid was putting forward the same ideal once more, with the same references to literature, sculpture and painting to validate the choices he indicated. There had been several intimations of this direction in Reid's previous writings, starting with *The Garden God* (1905), where the novelist had deliberately placed himself in this Uranian/ Hellenist tradition. He was to show an interest, sometimes scholarly, in nineteenth-century literature and its genres throughout his career.[3] But what might be seen as versions of these genres, as school stories or mytholigical tales, like *Pirates of the Spring* and *Demophon*, for instance, were not simply reworkings of Thomas Hughes's or Charles Kingsley's novels; taking their themes from mainstream nineteenth-century literature Reid's novels explore male same-sex desire in both its personal and social dimensions.

In one of the longest and most detailed criticisms of Reid's novels published between Russell Burlingham's biography (1953) and Taylor's, Peter Coveney analysed tendencies of the novelist's work. Or rather he identified weaknesses in Reid which might account for the decline of his reputation. This criticism culminates in Coveney's finding a central 'erotic intention' in the novels supported by 'intrusive references to Greek and Renaissance culture.'[4] While Greek references are undoubtedly present in the novels, Coveney's interpretation is that they are meretricious. He notes of *Brian Westby*: 'The central emotion in itself is not necessarily embarrassing. The embarrassment arises from the idealizing falsification. Everything safeguards the emotion from its central reality.'[5] This reality in Coveney's account is love, and although he appears to recognise the real restraints placed upon the novelist in approaching the theme of male same-sex desire and its fulfilment — what Coveney describes as the 'unacceptability of the emotional realites of this theme'[6] — the idea of falsification and dishonesty remains central to his objection. While there is a real evasion of many of the directions of contemporary literature, Reid is hardly alone in this evasion. My contention is that Reid's novels try to unite a personal erotic tendency with a sense of place and a direction in history.

This is the context in which I want to present Reid here. It must always be difficult to label him as a dissident; indeed, one might more easily see him as trying to harmonise elements in himself and in society — past and present, ancient and modern, sacred and profane, child and adult.

Rather than taking issue with the *status quo*, Reid might seem to be conservative, involving himself in a re-Edenising of society, a harking back
to an unsustainable state of wonder, of lack of the real pressures of work
and strife. Reid himself saw his narrative as coming out of a dream, a dream
of boyhood friendship experienced on the shore of some mythic sea. Yet
there is a less personalised emphasis in his work too, and it is the one
I dwell on here, that of the recent history of men like himself, men whose
sexual inclinations we call variously 'homosexual', 'gay' or 'queer'. And this
emphasis leads Reid on to consider the nature of these inclinations, particularly in relation to change and development both in terms of cultural
history and of the individual.

In placing Reid in this context, I am not claiming that he was a champion of what we might once have called 'gay rights'. The differences he
had with his friend the English novelist E. M. Forster, which I discuss below,
especially over the general direction of Forster's *Maurice*, indicate fundamental disagreements. Instead I am pointing here to a split which is not
a simple opposition but which is a symptom of plurality in the discussion of the issue of male same-sex desire for early twentieth-century
novelists. To do this I want first to explore some of the ways in which
Reid can be seen as departing from the expectations of his class and his
religion in Northern Ireland before I move on to the ways in which Reid
uses themes of Hellenism and of the development of sexuality in the Tom
Barber trilogy. I will also call upon Reid's autobiographical works, *Apostate*
(1926) and *Private Road* (1940), as well as unpublished correspondence
to make evident the importance of these themes for the novelist. My task
is to locate Forrest Reid within a debate on masculinity and sexuality, and
in this I want to challenge the idea of Reid as essentially an old-fashioned
and untroubling author who purveyed reassuring fictions notable for their
idyllic 'natural' settings. My contention is that the novels present an alternative view of the discussion of the nature of homosexuality.

Apostate is important for providing us with a way into Reid's novels. While
being a conventional record of the early years of his life, indistinguishable
from the lives of many boys throughout Britain at that time, through its
exploration of childhood it functions as a kind of artistic credo for an
artist whose major works place childhood so centrally as an experience.
And the critique of religion and the arts that disrupts the autobiography's
seemingly smooth surface helps explain the work's odd title. In *Apostate*
Forrest Reid records his early resistance to the religion of his parents —
the Anglicanism of the Church of Ireland. Even his beloved nurse Emma
could not persuade him to adopt her Low Church enthusiasm. Is this the
apostasy that has given his autobiography its name? I think it is in part;
but surely there were other aspects of Christianity that might have appealed

to him. It is significant that in his novels the other, and predominant, religion of Ireland — Catholicism — is conspicuously absent. This is odder when one considers that several of the literary characters to whom Reid was drawn were converts to Catholicism — Wilde and Dowson, among others; characters who had turned their backs on a dominant Anglican or Protestant orthodoxy and had accepted Catholicism. There is some evidence that Nineties converts found a correspondence in the marginality of their religous beliefs and their sexual practices, a kind of acceptance, 'a returning home', when they 'came to Rome'; two marginalities in British culture were brought together. In later life two of Reid's notable correspondents were Catholics: André Raffalovich (himself a Nineties convert) and François Mauriac. By the time of his correspondence with both of these men, Reid had futher hardened his heart against Christianity, and his comments to them on this subject are curiously abrupt and uncharacteristically rude. His silence on Catholicism has as much to do with the context of faith in Reid's Belfast. It would have been impossible for him to have considered a conversion to Rome. It would have placed him beyond the pale. Reid's apostasy is total; it is both a rejection of the religion of his forefathers and an embracing of ancient Greek religion. This in turn leads him, sometimes reluctantly, towards a rejection of the dominant sexual mores — not, I need hardly add, of Belfast and Northern Ireland alone, but of Britain. That this understanding of his own sexual nature was painful and mixed is borne out less in the fictional works than in Reid's extensive correspondence. This correspondence is, significantly, often on the subject of homosexuality although the term is not used and neither are alternatives like 'Uranianism' or 'Urism'. Reid remained torn about the practice of his sexuality, however (a fact which I shall discuss in detail in this chapter); while his apostasy is a rejection of Christianity, its application is towards an alternative sexuality, 'the Greek'. And yet his apostasy might be seen as a rejection of those aspects of an emerging 'gay' subculture — the physical consummation of that idealism embraced and described by Reid in his novels. Although he 'perverted' from Christianity, with defiance and openness, Reid remained an apostate in terms of his homosexual peer group also.

Apostate does not present its final message of belief with any sense of its having been temporary, reversed at a later date or replaced by a more sophisticated set of beliefs. These beliefs hinge upon his reading of Greek mythology and Greek poetry and drama, although he takes pains to deny some of the more scholarly attitudes to these subjects, attitudes that would have characterised the writings of an earlier generation of (gay) classical scholars. Reid presents his ideas on this subject as being both close to nature, coming out of nature, as it were, and 'natural', almost unsophisticated. The more sophisticated version of these beliefs might be seen to be presented by Pater and Symonds, both of them controversial figures in the 1880s and by the anthropological concerns which Reid acquired from Frazer in the 1900s. 'The darker, more mystic element interwoven with the worship of Dionysus (the *truly* religious element, doubtless, with its blood-sacrifices and ecstasy, and mingled lust and madness), this was repellent to me because of the cruelty bound up with it.' The gods Reid preferred were Pan and Hermes 'because they had human limitations, were beautiful and strong and passionate, were neither solemn nor sad, and had morals not very different from my own' (*Apostate*, p. 211). The appeal of Greek mythology, then, was of youth and simplicity, Theocritus rather than Pater, humanity rather than deity. The generational split is an interesting one. Pater's stressing of the complexity of Dionysus, Demeter and Persephone as symbols, and their substitution by Christian religious symbolism, belonged, however obliquely, to the world of religious, Anglican discourse, an Oxford movement not towards Rome but towards Athens. Reid's position is taken up against this dark complexity of metaphor. The 'lesser-gods', Pan and Hermes, allow Reid to see religious experience as something essentially bound up with childhood and innocence. Significantly, the distaste Reid felt for Dionysus is close to his feelings for Christ. In *Apostate* he tells us that

> in spite of his sinlessness, I did not feel drawn to Christ. I could not banish from my mind the pictures of him I had seen — with always something over-sweet about them, something mawkish and effeminate — the beard, the eyes, the lifted finger of gentle admonishment — and the actual words of the Gospels produced upon me, in another way, much the same effect. (*Apostate*, p. 130)

This rejection of the symbol of Christ as 'effeminate' echoes Pater's description of Dionysus in *Greek Studies* (although Pater is less disapproving and more dispassionate, cataloguing the ways in which Dionysus might be characterised). In one of his earliest published writings, 'Pan's Pupil', the young writer had written of Pan, Dionysus and Christ in ways devised from both Pater and Wilde: 'Like Dionysus he came out of the East, and was pale with the burden of his dreams.'[7] Reid is a classicist of a type which existed in the early part of this century, one for whom the spirit of Greece had been modified by a version of the 'muscular Christianity' of the 1850s. His attitudes and beliefs are close to those of the Uranian poets and critics who were active from the 1890s to the 1920s. His early rejection of Christianity is contrasted with his embracing 'the poetry and religion and art of the Greeks'.[8] The discovery of an alternative is presented as coming out of Reid's very early sympathy with animals and with his feelings of connection with the world of nature at large:

Long before this, independently, I had arrived at the Greek view of nature. In wood and river and plant and animal and bird and insect it had seemed to me there was a spirit which was the same as my spirit. And here, in this poetry, every aspect of nature seemed to be perpetually passing into divinity, into the form and radiance of a god, while the human passed no less easily into tree or reed or flower.[11]

This early vision of the world of nature was to remain with him and inform the later novels, particularly the Tom Barber trilogy (written between 1931 and 1944).

In the manner of adolescents, the young Reid hung prints of his heroes on his bedroom wall: Socrates and the Hermes of Praxiteles, 'my guardians', as he describes them, 'human and divine'.[10] These were the outward signs of the young man's paganism, symbols of his understanding of the intellectual and aesthetic appraisal of male beauty. However disguised initially, this was always central to his fiction and it became a cause he defended in his later writing; it began with the aestheticised Pan-worship of 'Pan's Pupil' in 1905, a minor short story never republished, and it continued throughout his major works.

Having produced a first novel which he felt ashamed of, on a theme 'entirely outside [his] experience, and even the natural scope of [his] sympathy',[11] Reid attempted, with his second novel, to get to the core of what touched and interested him. *The Garden God* (1905), is about 'friendship', a term used as a code for homosexual relationships in some circles.[12] He dedicated the work to Henry James, whom he admired and who had received the gift of Reid's first novel, *The Kingdom of Twilight* (1904), with friendly politeness. When *The Garden God* reached him, complete with dedication, the nature of the 'tale of two boys' hit home; James was shocked, and the correspondence between the two writers ceased. Reid was naïvely confused about this incident, seeing the novel as innocent and the dedicatee's reaction as one of 'repressed exasperation'.[13] As Reid observed of his former hero, 'In the preface to *The Turn of the Screw* he makes the same protest of ignorance, which cannot be sincere, since the internal evidence of the story points to a quite definite knowledge. The attitude appears to be prompted by a strange moral timidity, which refuses to accept responsibility for what deliberately has been suggested.'[14] However astute Reid is about James, he cannot seriously have believed that his work might not have compromised the older novelist. He himself was curiously oblique in these matters, refusing to understand the comments of a publisher's reader on *Pirates of the Spring*, a school 'friendship' story where the sexual undertones are more disturbing *because of* their covertness.

The Garden God is written as a narrative within a narrative, a 'dream within a dream', if one takes the suggestion offered by the quotation from

Edgar Allan Poe on the title-page. It describes the romantically fulfilled friendship between two young men whose most significant encounter takes place on the afternoon of the death of one of them. This encounter consists of the arranging of one of them in classical poses, in imitation of ancient Greek sculptures — a Faun, the Adorante, the Spinario. The narrator, in remembering that afternoon, reveals an aesthetic attitude to life, a desire for the world to be perfect, a work of art. This world is perfected by the narrator's rearrangement of his friend's body into these artistic poses, and it undergoes a further perfection through the action of memory.

Reid is here very close to the fulfilment of his dream ideal, a novel about masculine friendship. The responsibility for taking decisions which might lead to the possibility of sexual fulfilment is taken away by death. No matter that the narrator lives out the rest of his life in bitterness — one moment had been perfect, and unspoilt by sexual consummation. The friendship was erotic but not sexual.

In identifying masculinity with sculpture, I see Reid as following on from Pater's suggestions made in *Studies in the History of the Renaissance*, with its infamous 'Conclusion', and *Greek Studies*, where the potential eroticism of the male figure is described in terms elaborated from Winckelmann.[15] Pater's identification of great sculptures with masculine qualities — calmness and passivity rather than energy and activity — has its echoes in Reid's list of the *poses plastiques* taken up by Harold in *The Garden God*. While it is true that these motifs in Reid's fiction are part of a cultural history of homosexuality, they also represent an idiosyncratic sexuality with particular desires and directions.

Reid's participation in a debate on homosexuality can be pieced together from his correspondence with two 'gay' contemporaries, E. M. Forster and André Raffalovich. Their perceptions of him are revealing, one tending to oppose himself to the particularities of Reid's sexuality, the other broadly to agree with them. Forster differed from his friend on several occasions and in several ways, and yet loved and admired Reid too. The biggest divergence between the men was on the issue of fulfilment of homosexual desire. Where Reid denied the value of consummating relationships (for himself and for his fictional characters), Forster saw consummation as desirable and necessary. He claimed that Reid, essentially, disapproved of '*all* carnal relations even matrimonial' (Forster's emphasis).[16] This divergence has one other feature, Forster's tendency to gravitate towards working-class men (as opposed to middle-class boys). He satirises the predilections of the two writers thus: 'I am for men and cats, rather than boys and dogs' but he certainly prefers Reid's choice over 'women and horses'. But there is a fundamental objection in Forster's reception of his friend's novels — an objection rather than a disapproval — and that is

in the transitory nature of the love of boys: 'Boys — you'll have seen by
now why these get ruled out by me. No permanent relation to them, except as a memory, is possible, and Maurice can't live on memories.'[17]
Memories are the motive force of *The Garden God*, which is above all a
novel about recalled beauty, love, loss and pain. Forster's own tendencies
are to follow sexually active relationships with men. His observations on
Reid's failure to follow through the potential of these relationships in his
fiction (as well as in his life) are deliberately wry: in *Demophon* he cannot
understand why the hero lets the waggoner go on. 'However that's my personal limitation', he says with obvious irony;[18] in *Uncle Stephen* he regretted the loss of scenes between Tom and the poacher Deverell and described
his own motives for wanting to read them as 'the worst';[19] in *Young Tom*
he preferred James-Arthur to the hero.[20]

If Forster is amusing and even flippant at times about Reid, he did see
a particular direction in the work, and it was one with which he disagreed.
Instead of chaste, pure and 'remembered' writing on male same-sex desire
he sought affirmation from Reid, affirmation on the moral neutrality of
homosexuality. He saw Reid's position as compromised by fear of sin and
by a consequent celibacy: 'I have wanted very violently to comfort you
and to tell you that your sense of sin is a delusion . . .'[21] There is a note
of impatience too in Forster's letter regarding *The Garden God*, published
some eleven years earlier: 'The only thing in daily life that seems to you
beautiful *in itself* is school friendship and if you wrote about it there would
be a warmth and charm you don't get otherwise. There is in *The Garden
God* which I (and others I know) have enjoyed. If you wrote such a book
now you would be much more conscious and external, yet I know why
you shouldn't write it.'[22] There is both understanding and frustration in
such criticisms of his friend.

Raffalovich and Reid were closer as types than Forster and Reid. Reid
confided in both men when he had received a reader's report from T. Fisher
Unwin concerning his novel *Pirates of the Spring* (1919). This report apparently claimed that 'sodomy was the *leit*' of the novel, a claim which
caused the novelist pain.[23] Both of his correspondents failed to see what
the reader was driving at. Forster, as upset as Reid, replied, perhaps over-
reassuringly: 'No one who has the least sense either of you or of literature
could have drawn such an inference.'[24] Reid explained what he saw as the
'thesis' (rather than the 'leit') of the novel to Raffalovich during a discussion of a novel, *L'Erreur*:

> With the thesis of the book I am in entire agreement. Although it may
> not be obvious, in *Pirates of the Spring* there is an underlying idea of
> a similar sort. The most satisfactory friendship is one in which the

mistake is *not* made: all others are doomed, and though the ending need
not be tragic, if it is not, it will be a mere fizzling out. I had this belief
even when I wrote *The Garden God*. It may have been subconscious, but
still the form of that story seems to me to show that it was there. Such
a relation has a beauty and a bloom that pass quickly I am afraid. At
any rate I cannot myself imagine it, with any of the beauty left, surviv-
ing the period of boyhood.[25]

Here Reid is paraphrasing, perhaps unconsciously, the Platonic view of
love and the higher life. Raffalovich's reply was typically obscure but had
all the intimacy of a conversation: 'How you interest me: I had seen the
Thèse in life: in your novel it is unexceptionable. But it is only a limited
number of men who can as you do restrict the bloom and beauty to a sort of
Golden Age.'[26]

    In the continuation of this letter Raffalovich may be fishing for informa-
tion on Reid's private life, information which was not forthcoming in any
detailed form:

One word more, if I don't bore you, as to the *Thèse*: to feel to the full
the happiness of a true friendship *sans L'erreur* one has to know in some
measure what a friendship with L'erreur is like? Your boy in the Pirates
learnt through the Evan episode. Would he without it have known so
well? I once wrote for Lacassagne *I think* (it is so long ago) that platonic
love *repressed* and *restrained* what friendship did not experience.[27]

This is in line with the defence of homosexuality which Raffalovich published in 1896 and which saw sex between consenting males of a similar age
and mental development as perfectly acceptable.[28] At the same time, he
has an evident sympathy that allows him to detect the underlying theme
of the novel (while it might be detectable only to the 'aware'). He saw the
transformation of beauty — physical and material beauty — into a 'moral
beauty'.[29] This sympathy encouraged further confidences. The idea of the
'error', for example, is taken up in Reid's next letter: 'It is possible to write
a poem to a friend, but it must not be a love poem. Even the faintest tinge
of eroticism in such a thing would strike me as a deplorable error in taste;
and bad taste is always ugly.' And then, paying tribute to the ease with
which he could communicate with Raffalovich (whom he never met in
person), he continued:

When I was a little boy — not more than nine, I think — I had a dream
of another boy:— I met him in a garden overlooking a stretch of sand
with the sea breaking on it. He was an actual boy, but the curious thing
is that I had no consciousness of any particular deep affection for him
until I met him in this dreaming way. Yet the next morning when I met
him again in the flesh, everything was altered, and I appeared to have

become suddenly intimate with him. That is to say the dream seemed to have affected *him*, though doubtless what really affected him was only the change in my own manner. A few months later he went away. I never saw him again. But for years, until I was nearly sixteen, I dreamt of this sea garden. It was always the same, and always I met this boy there. He grew older, and changed, I expect, quite beyond recognition, but I was never conscious of the change. These dreams grew much rarer in later life, and the *time* now began to move backward. I remained, and the dream boy remained, at an age somewhere about 15 or 16. The last time I had this dream was not quite a year ago, and I was again a boy of that age. These dreams are infinitely the happiest hours I have had in my life, and I regret extremely that I am losing — I may say indeed that I have lost — the gift of getting back to my garden. At the same time when they came frequently I was innocent, and always, later, got back that innocency of mind. I believe if the physical side of life had remained unknown to me I should not have lost this power.[30]

Reid told Raffalovich that this dream was the source of his fiction and that he had attempted 'to extend the field of its operations'. This extension, and the diminution of the dream's force as he had grown older, had led to the dying out of the 'lyrical element' in his writing. The 'physical side of life' now known, the error having been committed, in other words, the artist must reconsider his perceptions and is in some ways diminished. It is strange that Reid thought at this date (1920) that he would never write a book about boys again. One might see the subsequent direction of his fiction and the defence of his thesis as a renewal of his powers and a reworking of some of this essential 'dream' material. Certainly the Tom Barber trilogy is, in some respects, an overview of this material, and to it one might add *Brian Westby*. These are works which describe, analyse and defend 'the dream' and yet which place it in a social and historical setting which makes the personal element apparent.

The correspondence was never again so intimate on Reid's part; it takes on a businesslike tone thereafter. Raffalovich's reply may have intruded too far into Reid's privacy, or it may have shown too professional an interest in the whole subject, an interest shown in the use of a certain medical vocabulary. 'I am deeply interested in what Henry James would have called your case, but which may be called your adventure, your discovery. . . . I sometimes tell people that God is the supreme novelist. Your novels, your experience, should inspire you with joy and gratitude.'[31] Raffalovich's tone here — the 'case', the reference to God and his subsequent citation in the letter of Havelock Ellis's interest in the 'case' of J. A. Symonds — may have alerted the novelist to an undesirable direction in his correspondent's thinking.[32] Yet Raffalovich's identification of a thesis in Reid's fiction and Reid's at least partial admission show the works to be less transparent than might first be thought. Reid returned to writing about boys in the late 1920s because he was able to extend his field of reference by taking a less personal view of the subject and by dealing with the development of sexuality, and with stages of development, in the personality of one character. In doing so, Reid appeared to indulge his passion for boys but, in effect, dramatised and analysed it. In this shift in emphasis the novelist was undoubtedly influenced by the writings of authors who examined childhood systematically (such as Aksakoff, whose *Days of Childhood* appeared in a popular edition in 1923) or by current writing on child development (such as Cyril Scott's *The Autobiography of a Child* or Albert Moll's *The Sexual Life of the Child*).[33]

Pirates of the Spring proved to be central to a change in Reid's work. In writing it, he recognised that the school story could be extended into a dialogue about the real nature and operation of masculinity and, in particular, male same-sex desire. Reid took pains to see his characters as individual representatives of moral alternatives, so much so that his plot creaks under the weight of the exposition of their traits and characteristics. The novel explores the microcosmic nature of school and the relationships it engenders among adolescent boys. We can see the novel as being an examination of the 'homosocial' structure of society (to borrow a term from Sedgwick).[34] Indeed, there is a strongly anti-homosexual strain in the story, and physical relationships between males are silently vetoed. Sports such as boxing stand in for sexual acts. The book sees two classes of boys — insiders and outsiders. The insiders include the hero, Beach Traill, and his old friend, Palmer Dorset. The outsiders are Cantillon and Hayes; one is despised, the other loved, by Traill. As elsewhere in Reid's novels, the beauty of real, living people — as opposed to that of sculptures and paintings — is morally supect and perhaps even dangerous. So Evan Hayes, perceived by Traill as handsome (and at one point 'like a young faun'), shows himself to be utterly cowardly and morally weak. Yet there seems little doubt, although it is never stated in these terms, that Traill has fallen in love with Hayes and that his admiration for his physical charms flaws his judgement. This is the 'error' discussed by Raffalovich and Reid in relation to *Pirates*. In the figure of Cantillon, on the other hand, we have a stereotype of the Wildeian dandified homosexual, his fingers ringed, his hair oiled, his appearance unhealthy. He persuades younger boys to break the school's rules (although we are never told precisely what they get up to), and gravitates towards the town and its racy pleasures rather than to the semi-rural innocence of Trailla and his friends. Dorset, the most manly of the boys, tells Traill: 'Nothing [Cantillon] ever did in his life was decent. He's an outsider, and he'll be fired before all's over — the sooner the better.'[35] In this homosocial structure, being 'fired' (expelled) is the fate of those who transgress the school's rules. Those who transgress the unwritten rules of the boys — based on ideas of chivalry, loyalty, and honour — are shunned. The novel might have been the product of a memory of the Wilde–Douglas affair and the ways in which the 'error' can draw in and corrupt others around them.

Pirates of the Spring sets the tone for Reid's subsequent exploration of the ways in which moral alternatives are explored, accepted or rejected by adolescents. And yet what is at first simply an extension of this enterprise became an expansion into the entire developmental states of boyhood, taking a boy with a homosexual sensibility as its subject. The simpler homosocial structure of *Pirates*, with its plot of social acceptability / unacceptability and its 'hormonal' ending (the sudden burst of physical activity), was replaced with a single, perhaps unique, hero, who experiences the complex structures of the world in the form of historical continuities and disruptions. These include magical phenomena and shifts backwards and forwards in time as well as biological and hormonal changes. The trilogy form helped Reid to trace the effects of these processes on Tom, as Aksakoff was able to do in his celebrated three-part autobiography.[36] We might say that whereas *Pirates* is about becoming a gentleman, the Tom Barber trilogy is about becoming a man, and whereas *Pirates* is about convention and of wanting to be accepted, the trilogy is about unconventionality, in particular about the recognition and acceptance of one's own sexual unconventionality, about self-acceptance and self-recognition.

This brings us to Reid's reception of two books by 'Arthur Lyon Raile' (pseudonym of Edward Perry Warren), *The Wild Rose* and *A Defence of Uranian Love*, the first of which he reviewed when it was reprinted in 1928. (He actually requested the book and reviewed it for the *Irish Statesman*.) The other was given to him by Osbert Burdett, and their correspondence on this and related subjects is an interesting one to chart. In considering it, however, we have to see that Reid was not an isolated provincial gay man, simply mouldering away in a forgotten corner of the British Isles, but that he had met several leading supporters of the Uranian movement when in Cambridge and had kept up his friendship with E. M. Forster through correspondence as well as annual visits. One of his earliest correspondents was Osbert Burdett, later to have a reputation as a literary critic and biographer. It is worth quoting at length from Burdett's first letter to Reid, dated 1907:

> I am taking the all but too great liberty of writing to you, because I would venture to tell you how very much struck I was with your recent book *The Garden God*.
>
> If you will excuse my saying so it seemed to me to be by far the best

book on the subject that I have read. The fine eclecticism which enabled you to catch the spirit of friendship seemed to me beyond praise.

And the way in which the Hellenic ideal suffused and coloured, being indeed the motif of the whole book was, I think, the outcome of a rare Scholarship.

With what a sense of relief I traced that discreet art which enabled you to say so little or to imply so much!

I would only venture to add that if you ever think of treating the subject again I hope it might be treated from the strictly modern standpoint.

Surely if the thing is fine or rare at all, the quality of fineness, or rareness, are intrinsic virtues, not dependent at all upon the *Greek* conception of philosophy as 'the science of love'.

It is at least certain that boyfriends would account for it on other than Greek grounds. We have then but to wait till the modern aspect of friendship, which the Christian ethics have permeated, (and which is not Pagan in the good sense of that good word,) is treated on its own ground, and who should be so fit as the author of *The Garden God*.[37]

It is clear that Burdett's hopes are for a literature that recognised homosexuality ('friendship') and that he saw Reid as the champion of such a literature. In another letter written in the same year Burdett raises some of the issues of Reid's first two novels:

There is, please don't laugh at me, something almost sacred . . . in your books at least to me, something that I can only describe as 'so intimate', so soul-piercing that I sometimes wonder that you ever published them. . . . And I believe I am right in at least this sense that these two books at any rate will never become very widely known: there are only a few of us who can love them well enough!

You have transcended Pater by giving his peculiar 'dream of a world' a more human note, and have therefore touched not my emotions merely, as he did, but my heart.[38]

In 1928 Burdett contacted the novelist to inform him of the publication of a 'new and enlarged' edition of *The Wild Rose*, a volume of poems by 'Arthur Lyon Raile' (the first edition had been published in 1909, and this edition represented not that volume alone but also some of Raile's poems from his other volume, *Itamos* (1903).[39] 'Do you know these poems, very Greek in their inspirations?' Burdett asked Reid. More than a year later Burdett wrote again, this time mysteriously, of Raile, whom he does not name: 'If you will be in London during this summer, I shall have a rare book for you, a book as certain to interest you as any book that you have not read, and by an author whom you once praised, that will explain why I am sparing of details'.[40] This book was Raile's *A Defence of Uranian Love*, a three-volume work, privately printed by the Cayme Press and distributed among

Raile's friends, who, apparently, did not share his enthusiasm for the theme.[41] In 1941 Burdett became joint biographer of Raile, with E. H. Goddard, but did not analyse the work, obeying his subject's wishes by this silence.[42] His original coyness over the title and author of the book he had waiting for Reid was undoubtedly due to the subject, and he might have feared the construction put upon his and Reid's interest in the work should the letter have fallen into other hands. Burdett wrote to Reid from Paris in August 1929:

> Please keep the books, as one of the few likely to appreciate them, and the first part, as you say, needs to be read more than once.
>
> No doubt, a personal preference was the point from which he started. Oxford and England were a kind of reprieve after America, and at Oxford the author became immersed in Greek, and when he left, being a rich man, he was able, with a friend, to devote his life to collecting Greek antiquities, and the two really formed the Greek section of the Boston museum. . . . His sensitiveness to Greek art was of course a great help, and then, being an independent man, he was able to inhabit a house and to order his life on Greek and aristocratic principles. . . .
>
> He was only really at home in his own world, and though in a sense eccentric, he was natural.[43]

Reid's review of Raile's *The Wild Rose*, written for the *Irish Statesman*, is interesting for the way in which it negotiates a position of appreciation between an understanding of the content ('unusual') and the manner ('difficult'). This may seem something of a Hobson's choice, but Reid finds that the 'chief merit' of the poems lies 'in a remarkable constancy of spirit and faith'. He continues: 'The mood may vary in different poems, but never the underlying faith. For faith it is, though not a faith in Christianity, and the only god evoked is pagan. It is a faith in three or four human qualities — courage, fortitude, loyalty, faith itself . . .'[44] Yet beneath this observation of Reid's we can perhaps discern a more personal and a less disinterested voice. What constitutes this courage, this fortitude, loyalty and faith? What are they for, what are they about? Reid quickly identifies them as the courage to be oneself, to have one's sexuality, one's realisation:

> With the exception of a few pieces the entire collection really forms one single poem — an *apologia pro vita sua*, a confession, a creed. There is neither complaint nor self-pity, yet beneath the stoical reserve one becomes conscious of an undertone of pain. There may be here and there, happiness, hope, pride, but the fundamental note is the realization of exile, of captivity, of loneliness. Therefore the poet turns backward to an antique, legendary land, in which he can imagine his dreams coming true; the spirit of the book is pagan, though not completely pagan — how can it be, when it finds it necessary to explain itself, to defend its choice, to make a choice at all?[45]

Reid's choice to review this crabbed and difficult volume might be seen as an attempt to define his own work. Timothy d'Arch Smith has seen Reid's description of Raile's poetry as applying 'more to Reid's novels than Raile's poetry'.[46] And this would certainly seem to be true of the last paragraph of the review:

> . . . the gaze of the poet is fastened on his own soul, the very landscapes are subjective. What he gives us, nevertheless, is no sentimental reverie. . . . And the experience itself? That in one sense is individual, and in another it may be, universal. It is the desire for that complete union with another being in which the very idea of self is lost and found. Out of this desire the mythopoeic imagination of boyhood creates a dream image, a breathing shape, the soulmate who never was and never can be.[47]

It is interesting that in these extracts Reid sees Raile as defending a choice, this before he knew, apparently, the title or drift of Raile's *magnum opus*.[48] And he attributes an overtly Platonic edge and motive to *The Wild Rose* which is central to Raile's *A Defence of Uranian Love*. In many ways Reid's understanding, and his acceptance, of *A Defence*, show him to be as outside his own period as Raile himself was. The book is misogynistic and patrician; in some ways it is an expansion of an argument from such turn-of-the-century books as Carpenter's *Iolaus*, but without the radical, democratic edge. Yet it is my contention that the book allows Reid to see, at a crucial stage of his career, a way of putting forward a thesis on the development of a young male character, one which has a theoretical base but which does not preach, one in which a tradition and history of a type of character can be enwrought with a realist plot. Raile's thesis is that modern society has replaced the masculine as good with the feminine as good (he almost sneers at women in his attempt to place them in relation to men) and that a true understanding of the relation of things would bring about the acceptance of the Uranian ideal, i.e. the male as central, the recognition of male beauty, and the return to high philosophical pursuits:

> The Uranian doctrine would assign a high value to the masculine qualities; it would give authority to man. . . . The recoil from (Platonic abstractions) lies to a great authority in mankind across the ages, toward the scholarship which is the memory of the world, the study of our record of nobility, a Christian and pagan: in short, toward great men and women. The Christians disregarded the Pagans; modern thinkers disregarded the Christians; the Greeks disregarded women; we have disregarded men.[49]

It is not in misogyny that Reid follows Raile but in the re-centring of a masculine aesthetic and the appeal to 'the memory of the world' as authority, although there is a sense in which this history is an attempt to validate the dismissal of women's power in society and to argue for a return to the domination of the male — what Raile describes as the simplicity and severity of the male. One might see some of Raile's theory as close to the 'new Chivalry' of Anglican pederastic circles of the previous century, but Raile's dislike of Christianity, its effeminacy and softness, makes his conclusions quite different. Reid, as we have already seen, was similarly opposed to Christianity and as attracted to Greek religion as Raile. By appealing to classical Greece, Reid is subverting the Christian, specifically Protestant, tradition of mainstream culture in Britain, which had, as 'high' culture, paid homage to Greece, but which, as 'popular' culture, had maintained a steady philistinism. Reid recognised that a classicising language could be subversive and challenging, as it had been for an earlier generation, but also that it could have an insidious effect. The tragic and fatal elements of this classicism are mediated by the novelist's rejection of large themes and his dwelling on small, familiar motifs. And in choosing to 'rationalise' his approach to childhood, Reid challenges an orthodox view of childhood as 'natural' and unsexual.

The very difference between Reid's boy hero, Tom, and the other boys we encounter in the novels which feature him points to the exceptional nature of his character. Is this special pleading? I think not. In this singularity Reid does not ignore the ways in which his character's attitudes impinge on the (sexual) interests of others. This is strikingly true in *Uncle Stephen*, where the young poacher Deverell has a barely disguised passion for Tom. *Young Tom*, however, finds the hero on the other side of the conundrum of sexual attraction. And Reid is careful to indicate the precise state of development of his hero. The boy is greatly drawn to James-Arthur Fallon, a farm-hand, and when the two meet by the river Tom persuades the older boy to swim. James-Arthur's reluctance, which is mysterious to Tom, is due to his age and size: he fears a passer-by, especially a female, catching sight of him. Eventually he is persuaded, and the following passage describes him as he prepares to enter the water:

> James-Arthur was as fond of the water as Barker [one of Tom's dog 'friends'], and now, while he stood up on the bank in the sunlight, he slapped his sturdy thighs in pleased anticipation. Even at this early date of summer his body was sunburnt, and in Tom's eyes he somehow did not look naked. He had simply emerged from his soiled and much-patched clothing like a butterfly from a chrysalis, and the contrast between his fair hair and the golden brown of his body and limbs appeared to the smaller boy as attractive as anything could be. In fact James-Arthur, merely by divesting himself of his clothes, had instantly become part of the natural scene, like the grass and the trees

and the river and the sky, and the dragon-fly asleep upon his water-
lily. (*YT*, p. 33)

Tom is puzzled by James-Arthur's other friendships, which he fears ex-
clude him from being the older boy's 'chum', and he is surprised by James-
Arthur's friendships with women (*YT*, p. 41). Tom's admiration is sometimes
for the farm-hand's moral judgement, sometimes for his knowledge — how
to call down owls, for instance. But the aesthetic appreciation of James-
Arthur's physical appeal, compounded of strength and beauty, is striking,
and in several scenes Reid appears to mimic some of the idyllic rustic
scenes of painters like Fred Walker and Henry Scott Tuke which feature
young working men. The vision of this 'natural' beauty and Tom's appreciation of it are brought together in chapter 20 of *Young Tom* when the boy
approaches his friend at work digging potatoes in a field. Tom has come
to seek advice about the theft of a rifle. It shows the male as an object
both of intellectual and physical admiration:

> James-Arthur, the sun streaming down on his flaxen head and open blue
> shirt and bare arms, stood motionless, leaning on his fork, while the
> story was poured out. . . .
>   James-Arthur spat on his hands, which were broad and powerful, and
> plunged his fork energetically into the ground. But it was a solitary
> plunge; he left it there; and proceeded to wipe his hands on his dirty
> corduroys. . . .
>   James-Arthur scratched his head in silence, and Tim immediately said:
> 'Don't; your hands are all earthy.' But this was involuntary, and because
> James-Arthur's hair was exactly the colour of very ripe oats, and looked
> as if it would show the slightest mark: next moment he returned to the
> matter he had come about. (*YT*, p. 138)

These instances introduce us to a language of emotion, a direction of the
author's thinking which demonstrates that these novels both cover and
uncover the nature of Tom's sexuality, expressed here as a simple preference.
  The first of the Tom Barber novels, *Uncle Stephen*, may strike us on a
first reading as a fiercely conventional book. My reading of it is that it
is deliberately unconventional and subversive, and that in constructing
its plot Reid recognises two audiences, one that will be seduced by the
purely literary conventions of the novel (the fine writing and particularly
the descriptions of nature) and another for whom the sexual nature of
the plot is clear. But even the plot contains subtle assaults on the *status
quo* — the role of the conventional family and the positions taken up by
the representatives of the church, the law business — represented by Mr
Knox, Mr Flood and Uncle Horace. Elsewhere in the trilogy medicine is
represented by Dr MacCrory and science by Tom's father. There is a clear

sense of Tom's being in a discursive relationship with these forces both of social control and access to knowledge. In this structure Uncle Stephen represents magic, 'forbidden' learning, of course, and the art and religion of ancient Greece. However, the tension of the novel and the sympathy of the reader are retained by Tom's being something of a go-between; he mediates between this conventional world and the unconventional, even lawless, world of the poacher, Deverell. In part this plot is conveyed through overt references to Tom's own unorthodox ideas and his fears of them. But it is also plotted into the work by the subtle use of dualities, of doubles, and opposites: age and youth, inside and outside, past and present, dream and reality, polarities of class also playing their part. To negotiate these alternatives, Tom must make his own way between his unorthodox instincts and the demands of society. This is illustrated clearly in the making of a path between the Manor House, where Uncle Stephen lives, and the deserted house where 'Philip' has taken refuge. That this path of Tom's is also more 'natural' is also made apparent, for it is taken up quite quickly by wild and domestic animals, while it — and indeed the very existence of the 'other' house (the ruined old house) — is ignored by all the other characters.[50]

Reid intended us to see part of Tom's unorthodoxy as sexual in nature. Tom recognises 'two kinds of love' and is drawn quite openly to physical contact with other males which culminates in scenes where kissing, hugging and caressing are all countenanced (although still seen as unusual). The novel's success lies in seeing these encounters as entirely reasonable for the participants. Reid brings together Uncle Stephen and Tom in a kind of collaboration — a collusion (*US*, p. 267) — to fight a prevailing orthodoxy which is described as well as alluded to several times in the novel; Tom's thoughts struggle for a definition: 'Happiness depended on kindness and understanding and — and — on not insisting that everybody should have the same feelings and thoughts (*US*, p. 202). The novel ends with a resonant note on this subject: having decided that they have worked out a future for themselves, Stephen is questioned by Tom as to the reactions of Mr Knox (the clergyman) and Mr Flood (the solicitor):

> 'Is it all right?' Tom questioned eagerly, his eyes searching Uncle Stephen's face.
> 'From our point of view — yes.'
> 'And from theirs?'
> 'Well, theirs isn't ours, I'm afraid.' (*US*, p. 207)

Seeking this future and avoiding convention leads to a resolution: they should travel to Greece and Italy together. The choice is revealing. For Stephen it is a way of retracing his steps, of relearning the things which had obsessed his adult life — religion, art and 'magic'. For Tom it is a way of becoming adult (just as Stephen had done after he had run away from home half a century before). The repetition of the travel is one of those dualities referred to above, revealing both the unorthodoxy of Reid's view of what is good for Tom (*not* going into business, *not* continuing his formal education) and his dependence on the 'gay' scholarship of the previous century, where classical civilisation is held as preferable to the conventions of Christianity. If any single sign of the profound sexual unorthodoxy of Stephen were needed, this espousal of the Greek way of life, not simply as a mode of scholarship but as a way of living, would be it. Tom is collusive in this choice; he revitalises it for Uncle Stephen and makes the (Greek) world new again for him. Tom is led to this world at first by instinct and later by Stephen, but also, significantly, by Hermes, the god who 'cares for boys' (*US*, p. 217) and for whom Tom develops a priestly devotion, falling on his knees 'in a spirit of love and worship' (*US*, p. 204) beneath a sculpture of the god.

Yet one might say that the whole history of Tom and his uncle starts and ends in the Mediterranean, and particularly the Greek world and the constructions put upon it since the eighteenth century. This theme is represented in *Uncle Stephen* by Hermes and in the conscious Hellenising of the adolescent Tom. (Before this stage is reached, Reid is careful to present Tom's life as un-Hellenised. In *The Retreat*, where magic is a recurring motif, one can see a kind of medievalisation of the boy's life. One of the notable features of Reid's reverse history of Tom Barber is in the way in which themes are introduced and erased: Tom's perceptions of magic in the 'first' book, *Uncle Stephen*, are erased gradually, Hellenised, and rationalised throughout the novel, but are reintroduced in the 'second' novel, *The Retreat* covering an earlier phase in Tom's life, to recomplicate the idea of development of the boy's character and perceptions.) Reid's understanding of the homosexual nature of 'the Greek world' is essentially homoerotic, a world where a knowledge of love, sex, the body and social relations is seen in terms of male same-sex relationships. In many ways, Reid's understanding of this world does not depend on a close reading of Greek philosophy or history, but on his understanding of Plato and *fin-de-siècle* perceptions of his teaching.

Hermes is a recurring motif in the Tom Barber trilogy. Reid takes pains to replace Orpheus with Hermes at an early stage in Tom's development. In *Young Tom*, set at a time when the boy has only just heard of his uncle and of his notorious book, Tom's curiosity is expressed in a conversation with the family doctor:

> 'Is there anything about Orpheus in Uncle Stephen's book?' Tom asked. . . .
> 'In the book you lent me there was, but only a little.'

'I'm afraid I don't remember: it's a good many years now since I read it. . . . I know there's a great deal about Hermes in it. Are you particularly interested in Orpheus?'

Tom hesitated. 'It's just what it said about him in that book of yours — that when he played his music, all the animals and birds followed him and wanted to listen.'

'And you'd like them to follow you?'

Tom laughed. 'Of course I know it's only a story. Still, it could have happened, couldn't it? And there might be something about it in Uncle Stephen's book, because it says in your book that maybe it was Hermes who gave him his lyre.'

'Does it? I'd forgotten that too. It's usually supposed to have been Apollo.'
(*YT*, p. 57)

This shift from the 'natural', unspecific Orpheus to the specific god of boys and boyhood is an important one. Earlier in their conversation about nature Dr MacCrory tells Tom that his, Tom's, love of natural history has nothing to do with science but is because of his fondness for animals, 'which is a spiritual quality' (*YT*, p. 56). Tom's mind is Greek in its very naturalness.

One might see the direction of the Tom Barber trilogy, therefore, as tracing the development of a 'natural' Greek mind misplaced in a provincial north of Ireland setting, a mind quietly in rebellion against the *status quo*, towards a realisation of the consequences of that mind, and those tendencies, sexual and moral, in an adult fulfilment. Hermes is a link in that chain, and there are indications at the end of *Uncle Stephen* that he has already been outgrown though not forgotten.[51] This would be the case too for Uncle Stephen, who still sleeps beneath a statue of the god. That this is a magnification of Reid's own interests is clear. Reid's emotional closeness to boyhood, even in old age, is the spirit out of which these observations are made possible. In his translation of the poems from *The Greek Anthology* he includes verses to Hermes, as in a piece by Leonidas of Tarentum: 'These toys of his boyhood — his lucky ball, his noisy boxwood rattle, the knucklebones he loved, the top he span — Philokles hangs up here as gifts to Hermes.'[52]

But in creating a boy who had the Greek character 'naturally', Reid enters upon a thesis, a defence even of that kind of nature. Reid is hopeful for 'the Greek character': neither Stephen nor Tom have come to grief, have not killed themselves, nor become social outcasts, a significant move from the dreadful fate of the chief characters of *The Garden God*. Tom, while changing and growing himself, is also the contact point for several other characters in understanding themselves in relation to this love. Tom might himself be Hermes, a guiding spirit, and his charm a kind of grace (although Forster implied that this charm was somewhat overdone).[53] His natural charm subverts any attempt by a hostile reader to see the boy's feelings as somehow perverse, and his relative lack of contact with social institutions, like schools and churches, avoids the charge of viciousness on the part of those institutions. There is no call in the trilogy to praise or blame public schools or perverted clerics. Indeed, Reid has set up a 'hermetic' world in which he can scrutinise his subject and limit its interaction with other forces, although these are experienced by Tom in a series of encounters.

One of the most noteworthy of these encounters is with James Deverell in *Uncle Stephen*, a character who presents himself as a rival for Tom's affections against his own family and friends — his own class, in other words. Deverell is persistent in his love for the younger boy, admitting his feelings openly, although quaintly and without finesse: 'You're the only one I've ever cared for. I would have been a good pal to you, but it can't be now. I'd have gone straight with you, and this would have never happened' (*US*, p. 160).[66] This dialogue, and others like it, is precariously close to that of the Victorian romantic novels so loved by Reid in his boyhood. Yet there is something daring about the putting of such words into the mouth of a teenage boy in conversation with another boy, the mouthing of romantic clichés from a boy who might have heard them from others. These words have a poignancy too within a discourse of male same-sex desire and almost mock the 'friendship' vocabulary of the Uranian poets. But Deverell's feelings are unilluminated by that Greek atmosphere, that classical light and air that Tom has found instinctively. When ruminating on his recent adventures at the end of the novel, Tom remembers his swain:

> If it had not been for Uncle Stephen he might have gone away with Deverell, and what would have happened then? What would have become of him? . . . Why had Deverell loved him? What was it he had loved? Not his beauty at any rate, for he had none. . . . Deverell's chances had all been unlucky. He had gone very likely straight into the darkness. He might find somebody else to love, but it was improbable. (*US*, p. 268)

From wanting to 'go straight' to going 'straight into the darkness' — a punishment, one might think, for those who are too raw, too close to their emotions. For all his affection for the poacher, Tom cannot consummate his love, and in one of those oppositional dualities of the novel Reid contrasts the emotional leave-taking of Deverell to the threatened departure of 'Philip'/Stephen (see *US*, pp 169, 198). The 'error', as Reid described it to Raffalovich, has not been committed, but it had been sighted, reflected upon, and rejected.

In rejecting Deverell, with no matter how many regrets, Tom is enacting Reid's thesis of the Platonic (or Socratic) aristocracy of homosexuality, of the suitability of same-sex relationships within a tightly structured social world. In this he is departing from one of the most important tendencies of homosexual awareness in late nineteenth- and early twentieth-century Britain: the healthy and desired breakdown of social class that same-sex relationships offered as an advantage over heterosexual relationships. Jeffrey Weeks describes these democratic, socialist tendencies in *Coming Out*, particularly how they cluster around political and other groups in Britain. Laurence Housman was involved with both the Order of Chaeronea and the British Society for the Study of Sex Psychology as well as the early feminist movement, seeing a genuine connection between these movements and what might be seen as 'liberation'. Laurence Housman wrote to C. R. Ashbee about comradeship: 'I haven't a doubt of the extraordinary humanising and educative values which come out of these rapprochments — especially when it is between class and class that the union takes place. . . . Comradeship with women made me an ardent suffragist; comradeship with man makes me more and more of a socialist.'[54] The tendency comes out of Whitman and Carpenter, and it was one which Reid was familiar with.[55] Yet one might say that there is a consciousness of the debate around inter-class comradeship in Reid's mature works, and that the subject reappears, even if only as a foil, in the Tom Barber trilogy. In other words, it is apparent that the tender, even loving relationships represented by James-Arthur and Jim Deverell can come to nothing because of an underlying Socratic belief on Reid's part in the unsuitability of such friendships. They do not represent the perfect; nor do they reflect the 'classed' models of same-sex partnerships of the *erastai/eromenoi*. Such relationships have other implications. As Robert Aldrich has noted recently of Aschenbach's obsession in Mann's *Death in Venice*, 'the ideal relationship between man and boy is a replication of the Greek model, posited on the assumption that physical love is the way to spiritual love and that love leads to knowledge.'[56] Yet Reid's problem in *Uncle Stephen* is to bring the relationship between uncle and nephew within the bounds of an acceptable 'Greek' relationship. This would help explain the reappearance of Stephen in the guise of 'Philip', the incarnation of Stephen some fifty years before.

In Tom's second phase (in *The Retreat*), his oddity is revealed, discussed, and accepted, up to a point, by the other characters. In several episodes the boy is described as 'queer' or 'odd', and a connection is made between this oddity and his family (from his mother and her uncle, 'Uncle' Stephen). Tom, here and elsewhere in the trilogy, is described as 'plain' and yet as 'magic', or rather as having magic 'in him'. At the same time, as I have pointed out about his character in *Young Tom*, there is no sexual ambiguity about the boy; his pursuits, hobbies and friendships are the same as those of many young boys, and he has a tendency to fantasise, particularly about past lives. And yet his sexual proclivities are quite formed, if nameless, at this early stage (he is about eleven years old). These proclivities show themselves at the very height of the 'normalised' activity, playing games. During a practice game of cricket Tom gets into a row with his own team and the opposition because he stopped playing suddenly. 'In a dream he had stood there — and the awakening had been rude.' Tom had been 'so much struck by the appearance of the bowler that he had made no attempt to defend his wicket. . . . Tom had been thinking how nice he looked.' (*Retreat*, p. 64). Elsewhere Tom expresses a desire for an ideal friend (p. 65), and a preference for fair hair (p. 141) among other things. Tom's consciousness of his own plainness is a part of this tendency to see the beauty in other males and in nature itself.[57]

While one might see the intense engagement with the natural world as part of Tom's 'Greek' nature as commented upon by Dr MacCrory, this part of the plot is subsumed by a general extension of the Edenic theme present in other parts of the books. Here, however, the Edenic quality of Tom's life, his ability to transform the banal and the familiar into the magical and strange, is seen in opposition to a 'real' Eden visited by Tom during a nocturnal flight with Gamelyn, the angelic figure who visits him. This comes out of Tom's ruminations upon the exact location of Eden and what exactly had happened to it during the Flood. He meets the serpent, whom he grows to like, as well as a dog and an albatross, and it appears from his conversation that God never visits the garden, that Adam had died, and that the snake is a misogynist. The snake's discourse about Eve (Eva) is curiously vicious and cruel and is punctuated with violent images. On the other hand, the snake liked Adam and regretted his ensnarement by Eve. The ambiguity of Tom's reception of these ideas reflects his ambiguous feelings towards men and women in his own life — his father and mother and, more particularly, Mr Holbrook and Miss Jimpson. At one point Tom's interest in music is seen as a mirror of Mr Holbrook's own, and in opposition to the philistinism of Miss Jimpson. This incident reveals Tom's masculinity to Miss Jimpson: 'I thought you were different, but I see you really aren't', she tells him (*Retreat*, p. 60). The aesthetic appreciation of opera is beyond her, and it makes her feel unworthy of Mr Holbrook. Later they reveal their engagement to Tom, and she shows signs of wanting to kiss him:

> . . . they stopped, and shook hands, and the dangerous moment went by. Miss Jimpson didn't kiss him — though he still believed she wanted to, and indeed he might have let her if Mr Holbrook hadn't been there. He suddenly found himself feeling a little sorry for Miss Jimpson — and understanding her — understanding her better than Mr Holbrook did perhaps. (*Retreat*, p. 205)

This moment is not explained in the novel, and it may be supposed that the kind of manhood yet to be experienced by Tom and which had just been revealed to him was sufficiently different from that of his music teacher to make Tom aware of the failures of men in living up to the expectations of women.

The Eden theme, then, might help explain differences in the sexes while not explaining to Tom an essential thing about his own nature — *his* sexuality. He likes to see the Bible as a fairy story, and in a conversation with his mother on the subject is severely chastised:

> 'I think the Old Testament is more interesting [than the New]. . . . The Flood, and Jacob's Ladder, and the Witch of Endor, and Lot's wife, and Balaam's ass, and Jonah in the whale, and Moses turning his rod into a serpent — they're just like the *Arabian Nights*.'
> 'They're not in the least like the *Arabian Nights*,' Mother contradicted, 'and it's very wrong to talk in that way.' (*Retreat*, p. 79)

Although Mother warns him firmly that 'God is not a magician', we do not feel that Tom is convinced. Excluded from the morality of Christianity, he is here negotiating a place in relation to it, desiring a magical change to the very order of things, the order created and sanctioned by a Christian culture. This accounts for the strongly expressed wish to meet his uncle, whom he believes to be a magician. He discovers him instead, in the novel that bears his name, to be a classical scholar and a recluse whose way of life is a conscious rejection of the religious and social standards maintained around him.

The Retreat marks a pivotal moment in Reid's trilogy, in the life of his fictional character Tom Barber, and in the novelist's thesis of change and development in his hero's sexual nature. Reid sees the pressures upon the individual as profoundly cultural and plural. Yet Tom's self is resistant, questioning and formed. The idea of becoming a male, so central to Raile's *Defence*, is part of the thesis of Reid's trilogy. At the end of *The Retreat* there is a suggestion that, at this stage of his development, Tom's life might stop being interrupted by fantasy and elaborate visions and that he will begin to settle down and mature. He will become a young man (like the final version of Gamelyn, who has appeared to him three times in the novel). Tom will achieve stability with his coming of age, but the promise of that stability and happiness is somewhat modified by his ruminations in *Uncle Stephen*. As I have indicated, Tom and his uncle eventually decide to travel in order to study the classical culture of the Mediterranean. This, I have suggested, is a way for them to be themselves and to enact a destiny for gay classical scholars of the generations preceding them.

While I have traced here the origins of Forrest Reid's defence of homosexuality to a discursive, non-democratic — even patrician — version of a debate revived in the nineteenth century, I claim that this defence is still challenging to his readers. His Tom Barber trilogy is less about nature and magic and more about the alternatives which they obscure — the natural inclinations of Tom and the hidden history that would vindicate them.

Abbreviations

Apostate	*Apostate* (1926), London: Constable, 1928
Retreat	*The Retreat* (1936), London: Faber, 1946
US	*Uncle Stephen* (1931), London: Faber, 1946
YT	*Young Tom*, London: Faber, 1944

Notes and References

1   *Uncle Stephen, The Retreat* and *Young Tom* were published in one volume as *Tom Barber,* New York: Pantheon Books, 1955, for the American market.

2   See Linda Dowling, *Hellenism and Homosexuality in Victorian Oxford,* New York: Cornell University Press, 1994, for a discussion of the Hellenist tendency in nineteenth-century culture.

3   Reid published several essays and articles dealing with nineteenth-century literature including 'Minor Fiction in the Eighties' in *The Eighteen-Eighties: Essays by Fellows of the Royal Society of Literature,* Cambridge University Press, 1930. His *Illustrators of the Sixties,* London: Faber & Gwyer, 1928 demonstrates another aspect of this interest, periodical literature.

4   Peter Coveney, *Poor Monkey,* London: Rockcliff, 1957, p. 227

5   Ibid.

6   Ibid., p. 228.

7   Forrest Reid, 'Pan's Pupil', *Uladh,* i, no. 3 (May 1905), p. 19.

8   Ibid., p. 205.

9   Ibid., p. 207.

10   Ibid., p. 205.

11   Forrest Reid, *Private Road,* London: Faber, 1940, p. 27.

12   This tendency has some of its origins in Whitman and found expression in the writings and theories of J. A. Symonds, Edward Carpenter (*Iolaus: An Anthology of Friendship* was first published in 1902) and Laurence Housman (who gave a lecture in 1916 on 'The Relation of Fellow-feeling to Sex'). For discussions of this tendency in Britain see Jeffrey Weeks, *Coming Out,* Quartet, 1977; Richard Dellamora, *Masculine Desire: The Politics of Victorian Aestheticism,* Chapel Hill: University of North Carolina Press, 1990; Phyllis Grosskurth, *John Addington Symonds: A Biography,* London: Longmans, 1964.

13   Reid, *Private Road,* p. 69.

14   Ibid., p. 70.

15   For discussions of Pater's understanding of Winckelmann see Dellamora, op. cit., ch. 5: 'Arnold, Winckelmann, and Pater', pp. 102-16; Robert Aldrich, *The*

Seduction of the Mediterranean: Writing, Art and Homosexual Fantasy, London: Routledge, 1993, ch. 2.

16 Forster to Reid, 17 Mar. 1915.

17 Forster to Reid, 13 Mar. 1915.

18 Forster to Reid, 24 Sept. 1927.

19 Forster to Reid, 28 Oct. 1931.

20 Forster to Reid, 12 June 1944.

21 Forster to Reid, 23 Mar. 1915.

22 Forster to Reid, 31 Mar. 1915 (Forster's emphasis).

23 Reid discussed a reader's report for T. Fisher Unwin, who finally published the novel in 1920 with the Talbot Press, Dublin, and the American company Houghton Mifflin.

24 Forster to Reid, 22 Nov. 1919.

25 Reid to Raffalovich, 6 May 1920. I have not been able to trace the novel *L'Erreur* discussed at the beginning of this extract.

26 Raffalovich to Reid, n.d. (but May 1920). I have retained Raffalovich's own punctuation in this and other extracts from his letters.

27 Ibid.

28 André Raffalovich, *Uranisme et Unisexualité: Études sur différentes manifestations de l'instinct sexuel* (Lyon: Storck; Paris: Masson & Cie 1896).

29 Raffalovich to Reid, 19 Mar. 1920.

30 Reid to Raffalovich, 20 May 1920.

31 Raffalovich to Reid, 22 May 1920.

32 Raffalovich had already sent Reid a copy of his archives on homosexuality, and Reid may have felt too scrutinised, perhaps as another 'case' for the same collection.

33 My information is from an examination of Reid's own copies of these books, which contain marginal annotations in his handwriting.

34 See Eve Kosofsky Sedgwick, *Between Men: English Literature and Male Homosocial Desire,* New York: Columbia University Press, 1985.

35 Forrest Reid, *Pirates of the Spring,* Dublin: Talbot Press, 1920, p. 64.

36 Serghei Aksakoff (1791-1859) published his autobiography *Years of Childhood* in 1858. The Oxford University Press World's Classics translation was published in 1923; Raffalovich may have known this work in its original Russian, but he and Reid (and several of their correspondents) must have read the book in this version.

37 Burdett to Reid, 21 Feb. 1907. I have been unable to trace Osbert Burdett's executors for permission to quote passages from his published and unpublished works.

38 Burdett to Reid, 18 Oct. 1907. It is not my intention to expand upon the 'dream' element in Reid's fiction, nor on the perception of it by other writers, Reid's correspondents, etc. For a fuller discussion of this subject see Brian Taylor, *The Green Avenue: The Life and Writings of Forrest Reid 1875-1947,* Cambridge University Press, 1980, and my introduction to *The Garden God,* London: Brilliance, 1986.

39 For bibliographic information on *The Wild Rose* see Timothy d'Arch Smith, *Love in Earnest,* London: Routledge, 1970; Brian Reade, *Sexual Heretics,* London: Routledge, 1970. And see too David Sox, *Bachelors of Art: Edward Perry Warren and the Lewes House Brotherhood,* Fourth Estate, 1991, pt. III, ch. 2.

40 Burdett to Reid, 26 May 1929.

41 See Sox, op. cit., pp. 84-7.

42 Ibid., p. 87; see also Osbert Burdett and E. H. Goddard *Edward Perry Warren: The Biography of a Connoisseur,* Christophers, 1941, ch. 15.

43 Burdett to Reid, 28 Aug. 1929.

44   Forrest Reid, 'Arthur Lyon Raile' in *Retrospective Adventures*, London: Faber, 1941,
     p. 171. (This review was reprinted from *Irish Statesman*, 14 Apr. 1928.)
45   Ibid., p. 172.
46   d'Arch Smith, op. cit., p. 300. As I have shown above, Reid's review of *The Wild
     Rose* was written before he received *A Defence of Uranian Love* from Burdett.
47   Reid, *Retrospective Adventures*, p. 175.
48   Warren himself referred to the work as *Magnum Opus* (see Burdett and Goddard,
     op. cit., p. 300). As I have shown above, Reid's review of *The Wild Rose* was writ-
     ten before he received *A Defence of Uranian Love* from Burdett.
49   'Arthur Lyon Raile', *A Defence of Uranian Love*, 3 vols, Cayme Press, 1928-1930.
     My quotation is from vol. III, 'Conclusion', p. 77.
50   This split, between the house and the grounds appears to have been a central
     motif of Reid's projected school novel *The Green Avenue*. Brian Taylor, op. cit.,
     p. 186, cites Stephen Gilbert on this novel: 'While the avenue was green and at-
     tractive, the house, unseen from the gates, was a far less happy place.'
51   Tom says goodbye to the garden statue of the boy by kissing him. The moment
     is revealing: 'When Tom's lips pressed on those other lips the eyes were looking
     away from him, and dimly he felt that this was a symbol of life – of life and
     of all love. No, no – not all – not Uncle Stephen's. . . .
     He hurried from the garden, trying as he went to shake from him this incom-
     prehensible mood and return to actuality. Surely the present crisis was absorbing
     and exciting enough, and the future was there, beckoning eagerly, filled with hap-
     piness.' (Reid, *Uncle Stephen*, p. 269)
52   Forrest Reid, *Poems from the Greek Anthology*, London: Faber, 1943, p. 27.
53   Forster to Reid, 28 Oct. 1931. Forster commented on a draft of the novel: 'The
     fewer incidental characters Tom charms the stronger will be his essential charm.
     He ought to leave many people quite indifferent.'
54   Quoted in Weeks, op. cit., p. 125.
55   See, for example, Carpenter's *Days with Walt Whitman*, London: George Allen, 1906.
     Reid possessed a copy of Carpenter's *Iolaus* given to him by James Rutherford in 1907.
56   Aldrich, op. cit., p. 9.
57   One can contrast the 'plainness' of Tom with the handsomeness of Evan in *Pirates
     of the Spring* (see esp. p. 346) and the different moral characters of the boys. Reid
     referred to his own 'somewhat Socratic ugliness' in *Private Road* (p. 58) and may
     be linking himself, Tom and Socrates in the novels.

Acknowledgements

This chapter could not have been researched without the generosity and co-operation
of the following: Stephen Gilbert, who allowed me access to Forrest Reid's correspondence and who shared his ideas and memories with me; the English Province
of the Order of Preachers, and particularly their archivist in Edinburgh, Father Bede
Bailey, who allowed me to consult the correspondence of André Raffalovich; the Rev.
David Sox, who shared information on, and material by Edward Perry Warren (Arthur
Lyon Raile). My special thanks to them all.

I would like to thank librarians and staff at the Linen Hall Library, Belfast; the Belfast
City Library; the University of British Columbia (the Colbeck Collection); the University
of Keele; and the University of Staffordshire. My thanks, too, to Terry Cartlidge for
his many suggestions when we first read Forrest Reid.

4 Lost Time
The Smell and Taste of Castle T

Roz Cowman

The primary concern of this essay is to establish the displacement of sexuality onto an eroticised landscape in the Irish RM fictions of Somerville and Ross (Edith Œnone Somerville and Violet Martin). Through their letters and autobiographical writings I shall examine the relationship between these two women both as a writing partnership and as a unique bond of love. I shall explore the strategies by which they linked concepts of gender, sexuality, racial identity, religion and social class, thereby devising their particular ethos. The focus of the essay will be an examination of this ethos, and the process by which Somerville and Ross transformed it into an aesthetic. I have selected from their fiction *Some Experiences of an Irish RM* and *Further Experiences of an Irish RM*. These works embody most clearly the essential structure of this aesthetic: the construction of a mythology of the Anglo-Irish as a race and caste, and the consequent displacement of sexuality within this mythology onto landscape.

THE PERSONAL RELATIONSHIP

Because Somerville and Ross lived within a concentrated family network, and at the centre of a complex social system, we have to evaluate their relationship, their sense of self-definition and personal identity, in the context of their extended family and social circle. Here a brief biographical note will serve as a reference point. Since in their letters they refer to each

other as Edith and Martin, I shall refer to them by these names. Edith
Œnone Somerville was born in 1858; her family home was at Drishane
House, Castletownshend, in West Cork. Her cousin Violet Martin was born
in 1862 at Ross House in Co. Galway. They met for the first time in 1886,
when Violet Martin paid a visit to the Somervilles in Castletownshend.
Both cousins, belonging to the landowning Anglo-Irish class, were
chatelaines of large country houses. Edith was training as an art student
in Paris, and Martin had returned from a girlhood spent in Dublin to Ross
House in Galway, which was in need of repairs and money.

Biographers have discussed in greater detail the relationship between
Edith and Martin. One biographer, Maurice Collis, describes Edith's feeling
for Martin as ' . . . a passion, an obsession from the depths of her being'.
Collis bases this claim rather insecurely on the double proposition that
Edith had 'a profound distaste for the opposite sex'[1] and that 'Edith
could only fall in love with a woman'.[2] The first is inaccurate: in her fiction, letters and autobiographical writing, Edith clearly likes and enjoys
the company of men. Her love for her brother Boyle is sufficient to make
that clear. The second proposition must remain forever unexplained; since
we need not doubt her love for Martin, it seems pointless to isolate it within
such dismal *faute de mieux* parameters. Gifford Lewis refutes Collis's analysis
in her excellent biography, *Somerville and Ross: The World of the Irish RM*
She completes and puts in context the quotations which Collis uses to
support his argument, restoring them as descriptions of ordinary family
interactions, and by no means the hysterical illnesses and dramas which,
Collis suggests, 'could only be fully explained by a psychiatrist'.[3]

If we examine the relationship from internal evidence, it can be seen
that their way of life in nineteenth-century Anglo-Ireland would render
unlikely any physical sexuality between them. There is a deep and exclusive love implicit in the letters, and also a series of uneasy references
to sexuality, especially on Martin's part. She writes to Edith on 11 March
1895 about the 'Ballad of the Nun', which has just appeared in *The Yellow
Book*: 'I wish it were a little less degraded. I do wish people would give
up making the central physical fact of life its central point of happiness,
of intellect, of interest' (*Letters*, p. 221).

Martin's concept of sex as the central physical point of life isolates it
from emotional, spiritual and erotic potential. She encourages Edith to
be the judge of acceptable sexual references — referring to a countrywoman
speaking of 'one child and the invoice of another', she asks Edith: 'Is this
very improper? I feel it is, but am not sure' (*Letters*, p. 132). In a later letter, written on 6 September 1889, a good example of the extraordinary
physical toughness and sexual prudery peculiar to her, Martin describes
a rare experience of horror:

I looked through *Nana*, Zola's book. I feel ashamed of having opening it . . . but it is not as bad as Ouida or Swinburne. . . . I am sure you despise me a good deal, and I certainly think it is not a book to read as there is no use in getting familiarised with bad things. . . . I thought I should feel better if I told you. (*Letters*, p. 154)

Then she goes on to describe the circumstances in which she has read the book:

A very weird room — on the ground floor — with an earthy smell . . . a horrid long dark passage leading to the door and nothing else . . . in the top of the door glass put in . . . so the door and passage seem to stare with those square eyes. . . . Mrs Persse assured me they [rats] couldn't get into the room but the noise they made was intolerable, and I slept very badly. . . . I wasn't frightened, just bored by them. Neuralgia, the earth smell, and rats over the ceiling and down the walls . . . and Zola's dreadful facts steaming and reeking in one's mind. (*Letters*, p. 154)

In this poignant letter we can see the strange contradictions — the noise of rats keeps her awake, she is fully aware of the sinister aspect of the room, but it is the horror and sexual shock of what she has read in Zola that leave her feeling brutalised, and needing to be reassured by Edith.

Apart from this internal evidence of a shunning of physical sexuality, we find Elizabeth Bowen, herself a member of the landed class and a contemporary, though not of their generation, referring to Edith and Martin's relationship: 'Nor was its nature — as it might be in these days — speculated upon. . . . The upper class, the Anglo-Irish, were then non-physical — far from keen participants even, from what one hears of them, in the joys of marriage.'[4] Pat O'Connor in *Friendships Between Women*, examining the forces that shape women's relationships, quotes Faderman: 'It was virtually impossible to study the correspondence of any nineteenth-century woman . . . and not uncover a passionate commitment to another woman, at some time in her life', although 'most of these relationships were not lesbian in the sense that they were genital'.[5] Both Edith and Martin were familiar with the legendary friendship between Maria Edgeworth and their great-grandmother, Mrs Bushe. The form this friendship took was a lifetime of effusive letters from Miss Edgeworth and considerably calmer replies from Mrs Bushe, with rare meetings. Edith refers to this as Edgeworth's 'falling in love with Mrs B'. Edith and Martin were familiar also with the close family relationships usual among women of their class, with a sister or a cousin, in which they would support each other through the trials of marriage and family life. In other words, the intensity of their own relationship did not appear unusual to these women, nor to their contemporaries.

It is difficult to imagine nowadays the obstacles that existed to a friend-ship between two women at the end of the nineteenth century. If we assume that shared interests, leisure, liberty, regular meetings, transport and money are some of the factors that underlie a modern friendship, it is sobering to realise that shared interests were the only factor available to Edith and Martin. We can see how their position as chatelaines in the landowning class both increased and diminished the possibilities of a partnership. It is significant that their first meeting took place when both were in their twenties. Since the degree of cousinship was close, the delay in their meeting reminds us that over one hundred miles separated their homes. At that time such a journey would have taken at least eight hours by public transport. We read in the letters of Edith, when finances were troubled, offering to pay Martin's travel expenses so that they can work together on a book, and of paying for her keep when she visits Martin. This ex-pense of time, effort and money in order to meet must be considered in contextualising their friendship.

Because they were both family-centred, it appears to have been their intention to remain family-bound. Certainly the way of life of the Ladies of Llangollen, Lady Eleanor Butler and Sarah Ponsonby, was repellent to Edith and Martin. These Anglo-Irish women had defied their families and the socio-sexual mores of the eighteenth century and set up house together in Llangollen in 1778. Like Gertrude Stein and Alice B. Toklas in twentieth-century Paris, they had become the objects of social and literary pilgrimage. Edith's and Martin's response to the scene of this long-dead relationship, when they visited Wales in 1895, is that of puzzled disapproval that people should choose to live in isolation from their families. They appear ge-nuinely surprised at a situation so foreign to the tribal enclave of the world of Somerville and Ross. Martin's comment is telling: 'I never could tell the wearisome grind of those blessed hags of Llangollen' (*Letters*, p. 170). Their decision against marriage I shall refer to later, but Edith, in *Irish Memories*, makes it clear that in retrospect at least she was aware of a choice between art and marriage. Referring to her great-grandmother Bushe, her comment is: 'She had a rare and enchanting gift as an artist which could scarce have failed to make its mark had she not devoted herself to "mak-ing originals instead of copies". . . . In her time there were few women who gave even a moment's thought to the possibilities of individual life as an artist' (*IM*, p. 52).

In the letters, a picture of this relationship between the cousins begins to emerge. In the early letters written shortly after their first meeting, the tone is unsteady, certainly on Martin's part. She is still a girlish twenty-four-year-old, a bit dazzled by a first visit to Edith and her overwhelming family; she is clearly a little offended that Edith, significantly, has not replied from Paris to an earlier letter. There is a certain tone of flirtatious scolding: 'There are people to whom it interests one to write, irrespective of their bad qualities and behaviour . . .' (19 May 1886, *Letters*, p. 6). This is half serious, as close to a direct expression of mutual affection as we will find. Nine years after their first meeting, Martin appears permanently nervous of expressing affection openly to Edith: 'My dear — if it were not so awfully foolish, I could put xxx's in that place like the children — you will understand that I have not done so because I don't want you to laugh at me' (*Letters*, p. 17). Martin's letter to Edith, who has just returned to Drishane and is mourning the loss of a little dog, closes on a note of tenderness: 'My heart aches for you when I think of you arriving in Drishane — goodbye — Edith, my dear' (*Letters*, p. 38). This rare tenderness is made permissible by grief or mourning, and is always evoked by dogs, in sickness or health. They speak freely of family love; they grieve for deceased pets, and console each other tenderly for such mourning. Affection between them is mainly expressed as a coded sharing of private jokes and of social standards, and a use of Hiberno-English to defuse the emotion — 'I'll never forget it to you.'

The letters give us some idea of the logistics — the long distance that separated their two homes, the endless busy-ness with maintaining an estate without enough money, the endless round of entertaining, mainly with family and neighbours, an account of a good day's hunting. Edith describes a typical week in Drishane, in a letter of 10 September 1888: 'Edith and Jim went by midday today. Tomorrow a hideous tennis function at the Broughams. Wednesday, Herbert goes — some of us . . . to the Powells. Thursday, we have a tennis party . . . on Friday, we have a dinner. . . . We are all so tied together — whatever is done must be done by everyone . . . and as the majority prefer wasting their time, that is the prevalent amusement.' The letter continues: 'We shall be leaving for Bristol on about the 28th of this month so it [Martin's visit] would not be worth the expense, the long journey. . . . Boyle's leave expires on 20th of October. The guests disperse on the 5th, and what he is to do in the meantime is the question. We can't . . . stay with the Bideford woman for more than . . . 5 days. Boyle . . . will have ten days to fool around in, and has no money to fly backwards and forwards.' Anyone catering for a large, adult household without enough money will understand the pressures that this letter reveals — Edith owes herself to her family, and the endless sapping domestic and social problems, exacerbated by travel, use up her mind. Later in the same letter a note is struck which makes clear how she used any opportunity to restore her creativity: 'Boyle and I had a really peaceful afternoon. We drove to a cottage on the way to Rineen — sent the trap home, and then sketched till dark and walked back. The bonds fell from us for once — and we were temporarily free' (*Letters*, p. 50).

In a further letter, written in January 1889, Edith sent Martin a 2,000-word description of a run with hounds. They hack to Skibbereen (about five miles), box the horses in Ballineen, ride to the meet at Manch House (at about 9 a.m., I would estimate), their fox goes to ground at about 4 p.m., they ride four miles back to Manch, and the railway station, and back to Drishane again, a twelve-hour day. Edith comments on this: 'I am a bit stiff today' (*Letters*, p. 117). In length, this would be a normal day with hounds; for Edith it merits description only because of hunting with a strange pack and the unfamiliar practice of travelling by train to the meet. Hunting on this scale was a social duty for Edith, apart from being an irresistible pleasure. However, in spite of the family being landowners, lack of money would have made this magnificent day impossible 'only that Mrs Chare most nobly gave us £1 each at Christmas' (*Letters*, p. 150). In February 1889, after this letter, Edith spent three months in Ross, where a less intense but equally time-consuming way of life would have interrupted, as usual, their literary collaboration.

WRITING RELATIONSHIP

The fact that they were apart so often naturally raises the question, how did their literary collaboration occur? The physical facts are simple; sometimes they were able to spend time together and worked on a new project. When apart, they wrote comments and suggestions to each other. Edith did the illustrations. They wrote to meet a perceived public demand; their first book, *An Irish Cousin*, was intended to belong to the 'shilling shocker' class. Edith's description of the collaboration is found in *Irish Memories* (p. 133):

> One or the other — not infrequently both, simultaneously — would state a proposition. This would be argued, combated perhaps, approved, or modified; it would then be written down by the (wholly fortuitous) holder of the pen, would be scratched out, scribbled in again; before it found itself finally transferred into decorous MS; would probably have suffered many things, but it would, at all events, have had the advantage of having been well aired.

Martin's view of their shared authorship can be found in a letter of September 1889: 'The reason few people can [write together], is because they have separate minds upon most subjects; I think the two Shockers [family name for Edith and Martin] have a very strange belief in each other, joined to a critical faculty' (*Letters*, p. 213).

To understand the writing aspect of their partnership, we need to study an essential chapter from *Irish Memories*, 'When First She Came'. This work, published in 1917 by Edith after Martin's death, is a nostalgic, commemorative work detailing episodes from family history and, in particular, episodes from Edith's and Martin's shared lives. The most powerful of these recollections is that of the summer of 1886, their first summer together:

> It was one of those perfect summers that come sometimes to the south of Ireland, when rain is not, and the sun is hot, but never too hot, and the gardens are a storm of flowers, flowers such as one does not see elsewhere, children of the south and the sun and the sea; tall delphiniums that have climbed to the sky and brought down its most heavenly blue, Japanese iris, with their pale and dappled lilac discs spread forth to the sun . . .; peonies and poppies, arum and ashphodel, every one of them three times as tall, and three times as brilliant and three times as sweet as any of their English cousins, and all of them and everything else as well, irradiated for me that happy year by a new 'Spirit of Delight'. (*IM*, p. 214)

She writes of the same period:

> those blue mornings of mid-June . . . lying on the warm, short grass of the sheep fields . . . listening to the curving cry of the curlews and the mewing of the sea gulls as they drifted in the blue over our heads; watching the sunlight making dancing stars to light in the deeper blue firmament below . . . not in the golden world did the time fleet more carelessly than it did for all of us that summer. (*IM*, p. 126)

This is the Golden Age, the Lost Paradise incorporated in a landscape of eroticised beauty, which appears in much European fiction from around this time onwards. Proust's thousand-word description of a hawthorn hedge in *Du côté de chez Swann* is of greater intensity, but its combination of the erotic and the aesthetic springs from the same source. In either case this source is involuntary memory and synaesthesia (the transposing of sensory images), gifts shared by both Proust and Violet Martin. The narrator's total recovery of an experience from the past, triggered by the flavour, scent and texture of a madeleine soaked in lime-flower tea, is one of three such episodes in *À la recherche du temps perdu*. Martin leaves only one record of synaesthesia and involuntary memory. In a letter of January 1887 she writes to Edith from London:

> Just as we were stumbling into the dark dress circle, the orchestra began 'Die Blume' — I felt almost faint from the smell and taste of Castle T[ownshend] that it gave — everyone's voices, everyone's dress (notably you in the tea-gown, playing it), the look of the room with the lamps lit — a kind of vision . . . (*Letters*, p. 56)

This is an exceptional experience of synaesthesia — a total sensory recovery of the past, similar to that to be experienced by Proust in January 1909. While Martin does not describe again any episode of equal intensity, we can nevertheless assume that this was not an isolated occurrence in her life — synaesthesia and involuntary memory tend to be recurrent phenomena.

In fiction, they facilitate the retrieval of a lost experience, particularly the retrieval of sensory impressions as experienced in childhood, and of life as it *felt* at a particular time. Gabriel Josipovici expands on this in *Proust: A Voice in Search of Itself*: 'The real law of the lost paradise . . . is that it is not until something has been lost that it can truly be found. Involuntary memory does not just call up a moment of the past, it holds together something that is common . . . to the past and to the present, and which is thus more essential than either.'[6] He goes on to quote Proust: 'But let a noise or a scent, once heard or once smelt, be heard or smelt again in the present and at the same time in the past . . . and immediately . . . the essence of things is liberated . . . and our true self which seemed to be dead . . . is awakened and reanimated as it receives the celestial nourishment.'[7]

Proust's narrator Marcel is frustrated by his inability to 'hold' his vision as it first appears to him, and looks for a person to embody that landscape. This is the equivalent of Eliot's 'objective co-relative', an unrelated object which can be relied on to evoke certain associations. Edith's and Martin's differing accounts of the origin of *An Irish Cousin* show this process at work. Martin writes in 1889, just after its publication: 'you told me of the old maniac's face at the window' (*Letters*, p. 41), referring to an event which was central to the composition of the novel. Edith, in *Irish Memories* (1917), describes the same event as if both she and Martin had experienced it together. They ride to visit an isolated cousin in Castletownshend, and as they leave in an October twilight they see 'a window, just over the hall door . . . a white face . . . we saw the face glimmer there for a minute and vanish'. The countryside is described: 'We rode home along the side of the hills, and watched the fires of the sunset sink into the sea, and met the crescent moon coming faint with light' (*IM*, p. 130). It is possible to see from these two very different accounts how Edith situates Martin in a landscape and makes her presence central to the aesthetic impact of the scene. In this way she recreates the past in a lasting form.

THE IRISH RM NOVELS

Landscape pervades the Irish RM novels, and it is the one constant in a world where categories are otherwise blurred. In these stories the

Anglo-Irish amongst themselves acquire an overall androgyny, where males are not expected to be masculine, and females are not necessarily feminine; males are often incompetent, females hunt hounds, break in young horses, run estates. The matriarch Lady Knox says: 'Bernard Shute has gone off to the Clyde, and I had counted on his being a man at my dance next week' (*EIRM*, p. 132). Here the ambiguous Anglo-Irish suggests that Bernard Shute can assume or discard manhood at will. Major Yeates, faced with an angry dowager, says: 'I wished myself safe at Shreelane, with the bedclothes over my head' (p. 200). Faced with his inadequacies as Master of Foxhounds, he prays that his huntsman will look on him, at best, as 'Parsifal . . . a blameless fool' (p. 130). Speaking of Bernard Shute, his sister, in a passage of Wildeian inconsequence and ellipsis, says: 'I should never have allowed him to take up gardening. It only promotes intimacies with dowagers' (p. 294).

However, apart from the presentation of the Anglo-Irish as androgynous amongst themselves, there is also a very different perception of the Anglo-Irish *vis-à-vis* the native population. This perception accords with the discourse of Celticism, as developed in the nineteenth century from contemporary philogy, ethnology and anthropology, by Ernest Renan and Matthew Arnold. Celticism, as an argument, begs the question; its premise and conclusion are identical: that feminine is inferior to masculine, and that some races can be classified as Celtic and feminine. Renan's *Poesie des races celtiques* (1877) assumes the existence of, and equates, racial and gender psychological traits: 'If it be permitted us to assign sex to nations as to individuals, we should have to say . . . that the Celtic race . . . is an essentially feminine race.'[8] Arnold, influenced by Renan, expands this proposition to justify the process of imperialism. The Celtic or Irish race, with its 'feminine' qualities of emotional weakness and excitability, is complemented and made whole by the Teuton, Saxon, or English race, whose characteristics are the 'masculine' attributes of steadfastness, organisation, and calmness: 'Then we may use German faithfulness to Nature to . . . free us from insolence and self-will; we may use the Celtic quickness of perception to give us delicacy.'[9] Thus the discourse of Celticism offered considerable advantages to the self-image of England as an imperial power, and even greater advantages to the Anglo-Irish as perceived by Somerville and Ross in the Irish RM novels. We find an intensification of erratic, fey behaviour on the part of the Anglo-Irish, an increase of Celtic qualities (hysteria, disorganisation) when faced with English visitors or with any Saxon-Teutonic display of organisation, inflexibility or authoritarianism. However, in the presence of 'the people', to whom I shall refer presently, the Anglo-Irish become Teutonic, imposing order, being stoical and firm.

This Janus-like ability to face in opposing directions has been aptly categorised by David Cairns and Shaun Richards in *Writing Ireland*: 'For the Anglo-Irish, Celticism offered the position of Ireland's resident Teutons.'[10] These writers include another aspect of Celticism which is also familiar from the Irish RM novels, the 'idealised Gaelic tribal society, based on identifying the warrior chiefs with the Anglo-Irish and the chiefs' followers with the peasants, denying the Catholic bourgeoisie a role'. Thus Celticism enabled the obliteration, at least in theory, of an entire class, the rising Catholic middle class, to which Somerville and Ross are certainly hostile in their letters and in the Irish RM novels. Many of their letters attest to a naïve belief in the 'loyalty' and personal devotion of tenants. While this belief is a colonial stereotype, we can see how it gains credibility for the Anglo-Irish when validated by a pseudo-scientific discourse. In letters Edith and Martin refer to themselves as Irish, to the English as Saxons, and to the Irish tenant class as 'the people'. This is another colonial assumption, that the colonised population has no nationality and can be classified as aboriginal. Thus, Edith and Martin used the racist theory of Celticism to equate caste, race and gender. For them, the Anglo-Irish take on the 'masculine' attributes of power, control, honesty, in contrast to the 'feminine' traits — cunning, emotionalism, lack of power — of 'the people'. A letter from Martin discussing votes for women makes clear how gender is perceived:

> I certainly think it absurd that the people Mama employs would have a vote and that she herself should not have one; after all, most women who have to stand alone and manage their houses or places themselves are competent to give as intelligent a vote as Paddy Griffy or Sam Church.
> (*Letters*, p. 141)

Note the definitions here: 'women' are women like Mama, Anglo-Irish, empowered, masculine in gender because they employ men of 'the people' who are now feminised by the context.

Gender is also affected by religion, in that Catholics, particularly those of the middle class, are feminised or disempowered, regardless of biological sex. In the *Experiences of an Irish RM* a young Catholic male, sexually and socially active, is feminised by name ('Curly' McRory) and is further emasculated by description — too well dressed, too handsome — and by suggestive imagery: 'his lily-white flannels, his voice an unmistakable Dublin light tenor' (*EIRM*, p. 302). Major Yeates, the protagonist of the novels, refers to a young female fellow-guest as: 'a fluffy-haired, certainly rather pretty little abomination, a creature who was staying with the McRorys' (p. 295). When we decode 'McRorys' we can understand the full impact of this description. The McRorys are a Dublin ex-coalmerchant's family, belonging to the Catholic bourgeoisie which is becoming increasingly upwardly mobile. This is the class which is presented as most threatening, and most innately vulgar, in other works by Somerville and Ross and in other Anglo-Irish novels, for example *The Real Charlotte* by Somerville and Ross, George Moore's *A Dream in Muslin* and Maria Edgeworth's *Castle Rackrent*. These works manifest the same dread of this social group, which was rapidly expanding to fill the professional gaps and to buy up the abandoned 'Big Houses' left by the departing Ascendancy.

Within this gendering of the Anglo-Irish, androgynous amongst themselves, or male in opposition to native Irish as female, we also find that ethical and aesthetic standards are linked to these new groupings. In the *Experiences of an Irish RM* the first-person narrator, Major Yeates, belongs to the Anglo-Irish class, and authorial ideology and approval are vested in him. Thus in a scene where old Mrs Knox refers to a young servant as 'a barefoot slut out of a cabin' the narrative endorses Mrs Knox's voice as 'well bred and imperious', while that of her opponent, a proprietress of a commercial establishment, is described as 'shrilly tremulous with indignation' (*EIRM*, p. 31). The narrative already indicates support for Mrs Knox as an aristocrat with an inherent (not acquired) ruling quality of voice; the brutality of content of her speech is not commented on. Her opponent's reply, 'I consider your conduct is neither that of a lady nor a Christian' (p. 31), is devalued by the speaker's being presented as uncontrolled, hysterical, like a terrier after a rat. Its content, dignified and restrained (and very 'upper-class' in its rhythm and syntax), is not commented on. This exchange epitomises the ethos which underlies this idealised aristocracy. Everything the 'peasantry' do is wrong, because they cannot be right. Even when they defeat the aristocracy in an exchange, as Major Yeates is often defeated, this only reinforces the identity of the 'inside' group by emphasising the efforts of the outside, the 'other'.

Once we appreciate the authorial stance on ethical issues, we can appreciate that the same stance will idealise all attributes of the Anglo-Irish in these novels. Aesthetic values relate mainly to clothes and décor. Their dirty, shabby or luxurious homes are intrinsically correct; the dirty, shabby or luxurious homes of 'the people', and especially the bourgeoisie, are intrinsically wrong, the result of inborn dirtiness, fecklessness, or of vulgar effortfulness: 'Detestable soup in a splendid old silver tureen . . . a perfect salmon . . . on a chipped kitchen dish' in Aussolas Castle (*EIRM*, p. 35), but in the *nouveau riche* McRory home 'a soup tureen full of custard, a mountainous dish of trifle. . . . Philippa had on one side of her plate a cup of soup, and on the other a cup of tea' (p. 303). Similarly, the domestic animals and fowl wandering in and out of Aussolas Castle are not the same as those wandering in and out of a tenant's cottage. The Miss Flynns' house is a good example. In their farmhouse 'a cascade of white paper flowed glacially from the chimney to the fender, the gloom was Cimmerian, and unalterable, owing to the fact that the blind was broken; the cold of a never-occupied room ate into our vitals'. Presently 'the daughters of the house made their entry . . . in gowns suggestive of a theatre, or a tropical garden party, and in picture hats, necklaces, bracelets and lavish top dressing of powder' (p. 234). These, in fact, are the famous young ladies who are so refined that 'they hardly knew the way to the stables' in their own home, and very different in their exaggerated femininity from the women of Major Yeates's circle.

So in these novels, landscape and the beauty of country life are the only unchanging quantities. Landscape is a character in these works and embodies the emotional source of their authors' writing. 'The horns . . . blew their summons antiphonally into the immensities of sea and sky, and summoned only the sunset and after it the twilight' (*EIRM*, p. 240) . . . 'The sunset had waned, and a big white moon was making the eastern tower of Aussolas look like a thing in a fairy tale' (p. 34) 'A mountain towered steeply up from the lake's edge, dark with the sad green of beech trees in September' (p. 43) . . . 'The rich and southern blue of sea filled the gaps between scattered fir trees; the hillside above was purple with heather' (p. 161) . . . 'the smell of mignonette . . . the summery rattle of a reaping machine, the strong and steady rasp of a corncrake, and the growl of a big steamer from a band of fog that was advancing, ghostlike, along the blue floor of the sea' (p. 184) . . . 'rough heathery country . . . with a string of little blue lakes running like a turquoise necklet round the base of a furry hill, and patches of green pasture . . . amid the rocks and heather' (p. 13).

I believe part of Edith's and Martin's response to landscape was connected to the strenuous activity of following hounds over it. We are aware nowadays of the beneficial chemical changes induced by exercise – the 'exercise high'. Not even this degrading cult name, nor an understanding of its chemical basis, alter the overwhelming feeling of pleasure that comes from exercise. For Edith and Martin, the joy of exercise was increased by the tactical excitements of hunting – anticipating where the fox would break, watching hounds work, the relationship with their own horses, the behaviour of others in the field, anticipating the weather – all these still contribute to an overall feeling of achievement and unity, of being part of a process of nature, which is not to be underestimated. And repeatedly in *Some Experiences of an Irish RM* and *Further Experiences of an Irish RM* this experience is described – in terms which are often those of sexual response. When Major Yeates introduces his wife to hunting, she becomes addicted very easily, and reminds her husband as they wait by a covert: 'Sinclair, . . . remember if they find, it's no use to talk to me, for I shan't be able to speak' (*EIRM*, p. 118). Later, in the same episode, describing hounds finding a scent: 'The first ecstatic whimpers broke forth. In a moment it was full cry, discordant, beautiful, and soul-stirring, as the pack spread and spread, and settled to the line. I saw the absurd dazzle of tears in Philippa's eyes' (p. 126). 'It was a day when frost and sunshine combined went to one's head like champagne' (p. 130). On another occasion 'the cry of the hounds filled the air with a kind of delirium' (p. 140), and, most significantly, 'pure ecstasy stretched his grin from ear to ear, and broke from him in giggles of delight' (p. 239).

Even the house becomes animated in the writings of Somerville and Ross. Molly Keane, in her perceptive foreword to the *Selected Letters*, refers to 'a sexual love for the house and its demesnes' (p. xviii). All those who have read her marvellous description of bleak 'Temple Alice' (in *Good Behaviour*), a comfortless house as frigid as the family that inhabit it, will remember the apotheosis of the same house in a happy summer full of sexual possibility for the narrator, when the shabby old house becomes incandescent in its beauty. Keane is aware of how landscape and buildings are transformed by Eros. In the *Experiences of an Irish RM* houses do not take on this erotic glamour in the same way, but they become part of nature. This is a apparent in the description of Aussolas Castle: 'A couple of young horses outside the windows tore at the matted creeper on the walls, or thrust faces that were half shy, half impudent, into the room. Portly pigeons . . . on the picture frames kept up a hoarse and pompous cooing' (*EIRM*, p. 81). This is the interiorising of a Greek pastoral idyll — where animal and human cohabit and are not distinguished, the atmosphere of 'L'après-midi d'un faune' where the animal is almost human, the human almost animal ('the petulant, fractious manner of goats that so ill-assorts with their Presbyterian beards' (p. 267)). In fact, Mrs Knox, the owner of this ménage, has married her husband, 'Badger' Knox, to save his pack of hounds. The house is guarded effectively by an old mare and young unbroken colts that run wild in the park ('There are plenty of people afraid to come here at all. There are scores of them running wild like deer in the woods' (p. 33)). The accepted presence of rats in Martin's letter about Zola has already been referred to; Major Yeates refers to his bachelor life in Shreelane: 'long, lonely evenings there with the rats for company' (p. 84). With these, and jackdaws in the chimney, country homes were inhabited to a degree that now belongs to myth or fairy tale, and this was taken for granted; just as dropping a goose down the chimney was the accepted chimney-scourer. An external example of the myth-inducing power of this fiction, the story of 'Trinket's Colt' contains the ancient archetype of the severed horse's head; Major Yeates, crawling on his stomach through a furze covert, is 'confronted by the long horrified face of Mrs Knox's colt, mysteriously level with my own' (p. 41). A rival of Flurry Knox's is hunted by Flurry's hounds. The result? 'He lost his brush. . . . Old Merrylegs tore the coat tails off him. . . . Flurry has them to nail to his kennel door' (p. 29) (like a fox's brush). Nor must we forget the Gannon family, related to Flurry Knox, who live secretly like nesting rats in Major Yeates's stable-loft; Flurry's hounds following a fox that goes to ground in the loft reveal all to the assembled hunt: 'Never will . . . Flurry Knox . . . hear the last of the day that he ran his mother's first cousin to ground in the attic' (p. 15).

These extracts make clear that, although we are on the surface reading an Anglo-Irish comic novel, the stereotypes it appears to present are in fact the familiar contents of myth where there is no clear distinction between animal and human. It brings us back to a golden age of pastoral myth, and the freedoms that implies. This brings us to the presence of the erotic demiurge, Dionysios himself, the dismemberer of animals, the source of the Dionysia, the focus of the Bacchantes. He is omnipresent in the *Experiences of an Irish RM* — in the person of Flurry Knox, that least erotic of squireens. How can we read Flurry as an incarnation of Dionysios? He does indeed possess many of the right attributes: 'the slow, sing-song brogue, the hypnotic voice' (*EIRM*, p. 4) of Dionysios in Euripides' Bacchae; the androgynous appearance — 'a fair, spare, young man'; the outsider in appearance — 'a stable boy among gentlemen, a gentleman among stable boys' (p. 4); the bland expression — 'he seldom laughed, having . . . the gravity of manner that is bred by horse-dealing' (p. 5); 'a grave and almost religiously gentle young man' (p. 73); the sibylline speech — all Flurry's speech is ironic, with a subtext unavailable to the harassed narrator, Major Yeates. His name, also, is androgynous — 'Flurry' is the diminutive of 'Florence', a forename still given to males of the McCarthy clan in Ireland. As the local Master of Foxhounds, he is the leader of the Bacchantes, the hunting women obsessed by blood-lust (such as Philippa, Major Yeates' wife, whose name means 'horse-lover'). Flurry is the dismemberer of animals — the fox, and dead beasts to feed hounds on; his residence is like the shrine and altar of a mountain deity: 'the fir trees around were hung with gruesome and unknown joints' (p. 38). He is the Lord of the Animals; his ancestry marks him (he is the grandson of Badger Knox, part animal); he inherits from his grand-uncle Denis (which Latinised is, of course, Dionysios). Even the name of his house is Dionysiac — Tory Cottage; *tory* is the pine cone, the Greek thyrsos, the phallic emblem of Dionysios.

Animals, hunting and the countryside described with an intimate, detailed passion are profoundly eroticised. The language of the narratives devoted to landscape and hunting is emotionally charged, the images are sexual, and a pagan, pantheistic, pan-erotic Arcadia expands before the reader, a world that existed before we could distinguish between human and animal. Major Yeates refers to the 'prehistoric age' in south-west Ireland. This is at once the world of pre-genital childhood, and the world of Greek mythology, where the genital lurks everywhere, anthropomorphically. Flurry, his hounds, horses and heartland are the core of the *Experiences of an Irish RM* in them Edith and Martin have used this comedy to express, unconsciously, archetypes of orgiastic excitement, which may never have occurred to them as possible in physical sexuality, but which were nonetheless a repeated experience in their lives.

It would appear that Edith and Martin used all circumstances of their lives as Anglo-Irish chatelaines of a diminishing social order to further their relationship, and, more importantly, used the social, religious, aesthetic and gender divisions inherent in their position as colonisers to produce at least one work, the *Experiences of an Irish RM*, which would present a manifesto of erotic joy. Just as E. M. Forster and Kenneth Grahame used the images of Hellenism and Arcadia in their writing as a coded expression for forbidden, uncertain or unconscious sexuality, so these writers converted Ascendancy life in post-Famine Ireland into the images of Greek pastoral idyll, a land of centaurs and fauns.

Long after writing of this Irish Arcadia, and some thirty years after her first meeting with Martin, Edith completes the connection between this eroticised landscape and her own relation to Martin, and it is a crucial moment in her writing. In *Irish Memories* Edith describes the summer of her first meeting with Martin. I have quoted part of this already, here is the complete text:

> It was one of those perfect summers that come sometimes to the south of Ireland, when rain is not, and the sun is hot, but never too hot, and the gardens are a storm of flowers, flowers such as one does not see elsewhere, children of the south and the sun and the sea, tall delphiniums that have climbed to the sky and brought down its most heavenly blue; Japanese iris, with their pale and dappled lilac discs spread forth to the sun . . .; peonies and poppies, arums and asphodel, every one of them three times as tall, and three times as brilliant, and three times as sweet as any of their English cousins, and all of them, and everything else as well, irradiated for me that year by a new 'Spirit of Delight'. It was, as I have said, though then we knew it only dimly, the beginning, for us, of a new era. For most boys and girls the varying, yet invariable, flirtations and emotional episodes of youth are resolved and composed by marriage. To Martin and to me was opened another way, and the flowering of both our lives was when we met each other.
> (*IM*, pp 124-5)

Abbreviations

EIRM   *Experiences of an Irish RM*, London: Dent, 1970 (combined
         edition of *Some Experiences of an Irish RM* (1899) and
         Further Experiences of an Irish RM (1908))
IM   *Irish Memories*, London: Longmans, 1917
Letters *The Selected Letters of Somerville and Ross*, ed. Gifford
         Lewis, London: Faber, 1989

Notes and References

1   Maurice Collis, *Somerville and Ross: A Biography*, London: Faber, 1968, p. 32.
2   Ibid., p. 37.
3   Ibid., p. 96.
4   Elizabeth Bowen, *The Mulberry Tree: Selected Writings of Elizabeth Bowen*, ed. Hermione Lee, London: Virago, p. 186 (review of Violet Powell, *The Irish Cousins: A Biography of Somerville and Ross*).
5   Pat O'Connor, *Friendship Between Women*, Hemel Hempstead: Harvester Wheatsheaf, 1992, p. 13.
6   Gabriel Josipovici, *The World and the Book*, London: Macmillan, 1994, p. 18.
7   Ibid., p. 18.
8   Ernest Renan, *Poetry of the Celtic Races*, London: Walter Scott, 1897, p. 8.
9   Matthew Arnold, 'On the Study of Celtic Literature' in *English Literature and Irish Politics*, ed. R. H. Super, Ann Arbor: University of Michigan Press, 1973, p. 383.
10 David Cairns and Shaun Richards, *Writing Ireland: Colonialism, Nationalism and Culture*, Manchester University Press, 1988, p. 50.

5 Women and Desire in the Work of Elizabeth Bowen

Patricia Coughlan

> 'She abandoned me. She betrayed me.'
> 'Had you a sapphic relationship?'
> 'What?'
> 'Did you exchange embraces of any kind?'
> 'No. She always was in a hurry.'
> ELIZABETH BOWEN, *Eva Trout*, p. 184

The array of analytic tools available today to anyone thinking about issues of homo/heterosexual definition is remarkably little enriched from that available to, say, Proust. . . . Most moderately to well-educated Western people in this century seem to share a similar understanding of homosexual definition, independent of whether they themselves are gay or straight, homophobic or antihomophobic. . . . That understanding is . . . organized around a radical and irreducible incoherence. . . . Enduringly since at least the turn of the century, there have presided two contradictory *tropes of gender* through which same-sex desire could be understood. On the one hand there was, and there persists, differently coded (in the homophobic folklore and science surrounding those 'sissy boys' and their mannish sisters, but also in the heart and guts of much living gay and lesbian culture), the trope of inversion, *anima muliebris in corpore virili inclusa* — 'a woman's soul trapped in a man's body' — and vice versa. . . . One vital impulse of this trope is the preservation of an essential *heterosexuality* within desire itself, through a particular reading of the homosexuality of persons: desire, in this view, by definition subsists in the current that runs between one male self and one

103

female self, in whatever sex of bodies these selves may be manifested. . . . The persistence of the inversion trope has been yoked, however, to that of its contradictory counterpart, the trope of gender separatism. . . . Far from its being of the essence of desire to cross boundaries of gender, it is instead the most natural thing in the world that people of the same gender . . . should bond together . . . on the axis of sexual desire. As the substitution of the phrase 'woman-identified' for 'lesbian' suggests, as indeed does the concept of the continuum of male or female homosocial desire, this trope tends to reassimilate to one another identification and desire, where inversion models, by contrast, depend on their distinctness. Gender-separatist models would thus place the woman-loving woman and the man-loving man each at the 'natural' center of their own gender, in contrast to inversion models that locate gay people — whether biologically or culturally — at the threshold between genders.

EVE KOSOFSKY SEDGWICK[1]

I

This essay is a discussion of Elizabeth Bowen's representations of woman-to-woman attachment in her work. I have chosen at the outset to place my appraisal within the context of Eve Kosofsky Sedgwick's views, as one of the most effective summary accounts of our current state of thinking about same-sex desire. Did Elizabeth Bowen hold one of the two positions outlined (according to the 'two contradictory tropes of gender') by Sedgwick? If so, which? At first glance, it seems to have been the former. Whenever she explicitly represents lesbians, she often adopts the 'inversion' model, using schemas of boyish or mannish appearance in narrative description; and she avails besides of other aspects of the Twenties stereotype of the emotional life of lesbians when she renders them as tempestuous and unstable. Yet one has not quite said everything even when one has, as I shall try to do, examined in more detail some of these explicit representations of alleged female 'inversion'. As I hope to show, the 'lesbian continuum' model is perhaps ultimately more useful as an approach to Bowen: that is, the concept, classically inaugurated by Adrienne Rich in 1980 but already developing during the 1970s, of a continuum of woman-to-woman interaction within which recognition may be given to virtual or symbolic mother-daughter feeling and all other kinds of attachment between women as 'woman-identified' and not different in kind from the lesbian.[2]

Women's mutual bonds, loving or obsessive, do not get much attention in the author's own general descriptions and judgements *qua* narrator in Bowen's fictions, or in her scant meta-commentary (reviews, the available passages from private letters, her published criticism) on these matters. Nevertheless, the fictions engage in a meditation so intense and piercing on female bonding, including symbolic and literal mother–daughter relations, that the topic cries out to be discussed.[3] Power, mothering, sexuality and the successful or failed constitution of selfhood are bound up together in Bowen's writing with an exceptional and even dismaying intimacy; and tangles between 'desire' and 'identification' of women for and with one another (however much these two terms are clearly separate in Freud's psychology) certainly mark deeply her representations of social and psychological life.

On the other hand, there are still major disputes within lesbian theory about the legitimacy, or usefulness, of such a blurring of desire with identification in reflecting on women's interrelations. Is the 'continuum model' of lesbianism productive and enabling, or does it fatally risk the consigning of women's mutual love to the infantile, the pre-Oedipal and in some sense pre-sexual domain, and therefore blot out the possibility of adult same-sex desire, a focused lesbian erotics?[4] Sedgwick has usefullly insisted on the continuing coexistence of these two main models of same-sex relations, however contradictorily, in our minds. In the light of our increasingly focused understanding of the complexity of women's mutual relations, there is a more and more urgent need to conduct a broad investigation of Bowen's imaginative conceptions of relationships between women in all their various forms.

There are three topics contiguous to this investigation, which would also merit detailed study, and which I shall now briefly mention but not explore in detail. First, Bowen's references to gender itself are evidently relevant. By these I mean her interest in representing some equivocal quality in the usual social signals of 'femininity' or 'masculinity' in a character's self-presentation, counter to their apparent gender appartenance, or a quality of cross-gendering in their emotional life, whether or not this is primarily in the context of sexuality; or in the terms she herself tends to adopt, a 'womanishness' felt in male characters, and a 'boylike' or 'boyish' air in female ones. It would be useful to examine this blurring and occasional swapping over of some of the conventional markers of femininity and masculinity in the social world of the novels, and the relevance of this unsettling volatility of gendering to our thinking about the homoerotic.

The second relevant issue is that of the nature of desire itself, irrespective of gender. In Bowen, desire has a strikingly labile quality, seeming to be imagined as not always safely (or dangerously) vested in persons, but to be conceived as a force or form of energy in itself. It tends to be an aura (or perhaps a miasma), something which floats around a sexually attractive character and is experienced by others of either gender. It affects, for instance, the golden-haired girl Jane in *A World of Love*, whose outstanding beauty is felt by all the adults in the household and draws all to her, even, in a characteristic piece of uncanny plotting, the dead Guy. Sydney Warren in *The Hotel* is similarly afflicted, becoming, like Jane, a kind of unwitting conductor of emotions. Marda in *The Last September* also attracts others, without or largely without *doing* anything to produce this result, and moreover without self-engagement in the process: she does not flirt, and indeed finds herself affectively detached, to and beyond the point of *ennui* and existential isolation. This is another reason why it is difficult neatly to hive off woman-to-woman attraction, delimit and define it, and discuss it in isolation from the phenomenon of desire as a whole in Bowen's fictions. It is an aspect of Bowen's modernity that she so conceives desire, as what Sedgwick calls 'an unpredictably powerful solvent of stable identities'.[5] W. J. McCormack's discussion of *The Heat of the Day*, a novel in which the presence of desire in this sense is especially marked, shows how that novel's concern with the volatility and unknowability of personality as a whole is a function of its ideological and historical moment (or perhaps vice versa: history conceived as some kind of rationally apprehensible progress is decomposed by, among other things, the failure of stable selfhoods).[6]

The third and related question which requires attention is: to what extent does Bowen rewrite sex as power? This is Henry James territory, and Bowen has a striking kinship with James both in moral vision and literary form. Are her representations of sexuality itself Jamesian also? What is the role of Irish repression (or, as she says, 'sublimat[ion]' or sexless infantilism) in them? In the Irish Gothic writer J. S. Le Fanu, who influenced both herself and James before her, she names 'another terror-ingredient, moral dread'.[7] She differs from James in the degree to which she links this quality with specifically sexual manipulation; how are those links effected and sustained? And what, if anything, have these links — the conscious use of others' sexual attraction, passion or need for love to produce effects in the world — to do with gendering, especially 'inverted' gendering, so-called? (Commenting later on *The House in Paris*, Bowen herself saw the sickroom of Madame Fisher, that laboratory for practising the witch-like manipulation of others, as a '*bois dormant*', which makes Madame Fisher, widowed in youth, a Sleeping Beauty but loveless and unawakened by another, who has had to be her own Prince Charming — both genders in one, as it were.)[8]

This is a painful question. The manipulators in Bowen's fictions are usually women, and so are most, though not all, of those they work upon; what are we to make of this intense consciousness of female power, albeit darkly used? How may we distinguish it from the stereotype of the Destroying Mother or witch? In Bowen, mothers literal and symbolic may forsake their children, voluntarily or otherwise (see Portia's mother Irene, who dies,

Edward's mother Elfrida, who 'ruins' herself, Leopold's mother Karen, who cannot acknowledge him, and Eva Trout's beloved teacher Iseult Smith, who shies away from a committed care for Eva). They may exact compliance in the social order (Mrs Michaelis from Karen, Aunt Myra from Lois), ruthlessly appropriate the young as puppets in their own drama (as Madame Fisher does with both her own daughter Naomi and Karen her charge), or do as Mrs Kerr does to Sydney Warren: coldly and cruelly engage her affections, then transfer her attention to someone else, purely, it seems, for the Sadeian pleasure of seeing her power in action. For Phyllis Lassner, it is *male* dread of women which looms large, along with constricting social forms, in Bowen's fictions; but though Lassner has by her robust recourse to psychoanalytic perspectives on male–female relations greatly helped to remove Bowen's work from the context of woman's-novel gentility to which it was for too long and quite inappropriately consigned, there remains a great deal more to be said about Bowen's staging of gender and sex, and in particular about her intense interest in inventing manipulative and/or evil mother-figures.[9] Still, to return to the opening question of this paragraph, in Bowen desire is not so totally transformed into, and rewritten as, power as it is in James; therein lies some of the intense interest the matter holds for our purposes. We may imagine power and sex as each a different axis, which sometimes cuts across the other, just as the drive of characters to insist on a fuller subjectivity for themselves, to assert more agency and resist objectification, sometimes also intersects with one or both of the other axes.

These three topics are properly concerned in any investigation of sex and gender in Bowen; but I leave them aside now, in order to concentrate mainly on some of Bowen's explicit representations of woman-to-woman feeling.

II

Discussing the role of same-sex attachment in literary texts is, of course, always a delicate and complex business. It is never more so than when the author of those texts is concerned, as Elizabeth Bowen was, to distance herself from any overt interest in or attraction towards the lesbian. In his introduction to the present volume Éibhear Walshe has already cited one of her disclaimers of such interest, made in the 1930s, and has noted the equal or even greater concern of her biographer, Victoria Glendinning, to register Bowen's alleged rejection of lesbian relationships in her life.[10] We must respect such surfaces, but may also notice where they may mask a nexus of anxiety, a need so to constitute and perform the self as to appear adequately, suitably, feminine (given the desexing nature of the prevailing lesbian 'invert' stereotype).

À propos of the alleged physical signs which assisted observers to apply this stereotype, many descriptions of Bowen's own appearance by her contemporaries stress her large frame and assertive physical presence. Phyllis Lassner summarizes these: 'She was tall and large-boned, and gave an impression of having masculine qualities in her movements, strong face and forthright opinions.'[11] Bowen's unusual social role, as the sole heir of a landed family, however impecunious it was by then, contributed also: her parents had expected a son, and even chosen the name 'Robert' (the first name, incidentally, Bowen gave to both Stella Rodney's lover and the man surveilling her in *The Heat of the Day*). We would, of course, ourselves be putting the mannish-lesbian stereotype into action if we drew conclusions about Bowen's own choice of sexual modes or acts; all this is more of a comment on the narrowness and regulatory character of prevailing prescriptions for femininity in the period from about 1900 till the very recent past.

A wide range of critics now refer openly to the fact that, whatever about the nature of her marital life with Alan Cameron, Bowen had sexual affairs with men. It is scarcely necessary to point out that this does not preclude attraction to or love of women on her part. As regards Glendinning, her work is intelligent, sensitive and rich in detail, and is indispensable to the study of Bowen. But, writing as she was in the mid-1970s, and no doubt hampered by the then stricter limits on what could be said about sexuality, her biographical style is discreet to what now seems an unnecessary degree. The biography tends to take on the tone of her subject's letters and of the social intercourse of the period so fully as sometimes to muffle its own analytic potential. Thus a careful reading of the passage where Glendinning directly addresses the matter of Bowen's possible sexual self-identification leaves a distinct impression of ambivalence and constraint. On the one hand, Glendinning says:

> Enough lesbian sensibility has been discerned . . . in [Bowen's] manner for some people to have presumed that, however conventional her married life, it was towards women that her true inclinations lay.[12]

and on the other, she asserts that

> For a heterosexual woman, a close friendship with another woman *is precisely that, and no more.* For a lesbian, nearly all relationships with women must be coloured by the possibility of love (my emphasis).[13]

The development of consciousness about bisexuality, contrasexuality and gender as performance would lead us now to query such a crisply announced dichotomy between heterosexual and lesbian, which would preclude the very possibility of either a bisexual orientation or a gradual, sometimes almost lifelong, arrival at a dominant sexual preference — whether or not such a process culminates in any 'coming out'. All this is admittedly (as Sedgwick very well demonstrates) a minefield; at times in the biography there seems a risk of implicitly accepting the inversion model prevalent in the earlier part of the twentieth century, and as a result of collapsing 'lesbian' into 'masculine'. Thus: *'there was a good deal that was masculine* both in Bowen's physical self and in her mentality' (my emphasis). Glendinning also draws on a certain 'worr[y] about herself as a woman' perceived in her by 'a few of her friends', reading Bowen's 'fondness for cosmetics, her concern for her appearance' as a kind of behaviour she calls 'anxiously feminine'.[14] She further instances Bowen's curt rejection of sexual overtures by particular lesbian friends, implying that this amounts to a dispelling of any likelihood of lesbian orientation in general. It is only fair to say that Glendinning has a consistent policy of delicacy and is, in heterosexual matters also, less ready to call a spade a spade than many of those who have discussed Bowen in the two decades or so since she wrote. She is far from explicit about Bowen's several affairs with men in the 1930s and 1940s, no doubt understandably, given the far larger numbers of Bowen's contemporaries living at the time she was writing. The now much greater freedom about the discussion and the understanding of all these categories — 'masculine', 'feminine', 'lesbian', 'heterosexual' — should help us to acquire more subtle conceptions of the complexity of experience and of the self-performance of gender and sexuality in the real world and, still more, in the highly complex set of social and sexual representations in Bowen's work. The whole matter can hardly fail to be intriguing to anyone thinking about Bowen, but, while I do not propose a total severance, in the formalist manner defined by T. S. Eliot, between 'the [wo]man who suffers and the artist who creates', and still less do I suppose an oppositional relation between the two, the ultimate *raison d'être* of this essay is Bowen's art, which is even more interesting than her life.

At the end of that life there is a discernible shift in her own writing about this subject. The way she discusses the possible lesbian relationship of Somerville and Ross in her 1970 review of Violet Powell's *The Irish Cousins* is illuminating:

> When the cousins met . . . there occurred one of those fusions of personality which in one way or another can make history. Their from then on total attachment incurred no censure, and — still stranger, given the habitual jocularity of their relatives — seems to have drawn down no family mirth. Nor was its nature — as it might be in these days — speculated upon. Absolutely, the upper class, Anglo-Irish were (then)

> non-physical — far from keen participants, even, from what one hears
> of them, in the joys of marriage. (*MT*, p. 186)

At first glance, this might seem to play down the 'total attachment', especially
when she goes on to mention the 'Ladies of Llangollen', citing Somerville
and Ross's opinion that they were 'extremely silly', and then again when,
in a lightly humorous but significant passage, she insists on the asexual-
ity of Ascendancy culture:

> This couple of gentlewomen from Ireland were encased, armoured, in
> the invincible heartiness of their extroverted tribe and specialized class.
> Round and upon them blew prevailing gales of clean fun, anaphrodisiac
> laughter. Anything 'extreme' was comic: that went for passion, that went
> for art. Dogs, jokes, were the accepted currency. Their initial literary
> endeavours, daylong disappearances, together, to the neglect of tennis,
> side-split brothers and sisters, uncles and aunts. Only when books 'ap-
> peared' did menace begin. The two now ceased to be amateurs: things
> looked serious. The actual crux, or crunch, was *The Real Charlotte*. (*MT*,
> pp 186-7)

But when one examines these passages carefully, it becomes clear that what
Bowen says is, first, not that they were not lesbians, but that if they were,
they got by without censure in their milieu; and, second, that they were
able to do so because of the formidable repressions of sexuality and the
body which characterised that milieu. So, though Bowen certainly, and
with entire prudence, avoids a direct judgement or naming of the
undeniable mutual love of the cousins as a lesbian one, at the same time
she discerns in that attachment a quality of opposition to their given community and its values, a quality which emerges clearly and incontrover-
tibly in the fruits of that attachment, their writings. In spite of the implicit
assertion of a change since their time, when 'the upper class, Anglo-Irish
were (then) non-physical', we may see an element of autobiographical
reference in what she says about those other daughters of the Big House
who grew up in rural Ireland a scant decade or so before she herself was
born in 1899. (The tennis party in *The Last September* comes to mind.)

In this passage there is also an implicit equation being made between
the realms of freed desire and of art as spaces where social constriction
is to be overcome, or at least combated. Passion, art, power, desire are all
linked. Usually this 'desire' (figured primarily as sexual and indeed as
heterosexual in the plots of most of the novels) is antithetical, even fatal,
to the presumptions of the social world which is the habitat of the
characters. How antithetical may not Bowen's perhaps corresponding
aesthetic 'desire' have been to her own social world? By aesthetic desire
I mean the narrative force or urge to go beyond, which at the meta-level

of the author drives plots towards their resolutions and, much more, proposes their ideological, their moral, meanings. The cataclysms in both cases are generally muffled by the effect of a devastating irony recalling that of such a radical sceptic as Laclos, which saves the appearances of civility but hollows out their moral being to a shell. In what she has to say about Somerville and Ross she makes no bones about naming their passion and their art in the one breath; she goes on to note how they 'cut the cable' in *The Real Charlotte*, making their own 'a terrain of outrageousness, obliquity, unsavoury tragedy, sexual no less than ambitious passion' (*MT*, p 187). There can be no doubt of Elizabeth Bowen's own taste, under the highly polished surfaces, for the monstrous, the perverse, the necessarily antithetical (an 'antithetical' perhaps in Blake's sense, borrowed subsequently by Yeats).[15]

In all except her late work any specifically lesbian manifestation of that resistance to norms is usually projected as marginal, kept sleekly in check or, sometimes, conceived as predatory; but an imaginative fascination inheres even, perhaps especially, in these instances of predation: what reader of *The Hotel* does not feel the real silken cord of the book drawing tight between Sydney Warren and Mrs Kerr? Mr Milton is a sideshow to it. And the, so to speak, daylight modes of female empowerment, such as Karen's in *The House in Paris*, tend to be upstaged by the dark destructive designs of Madame Fisher and her like (of whom Karen thinks 'she is a woman who sells girls; she is a witch' (*HP*, p. 155)).[16]

III

We have seen how Elizabeth Bowen decisively disclaimed any attraction in her own life towards lesbian sexuality in general, and individual lesbian women in particular. When in her fictions she created explicit representations of adult lesbian characters, she tended, as I have said, to place them in the margins, and with a high degree of irony, distance, and even moral disapprobation — not, to be sure, specifically of their presumed sexual acts, but of a range of characteristics with which she chose to endow them, characteristics sometimes including over-emotionality, sometimes manipulativeness. There are several glancing mentions, often humorous and, I think, all distancing except in *Eva Trout*, of the 'crushes' of adolescent girls. In *The Death of the Heart* Portia's school companion, the 'more than doubtful' Lilian, has had to be taken away from an earlier school 'because of falling in love with the cello mistress, which had made her quite unable to eat' (*DH*, p. 51).[17] And when Mrs Kerr in *The Hotel* mentions Sydney's attachment to her in a tone of carefully calculated ruefulness, her son Ronald remarks: 'I thought you couldn't tolerate *schärmerei*' (*sic*; *TH*, p. 94).[18] But strong attachments between adolescent girls, or between young adult and older women, receive a more complex treatment, which, as I have suggested above, tends to represent the older woman in question negatively, whether as more or less predatory or as *distraite* and therefore emotionally irresponsible. Much of this, viewed piecemeal, may seem to readers to distinguish itself only slightly from such earlier versions of the quintessentially designing woman — coded, if not stated, lesbian — as Dickens's wicked Miss Wade, who sets out to alienate the affections of Tattycoram in *Little Dorrit*. This impression is, however, I believe, radically misleading.

And in her very late work there is a decisive shift in these patterns: both *The Little Girls* (1964) and *Eva Trout* (1968) concentrate predominantly on female attachment, and both explicitly, if inchoately in the case of *The Little Girls*, explore lesbian desire.[19] There is a poignant awkwardness about both these novels, which critics, I think rightly, put down to that radical distrust of language itself, not to speak of fictional form, which is such a marked and progressive development in Bowen's work even from *The Heat of the Day* (1949) onwards. It is also relevant however, that it was only in her sixties that Bowen, widowed, having finally lost or perhaps rid herself of her Irish family home, and trying to achieve a stable base in south-east England, the scene of the intense years spent *à deux* with her mother from the ages of seven to thirteen, found herself able more or less directly to address questions of women's mutual attraction. This too must lie beneath the tongue-tied, halting utterance not only of the characters but even sometimes of the narrator in these novels. Bowen addresses such attraction, and some of the larger implications about a woman's life as a whole which it has, very much more satisfactorily in *Eva Trout* than in *The Little Girls*. The narrative pace of this novel is less than compelling, and to read it is to have the sense of a flailing immobility recalling the 'festination' — the repetitive embroilment in the same perpetually uncompleted actions — which in life besets people with certain neurological disorders. The only passage in which the '"l"-word' is actually mentioned offers, perhaps not accidentally, a particularly vivid example of this effective mental and psychological arrest:

> '. . . And apart from that, also, I often bore him — nor, I may say, is
> he the first I've bored. But then, boredom is part of love.'
> 'That I deny!'
> 'Well, of affection.'
> '*That* I doubt.'
> 'Then you've no affections. — Mumbo, are you a Lesbian?'
> 'Anything else, would you like to know? . . .' (*TLG*, p. 197)

It is interesting that being a lesbian is apparently equated by Sheila with a denial of affections: that is, an unnatural state.

Eva Trout also has male homosexual characters, who are treated with a conspicuous hostility, as outstandingly manipulative and calculating, artists in scripting the suffering of others.[20] Bowen seems not really to have been interested in giving much more than a thumbnail sketch of these characters, and by no stretch of the imagination could they — Constantine and the trendy cleric Clavering-Haight — be said to be positive, valorising versions of gayness; instead Bowen restates the stereotypical connection between scheming and homosexuality, presenting these characters as either parasitic (Constantine and the clergyman, named out of Trollope) or deluded (Trout senior).

The characterisation of bisexual Eva, however, is, as we shall see later, strikingly different. She is shown as capable of explicit desire for both men and women, and is nevertheless not marginalised, treated as a caricature or morally discredited, all fates which befall the lesbians who are limned in more-or-less thumbnail sketches in Bowen's earlier work.[21] I shall discuss some of these earlier examples, and return later to Eva.

IV

The early and excellent short story of Bowen's, 'The Jungle' (1929), is set in a girls' boarding-school and deals with how the heroine, Rachel, forms an intense and troubling relationship with a younger girl, Elise. The setting is significant: it seems to have been acceptable in the period to show same-sex attachment in this conventional context. This presumably allowed readers to make the equally conventional — and implicitly regulatory — assumption that such attractions are a function of immaturity, that girls grow out of them and into proper adult heterosexual relations, and even that they can be seen as practising the rhetoric and rhythms of an emotional attachment on one another in advance of the real thing, falling in love with a man. The friendship of Eva Trout with Miss Smith, which is being discussed in my first epigraph, took place at school; the coming into her own of Theodora Thirdman in *Friends and Relations* is also effected during her boarding-school time.

The title of 'The Jungle' refers to the tangled small wood that the solitary Rachel has discovered by breaking the school bounds. Without a special friend one term, she meets Elise Lamartine, who is in certain ways markedly different from Rachel (and from the norm in the school community). She has French ancestors (and, the reader sees, a poet's name), and is exceptionally talented at physical pursuits such as gym and lacrosse. She has 'her hair cut short like a boy's', and after the friendship is established she takes the upper hand, ordering Rachel around in spite of her own inferior school status. The character of Elise is thus heavily coded, indeed it is overdetermined according to the gender/sex semiotics of the period, which as Sedgwick points out remain very much with us today: she is not only somewhat French (are we to read amorously advanced and precociously developed, sophisticated, or just 'other'?) but more than evidently tending towards the 'inverted' (over-given to physical prowess, tomboyish in tastes and appearance, masculinely authoritative). Bowen gives Rachel two foreboding dreams near the start of the story which quite directly make the relationship with Elise something uncanny and threatening to normality:

> Rachel had one terrible dream about the Jungle and woke up shivering. It was something to do with a dead body, a girl's arm coming out from under the bushes. . . . A few nights afterwards she was back there again, this time with some shadowy person always a little behind her who turned out to be Elise. When they came to the bush which in the first dream had covered the arm she was trying to tell Elise about it, to make sure it *had* been a dream, then stopped, because she knew she had com- mitted that murder herself. She wanted to run away, but Elise came up beside her and took her arm with a great deal of affection. Rachel woke up in a gush of feeling, one of those obstinate dream-taps that won't be turned off, that swamp one's whole morning, sometimes one's whole day. (*CS*, p. 232)

Later, on their first visit together to the Jungle, Rachel recalls her dream-experiences, a heady mixture of sexual feeling, dismemberment and self-condemnation ('she knew she had committed that murder herself'):

> Here was the place where the dead girl's arm, blue-white, had come out from under the bushes. Here was the place where Elise, in the later dream, had come up and touched her so queerly. (*CS*, p. 235)

It is worth spelling out what is happening here. The arm appears where it should not (in accordance with Freud's classic definition of the uncanny) — and so does Rachel's desire for Elise. The self is lawless, a jungle. Elise takes her arm and thus releases her longing. At the climax of the story, after an estrangement between the two girls, Elise is discovered lying with one arm flung out on the ground, asleep, in the Jungle; it ends with her curling up on Rachel's lap and falling asleep once more: 'The round cropped head like a boy's was resting on Rachel's knees. She felt all constrained and queer; comfort was out of the question' (p. 241). Rachel, though a more senior girl, is as if bewitched by Elise's force of personality and by Elise's very capacity to show indifference to her. The dream has climaxed with an uncontrollable excitement, rendered in a metaphor with unmistakable sexual suggestiveness: 'a gush of feeling', a tap that cannot be turned off.

This story is beautifully managed. The importance in the school society of peer interaction and conventional distinctions such as parity of age among friends is evident, and the Jungle aptly represents Rachel's unregulated inner, sexual and emotional, self, to which in some trepidation she admits Elise. The motif of Elise's sleepiness humorously suggests the fairytale analogue of the Sleeping Beauty, a favourite motif of Bowen's, which would make Rachel her prince — a suggestion lightly acknowledged by the narrator during the scene: 'Rachel stood looking down — the only beautiful thing about Elise was the cleft in her chin.'

This protagonist, Rachel, appears in an earlier story, 'Charity' (1926), which also concerns a friendship with another girl, but while it deals with relations of power between the two and between the friend named Charity and Rachel's older sister, it only lightly touches on physical contact, and parodies rather than actually enacts erotic relations. The girls are twelve. Charity comes to stay with Rachel during the holidays, and while eating a late supper they play romantic roles:

> They lit one candle, and Charity, who could be very funny, sat languishing in the light of it, fluttered her lashes and ate off the tip of her fork. Rachel was a Guardsman, very adoring, and kept offering her champagne and cocktails. . . . Rachel . . . jumped up, flung an arm round Charity's neck and kissed her violently. 'Oh, be *careful*, Captain de Vere', squeaked Charity; 'you are dripping champagne from your moustache.' (*CS*, p. 195)

The distinction between the stories is that between a true, disturbing engagement of the self, and the consciously ludic playing of roles conceived as adult, which are themselves guyed in this performance. In 'The Jungle', I would say, there is no doubting the strong lesbian feeling, and I detect no ironic or even distancing impulse in the narration or in the totality of the story. The focalisation through the naïve protagonist, in this case Rachel, is a technique in which Bowen, even in her earliest work, shows a skill connected with the thematic importance of innocence in her vision. In 'The Jungle' the innocence of Rachel may be read as signifying doubly: it is an innocence of the erotic, or an inability to name the experience of sexual desire as such, but it is also an innocence of psychological manipulation (for all her and her schoolmates' counting themselves sophisticates). She encounters the two in one, in her time with — and then, painfully, without — Elise.[22] When Elise aims (as the reader discerns) to produce an effect, the effect of hopeless longing, in Rachel, she has 'the most wonderfully natural way of not seeing one' (p. 239). This is the avatar of Mrs Kerr's artlessness with the hapless Sydney in *The Hotel*

(1927), Bowen's underrated first novel. In 'The Jungle', then, Bowen is already exploring both desperate desire and manipulativeness in the context of emotional attachment between females as played out by romantic and erotic flirtation and invitation.

V

With the one exception of her involuntary gift for rich dreams, the Rachel of 'The Jungle' and 'Charity' does not show conspicuous talent at anything except perhaps the capacity to suffer. Sydney Warren, the heroine of *The Hotel*, is quite different. With her man's name and her unwillingness to suffer fools gladly, her striking, sometimes boyish good looks and her air of having a tempestuous inner life, Sydney stands out in the small, claustrophobic expatriate society of the English wintering on the Italian Riviera. The novel has a curious uncertainty of tone, wavering between social comedy and *Bildungsroman* effects. But it attends to women's inter-relations more intensely than most of Bowen's later work. Indeed, Bowen opens and closes the novel with a pair of bit players, Miss Fitzgerald and Miss Pym, whom it is difficult not to read as a distant echo of the Ladies of Llangollen.[23]

At the beginning of the novel we join these two characters in mid-quarrel, or perhaps tantrum. High-souled, religious, given to sketching landscapes, and deeply mutually attached, this pair at first appear to be a fairly sharp satiric parody of intense romantic friendship between women, Edwardian-style. In the pattern of the novel Bowen uses them half as foil and half as analogue for the relations of Sydney and Mrs Kerr. Of course, Bowen's effects are delicate, though rarely precious in the negative sense, and it is always difficult to be sure what is ironic and what is not. Further obstacles to interpretation are the cataclysmic shifts in social life which have taken place since the 1920s, the volatility induced by modernity, of which the character Sydney Warren is herself a living instance, and the arcane quality of English upper-class culture. One may be misreading all kinds of signals; but for all Miss Fitzgerald's and Miss Pym's role as butts of the narrator's humour at the start of this text, I would argue that ultimately they are, as the Bible says, not mocked. Their attachment stays firm, and though they make each other intermittently wretched and entirely lack aesthetic grace, there is about their partnership an authenticity entirely foreign to the bewitching Mrs Kerr. In this they resemble foolish Major Brutt in *The Death of the Heart* (1938), who together with the wronged heroine Portia attracts the epithet 'pure in heart'.

Mrs Kerr is Sydney's older, widowed friend, who has a witch-like power.

The clergyman Milton, briefly Sydney's fiancé, is shown feeling that power in a very Jamesian passage with her. He has been summoned to sit with her, ostensibly to be congratulated on the engagement:

> He reproached himself for a suspicion of being closed in on, and of their oasis of silence, light and solitude having become for him a rather remote and dangerous island. Her personality had a curious way of negativing her surroundings, so that unless one made instant resort to one's senses the background faded for one and one conjured up in one's half-consciousness another that expressed her better, that was half an exhalation from herself. . . . He felt again, through that window behind her, that dark garden distressed by the wind; around her those undisturbed shadows, that never-ebbing, mild light. (*TH*, pp 135-6)

The brittle surface of the social scene is here definitively breached by an effect which can only be called uncanny: Mrs Kerr here more suggests Purcell's Sorceress working to wreck Dido's romance than the poised, graceful woman who has attracted Sydney's admiration, even hero-worship, who has distinguished Sydney by her special friendship — perhaps the phrase is 'made Sydney her pet'. The novel is, it eventually becomes clear, one story inside another: not really in the end the narrative of Sydney's development, her *Bildung* in the usual sense — that is, her arrival at marriage or even vocation or, more vaguely, a state of 'maturity' — the business of the text is rather the unmasking of Mrs Kerr. The book's true climax comes in the highly satisfying scene in the penultimate chapter, chapter 24, where Sydney actually gets to tell her erstwhile tormentor that she has understood the whole intrigue.

There is, of course, no gross proof that Mrs Kerr's designs upon Sydney are specifically lesbian designs, certainly in the mere physical sense; but it is hard to account for Mrs Kerr's power over Sydney in any other way than as an erotic plot-motif.[24] Perhaps for her — as I have suggested earlier — the equivalent of sex is power, which too has its excitements, its arousals and climaxes. Mrs Kerr's physical attraction is nevertheless carefully emphasised. As a young adult her son Ronald, who is made the instrument of his mother's manipulation of Sydney, is still vividly conscious of this bewitching beauty, which, in keeping with the book's Italian setting, is represented in terms of cultural icons (Madonnas, the women in Pre-Raphaelite pictures):

> . . . behind the mask of her face she perceptibly retreated from consciousness, in the attitude of the Beata Beatrix. Looking down at her he went back through his memory, past his admiration for Rossetti, to the day when at six years old he had called his mother 'My Beautiful'. (*TH*, p. 96)

VI

In *The Hotel* Bowen makes Sydney both *ingénue* heroine and sexually ambiguous. In the slightly later *Friends and Relations* she divides these roles, assigning the former primarily to Janet Studdart, and the latter to Theodora Thirdman. Sydney Warren also combines self-will with these other roles and attributes: in *Friends and Relations* the problem of women's appropriate self-determination arises, however differently, in the case of both Janet, the 'feminine' heroine, and in that of Theodora, the — one would almost have said 'butch' — lesbian. (Bowen complicates the issue by also having Theodora desire Janet.) Apart from, or as well as, her lesbian characterisation, Theodora is one of a type in Bowen; to this type belong all those awkward and inconveniently perceptive teenage girls dotted about the novels who, like Pauline in *To the North*, are being 'brought up by a committee of relatives', or, like Theodora herself as she first appears, 'spectacled, large-boned . . . awkwardly anxious to make an impression', and wearing a totally wrong hat ('"What a terrible girl," said Lady Elfrida' (*FR* pp 12-13)).

In Bowen's early and middle work, such characters glower from peripheral niches in the plots, while the protagonists gliding up the central aisle of the story generally have beauty, social poise, parents, the warmth of human regard, or some combination of three of those four which makes them adequate to life.[25] Eva Trout's strengths are sympathetically registered, in the 1968 work, as it seems Theodora's cannot be, at least overtly, in the 1931 one. For all the rapier-sharp and comic perception of Theodora which Bowen is able to give the narrator — 'her personality was still too much for her, like a punt-pole' (*FR*, p. 13) — one cannot say that Theodora is constructed with pity, or even with charity, as Eva is. But Theodora undeniably has agency: she is the author of many of her own most entertaining scripts. After early chagrin at her felt exclusion from the ranks of the acceptably feminine ('she did not seem likely to have a figure at all', thinks her mother), she strikes back with growing enthusiasm and flair at those within, and learns to vary herself and then to perform that repertoire of selves superbly. She invents a parodic persona, 'Lady Hunter Jervois', and in her 'mature, pleasant voice' telephones members of high society in the guise of this *alter ego*. She does this not to conceal herself, in a self-closeting or socially self-protective way, but goes on the offensive and uses her talents to confound that society which has no room for her. The novel's most hilarious bits attend her. In the role of Don Juan at school, she creates a disruptive stir of attraction from the others and admiration for her simulacrum of masculinity:

'How different you are with no spectacles,' said Dona Anna, lingering
by the bathroom door.

'We've never had so much love in a play before,' said Hester, joining
them. 'Generally, we just arrange for lovers to go off tenderly. I mean,
I do think Theodora's extraordinary . . .'

I suppose I can't imagine feeling self-conscious,' said Theodora, strad-
dling a little. (*FR*, p. 45)

(Theodora's virtuosity is, of course, reckoned transgressive: 'But next week,
Miss Byng rather strongly suggested they should dramatize folk-songs. She
said she liked their programmes to vary' (*FR*, p. 45).) Her talents consist
in the reinvention of selfhood, in creatively breaking ranks: her mother
ruefully realises Theodora's spiky difference from her own adolescence,
sketched as the correct course followed by the kind of 'dutiful daughter'
Adrienne Rich called the male-identified woman — 'herself, she had practised the piano a good deal, said, "Very well, Father," when Father objected;
her figure began, she braided her back hair' (p. 29) — while Theodora,
significantly, 'improvised but did not practise'. In this character Bowen has
represented a figure far more complex than the stereotypical invert:
Theodora seems both less and more than the 'normal' woman projected
by her society: less feminine, less acquiescent, less pretty, but more
intelligent, more steely, more active, and bigger. Viewing the girls' pet guinea-
pigs at the progressive school where Theodora is to be sent to 'finish' her,
her father says: '"She has a brain," . . . staring into the cages (the brain
his son would have had), but unsteady, variable' (p. 29).[26] At a crucial
moment in the novel's main plot Theodora's strength shows itself negatively,
when she sends the letter which brings about the emotional catastrophe
of the main characters. She does this for emotional revenge, because Janet
cannot return her regard, or even her attention; this kind of motive she
has in common with Eva Trout, but the planned and willed quality of
her act, and the pleasure she has in watching the effects of her actions,
a motive one would call 'Sadeian' in relation to Mrs Kerr in the preceding
novel, differentiate her sharply from Eva, whose actions are only incidentally destructive. Theodora is much funnier, but then a convention seems
to be operating in the novel whereby she is understood as a kind of
grotesque whom the reader is expected not to take seriously — until, that
is, she maliciously brings down the house of cards about the ears of the
others, the straight women and their families. Even then, the narrator does
not give her the degree of interiority which belongs to the characterisation of the novel's heroine, Janet, unambiguously named as object of
Theodora's desire. (Janet tolerates Theodora, classifying her as 'odd'.)
Theodora's *sprezzatura* and her flamboyant non-conformity have, however,
their echoes in the novel at what one might think the other extreme: the

flamboyant Lady Elfrida, mother of the tormentedly conventional and respectable Edward, who as a young wife has 'ruined' herself by her sexual liaison with the big-game hunter Constantine but remains flagrantly unrepentant.

One especially interesting scene in *Friends and Relations* sets up the domestic life of the now adult Theodora and her flatmate Marise, formerly her school friend. Focalised through Theodora's mother, Mrs Thirdman, this little episode has a Jamesian *ficelle*-type function in terms of the plot, but plays a more important role thematically in the novel's meditation on women's possible lives.[27] The passage is curious in that its dry irony seems rather equivocal: it is not clear whether the bewildered, literalistic mother or the angular, eccentric younger women are the object of implicit censure. Perhaps this is because the ironic narrative voice — which Bowen must have learned very largely from Jane Austen and which announces a correct set of judgements on manners and morals — is predicated upon the existence of a set of incontrovertible social norms which attract the consent of a coherent social world, whereas such a consensus is no longer in being in the twentieth century.

Signalling its occupants' uncompromising modernity, the flat has 'a varnished colour-scheme of almost menacing restraint' in which 'there were scimitar-curves and discs and soaring angles', there are 'gramophone records, proofs and curious drawings', but few comforts as Willa Thirdman would understand them — only 'very low' seating (probably, she thinks, because Marise and Theodora 'stood about so much'); and 'dust from the tea-leaves rose in a light film' when 'the alarming girl' Marise sets about offering hospitality (pp 124-5). Marise is a writer; a little later the manuscript of a novel she has written plays a background role in one of the climactic emotional scenes of this novel. Asked what it is 'about', Janet says: 'Oh . . . women's difficulties, difficulties about women: I don't remember. I didn't think it seemed very good' (p. 137). The lives of these two women are an implicit rejection of everything which has been expected of them; they prefer to be telephoned in advance of any visits, 'in view', says Theodora, 'of everything'. The narrator here adds:

> The two had perfected a system of half-allusion — it is not difficult for women to live together — and rarely had to say anything more direct than 'What are we out of?' or 'You are looking like death today'. (p. 124)

Mrs Thirdman, leaving, feels an obscure disappointment:

> An interesting life, she repeated. Yet twenty-six years ago she had borne Theodora — to what? For this? And an idea remained in her mind that the furniture in the flat was made of ground glass. (p. 126)

A moment characteristically balanced between ironic humour and poignancy follows: 'She wished she had a married daughter in London . . .'

VII

In Bowen's later texts there are important representations of female fellowship, admiration and attention which, while not, like this, explicitly coded as lesbian, leap to the eye of a reader whose consciousness has been at all raised about woman-to-woman relationships. There is Louie's admiration for Stella in *The Heat of the Day*, for example, and her capacity, alone among the novel's characters, for intuiting Stella's depair. The words 'a soul astray' form unbidden in her mind as her perception of Stella. Inarticulate, humble and isolated, Louie is lost in the world and, in herself, seems to lack all capacity to be the author of her own life, but to her it is given to discern Stella's pain and disinterestedly to admire her.

In the part of the story dealing with Stella and Louie, Bowen seems, most obviously, to be using the structure, highly conventional in comedy, opera and novels of manners, of setting up two characters as *alter egos*, or partial versions of one another. Louie becomes, like Stella, the mother of a son. With her husband away at war, she seeks attachments outside marriage and thus steps outside normative feminine behaviour, or 'virtue', as Stella has the reputation of having done (both in the past and again after Robert's mysterious death at what the newspapers call her 'Mayfair' flat (see p. 306)). Like Stella, she becomes oddly embroiled with Harrison, and so on. But it is important to distinguish between this *structural function* of the Louie–Stella parallel and the *emotional content* in their relation as characters. Accompanying the admiration she conceives for Stella, Louie also yearns for her. With renewed awareness she experiences her own permeability to the world, to whatever 'the air was charged with, night and day'. She feels herself to be so much 'receiver, conductor, carrier' that she cannot compose or discern herself as a separate entity; and it is in this context that, recalling Stella's warmth at their one meeting — 'But this is not goodbye, I hope? — she recognises what amounts to her passion for Stella: 'Lying in Chilcombe Street . . . Louie dwelled on Stella with mistrust and addiction, dread and desire' (p. 248). Her beauty, her class, her presumed wealth, certainly play a part in surrounding Stella with an aura of excitement for Louie, but beneath all these is a stratum of real and intense *combined* attraction and concern. This plot element in *The Heat of the Day* is a good example of what is a not infrequent phenomenon in the novels: the presence of a homoerotic motif or incident or feeling in the margins of the main action, slightly out of the direct glance of what the narrative theorist Todorov calls 'the narrator–reader couple', but there all the same, and perhaps the more suggestive for being oblique. (Naomi Fisher's mute attention to Karen in *The House in Paris* is another striking example.) In this case Louie's undischarged care for Stella, her perhaps rather maternal inexpressible concern for her, is touching.

Making a slight shift of perspective, let us consider Stella, apotheosis of Bowen heroines, in the context of gender, sexuality and empowerment. Stella has the smoothest of polished surfaces: she is beautiful, fashionable, and capable. She is apparently star-like, as her name suggests. But in fact not only is she literally being watched (like the circumscribed court ladies who were so ambiguously celebrated by Renaissance sonneteers as cold, distant guiding stars); she is beset by men who are all more or less inadequately phallic (to use a harsh word). Until well into the novel there is no intimation of female fellowship; Stella is alone, even exaggeratedly or markedly so, and so is Louie, when she distractedly half-tries to pick up Harrison in the opening scene.[28] On the other hand, the novel is full of instances of masculinity, but refracted and, glass-like, half-reflecting one another and split into shards or slivers. Bowen's verbal games with naming and with physical appearance as metaphor in this novel would not have disgraced a Freudian dream-text. Under surveillance by the shadowy Harrison, who literally looks crooked (his eyes are at different heights), Stella has a dead (and failed) husband named *Victor Rodney* and a scrupulously honourable but stiff and emotionally distant son, *Roderick Rodney*. In addition, she is in love with a wounded, limping man, whose unmanning at Dunkirk has coalesced with his oppression in childhood and his father's brokenness to bring about his secret treachery. This element of the plot, Robert's spying, scarcely or barely supports any attempt to give it motivation in realist terms, but functions strikingly as part of the novel's subtle and highly organised interrogation of masculinities, which is a motive on another level, namely the ideological and psychological. Robert's knee-wound, which, it is explained, is more disabling at some times than at others — he appears most physically wounded, limps worst, when he is *feeling* wounded — strongly recalls the displaced but recognisably phallic thigh- or buttock-wounds of medieval romance.[29] Harrison watches, knows and loves but cannot gain Stella; Robert loves her but has lost himself. Her son Roderick too loves her but is abstracted, not merely by his obsession with his role as owner of his newly inherited Irish estate. 'It had been clear', says the narrator with startling briskness, 'since Roderick was a child, that friendship with him would have to be one-sided' (*HD*, p. 60).[30] Between them all Stella is a specially intense example of Bowen's consistent representation of heterosexual women as 'other' to their men and isolated among them; a more extreme case still is Emmeline

in the earlier work *To the North*, who is destroyed by her desire for
the caddish Markie.

VIII

Between *The Hotel* (1927) and *Friends and Relations* (1931) came *The Last
September* (1929). This is almost as equivocal in its adherence to the
Bildungsroman genre as *The Hotel*. Its setting during the Irish War of Independence and its adoption of 'Big House novel' conventions (then seen
as inherited from Edgeworth, Trollope, Thackeray, and Somerville and Ross,
now definitively exemplified for many by *The Last September* itself) combine to complicate the story of Lois Farquar's passage to adulthood. Less
discussed than these, however, the novel has another aspect which may
be experienced as at the very least a variation on Lois's 'voyage out'. At
the opening of the novel she is self-consciousness in white muslin,
desperate for an escape from the emptiness attending the life-path which
she is expected to follow: a 'suitable' engagement, a marriage in due course
which will be devoted to stoutly sustaining her class and its way of life,
as her Aunt Myra does. Her cousin Laurence has at least Oxford to go
back to, and though he shares her ennui, he is not above irritatedly imagining her as 'a very pink bride'. All this functionlessness is, of course,
part of the book's stress on the façade, cardboard-like quality of the Anglo-
Irish Big Houses in their fragility and quasi-unreality compared to the 'wide,
light, lovely unloving country' described as 'the unwilling bosom' on which
the great houses were set (*TLS*, p. 66). But besides the historical aspects
of the novel, both the narrower and the wider ones — an anatomy of
Ascendancy uselessness, but also an intimation of international Twenties
malaise in general — it queries the prescribed narratives of femininity as
such. This interrogation centres on Marda, the 'Miss Norton' whose demure
name is given, tongue-in-cheek, to the middle section, which recounts her
visit to Danielstown.

Lois desires to desire. Her romance with Gerald, the English officer, is
dreamy but asexual; she cannot quite bring herself really to inhabit it.
But when Marda comes, Lois mutely admires her, wants to be with her,
longs for her regard. One of Marda's other functions in the book's design
is certainly as an older *alter ego*: ten years on from Lois and her friends
who are experimenting both in London and in Co. Cork with their first
exposure to adult social life, she has been there and done that. With a
broken engagement or two behind her, a just-avoided scandal, Marda has
had to capitulate to the script laid out for her and is about to marry. But
her lack of affect in the whole matter is striking: she is so purely following the rules, and her interior dissent from them is so plain. Exquisitely

poised and fashionable, Marda is a volatile element in the isolated world of Danielstown: not only Lois, but Laurence, and Hugo who is a whole generation older, all fall for her. So she attracts the desire of others, rather like Sydney Warren, but, also like Sydney, cannot herself become attached.

Turning to Lois's state of mind, it seems that Gerald fills a role which she needs to have filled as a kind of experiment, like her adventures in the stereotypical gaiety of youth such as dancing down the avenue to gramophone music. It is quite plain, even comically so, that Gerald's death is mostly a relief to Lois, whereas her attachment to Marda is what we might call emotionally in earnest. Marda in her turn attends to Lois in a way she is desperately in need of and which the likes of Aunt Myra or Francie do not.[31] It is another example, on a larger scale than the one in *The Heat of the Day*, of a woman-to-woman attachment which takes place in the margins of the accepted *social* narrative and which has little or no allotted place in the scheme of things (and, I might add, in most of the published criticism of Bowen to date). Accounts of the book which glide over Marda are, I would argue, defective to the extent that they ignore something Bowen placed, in one sense, at the centre of her design.

We should recall that Marda is about to move to England to make her marriage, a prospect for which Lady Naylor, who has never been able to see the point of the Home Counties, extends sympathy to her; the reader observes the implicit irony whereby Lady Naylor herself is about to be deprived by the forces of history of her own Irish home. The immolation of Danielstown in the book's spectacular final scene is so imaginatively satisfying because in it Bowen effects a virtual destruction not only of the Big House but also of that whole claustrophobic world within which Lois is so stiflingly confined. It is implied that modernity must afford Lois, at least, a purpose in life, even if Marda, for all the restless unchannelled force of her personality, has been obliged to capitulate to appropriately feminine uselessness.

Marda is not one of Bowen's manipulators, but is perhaps a prefiguring of Stella Rodney in *The Death of the Heart*: a woman straying without direction in the upper-class social world which is her milieu but which offers her no meaning. And Marda, like Lois, has conductivity: they are together when, in the rather uncanny ruined mill, they meet the book's second IRA man, who accidentally fires the shot which wounds Marda in the hand. When Marda leaves for the boat train, a ghostly wind blows through her empty bedroom and flutters the pages of the book lent her by the hopeful Laurence, which she has left lying there. In her invention of this disruptive figure, focus of the central part of the book, Bowen seems to distil and concentrate the other characters' search for purpose, and to show the failure of that search. All in all, the Marda narrative in *The Last September* might seem well suited for that kind of mental rewriting by lesbian-feminist readers described by Bonnie Zimmerman when she suggested

> that lesbian-feminist readers resist 'heterotexts' by privately rewriting and thus appropriating them as lesbian texts. There is a certain point in a plot or character development — the 'what if' moment — when a lesbian reader refuses to assent anymore to the heterosexual imperative and follows her own path.[32]

I have, however, grave doubts about this strategy. There are certainly cases where this specific application of the general 'resisting reader' policy originally defined by Judith Fetterley may prove fruitful, but the complex and subtle design and texture of Bowen's novels surely make them unsuitable objects for such simplifying upbeat readings. Given the paradoxical quality of Bowen's imagination and her multiple ironies, I feel one has one's hands full in attending to what *is* there, the endings that Bowen did actually write, however little purchase they may offer to perfectly understandable Utopian longings. I do not believe this judgement amounts to 'heterosexism' (after all, loving men scarcely gets the female characters of *The Last September* very far either); and my understanding of the novel is that, along with and among the other inheritances of traditional gentry society, the sex/gender system prevailing in it is being searchingly interrogated by Bowen in this as in other texts (and as we have seen it critiqued in her discussion of Somerville and Ross late in her life). Bowen's text characterises the relation of Lois to Marda with delicate impulses of yearning and attraction, but there are no false dawns: the light illuminating the book at the end is that of Danielstown burning down ('the door standing open hospitably upon a furnace').[33]

IX

I have been noting the insistent, if understated, importance of woman-to-woman attachment in Bowen's works from the end of the 1920s onwards, and the various modes of that attachment: the explicitly 'inverted' bond between the 'mannish' Theodora and Marise, the yearning of Louie for Stella, and, one might add, of Naomi in *The House in Paris* for Karen (herself tragically embroiled in her doomed passion for Max). Also insistently present are versions of mother–daughter bonds; what light may these throw on Bowen's representation of women and desire?

In recent decades psychoanalysts have increasingly stressed the fundamental role of the mother–child dyad in constituting identity. Elizabeth

Bowen's own childhood loss of her mother by death is a relevant biographical consideration here — a striking parallel with what happened
to Virginia Woolf. Rich's concept of a 'lesbian continuum', with its use of
motherhood as paradigm of woman-to-woman relationships, even contentious as that use is, also comes irresistibly to mind: does this to any
degree displace in Bowen the 'inversion model' of such attachments?[34] I
have mentioned the merging of desire with identification in 'woman-
identified' theories of feminine sexuality; at the end of this discussion
we shall see a striking expression of lesbian love as identification in *Eva
Trout: 'She is all I am . . .'*[35]

Certainly it is true that in Bowen's vision of relations between women
a crucially important role is played by mothers literal and symbolic, and
while there are both nurturing and destroying mother-figures, the destroying
ones predominate imaginatively. Mrs Kerr, Madame Fisher, and Mrs Kelway
in *The Heat of the Day* are all good examples of the destroying kind (and
so is Mrs Nicholson, another Jamesian manipulator, to the sad little boy
in 'Ivy Gripped the Steps'). But there are also important examples of the
'original nurturing love' of mother and daughter, and these examples do
make a remarkable use of the trope of love as identification, as distinct
from love as desire. These daughters' love is, as is perhaps true of all human
loves, never more intensely felt than after its loss. The Bowen novel in
which that love and loss are most memorably instanced is *The Death of
the Heart*, in which Portia's beloved natural mother Irene (which in Greek
means 'peace') dies. She finds herself in — or on — the hands of a cold
unloving stepmother, her half-brother's wife Anna. The book luminously
recalls the child Portia's and her mother's wanderings through inexpen-
sive Swiss hotels (because of Irene's illicit liaison with Portia's father, they
cannot come home, even after his death). In this passage early in the novel,
as Portia looks vaguely at her half-brother Thomas with whom she now
lives, he feels her abstraction:

> Thomas felt the force of not being seen. . . . What she did see was the
> *pension* on the crag in Switzerland. . . . Precarious high-upness had
> been an element in their life up there, which had been the end of
> their life together. That night they came back from Lucerne on the late
> steamer, they had looked up, seen the village lights at star-level through
> the rain, and felt that that was their dear home. They went up, arm-
> in-arm in the dark, up the steep zigzag, pressing each others' elbows,
> hearing the night rain sough down through the pines: they were not
> frightened at all. . . . They would lie down covered with coats, leaving
> the window open, smelling the wet woodwork, hearing the gutters run.
> (*DH*, p. 34)

Portia has a deep longing for maternal love and oblivion, which are strikingly merged in the scene where, overcome by the strain of Thomas and Anna's grand but chill house and beset by the manipulative Eddie (another vintage Bowen 'bounder') she falls asleep propped against the chimney-breast at afternoon tea.[36] The housekeeper Matchett's awkward efforts to offer Portia some surrogate motherly affection make a poignant strand in the novel's design. Herself starchy, proper and standoffish where the other servants and her employers are concerned, Matchett is nevertheless driven by her concern for Portia's lostness and a sense of her overwhelming emotional isolation to reach out to her in an awkward maternal moment, frozen at source by bodily repression:

> Matchett, reluctantly softening, inch by inch, unlocked her arms, leaned across the bed again, leaned right down — in the mysterious darkness over the pillow their faces approached, their eyes met but could not see. Something steadily stood between them: they never kissed — so that now there followed a pause at once pressing and null. Matchett . . . released herself and drew a judicial breath. . . . But Portia's hand, with its charge of nervous emotion, still crept on the firm broad back, the strong spine. (*DH*, p. 83)

This isolation is exacerbated by the prescribed repressions of upper-class femininity, not least by its denials of the body. Vigilantly watched over in the classroom by a headmistress whose 'rigid stillness quelled every young body, its nervous itches, its cooped-up pleasures in being itself, its awareness of the young body next door' (p. 55), Portia is ticked off for reading her letter from Eddie under the desk. Acutely aware of being above all an encumbrance to Anna and Thomas and inwardly desperate for someone's loving regard, Portia replays her life with her mother as an experience of complete mutual recognition and merging. Though from the viewpoint of respectability what they had was a 'shady . . . skidding about in an out-of-season nowhere', her memory is of a warm emotional union marked by mutual recognition, truly this lost daughter's 'original love':

> Untaught, they had walked arm-in-arm along city pavements, and at nights had pulled their beds closer together or slept in the same bed — overcoming, as far as might be, the separation of birth. (*DH*, p. 56)

This reminds us of the child Hermione in *Friends and Relations* who wakes with a nightmare and clings to her mother, crying: 'Oh, go on holding me tight, don't go; I wish we were the same person!' (*FR*, p. 110).

X

From these examples of mother—daughter attachment figured very much as identification, I turn to *Eva Trout* (1968). In this novel the highly finished protagonists of Bowen's earlier social worlds are supplanted by the raw, unfinished Eva, the great gawky girl who is first more or less orphaned — conveyed, in luxury, around the world after her distracted father and his exploitative lover Constantine; then emotionally wronged by her Miss Smith at school, who gave her some attention and held her out a promise of regard, but left her in a kind of psychological inchoateness and isolation:

> She desisted from teaching me. She abandoned my mind. She betrayed my hopes, having led them on. She pretended love, to make me show myself to her — then, thinking she saw all, she turned away. (*ET*, pp 184-5)

Becoming racked by 'long-ago' grief, she adds: 'I had never been. I was *beginning* to be. . . . She sent me back . . . to be nothing. . . . I remain gone. Where am I? I do not know — I was cast out from where I believed I was.' And later, Eva has come to see that Iseult hated her, 'hated the work she had feared to finish' (p. 185). Not at home in language, and unable to settle in any place, monster Eva is the ultimate avatar of all the too-strong but unfocused, 'unfeminine' women of the earlier fictions, of whom Theodora is the fullest exploration; her loves, all but one of which are for other women, are poignant, her fate early and violent death. Inheriting great wealth, she uses it to acquire a son by purchase, a deaf-mute with a prophet's name (Jeremy), an *alter ego* whose moment comes in the novel's intentionally weird climactic scene, just after Eva's own apotheosis when she appears dressed up for the pretend wedding she has planned in the gloom of Victoria Station. Jeremy accidentally (probably) and symmetrically shoots dead his virgin mother.

Eva is awkwardly large physically (and, we feel, psychically) and something of a poor fit as to social gender. A schoolfellow asks, 'Trout, are you a hermaphrodite?' and she replies: 'I don't know.' The possibility is not an entirely negative one: it comes supplied with potential, if odd ('queer'?) glory: 'Joan of Arc's supposed to have been' (p. 51). Looking back, Iseult Smith says to Clavering-Haight: '. . . she belonged to some other category. "Girl" never fitted Eva. Her so-called sex bored and mortified her. She dragged it about after her like a ball and chain' (p. 243). Her capacity for intense, helpless love, as for her mentor Miss Smith, has the effect of revealing the limitations of its objects. She strongly recalls the monster in *Frankenstein*, abandoned by its maker, righteously angry, and at first totally innocent. Eva does eventually come to display the same quality of agency shown earlier by clever Theodora, that other gender misfit; but where Theodora, as we have seen, employs her powers to discomfit others, and manoeuvres in a more or less Sadeian way to make them her puppets, Eva devotes her attention to making *herself* a life and wrenching free of her minders. In so doing, she has destructive effects, but not out of frivolity or deliberate malice. The book is a kind of study of will at work, in which the social surface is scantily, even perfunctorily, wrought. Bowen's interest in the internal pattern of psychological forces at play against one another and in Eva's eccentric but purposive self-development consumes her attention, making the novel more or less completely careless of Barthes's 'reality-effect'.

As to Eva's loves, her perception, registered with a flash of Bowen's earlier ironic poignancy, was that Iseult Smith was in too much of a hurry to 'exchange embraces of any kind' with her. There is, however, a touching scene in which Eva recites a passage of seventeenth-century poetry on the love of God, which evidently transfers to her own inexpressible love for her teacher:

> But thou art Light, and darkness both together:
> If that bee dark we can not see,
> The sunn is darker than a Tree,
> And thou more dark than either.
>
> Yet Thou art not so dark, since I know this,
> But that my darkness may touch thine
> And hope, that may teach it to shine,
> Since Light my Darkness is.
>
> O lett my Soule, whose keyes I must deliver
> Into the hands of senceless Dreames
> Which know not thee, suck in thy beames
> And wake with thee for ever.

Miss Smith's response (surely a tiny parody of 1950s 'New Criticism') is to talk about 'how pure language can be', with 'not more than two syllables — are there? — in any word' (pp 65-6). But in spite of that, in this instance of Eva's love for Iseult, Bowen gives her protagonist a degree of direct and expressible emotional investment which contrasts with the intentional inarticulateness of Rachel's unawakened sensibility in 'The Jungle' (with its not dissimilar school setting) and which elsewhere in her work is, as we have seen, more usually masked or deflected.

Still more clearly, Eva has also quite unambiguously loved her school room-mate Elsinore (can this, its *Hamlet* allusion a false trail, be a version of the 'Elise' loved by Rachel in the 1927 story?). This attachment is revealed in flashback, after their accidental meeting in America as adults. The adult Elsinore (now 'Elsi-nora') is described as still tiny, a suggestive complement to Eva's size: 'She had hardly grown. Inside the haze of thistledown hair her waif beauty was as it had been, not child's or woman's.' The accoutrements of her adult femininity seem like mere actress's props: 'The silver fox cape smothering her shoulders, the brilliants studding her ears might have been borrowed from an acting box' (p. 131). The contrast between the adult Eva's and Elsinora's appearance or self-presentation may seem to indicate what Sedgwick calls 'the preservation of an essential heterosexuality within desire itself', with Eva cast as 'man', as it were, to Elsinora's 'woman'; yet the trope of love as identification which is simultaneously present decisively displaces that of sexual difference. In this, the climactic passage, Elsinore, slight, fair-haired and ethereal, has attempted suicide by walking into the lake beside the school:

> *The hand on the blanket, the beseeching answering beating heart. The dark:*
> *the unseen distance, the known nearness. Love: the here and the now and*
> *the nothing-but. The step on the stairs. Don't take her away, DON'T take*
> *her away. She is all I am. We are all there is.* (p. 133; italics in original)

After a period of illlless during which Eva is allowed to be with her and, as we are only later explicitly told, love her, Elsinore's mother, who had earlier simply offloaded her at the school, suddenly turns up and takes her away. The passage above continues, in Eva's interior monologue:

> *Haven't you heard what is going to be? No. Not, but I know what was. A*
> *door opening, how is my darling? Right — then TAKE her away, take your*
> *dead bird. You wretch, you mother I never had. Elsinore, what happened?*
> *Nobody told me, nobody dared. Gone, gone, Nothing can alter that now,*
> *it's too late. Go away again.* (p. 133; italics in original)

It is difficult to read these passages in their context and think in quite the same way afterwards about almost any of the other woman-to-woman scenes and plot elements in Bowen.

XI

In conclusion, how may we draw these strands together? I have a number of very simple propositions. First, mother-attachment is a major nexus of feeling in Bowen's work, and it is invariably attended by one or more of the three emotions of love, grief or anger, each very intense. Sometimes that anger is projected onto the mother-figure, making her a 'destroying' or 'terrible' mother. Sometimes, as in the very early story 'Coming Home', it is part of a fantasy of destructive power within the daughter's self.[37] But, *pace* Adrienne Rich's view, in Bowen the mother–daughter bond is not, in my opinion, either felt or represented, nor can it usefully be conceived, as the source, origin or determinant of lesbian desire. Second, Bowen's fictions also show a sensitive awareness, remarkable for her time, of the shifting, sometimes evanescent, sometimes enduring interpenetration of desire and friendship in women's relationships, and she explores and represents such attachments across a spectrum from negative to positive. Third, her fiction shows a strong imaginative interest in the representation of specifically lesbian feeling and woman-to-woman relationships of desire, whether reciprocal or not. Finally, while in her work as a whole Bowen explores the desire for the other *as* other, whether between women and women or women and men, she attends with equal or greater intensity to desire as love of one's like, one's other self, in other words a desire which culminates in identification: *'the hand on the blanket, the beseeching answering beating heart. The dark: the unseen distance, the known nearness. Love: the here and now and the nothing-but. . . . She is all I am. We are all there is.'*

Abbreviations

CS	*Collected Stories* (1983)
DH	*The Death of the Heart* (1939)
ET	*Eva Trout* (1968)
FR	*Friends and Relations* (1931)
HD	*The Heat of the Day* (1949)
HP	*The House in Paris* (1935)
TH	*The Hotel* (1927)
TLG	*The Little Girls* (1964)
TLS	*The Last September* (1929)

Dates are the dates of first publication; references are to Penguin editions.
Quotations from Bowen's critical writings are from *The Mulberry Tree: Writings of Elizabeth Bowen*, selected and introduced by Hermione Lee, London: Virago, 1986, which is abbreviated as *MT*.

Notes and References

1   Eve Kosofsky Sedgwick, *Epistemology of the Closet*, London: Penguin, 1994, pp 85, 87-8.

2   Adrienne Rich, 'Compulsory Heterosexuality and Lesbian Existence' in Catherine Stimpson and Ethel Spector Person (eds.), *Women, Sex and Sexuality*, University of Chicago Press, 1980, pp. 62-91. See Sedgwick, op. cit., esp. pp 36-7 and 84-90, for a wide range of other relevant references to this argument.

3   Examples of the literal relations I am primarily thinking of are those recalled by Portia in *The Death of the Heart*, with her now dead mother, those in *The House in Paris* between Karen Michaelis and her mother, that iron hand in a velvet glove,

and those in the very early story 'Coming Home' (1923), which is a miniature study in the competing selfhoods of mother and daughter (*CS*, pp. 95-100).

4 I have drawn here (and elsewhere in this essay) on the following: Judith Mayne, 'A Parallax View of Lesbian Authorship' in Diana Fuss (ed.), *inside/out: Lesbian Theories, Gay Theories*, London: Routledge, 1991, pp. 173-85; Biddy Martin, 'Lesbian Identity and Autobiographical Difference(s)' in Anne C. Herrmann and Abigail J. Stewart (eds), *Theorizing Feminism*, Boulder and Oxford: Westview Press, 1994, pp. 316-38; Marilyn R. Farwell, 'Towards a Definition of the Lesbian Literary Imagination' in Susan Wolfe and Julia Penelope (eds), *Sexual Practice and Textual Theory*, Cambridge, Mass. & Oxford: Blackwell, 1993, pp. 66-84. Renee C. Hoagland's book *Elizabeth Bowen: A Reputation in Writing*, New York University Press, 1994 (in a series on Lesbian Life and Literature) has come to my attention just at the completion of this essay. It addresses Bowen in the combined perspectives of psychoanalysis, lesbian feminism, and the post-structuralist critique of traditional subjectivity. Hoagland's analysis of current thinking from these perspectives about the process of identification and its relation to desire is a useful one and bears on my own argument (see esp. p. 343 n. 32).

5 Sedgwick, op. cit., p. 85.

6 McCormack also insists, not incidentally, on the creative estrangement from realistic form which Bowen effects: 'Lucid with detail from the street and on the dressing-table, reliable as to rationing and blackout regulations, it turns away from realism into romance. This is no evasion of reality. It is the romance of irony which releases character from the iron cage of identification with the self. W. J. McCormack, *Dissolute Characters: Irish Literary History through Balzac, Sheridan Le Fanu, Yeats and Bowen*, Manchester University Press, 1993, p. 240.

7 In a well-known passage on Le Fanu's *Uncle Silas*, she wrote (as something specifically Irish) of the 'sublimated infantilism' of the Anglo-Irish milieu from which both she and Le Fanu originated, and added: 'In the story, no force from any one of the main characters runs into the channel of sexual feeling' (*MT*, p. 101). The remark about 'moral dread' is in *MT*, p. 112.

8 'The room, felt by the child [Henrietta] as "so full and still", is a case not of mere immobility but of immobilization. In a terrible way, it is a *bois dormant*' ('Pictures and Conversations', *MT*, p. 285). Madame Fisher's daughter Naomi says 'she is all mind and will, but she cannot make a *tisane* without flames running round the spirit stove' (p. 188).

9 See Phyllis Lassner, *Elizabeth Bowen*, London: Macmillan, 1990, esp. pp. 48-72.

10 See Victoria Glendinning, *Elizabeth Bowen: Portrait of a Writer*, London: Weidenfeld and Nicolson, 1977, pp. 189-91.

11 Lassner, op. cit., pp. 14, 5.

12 Glendinning, op. cit., p. 189.

13 Ibid., p. 140.

14 Ibid.

15 W. J. McCormack notes Bowen's employment of children and ghosts as conductors of one mode of such monstrosity, the uncanny (*From Burke to Beckett: Ascendancy, Tradition and Betrayal in Literary History*, Cork University Press, 1995, p. 409, drawing on the work of Giorgio Agamben).

16 In this connection, R. F. Foster cites Bowen's own warm approval of Portia in *The Death of the Heart* as a deliberate wrecker of the *status quo*, and approved of this destruction. Bowen disliked the tendency of readers and critics to emphasis Portia's victim position (R. F. Foster, *Paddy and Mr Punch*, London: Penguin, 1993, p. 103).

17 'More than doubtful' here is the phrase of Miss Paullie the headmistress, and is meant, I believe, to be read as a comment simultaneously on class and on a behaviour which infringes the close boundaries of feminine 'self-respect', i.e. flirtation (see p. 57).

18 *Schwärmerei* (Bowen, or the typesetter, incorrectly omits the 'w') in its usual twentieth-century sense means a rather irrational or excessive emotional attachment, and has often been used to name the attachments (or, more dismissively, 'crushes') of adolescent girls for each other or for older women, typically teachers or more senior girls, and especially in a boarding-school environment. Its older, more literary context was the special attention paid to the life of the emotions in the period of sensibility and Romanticism, between the late 1700s and the early 1800s. I am grateful to Beate Dreike for her elucidation of this word.

19 McCormack notes that the topic of homosexuality 'only breaks the surface' in these works, but after that is silent on the matter (*From Burke to Beckett*, p. 409).

20 Thus Eva Trout's dead father is presented in brief flashbacks as having been besotted by the silky Constantine, so mesmerized by his attraction as to be endlessly willing to be sponged off and, what is more to the point, to neglect and emotionally abandon the child Eva.

21 As Hermione Lee puts it, 'Though Elizabeth Bowen deals very unsympathetically with homosexuals in *Eva Trout*, there's a clear expression of understanding for lesbian feelings in the last two novels' [i.e. *The Little Girls* and *Eva Trout*] (*Elizabeth Bowen: An Estimation*, London: Vision Press, 1981, pp 208-9).

22 'She felt so sick for Elise that she prayed to be hit by a ball on the head every time she went out to Lacrosse' (p. 239).

23 Here, as very often, she plays games with names: for 'Butler' and 'Ponsonby', respectively Hiberno-Norman and quintessentially English-sounding, read 'Fitzgerald' and 'Pym', whose first name is even 'Eleanor' (like Butler's); in 'Pym' we might also hear an 'r' after the 'P'.

24 Diana Swanson's essay 'Subverting Closure: Compulsory Heterosexuality and Compulsory Endings in Middle-Class British Women's Novels' (in Wolfe and Penelope, op. cit., pp. 150-63), in a perceptive brief discussion of *The Hotel*, simply describes Sydney as 'in love with Mrs Kerr'.

25 Portia in *The Death of the Heart*, an exception, lacks at least three of these four, and to that extent prefigures Eva Trout.

26 When her parents return to their London flat after this visit they find that Theodora — like those guinea-pigs — 'has more than ever her caged air' (p. 30). On the 'brain his son would have had', compare the alleged expectation of Bowen's own parents about the gender of their child (see p. 108 above).

27 James applies the term *ficelle* (i.e. 'string') to characters whom he uses as often unwitting carriers of bits of information crucial to the plot: the symbolically named Miss Stringham is an example.

28 Louie's tough sidekick, the ARP warden Connie, who is introduced a bit later,

is one of a gallery of confidantes who are worthy of a whole discussion to themselves: it would include Lois's two friends Olivia and Viola (with their names borrowed from *Twelfth Night*, in which one falls in love with the other, resourcefully cross-dressed), and solemn Portia's slightly 'not-quite-quite' adviser Lilian in *The Death of the Heart*.

29 For an example in Malory see Catherine La Farge, 'The Hand of the Huntress: Repetition in Malory's Morte Darthur' in Isobel Armstrong (ed), *New Feminist Discourses*, London: Routledge, 1992, p. 265.

30 For this Stella tends to blame herself: a beautiful passage expresses her sense of having somehow been responsible for cutting him off fatally from the world in his childhood: '. . . when he was a baby she had amused him by opening and shutting a painted fan, and of that *beau monde* of figures, grouped and placed and linked by gestures or garlands, he never had, she suspected, lost interior sight. The fan on its fragile ivory spokes now remained closed: she felt him most happy when they could recreate its illusion in their talk' (*HD*, p. 61).

31 This recalls Marilyn R. Farwell's explanation of her own conception of the word 'lesbian': 'What is called lesbian does not depend on women loving other women genitally but, rather, on the presence and attention of women to other women that is analogous to the act of loving sexually another like oneself. In fact, words like *presence, attention,* and *sight* are used more often to describe this metaphoric lesbian' ('Toward a Definition of the Lesbian Literary Imagination', pp 73-4).

32 See Bonnie Zimmerman, 'Perverse Reading: The Lesbian Appropriation of Literature', in Wolfe and Penelope, op. cit., pp 134-49; this quotation is on p. 139.

33 One might also consider Marda as Lois's ego-ideal, in the Freudian vocabulary: one whom Lois can admire and look up to as a perfected version of oneself, a self *in potentia*.

34 See Farwell, op, cit, pp 71-3, for some excellent caveats and useful expressions of justifiable suspicion about the motherhood metaphor.

35 I owe this perception to Piaras Mac Éinrí, to whom I am grateful for this and other insights.

36 A moving scene which, like that of Rachel's dream, cries out for Freudian ex-egesis, along the lines of the hearth as figure for the absent mother.

37 This is according to a structure, illogical to the rational mind but perfectly coherent to the unconscious, familiar in psychoanalytic explanations of human behaviour — she's not there, so I'll make her disappear — which prompts one to wonder whether all Bowen's evil mother-figures are so constructed as a fantasy-revenge for their having gone. It would, of course, be reductive to read them as that and nothing else, but the thought is nevertheless not irrelevant.

6 Elizabeth Bowen
The Dandy in Revolt

DECLAN KIBERD

During the Easter Rising of 1916, while gunfire raked across St Stephen's Green as Countess Markievicz and her force engaged the British army, afternoon tea was served at the usual time in the lounge of the Shelbourne Hotel. We know this because Elizabeth Bowen records it in her elegant history of that Ascendancy institution. She was well aware, from personal experience, of the uses of such nonchalance; to her, polite behaviour was something which 'does really help to jack up morale' (*TS*, p. 128). When the Rising broke out, she was away at school in England. News of it was her first indication that something like a national revival had been afoot. Like many of the heroines of her books, she found herself well away from the scene of the action when something decisive was happening: the national revival had been judged far too inconsequential a thing for her own Anglo-Irish family to form any clear opinion of it. 'Who would ever have thought the Irish would turn out so disloyal?' (*TLS*, p. 46) might well be taken as typical of their reaction.

The Rising was, among other things, a systematic attempt to restore Dublin's metropolitan status, lost since the Act of Union; the Anglo-Irish gentry were by 1916 hopeless provincials, if by provincial one means to indicate people who have no sense of their own presence. Their world, as depicted by Bowen, is one whose members are constantly isolated from the wider society around them by the great walls encircling their demesnes: major events unfold on the other side of those walls, events which the aristocrats within make a point of not noticing. Unlike Edith Somerville, who studied the Irish language and kept abreast of the progress of the Gaelic League, the occupants of Bowen's Court in Co. Cork built their lives on 'the negation of mystical Ireland' (*BC*, p. 22). Her ancestors, she freely conceded, had driven Gaelic culture 'underground, with its ceaseless poetry of lament' (*BC*, p. 97); now, though a revival was in full swing, she showed no great curiosity about it. This was a mark of baffled incomprehension rather than ill-will: in her early years, she had been so sheltered that she had no idea that Protestants did not make up the majority religion in Ireland. An only child, she was shunted between Ireland and England, away from an ailing father and into the care of a mother who died suddenly when Elizabeth was only thirteen. If she grew up '*farouche*, haughty, quite ignorant of the outside world', the sort of self-invention necessitated by such a condition was perfectly typical of her class:

> It is possible that Anglo-Irish people, like only children, do not know how much they miss. Their existences, like those of only children, are singular, independent, secretive.[1]

The Anglo-Irish curbed their feeling because their prosperity was erected on 'a situation that shows an inherent wrong', the expropriation of the native Irish. Most relationships with the natives could only have issued in unpleasant accusation; it was better, therefore, to confine them to a few loyal cooks and retainers. For the rest, 'the new ascendancy lacked feeling, in fact feeling would have been fatal to it'. No wonder that Elizabeth Bowen became an expert analyst of the death of the heart. She saw hers as a class which, unlike its English counterpart, achieved its position through injustice — 'the structure of the great Anglo-Irish society was raised over a country in martyrdom' — and subsequently failed to justify its privilege by service.[2] It enjoyed power without taking responsibility for the wider countryside over which it ruled: instead it simply pulled up the drawbridge. That this suited the more lethargic and unambitious commoners as well as overlords was among the least of its recommendations:

> The Irish landowner, partly from laziness, but also from an indifferent delicacy, does not interfere in the lives of the people round. . . . The greater part of them being Catholics, and he in most cases a Protestant, they are kept from him by the barrier of a different faith . . . [and] a good-mannered, faintly cynical tolerance, largely founded on classes letting each other alone.[3]

This stand-off may have been less pleasant for both parties than she implies. *The Last September*, set in Cork during the War of Independence, tells of a Big House whose younger members yearn for some intrusion from the world of actual rebels; and a former insurgent himself, Seán

O'Faoláin, in reading the book could not help wishing for one of a different kind, a truly contrapuntal narrative about a Danielstown House 'that was at least aware of the Ireland outside . . . that, perhaps, regretted the division enough to admit it was there'.[4] Protesting against the elegant self-enclosure of the novel, he asked for Irish books which were not watertight compartments: Gogol in *Dead Souls* had linked divided worlds, and Chekhov had many stories about doctors who climbed walls. Bowen knew exactly what he meant, telling him in a subsequent interview in *The Bell* that when the Great Irish Novel would finally be written, 'I fancy you'll find that it has been written by a Protestant who understands Catholicism and who, very probably, has made a mixed marriage'.[5] For her own part, it was scarcely her fault if she had found such knowledge unavailable, encountering in her earlier years 'an almost sexual shyness on the subject of Roman Catholics'.

It might be added that what gives *The Last September* much of its bittersweet poignancy is the innocence of the Anglo-Irish as they go to meet their doom:

> If Ireland did not accept them, they did not know it — and in that unawareness of final rejection, unawareness of being looked at from some secretive, opposed life, that the Anglo-Irish naïve dignity and, even, tragedy, seem to me to stand. Themselves, they felt Irish and acted as Irishmen.[6]

This poignancy rises to a genuinely tragic resonance in the fact that, having blocked off feeling, these people now seem as admirably unaware of their own suffering as they once were so scandalously unaware of the pain which they inflicted on the dispossessed. A similar imperviousness, if not to feeling then at least to its overt expression, was noted in Elizabeth Bowen by friends and contemporaries. Like others of her kind, she lived at a certain remove from her own emotions, some part of her always held in reserve and able to monitor an experience, even as she submitted to it, with a cold, clinical precision. This observant detachment had long been a feature of Anglo-Irish writing, which achieved an almost anthropological status, seeking to view man as if he were a foreign, even non-human, witness of himself; but, in the writings of Bowen, existence takes on 'the trance-like quality of a spectacle' (*PC*, p. 23) not only for the author who anatomises it but for those caught up in it as well.

The English planters who had occupied Ireland were, in a sense, the first Provisionals, by no means certain of their tenure in a land where they would always be outnumbered by those whom they had extirpated. They knocked down the woods which had sheltered recalcitrant rebels, and huckstered off the leavings at sixpence a tree. If their grander houses seemed built for eternity, that was largely to allay the fear that they might be going home on the next boat: the exterior show of spaciousness and command was intended to mask an inner uncertainty. All they had to protect themselves against the avenging masses was an attitude, an assumed style. Elizabeth Bowen wrote that the Big House of rural Ireland was 'like Flaubert's ideal book, about nothing' (*PC*, p. 15), something which constructed itself around a lack, sustaining itself by the inner force of its style. This style, like the Yeatsian antiself, represented an ideal of courtly behaviour and *sprezzatura* to which the 'new Ascendancy' might aspire; it helped the founders of the line cope with the thought that their tenure might only be provisional, and it enabled the final descendants to maintain a semblance of defiant decorum long after the tradition had started to collapse. The training of the Anglo-Irish turned out to be an arduous preparation for the moment when style was all that they had left . . . for those takers of the toast and tea at the Shelbourne Hotel. The manner remained intact long after the men and women themselves had snapped.

For Bowen herself, all of this made a perfect sense in terms of her art. If the Anglo-Irish were a hyphenated people, forever English in Ireland, forever Irish in England, then she knew that better than most. At school in England, she played up her wild Irish side, yet she also tried to make herself more English than the English by her perfect decorum and style. Her truest sense of herself may have come when she was in motion, crossing from one country to another, in the manner of her heroine Lois in *The Last September*:

> She shut her eyes and tried — as sometimes when she was seasick, locked in misery between Holyhead and Kingstown — to be enclosed in a nonentity, in some ideal no-place perfect and clear as a bubble. (*TLS*, p. 89)

There is a real desperation here, for the bubble which she creates is grimly like the self-enclosed estate at Danielstown; and if you start out building a Utopia, you may indeed end up here.

Bowen's own style, mannered but functional, was formed (like that of the Big House) as a mode in which a desperate soul sought for an assured sense of identity; she turned to art for a stability which was unobtainable in the world. That style prefigured an ideal version of herself which she might yet live up to. It had the additional advantage of offering the marooned daughter an attitude with which to address a society: 'My writing, I am prepared to think, may be a substitute for something I have been born without — a so-called normal relation to society. My books *are* my relation to society.'[7] Nothing made full sense to her that was not in print. She wrote not so much to record as to invent a self, a self which lived on

the hyphen between 'Anglo' and 'Irish'. And she explored that moment when
the self peeps out of its cocoon in *The Last September,* the novel for which
she always confessed a special feeling of tenderness.

Set in the Troubles of 1920, the story centres on Lois Farquar, the orphaned niece of Sir Richard and Lady Naylor, owners of the Danielstown estate.
Outside, rebel soldiers engage in the final phase of a war of liberation against
the British, one of whose soldiers, Gerald Lesworth, falls in love with Lois;
inside, the Naylors and their visitors concentrate on tennis parties and
dances. The house epitomises order and continuity, the values on which
it is assumed that Lois will pattern her life; but it exacts a huge tribute
from its occupiers, condemning them to cold nights and claustrophobic
days. Lois feels haunted by the house, because its lack of an inner dynamic
seems a reflection of her own:

> And she could not try to explain . . . how after every return — awaken-
> ing, even, from sleep or preoccupation — she and those home
> surroundings further penetrated each other mutually in the discovery
> of a lack. (*TLS,* p. 131)

She is, therefore, immobilised by the very traditions which, in theory, should
uplift her.

It would be facile to present her life as a stalemate between self-expression
in Gerald's arms and doing the right thing by the Naylors, who disap-
prove of such an attachment. In truth, she trusts her own feelings too little to know whether what she experiences with the English soldier is love.
The forms of good behaviour have preceded her to every experience. In
the company of a world-weary older man whom she rather fancies, a Mr
Montmorency, she wonders how her carefree dancing up the estate avenue
must appear in his eyes:

> He had seemed amazed at her being young when he wasn't. She could
> not hope to explain that her youth seemed to her also rather theatrical
> and that she was only young in that way because people expected it.
> She had never refused a role. . . . She could not hope to assure him she
> was enjoying anything he had missed, that she was now unconvinced
> and anxious but intended to be quite certain, by the time she was his
> age, that she had once been happy. For to explain this — were explana-
> tion possible to so courteous, ironical and unfriendly a listener — would,
> she felt, be disloyal to herself, to Gerald, to an illusion both were called
> upon to sustain. (*TLS,* p. 32-3)

For Bowen, there is not necessarily anything ignoble about this willingness
of Lois to impersonate the kind of woman others may want her to be:

after all, this was the author who insisted that it is by illusions that people live. But in playing a role, Lois becomes dimly aware of a buried life within her which seems humiliated by such gestures. Like Christopher Dysart, similarly situated in *The Real Charlotte*, she feels enough to know that she should feel more, knows enough to sense how little she really knows. She is, moreover, effete, with the added hopelessness that she recognises such effeteness in herself. Caught in the open spaces between a role and a self, she finds a strange attraction in a house whose very architecture and furniture provide her with those stage directions which tell an actor how to perform: 'I like to be in a pattern, I like to be related; to have to be what I am. Just to *be* is so intransitive, so lonely' (*TLS*, p. 98).

Yet there is in Lois a real scruple about such pattern and relation: her mind is too fine to be violated by a single idea. She may envy those who know exactly who they are, but she also fears such certainty. When she finds her path on the estate crossed by a rebel in a trenchcoat, she feels a weird mixture of envy and terror:

> It must be because of Ireland he was in such a hurry. . . . She could not conceive of her country emotionally. . . . His intentions burned on the dark an almost invisible trail; he might well have been a murderer he seemed so inspired. (*TLS*, p. 34)

The 'lack' around which the house is sructured is a lack of a basic, animating principle: its members nervously rely on the mercy of rebels and on the efficiency of British soldiers to guarantee their own safety, yet they stand for nothing themselves. Lois is a good deal more compliant in these evasions than she would care to admit. When she overhears Mrs Montmorency speaking of her in an adjoining room, she panics and rattles the bedroom utensils, so as not to hear the rest: 'She didn't want to know what she was, she couldn't bear to: knowledge of this would stop, seal, finish one. Was she now to be clapped down under an adjective, to crawl round lifelong inside some quality like a fly in a tumbler' (*TLS*, p. 60). All she hears, therefore, is 'Lois is very —'; but *what* she is, she will never know.

The contemplation of the daily round at least allows for the postpone-ment of such ultimate questions; in this she is a good deal more compliant with Danielstown practices than she might care to admit. Sir Richard retreats into worries about dinner etiquette in order to spare himself think-ing of the dire destiny of his estate; and Lois, finding in Gerald's kiss 'an impact, with inside blankness', effectively cocoons herself inside the house which wants no truck with him. Identity is more to be feared than desired; that kiss is, in its way, as invasive and categorical as the prowler in the trenchcoat, promising this woman only 'a merciless penetration'.

Yet Lois is as much a victim of Danielstown values as the Irish rebel who crosses her path; for the Anglo-Irish are as guilty of ignoring the needs of the heirs within as of the dependants without. In return for nothing, the young are compelled to adopt a time-honoured set of manners and attitudes, to be 'sealed' and 'finished', so that the social forms may survive the death of their contents. Living in a period house, they are effectively told to embalm themselves alive, perform approved routines, and deny all feelings. Gerald is only an anachronism in the sense that he is fighting in Cork for an England of the mind, which still means something in gentry Ireland, but which his own country has long ceased to be. War has modernised the national manners: where once the English repressed feeling, now they express it.

A minor character in the novel, Mrs Carey, speaking to the wife of a British soldier, 'feared she detected in her a tendency, common to most English people, to talk about her inside. She often wondered if the War had not made everyone from England a little commoner' (*TLS*, p. 46). Lady Naylor, for her part, is quite dismayed by the new English propensity to 'tell one the most extraordinary things, about their husbands, their money affairs, their insides. They don't seem discouraged by not being asked. And they seem so intimate with each other: I suppose it comes from living so close together' (*TLS*, p. 134). She regards Gerald as a most improper suitor for Lois, not only because he comes from a lower social class, but most of all because he is modern, i.e. English. ('They tell me there's a great deal of socialism now in the British Army,' muses her distraught husband.) Gerald represents what England is becoming, while the planters believe instead in a pre-war England, which has now changed beyond all recognition, but whose lineaments they can still vaguely discern in the Ascendancy holdings of West Cork. So he must die for an ideal which, in his own country, has long been disposed of, offering protection to a people who do not even care for him. Elizabeth Bowen was all too aware of the accompanying ironies; by the time she wrote *The Last September*, her theme was historical ('in those days' is the phrase which opens the second paragraph), and she had seen the great life's work of her lawyer father on *Statutory Purchase in Ireland* outdated, even before its day of publication, by the Anglo-Irish Treaty of 1921.

This tragedy of irrelevance is made possible only by the unawareness of what is at stake among the rulers of Danielstown. Whether that ignorance is willed or deliberate depends very much on the individual. Sir Richard seems genuinely distracted by household affairs; his more practical wife, however, says: 'I make a point of not noticing.' This becomes the prevailing attitude adopted by occupants of the house not merely to outsiders but to one another. Lois turns away from Lady Montmorency's definition of her, and not merely though politeness, but as a protest against a world in which one is more likely to be talked at than talked to. She knows that if she overhears it all, she will be even less free to invent herself and more likely to be shaped by an implied pressure of social expectation. What is said in Danielstown is less often heard than overheard, as an unwelcome insight into what others may think of the overhearer.

Ideally, the young should have their part in shaping the house, in bringing in new blood; but instead sex seems 'irrelevant', and the house asserts its absolute right to shape them. In his anger and frustration, its heir Laurence yearns for 'some crude intrusion of the actual', adding that 'I should like to be here when this house burns' (*TLS*, p. 44). Lois also launches a covert counter-appeal to the values of the insurgents in an early conversation with Gerald, in which she marvels that, while nearby soldiers were dying, she was cutting out a dress that she didn't even need:

> How is it that in this country that ought to be full of such violent realness, there seems nothing for me but clothes and what people say? I might just as well be in some cocoon. (*TLS*, p. 49)

What she wants Gerald to do is to agree, and to admit that this is hardly a state of things worth fighting for.

Anglo-Irish self-control in such circumstances is patently ridiculous, but so also is the 'moral' English pretence that it would be ignoble to abandon such people. In a sharp outburst, Lois voices her rejection of the role of besieged maiden and devastatingly links her repudiation to the revivalist image of Kathleen Ni Houlihan:

> Can you wonder this country gets irritated? It's as bad for it as being a woman. I never can see why women shouldn't be hit, or should be saved from wrecks when everybody complains they're superfluous. (*TLS*, p. 49)

This appeal to Gerald, early on in the book, to come out in his true modern colours and stop playing the Galahad, is matched at a much later stage by the moment when Lois and her friend Marda, having stumbled upon a sleeping rebel in a mill, refuse to betray him to the authorities. Enraged by a society in which the true expression of feeling is inadmissible, Lois smoulders with much the same kind of resentment as the rebels; it is, of course, a kindness to Danielstown, as much as to the surprised rebel, that nothing is to be said.

During the encounter the insurgent's gun had fired 'by accident' (like the balloons which seemed to burst, spontaneously and pointlessly, at the British army dance). This evocation of a violence without agency conveys the sense of powerlessness of all individuals — nationalists, imperialists and gentry — in the vacuum of authority left by the Naylors. It also suggests that the Big House children are subconsciously willing the final conflagration. The rebels, like Lois and Marda, are simply marginal witnesses and participants in a history which eludes any final control by individuals; 'not noticing' is part of their ethic too. And yet somehow the rebellion frees both parties, returning Ireland to the Irish, and freeing Lois and her cousin Laurence to become themselves.

As always, Lois is somewhere else when the great events happen. By the time Gerald dies they are no longer lovers, so she denies herself any false romantic gesture over him, unlike the hypocritical Lady Naylor, who writes a letter to his mother praising the dead man's heroism and happy life. By the time that Danielstown is burnt down Lois is too far away for her response to be worthy of report. Yet there can be no doubt that the end of the house means that at long last she can escape the cocoon; she is free now to enter a world of risk and growth rather than languish in one of fear and inexperience. The next tragedy in which she participates will at least have the merit of being her own. Bowen's Court, of which Elizabeth was sole heir, did not burn: instead she maintained it, at large expense and emotional stress, until the burden became too great, and it was sold and razed in 1960. Many of her friends, Seán O'Faoláin included, considered her foolish to keep up the struggle for so long, but she felt the obligation very deeply, even though she betrayed characteristically little emotion on the day when she finally drove away from it. If the artist had shown a secret complicity with Irish insurgents[8] in causing Danielstown to burn, then it must be said that the same artist had created the state out of nothing: the rebel who smouldered within her was more than counterbalanced by the lady of the manor, who presided like a goddess over a world of her own creation. After Bowen's Court was gone, she began to look back with increasing tenderness on her own race and class; and the virtues of nonchalance replaced the imbecilities of 'not noticing' in her assessment of the Anglo-Irish:

> If they formed a too-proud idea of themselves, they did at least exert themselves to live up to this: even vanity involves one kind of discipline. . . . To live as though living gave them no trouble has been the first imperative of their make-up; to do this has taken a virtuosity into which courage enters more than has been allowed. In the last issue, they have lived at their own expense.[9]

However, this willingness to see such people even more tenderly than they saw themselves had been evident in *The Last September*. When Laurence announces that he wishes to be present when Danielstown burns, Mr Montmorency is outraged not just by the expression of such sentiments, but by the young man's insistence that they would all be so careful not to notice. To Mr Montmorency, life was 'an affair of discomfort, but that discomfort should be made articulate seemed to him shocking' (*TLS*, p. 44). To the cynicism of the modern undergraduate, he would infinitely prefer the desperate composure of the dandy: and if *The Last September* retains the power to move readers, that is, at least in part, because it is one of the very few works of literature to consider the dandy as a fit subject for tragedy.

Traditionally the dandy has been the stuff of comedy, especially in the brilliant Anglo-Irish example of Oscar Wilde. There are, in truth, many lines and passages in *The Last September* to which he would happily have laid claim, as when Lady Naylor voices her derisive opinion of a young suitor from a villa in Surrey, that bastion of transient modernity:

> His mother, he says, lives in Surrey, and of course you do know, don't you, what Surrey *is*. It says nothing, absolutely; part of it is opposite the Thames Embankment. Practically nobody who lives in Surrey ever seems to have been heard of, and if one does hear of them they have never heard of anybody else who lives in Surrey. Really, altogether, I think all English people very difficult to trace. They are so pleasant and civil, but I do often wonder if they are not a little shallow: for no reason at all they will pack up everything and move across six counties. (*TLS*, p. 58)

This neatly sums up the dandy's perennial problem: how to maintain an aristocratic hauteur and decorum in the absence of any available court at which to rehearse and play out such gestures. Self-conquest and self-discipline were the answers, according to Yeats, who said that there is always something of heroism in being sufficiently master of oneself to be witty. In Wilde's personal confession that he had to strain every muscle in his body to achieve mastery of a London dinner-table, Yeats found his pattern of such self-conquest: what seemed spontaneous and stylish was in fact the outcome of rigorous rehearsal.

This is why it 'takes a heroic constitution to live modernism',[10] because the resistance offered by the modern world to the *élan* of a person is out of all proportion to his or her strength, hence the dandy's intermittent desire for the relief of death. Mr Montmorency is not the only inhabitant of Danielstown who grows tired from the strain of maintaining a jaunty front; even Laurence and Lois in their more typical moments might be seen as types of the dandy-in-revolt:

> Lois thought how in Marda's bedroom, when she was married, there might be a dark blue carpet with a bloom on it like a grape, and how this room, this hair, would be forgotten. Already the room seemed full of the dusk of oblivion. And she hoped that instead of fading to dusk in summers of empty sunshine, the carpet would burn with the house in a scarlet night to make one flaming call upon Marda's memory. (*TLS*, p. 98)

The dandy's craving for oblivion is 'not a resignation but a heroic passion',[11] in fact the only form of heroism still practicable in the absence of a courtly backdrop. A hero thus becomes someone who knows and says and lives the truth that traditional heroism is no longer possible. Against the platitudinous salute to Gerald's death which causes Lady Naylor and her friends to say 'It was heroic', before looking down at their gloves and dogs, Lois sums up the dandy's crisis in conversation with a female friend:

> I wouldn't mind being properly tragic. . . . If one's not quite certain, one never knows where one is. . . . It's just that I feel so humiliated the whole time. (*TLS*, p. 87)

The problem is that there is nothing for such a one to do, as she tells Laurence: 'But I want to begin on something. . . . There must be some way for me to begin . . . what do you think I am for?' (*TLS*, p. 161).

Nobody at Danielstown, least of all Mr Montmorency, is capable of answering that. When asked what the British soldiers are dying for, he insists that 'our side is no side' — 'rather scared, rather isolated, not expressing anything except tenacity to something that isn't there — that never was there. And deprived of heroism by this wet kind of smother of commiseration' (*TLS*, p. 82). Nothing is left to such a man but beautiful manners and a perfect stylisation of every gesture, for here indeed is Walter Benjamin's essential dandy, 'a Hercules with no work'. Mr Montmorency, who had great plans for a new life in Canada, is left to attend to nothing more portentous than the folding of his wife's dresses. Of such a man might Benjamin have been thinking when he wrote his account of the dandy's tragedy, in which

> nonchalance is combined with the utmost exertion of energy. . . . There is a special constellation in which greatness and indolence meet in human beings too. . . . But the high seas beckon to him in vain, for his life is under an ill star. Modernism turns out to be his doom. The hero was not provided for in it; it has no use for his type. It makes him fast in the secure harbour forever and abandons him to everlasting idleness. In this, his last embodiment, the hero appears as a dandy.[12]

The point about such a one is that he is a descendant of noble ancestors, who must now live with the seismic tremors of the bourgeois market, learning how to conceal his horror at these shocking fluctuations and deteriorations with a pose of imperturbability. The dandies, who are the final, decadent flowering of their tribes, were expected to project an illusion of control in a changing, disintegrating society: to combine astute reaction with a relaxed demeanour and facial expression. All at Danielstown are in that sense dandies, operating under a dire stress which can never be shown. Lois and Laurence are simply the ultimate versions, who sense that being a dandy is yet another role, and who protect themselves against this humiliation by so distancing themselves from their relations that even their existence takes on the quality of a performance. Finding all about them strange on principle, they are doomed to isolation.

Lois and Laurence know that it is the dandy's tragedy to be able to play every part except his or her own, to become a martyr to performance. The available forms always seem to be appropriate to a prior experience, and never to this one. Their styles end up overriding the very experiences they should embody. Elizabeth Bowen noted how this decadence had manifested itself in Anglo-Irish writing, leading real people to make over their lives in terms of available literary images, whether Ascendancy Gothic or peasant buffoon:

> Propaganda was probably at its most powerful before there was a name for it. Both classes in Ireland saw themselves in this mirror: the gentry became more dashing, the lower classes more comic. We are, or can become at any moment, the most undignified race on earth — while there is a gallery, we must play to it. (*BC*, p. 194)

The relation between the Irish and English has been endlessly complicated by such play-acting, 'a mixture of showing off and suspicion, nearly as bad as sex'. The ambivalence felt by Bowen towards the English is, in the end (*HP*, p. 94), based on an outraged conviction that only the Anglo-Irish had, in the twentieth century, the courage still to live the myth of a traditional England. The property which had given them their high social position was, however, now preventing them from keeping it up, a bitter dandiacal paradox first recorded by Oscar Wilde, and crystallised by Bowen when she defined an Irish estate as 'something between a *raison d'être* and a predicament' (*CI*, p. 161).

Like all dandies, the Anglo-Irish were reluctant occupiers of the role, but once committed to it, they discharged it with verve:

> Husbands and wives struggled, shoulder to shoulder, to keep the estate anything like solvent. . . . The big house people were handicapped . . . by their pride, by their indignation at their decline and by their divorce from the countryside in whose heart their struggle was carried on. They would have been surprised to receive pity. I doubt, as a matter of fact, that they ever pitied themselves. . . . It is, I think, to the credit of the big house people that they concealed their struggles with such nonchalance. (*CI*, p. 161)

This is is, of course, an implied rebuke to those natives who put on the 'poor mouth' as a means of coping with impoverishment. But Bowen is also making the point that property, like an assumed style, helps to uplift morale and behaviour. A house for her is never a mere setting, but a coded set of instructions as to how its occupants should behave. The whining of the mendicant peasant, like the destructive rage of the rebel, might be traced to their lack of such a civilising influence: 'I submit that the power-loving temperament is more dangerous when it either prefers or is forced to operate in what is materially a void. We have everything to dread from the dispossessed'(*BC*, p. 338). That sentiment is wonderfully multivalent, since it also anticipates the autocratic madness of certain Anglo-Irish dispossessed, barking, like Beckett's Pozzo, their orders into an empty, contextless space.

The problem for those who choose to live only by style is that their performance is always liable to break down: the refusal to register suffering can all too easily shade into a reluctance to feel anything at all. It is summarised in the title of another of Elizabeth Bowen's novels: the death of the heart. Often this refusal of feeling, strangely compounded of inexperience and disillusion, is set against a background of social disintegration. Like Beckett's clowns, Bowen's ladies and gentlemen find themselves caught in a crisis of perpetual anticipation followed by inevitable disappointment, with all their days an expensive preparation for some splendid epiphany which never transpires. The dandy who begins with a taste for the heroic soon finds that there is no theatre in which to enact heroism, and so he or she is driven back into the studio and drawing-room, there to bemoan such frustration. Perhaps the most finished example of the type in nineteenth-century literature is Flaubert's Frédéric Moreau, a figure who arises in the interregnum between a lost *ancien régime* and its replacement by a clear new code. Still touched by romantic theory, Moreau can nonetheless feel the emptiness within; his plight is to be sure that society is a fraud, and yet to be unsure whether the self that makes this diagnosis is any better. Refusing all risk, he permits the world to overwhelm him. 'What have I to do with the world?', he asks in the manner of Lois Farquar. 'Others struggle after riches, fame, power — I have no occupation.'

Each self with which Frédéric Moreau experiments is not sustainable for long, for the intelligence which tells him that the world is corrupt is used finally and most formidably against himself. What makes him a poignant figure is also what makes Lois and Laurence so moving. If Laurence is a reminder that the dandy is forever in danger of falling into cynicism, Lois is a warning that the dandy must cultivate illusions, even after the chance to entertain any illusions has been lost. 'Illusions are art, and it is by art that we live, if we do,' wrote Bowen.[13] This is the option taken up by Lois. On one side of her is the cynic Laurence; on the other is the sentimental Livvy, who thinks *Mélisande* a beautiful poem and who marries the first soldier who crosses her path. Apart from the temptation to lapse into cynicism, the dandy may also be beguiled into indulging rather than transcending the self; if feeling can be denied by an assumed imperturbability, it can also be dissipated into easy sentiment by a realist, whose very nose seems already too 'experienced'. Lois, a true dandy, remains suspended between codes and worlds.

As did her creator, who remained a wanderer to the end, Elizabeth Bowen saw herself as a being without final context, and she understood the desperation behind the attempt to build a world on nothing but an illusion of style. This had been the complex fate of the Anglo-Irish from the outset, but it was the last ones like herself who lived it most fully:

> Tradition is broken. Temperament, occupation, success or failure, marriage, or active nervous hostility to an original *milieu* have made nomads of us. The rules we learnt in childhood are as useless, as impossible to take with us, as the immutable furniture in the family house.[14]

Yet, in that very disavowal of a native background or identity, she becomes a voice for all those uprooted, dispossessed Irish, from the Gaelic earls who fled in 1607, through the rapparees and exiled Fenians of later centuries, down to the Joyce and Beckett who had to put themselves at a distance from Ireland in order to convince themselves that the place had ever existed.

For the dandy's tragedy turns out to have been the story of the bards who woke up to find themselves wandering *spailpíní*, and of gentry who were reborn as tramps. All such nomads know the truth of Wilde's aphorism: that the first duty in life was to adopt a pose, a style, a way of being in the world, and what the second duty was nobody had yet discovered. Erecting a fragile world of words in the midst of the surrounding disorder, these artists were all hybrids, with that raffishness which is always the other side of the dandy's elegance. Bowen saw such complex persons as 'never being certain that they are not crooks, never certain that their passports are quite in order',[15] and above all, like those dandies who were prone to facial twitches, 'unnerved by the slightest thing'. That such a description applies as much to Gaelic as to Anglo-Irish writers and leaders may well be what makes Bowen the Aodhagán Ó Rathaille of her time and class. The great Gaelic poet who refused to call abjectly for help had his counterpart in the woman who, when she drove from Bowen's Court for the last time, refused to look back. The old order left her as stranded as any of her characters, and the new offered no place, so she was left with no choice but to invent herself:

I think we are curiouly self-made creatures, carrying our personal worlds around with us like snails their shells, and at the same time adapting to wherever we are . . . cagey, recalcitrant, on the run, bristling with reservations and arrogances that one doesn't show.[16]

Abbreviations

TLS	*The Last September* (1929), Harmondsworth: Penguin, 1987
BC	*Bowen's Court*, London: Longmans, 1942
TS	*The Shelbourne*, London: 1951
PC	*Pictures and Conversations*, London: Allen Lane, 1975

Notes and References

1 Quoted in Victoria Glendinning, *Elizabeth Bowen: Portrait of a Writer*, Harmondsworth: Penguin, 1985, p. 12.
2 Quoted in Edwin J. Kenney, *Elizabeth Bowen*, Lewisburg: Bucknell University Press, 1975, p. 23.
3 Ibid., pp 92-3.
4 Quoted in Glendinning, op. cit., pp 120-1.
5 Ibid., pp 164-5.
6 Ibid., p. 117.
7 Quoted in Kenney, op. cit., p. 38.
8 Glendinning, op. cit., p. 206.
9 Quoted in ibid., p. 160.
10 Walter Benjamin, *Charles Baudelaire: A Lyric Poet in the Era of High Capitalism*, trans. London: Harry Zohn, 1983, p. 74.
11 Ibid., p. 75.
12 Ibid., pp 95-6.
13 Quoted in Kenney, op. cit., p. 18.
14 Quoted ibid., pp 23-4.
15 Quoted in Glendinning, op. cit., p. 139.
16 Quoted ibid., p. 139.

7 Sodom and Begorrah, or Game to the Last

Inventing Michael MacLiammoir

ÉIBHEAR WALSHE

INTRODUCTION

For nearly fifty years Michael MacLiammoir, actor, dramatist, painter, designer, Gaelic scholar, theatre manager (and Corkman), dominated Irish theatre with his programme of experimental, poetic and continental dramas. In his own Gate Theatre, founded in 1928 with his partner, the Englishman Hilton Edwards, MacLiammoir provided a less insular, more cosmopolitan alternative to the state-subsidised Abbey Theatre and maintained a counter-balance to the peasant dramas and rustic comedies of establishment theatre with a programme of Wilde and Coward, Ibsen and Anouilh. In their own words, the aims of the Gate Theatre were to 'have in Dublin a permanent company presenting dramas of all nationalities, to experiment in new methods of production and design and to widen the sphere of Irish activity in the theatre.'[1] Terence Brown, in his *Ireland: A Social and Cultural History* considers MacLiammoir's contribution to Irish cultural life in the following terms: 'Only the work of a few individual poets, novelists and artists of the nineteen-twenties gave any hint that the dismal obscurity that Shaw feared might not envelop the country, as with MacLiammoir's presenting European drama at his Gate Theatre and his Irish language theatre in Galway.'[2]

Just as significant, MacLiammoir was also that most unique of figures within post-independence Ireland: the openly homosexual public figure. In a state where homosexual acts were criminalised until 1993, and the

150

homoerotic was censored and expunged from all official literary and cultural discourse, MacLiammoir and his partner Edwards survived, and even flourished, as Ireland's only visible gay couple. A strikingly handsome man in his youth, MacLiammoir maintained his looks into old age, Dorian-like, with the aid of paint and powder, and, theatrical, vivid, contrived, his face and figure were a familiar and popular sight on the streets of Dublin. This was no mean achievement within a culture where in 1941 Kate O'Brien, MacLiammoir's friend and contemporary, had an entire novel banned for one homoerotic sentence. When MacLiammoir died in 1978, the President of Ireland attended his funeral, as did the Taoiseach and several government ministers, while Hilton Edwards was openly deferred to and sympathised with as chief mourner.

Yet Michael MacLiammoir, Cork-born Irish actor and writer never actually existed. It was a name and a personal history conjured up by London-born actor Alfred Willmore, when he left England for Ireland in 1917. Alfred Willmore, born in Kensal Green in London in 1899, had no Irish connections whatsoever. He had been a success as a child actor, working with Beerbohm Tree amongst others and then had attended art college at the Slade School. However, just before graduating from the Slade, Willmore abandoned his studies and went travelling. In the short term, Willmore was fleeing Britain because of conscription and possibly because of the attentions of an older, wealthy, lover; as his biographer Christopher Fitzsimons argues, 'There is no reason to doubt that as Alfred's seventeenth birthday approached he would have been dreading the arrival of his call-up papers.'[3] More acutely, he was also seeking, in the aftermath of the Wilde trials, an acceptable persona within which to be both homosexual and, at the same time, visible. Alan Sinfield, in his study *The Wilde Century*, contends that a particular and threatening concept of 'the Homosexual' derived itself from Wilde's public persona and was implicated in his disgrace:

> The dominant twentieth-century queer identity, I will argue, has been
> constructed in this kind of process, mainly out of elements that came
> together at the Wilde trials, effeminacy, leisure, idleness, immorality, lux-
> ury, decadence and aestheticism.[4]

To escape association with this newly forged deviant sexual role, Willmore reversed Wilde's own journey of self-consummation by quitting London for Dublin, embracing Celticism, and remaking himself as an Irishman. Thus he found in the role of the Irish mystic artist a refutation of the taint of Wildeian aestheticism and decadence.

Throughout his life, in his various autobiographical writings, MacLiammoir was to tell and retell the narrative of this youthful decision to leave

London and to adopt Dublin as his theatrical base (each retelling involving a creative reordering of the narrative to accommodate and to justify MacLiammoir's assumed mask or persona). 'Here is London, a huge impersonal web of shadow and movement and like a vast motherly hen, the night broods and waits. . . . Home again to Ireland, to a new Ireland, maybe' (*AFH*, p. 25).

In essence, Alfred Willmore reconstructed himself as the neo-Celtic thespian Michael MacLiammoir, a disciple of Yeats and of the 'Celtic Twilight', because the Yeatsian mask would enable Willmore to dissent and separate from British masculinist heterosexuality. In other words, with the shadow of Wilde and the Wilde trials making the homoerotic suspect and questionable in Britain, the Yeatsian mode of artistic being offered a more acceptable role for the sexually ambiguous actor and dramatist, and so Willmore reinvented himself, taking on the mantle of the Celtic Revival. (Wilmore was not the only Englishman to reject or subvert his nationality because of his sexuality, and I would suggest something of a shared sense of alienation in the case of the spies, Burgess, Philby and Blunt.) However, to maintain this fictive persona, MacLiammoir's autobiographies turn on a series of evasions and screenings, obscuring his English origins and veiling his sexual identity, delicately treading a balance between artistic licence and downright 'fiction', i.e. invention.

(Perhaps a few words about MacLiammoir's disposition towards creative autobiography would be appropiate here. An attitude towards accuracy and exactitude in autobiographical writings is defined generously by Rebecca West, writing of Ford Madox Ford. West's view of Ford was that, although he was a fantasist, he was not a liar: 'Liars see facts as they are and transform them into fantasies, but in Ford's case, facts changed into fantasies in the very instant of their impact on his senses.'[5] MacLiammoir, like the consummate actor he was, saw his autobiographies as spontaneous creations, facts changing into roles as soon as he conjures them up. Each successive work of self-invention charts a lifelong journey towards validating a gay sensibility and homosexual identity.)

In this essay I have selected a few of MacLiammoir's dramatic and autobiographical writings for examination: *All for Hecuba* (1946), *An Oscar of No Importance* (1968), and *Enter a Goldfish* (1977), all volumes of autobiography, and two of his plays, *The Importance of Being Oscar* (1963) and *Prelude on Kasbeck Street* (1973). In concentrating on these particular texts to the exclusion of others, I intend to isolate those writings dealing directly with sexual identity, and the essay will therefore explore the strategies by which MacLiammoir accommodates himself within an Irish literary and cultural context.

Further to this, I will also argue that, once established as a neo-Yeatsian, and having written plays like *Diarmuid agus Grainne* (1935) and *Oidhche Bealtaine* [May Eve] (1932), and a volume of autobiography, *All for Hecuba* (1946), MacLiammoir discovered that such a persona was becoming less and less tenable. Therefore his theatrical work, especially during the 1940s and 1950s, became increasingly arid and uninspired. It is my contention that the emblematic figure of Wilde in MacLiammoir's memoir *An Oscar of No Importance* and in his one-man show *The Importance of Being Oscar* licensed the actor to bring his dissident sexuality more and more to the fore. In my view, his final play *Prelude on Kasbeck Street*, and his last volume of autobiography, *Enter a Goldfish*, are vitalised by a new centrality of the homoerotic.

By way of contextualising Michael MacLiammoir's visibility within the Irish popular imagination, I have subtitled this essay, 'Game to the Last', partly to reflect the continuous inventiveness with which MacLiammoir approached questions of sexual and national identity, and partly because of an autobiographical incident. MacLiammoir's gayness was so well known in Ireland that I can recall first hearing his name as a child, at a dinner party at home when one of the (male) guests told a joke about Michael and Hilton, walking in St Stephen's Green, with Michael falling into the duck pond. A drowning Michael calls to Hilton: 'A buoy, for God's sake, throw me a buoy!' — to which an admiring Hilton responds: 'Ah, dear Michael — game to the last!'

WILD(E) SONS FLEEING FROM THEIR MOTHER
(DENIS JOHNSTON, *The Old Lady Says No!*)

By his own account and also by that of his biographers, MacLiammoir's meeting with Hilton Edwards in June of 1927, in Enniscorthy, Co. Wexford, was a pivotal moment in the construction of the MacLiammoir persona. Private and public role, national and sexual identity, all of these were re-solved and anchored for MacLiammoir in his partnership with Edwards. (Alfred Willmore's decision to remake himself as the Corkman Michael MacLiammoir may have had something to do with the fact that he and Edwards, out of work and penniless, moved on directly from Wexford to Cork city, formulating plans for a new Irish theatre in the southern capital.)

In a professional sense, the actor/designer found the ideal director, with Edwards's exacting production values checking and harnessing Mac-Liammoir's excessive lyricism and self-dramatisation. On a personal level, the two were to live together for fifty years. However, in terms of MacLiam-moir's literary reincarnation as poet of the 'Celtic Twilight', Edwards pro-vided the perfect Saxon foil against which MacLiammoir could define his 'Irishness'. Irishness, for MacLiammoir, was a gendered racial identity, something sexualised. 'Ireland reacted to little but political frenzy. . . . A feline creature, I thought, Ireland is like a cat' (*AFH*, p. 215).

In all his autobiographical writings MacLiammoir plays this game again and again, the native-born son explaining the essentially inexplicable nature of Ireland and the Celtic imagination to the interrogating Englishman.

> We would pass by thatched whitewashed houses that looked rose-coloured in the moonlight, and by brown running streams whose voices seemed like the rushing of the world through space and, at times, I would try to explain Ireland to him. (*AFH*, p. 30)

> How, indeed, could we foresee, Ireland or I, that he, with the Englishman's uncanny knack for turning tables, would make both of us work far harder than we had bargained.[6]

(In actuality, it seems from biographical evidence that Edwards had more real Irish ancestry than Willmore.)

Added to this is a denial of any English connections. His rejection of London is seen as a racial necessity, the striving of the Celtic soul to free itself from the stranglehold of metropolitan culture:

> I had been brought to London an infant in a holland overall, and as a stage child in a sailor suit, I had loved it and then, adolescent, I had hated it again and fought to escape and here I was in a pin-stripe suit in 1935, a self-made alien, breathing the air that might have been my own. And I wondered was I right to choose the narrow Irish road and I know now that the choice was inevitable. Even my partner, had he wished, could not have changed that in me, though in all else I was putty in his hands. For good or for evil, the Irish way was part of myself, there really had been no choice at all. (*AFH*, p. 229)

Linked to this game of interdependent racial opposition is MacLiammoir's notion of sexual difference, a notion only made completely overt in his last writings. It is my contention that his invention of a necessary dialectic between Saxon and Celt in his relationship with Edwards reflected his parallel belief in a dichotomy between 'normal' masculinity and 'queer' or 'so' masculinity, thus rendering homoerotic desire explicable. The modes of racial characteristic, of binary opposition invoked by MacLiammoir in his creation of an artistic persona, especially in *All for Hecuba*, become modes of sexual opposition in later writings such as *Enter a Goldfish* and *Prelude on Kasbeck Street*, where MacLiammoir's 'theory' of homosexual attraction is made explicit.

ALL FOR HECUBA

> It is easier to remember when the eyes are closed.
> MICHAEL MACLIAMMOIR, *All for Hecuba*, p. 1

More than most autobiographies, *All for Hecuba* (1946) is a self-justifying, self-mythifying confection. MacLiammoir is at pains to find justification for the course of his life and career up to this point. This justification covers several aspects of his life and his artistic manifesto. Firstly, he sanctions his invented Irishness by dreaming up a Cork childhood and figuring Yeats as artistic mentor and muse. Secondly, he negotiates with his dissident sexuality through his evocation of his dead friend, Máire O'Keefe and her subsequent replacement with Edwards. Finally, he feels bound to explain his theatrical allegiance to Dublin and the Gate Theatre and a growing sense of artistic deadlock. In this first volume of auto-biography MacLiammoir turns this self-justification to his own advantage, reinterpreting his life as a Yeatsian quest for spiritual identity. His narrative style is a composite of name-dropping, tragic self-importance, casual racism, profound 'luvviness', evasion and invention, starting with his opening asser-tion 'I remember my mother, my father, my four sisters and a room that overlooks the river in Cork' (*AFH*, p. 1). As he retraces (and reinvents) his career from child actor to leading actor/manager, MacLiammoir is at pains to establish his connections within European theatre, casually placing Coward, Novello, Bernhardt and others in orbit around him and stressing the immense privilege he was affording Dublin by remaining there, as part of his Yeatsian programme.

MacLiammoir's theatrical career can be seen to have had three distinct phases: the Yeatsian phase — the 1930s and 1940s; an interlude of stagnation — the 1950s; and finally the Wildeian phase — the 1960s and 1970s. The nature of this Yeatsian programme needs to be considered. As I have said, Yeats afforded him a secure artistic mode within which to become an aesthete without the taint of Wildeian sexuality: 'Celticism has swept through, paling the colours and purging the fatty richness of a masterpiece and turning Wilde's monstrous orchid into a wet bulrush' (*AFH*, p. 45). MacLiammoir claims Yeats as an emblematic muse figure ('I had read Yeats' "Ireland and the Arts" for the first time at fourteen' (*AFH*, p. 32) and has Hilton Edwards railing jealously against the overweening influence Yeats has had on MacLiammoir, this attack, significantly, taking place on Howth head: 'Yeats was your god. He had shaped everything in your programme before you met him' (*AFH*, p. 215). Yet, how precisely did MacLiammoir engage with Yeats as a mentor figure within his own theatrical activity?

In *All for Hecuba* MacLiammoir places his decision to live in Dublin in the context of the death of his close friend and soulmate, Máire O'Keefe (This close relationship would, perhaps, have been something of a surprise for an Irish and English reading public, who knew MacLiammoir primarily in terms of his partnership with Edwards. It is only in later autobiographical work that MacLiammoir is more honest about the nature of his close attachment to her.) His deep grief at her death and his longing for Ireland is couched in Yeatsian terms: 'One vivid dream I had, a dream of a dark and well-beloved mountain at home, with a sky of lead and amethyst overhead. In Ireland I should awaken and life would begin again once more' (*AFH*, p. 23). There is, undoubtedly, some manifestation of Yeatsian influence in MacLiammoir's *Diarmuid and Grainne* (1935), an influence later acknowledged in his one-man show *I Must Be Talking to my Friends* and in his study *W. B. Yeats and his World* (1977), written with the poet Eavan Boland.[7]

However, it is important to note that in *All for Hecuba* there is no accounting for MacLiammoir's lack of contact with Yeats's own Abbey Theatre, or for the profoundly divergent programmes in these two Dublin theatres, or even for the fact that MacLiammoir, during Yeats's time at the Abbey, only appeared in two productions. His one recorded meeting with Yeats reflects something of the unease of their relationship:

> But I felt that he only half approved of me as an exponent of the Celtic Twilight, which in those days of self-conscious virility was at its lowest ebb, and I, in my heart, agreed with him. These were no times for echoing the vanished rhapsodies of the Nineties. (*AFH*, p. 70)

Towards the close of *All for Hecuba*, MacLiammoir writes of the death of Yeats and, referring to Ireland's artistic soul, asks the question 'What new stamp would be pressed into the changing wax, softened again into shapelessness with the death of the poet?' (*AFH*, p. 229). MacLiammoir may have been talking about Ireland and a loss of direction in terms of literary and cultural matters but there is also a sense that Yeats proved an unsatisfactory and inadequate personal muse for MacLiammoir himself.

He makes brave assertions about the need for a cosmopolitan theatre in Dublin:

> In the past, everyone in Ireland who could do anything ran off to London. We've given Shaw to that great smoking monster and Sheridan and Wilde and a hundred others. Think of the capital Dublin would have been if they had stayed at home. (*AFH*, p. 32)

— but nonetheless there was a sense that, by the beginning of the 1950s the Gate had failed to sustain itself as an integrated and consistent force within Irish theatre. As Terence Brown comments, 'Neither managed quite to create that sense of new awakening that had characterised the early years of the Irish literary theatre.'[8] In *All for Hecuba* MacLiammoir has Hilton attacking him for his obsession with his supposed Irishness, calling him a 'slave to racial fetishism' and blaming their enforced residence in Dublin for a certain staleness in their work. In his pamphlet *Theatre in Ireland* (1950), published by the Cultural Relations Committee of Ireland, MacLiammoir allows this: 'Yet that a period of uncertainty, even perhaps of stagnation, in the Irish theatre and its literature may be at hand seems likely.'[9]

There is, I would argue, another possible interpretation for this perceived sense of stagnation. Yeats dwindled as a source of inspiration for MacLiammoir because, ultimately, despite his protests ('Never, as far as I can tell, has he [Wilde] influenced my life, my thought or my action')[10] he found Wilde to be a more direct source of personal revelation. One of the code terms for the homosexual in MacLiammoir's time would have been 'unspeakables of the Oscar Wilde sort',[11] as employed by E. M. Forster in his novel *Maurice*. As MacLiammoir's career progressed into the 1960s the issue became one of making the unspeakable speak for him again.

THE IMPORTANCE OF BEING OSCAR

> Oscar Wilde has been a shorthand notation for one way of apprehending and living our sexual and emotional potential.
>
> ALAN SINFIELD [12]

Given that the name, and the texts, of Wilde had been employed throughout the twentieth century as a shorthand or code for homosexual identity, MacLiammoir's reading of Wilde, in his one-man show *The Importance of Being Oscar* (1963), was, as I will demonstrate, a very particular reading, shaped by MacLiammoir's need to find an acceptable version of Wilde and of his fate. Contemporary lesbian and gay theorists have been reclaiming Wilde as a powerfully disruptive figure, subverting through the dynamic of the homoerotic. For example, in *Sexual Dissidence* Jonathan Dollimore takes as Wilde's essential impulse the impetus towards a transgressive aesthetic:

> For Gide transgression is in the name of a desire and identity rooted in the natural, the sincere and the authentic; Wilde's transgressive is the reverse: insincerity, in-authenticity and unnaturalness become the liberating attributes of de-centred identity and desire and inversion becomes central to Wilde's expression of this aesthetic.[13]

However, in this version MacLiammoir fixes on the presentation of Wilde as tragic hero, with Hilton Edwards introducing the published text of the performance in the following terms: 'It shows him to have been aware, from the first, of the inevitability of his tragedy.'[14] In *The Importance of Being Oscar*, MacLiammoir chose to distance himself from Wilde, narrating his life and his writings rather than impersonating Wilde directly, and this allowed him to construct a Wilde of his own making. Edwards and MacLiammoir take Wilde's fall from grace as their theme and see that fall as consequent on his fatal glorification of the erotic: 'I did but touch the honey of romance/And must I lose a soul's inheritance?' (*IBO*, p. 15). However, the honey of Wilde's romance, in this version, is predominantly heterosexual, and Wilde's key act of transgression, his infatuation with Bosie, is referred to only once, in one telling phrase: 'That Tiger Life' (*IBO*, p. 37).

Setting a tone of world-weary despair and ennui, MacLiammoir keeps all his sexual referents gender-specific. In the first half of the presentation, Wilde's passion for Lily Langtry and his love for Constance, his wife, is recounted, and MacLiammoir's readings from *Salome* and *The Picture of Dorian Gray* concentrate on Herod's lust for Salome rather than on Salome's eroticisation of Iokanaan's body, and on Dorian's murderous instincts rather than on Lord Henry's and Basil's love for Dorian's beauty. At this point MacLiammoir chose to break the work, and, in the limbo of the interval, the 'Tiger Life' and the resulting trials are presumed to have taken place. In the second act, the consequences of Wilde's act are concentrated on, rendered with pathos and melodrama. Wilde's dignity in prison and in exile, his composed yet passionate reproach to Bosie in 'De Profundis', the stark anguished compassion of *The Ballad of Reading Gaol*, all serve to increase a sympathy with the erring outcast. His final fable, *The Doer of Good*, although dealing with lust and the despair of the erotic, is firmly normative in its gendering.

The Importance of Being Oscar came as a much-needed boost for MacLiammoir and Edwards, providing them with widespread commercial and critical success. This success led to a series of American and European tours and, eventually, a television dramatisation. However, playing Wilde, or at least interpreting Wilde, also led to questions that MacLiammoir was not quite ready to answer. In *An Oscar of No Importance*, he recounts an incident during his South African tour of the show when a woman journalist challenged him directly on the subject of Wilde's sexuality and, by implication, his own:

> 'You', began a small, plump, very firm-looking lady, gazing at me through her spectacles as though she would burrow into the depths of my soul, 'are going to act as Oscar Wilde?' 'Not act as him: I try to interpret him.' 'Well then, I would be interested to know, as you have chosen him rather

than another writer, what is your own attitude to the question of male homosexuality?' I gazed back at her in a prolonged moment of silence, as of deep cool waters whose apparent tranquillity might be haunted by many sharks. . . . Did she mean among cattle or human beings? But I never received an answer. (*IBO*, p. 138)

Neither, in point of fact, does the reader — yet! Although MacLiammoir and Edwards felt sufficiently confident as to the climate of public opinion in relation to Wilde (the 1950s being an important decade for the republishing of Wilde's texts and his rehabilitation as an artist), and were also emboldened by the success of the one-man show, there is evidence that they were still unwilling to highlight the homoerotic in their theatrical work. Indeed, it was not until MacLiammoir was in the final decade of his life and of his work that such a project was attempted. In the meantime his memoir, *An Oscar of No Importance*, is a revealing account of the way in which the one-man show on Wilde brought MacLiammoir to reckon with the nature of Wilde's sexuality and the implications for his own creativity.

AN OSCAR OF NO IMPORTANCE

The point is not just that the name of Wilde was a way to make the silence speak but that the silence didn't need to speak until Wilde's name was introduced.

ALAN SINFIELD[15]

In many ways *An Oscar of No Importance* (1968) is, as the title suggests, a mirror text for *The Importance of Being Oscar*, in that all of the evasions of the stage play are dealt with directly in the memoir. In considering the relation of the play to the memoir, it seems as if MacLiammoir found the public arena of theatre, as yet, an unsafe place in which to speculate on Wilde's sexual nature. (This issue of sexuality within the public domain of Irish theatre is one I wish to deal with later.)

As I have demonstrated, the play concentrates on the normative aspects of Wilde's life and writings; the memoir has no such reticence. MacLiammoir opens his narrative with surprising directness, relating a childhood incident where he quizzed his embarrassed father as to the exact nature of Wilde's unspeakable crime, eventually provoking this outburst: 'What was wrong with Oscar Wilde? . . . He turned young men into women' (*ONI*, p. 1). In the course of the memoir MacLiammoir explores his professional and personal bonds with Wilde — 'that magician whose name was my secret for evermore' (p. 4) — and allows himself to theorise on the significance of sexual difference in Wilde's life. Here he claims a more direct kinship with Wilde than in previous writings: 'Wilde was the invisible but by no means inaudible bond who made the road I was facing less chilly' (p. 24).

In relating the process by which he devised the one-man show with Edwards, MacLiammoir incorporates a quite candid and intensive account of Wilde's sexuality into the memoir, but adopts a tone of objectivity throughout. MacLiammoir's attitude to Wilde is one of worldly understanding — 'All right, so he was "So" (the twenties slang-word for the contemporary word 'queer' and almost as offensively overdone)' (p. 29) — and his account of Wilde's sexual history is forthright and clear-sighted:

> He had been initiated into homosexual practices, as the legend has asserted, by Robert Ross himself, and difficult as it may be for the mind of today wholeheartedly to believe that this was in truth his very first experiment, there is a great deal of evidence to show that he had been in fact passionately in love with his own wife, and had been strongly attracted throughout his earlier manhood by many other women. It was likely too that it was the experience with Ross that decided him to accept himself for the future completely as a pederast and to lose all his previous interest in the opposite sex. Robert Ross stated that the affair began in 1886, the same year that English law adopted the statute that nine years later was to cause Wilde's arrest and imprisonment: one could be forgiven for wondering could it have been the very same day that Queen Victoria signed the statute? at the very same moment, it may be, when Wilde decided to respond to the enamoured Ross, so closely the web seems woven about him. (*ONI*, p. 62)

Much can be deduced from the above account of MacLiammoir's own concept of homosexual attraction, a concept that also informs his later works, including *Enter a Goldfish* and *Prelude on Kasbeck Street*. Same-sex desire, as MacLiammoir presents it, is a matter of choice, a choice made from a bisexual nature, and he is anxious to frame the homoerotic within the context of heterosexuality. MacLiammoir makes a distinction — and a necessary duality — between the 'born invert' and the 'convert', a distinction that surfaces again in his later writings. He places Wilde within the second category and speculates as to whether Wilde's very public and very pronounced 'Tiger Life' was, in fact, a reaction to his earlier heterosexuality. 'Is it the enthusiasm of the convert? This, in Wilde's case, was perversely heightened by a violent and very personal sense of sin, which, in the born invert, is absent' (p. 63). In a sense, MacLiammoir finds Wilde's blatant disregard for potential notoriety disturbing and seeks to explain the almost suicidal disregard that Wilde had for public opinion and for the legal consequences of his sexual transgressions. Side by side with this unease at Wilde's supreme confidence is a need to find such openness commendable:

> Yet how fortunate he was. Not merely because without the catastrophe he would be remembered as the author of a handful of under-rated and little-read books and plays, but because, by the very nature of the scandal that ripped the last rags of decency from him, posthumous writers can discuss him and his work with complete frankness, as no other homosexual artist, leading a discreet and reasonable private life, can, even in our time, be discussed. Unless they pass into a vast immortality, of course, like Socrates or Shakespeare or Sappho or Michelangelo or Leonardo. It does not matter very much what we say of them: like the sun they are so undeniable, and like the sun they were born so long ago. But with later and lesser artists, the case is different, the life they had so wisely and so prudently hidden from the world succeeds at once in hiding their shameful secret from the world and in forever preventing their chroniclers from giving a full-length portrait. 'We may gather', one may read of many a splendid man or woman, 'that many slanderous rumours were circulated during the lifetime of this artist; that he (or she) was addicted to unnatural tendencies, and that the friendship with so-and-so was in fact . . . There is, of course, no solid foundation for such a theory.' These hints give us little more than a respectable retouched passport photograph: their discretion leaves us with a sense of incompleteness, and so we begin to guess, and to guess about the fundamental nature of the artist is a depressing and vulgar waste of time. (*ONI*, p. 131)

It seems as if MacLiammoir almost envies Wilde his open, unambiguous sexual identity, an openness not as available to MacLiammoir 'even in our time', or so he hints. In this memoir MacLiammoir is prepared to discuss Wilde's 'sin' frankly and openly, but always as the impartial, uninvolved outsider, rarely allowing his own connection with Wilde to surface, and keeping his own life apart. As narrator, he presents himself as judge and unbiased arbiter of moral conduct, fair-minded, rational, methodical, stripping away the prejudices against Wilde's aberrant sexual life and finding in his disaster a kind of achievement:

> Did I believe him to have been a bad man who, like so many bad men, provide an interesting study in abnormality? I do not believe him to be a bad man. His only 'badness' in my eyes is that he failed to fulfil the destiny imposed upon him by potentialities unguessed at even by those who idolised him at the hour of his triumph, perhaps especially by these. He himself was aware of them. Spiritually, if one may be allowed an outmoded, outworn term, he was a failure. Yet failure itself, bowed down with broken dreams, is essentially a part of him. (*ONI*, p. 223)

Yet, here and there, MacLiammoir lets his own personal stake in Wilde (and in Wilde's sexual nature) become apparent. At one point, discussing the difficulties of staging and playing *The Importance of Being Oscar*, and the tension brought to his relationship with Edwards, MacLiammoir confesses: 'Suddenly I saw what *The Importance of Being Oscar* threatened to do to our lives in the theatre. 'And our personal lives, too,' he [Hilton] added when I spoke of this' (p. 47).

PRELUDE ON KASBECK STREET

MacLiammoir's last stage play, produced in 1973, is also his most candidly 'out' play, and one where he finally permits himself to discuss the nature of same-sex desire on stage. The question must be asked: why, after forty years of a highly visible partnership, did MacLiammoir and Edwards wait so long to stage a play like this? Their biographer, Christopher Fitzsimons, offers the opinion that 'Had it been produced thirty-years before, it would have caused an uproar. . . . Both Edwards and MacLiammoir genuinely believed they were taking a risk.'[16] Even with the changing climate of public opinion on the subject of same-sex relationships and the change of legislation in Britain in 1967, MacLiammoir approached his subject with circumspection. As a result, *Prelude on Kasbeck Street* is, in parts, an equivocal play. Edwards, who directed the play, noticed this and wrote: 'There is a tendency to fear the theme and to dance off into comedy which is inclined to make the comedy obtrusive.'[17] However much MacLiammoir 'feared' the theme, it is significant that, at the end of his career, he was finally prepared to present the homoerotic on stage.

For *Prelude on Kasbeck Street* MacLiammoir chooses a contemporary setting, the 1970s, and a cosmopolitan milieu, Paris, to address connected issues of sexual and national identity. The protagonist, Serge, a celebrated ballet dancer, is also a displaced and reconstituted national subject, having started life as John Joseph Cassidy. Within this acquired pseudo-Russian identity, Serge exists both as artist and also as sexually different. The play opens with a violent row between two gay lovers, Serge and his 'companion' Jean-Louis, but this row is in French, thereby screening the vehement passion in their relationship, now on the point of break-up. Although it is mentioned that the lovers have had separate bedrooms and the word companion is used by Serge's housekeeper, Mrs Baty, to describe Jean-Louis, MacLiammoir leaves us in no doubt as to Serge's emotional needs and interests. This is effected through the overt use of symbol, signalling Serge's quest for love, in the title of the play.

The name Kasbeck is a reference to the 1913 ballet *Thamar*, presented by Diaghilev's company in London. MacLiammoir would have seen the ballet as a teenager in London, and here he parallels Serge's life with the historical story of Tamara, Queen of Georgia. Tamara, a tyrant of medieval Georgia, lived and ruled from her castle at the Kasbeck pass, and legend has it that she lured handsome young men into her castle, made love to them, and then had them killed (an historical fabrication, as the real Tamara was a shrewd and successful warrior queen).[18] Serge directly associates himself with this man-eating queen when he relates the legend to his housekeeper, Mrs Baty, thus explaining his attraction for 'normal', i.e. straight, men as being symptomatic of a self-destructive sexual destiny. Serge is the devouring Tamara, always involved with the wrong sort of man, those attracted by his fame and flattered by his attention, but always returning to women as their preferred choice of sexual partner. MacLiammoir is vague as to the true nature of the parallel between Serge and Tamara, but what is clear is that MacLiammoir is using the play to present his own concept of same-sex desire.

In this regard, MacLiammoir's concept of homoerotic attraction is, not surprisingly, very much akin to that of his fellow-countryman Quentin Crisp, who wrote in his memoir *The Naked Civil Servant*: 'Homosexuals set out to capture the love of a 'real' man'. If they succeed, they fail. A man who goes with other men is not what they call a real man.'[19] MacLiammoir replicates his earlier notion of necessary opposition between Celt and Saxon in this drama of sexual politics. This opposition has the effect of creating in Serge, the man who is 'so' or 'queer', a fated propensity to be attracted towards 'normal' men exclusively. This potentially destructive sexual dynamic is the driving force behind the play, and the course of the action follows Serge's attempts to escape this dynamic.

The defence and justification of homosexual desire is provided not by Serge, but by his friend and compatriot, Maggie (Madame Gonzales). When Jean-Louis leaves him, Serge fears loneliness and death because Eros signifies self-defeat for him. He turns to his friend Maggie for consolation. Maggie, another reconstituted national subject, attempts to comfort him by providing a broader perspective on his sexual destiny: 'Isn't your misery partly because of the world's attitude to your sort of person? . . . People always laugh at what they cannot understand. . . . They think your sort of person unnatural' (*PKS*, p. 12).

She continues in her defence of the homoerotic, much as Wilde did, by evoking Shakespeare and Michelangelo as exemplary gay men and admonishes 'the world for turning the whole thing into tart for tart's sake' (*PKS*, p. 14). Invigorated by Maggie's consciousness-raising, Serge gains a sense of empowerment:

> If my sort of person is represented in a book or movie as high or low
> camp, something both comic and contemptible, people will lap it up.
> If it is pornographic, it's acceptable permissiveness. But if it's given one
> shred of dignity or reality, God help us! (*PKS*, p. 14)

In his lament for the lost Jean-Louis, Serge rationalises his own compulsive need for love with someone 'normal', someone unartistic. Maggie
concurs, comparing him directly to Tamara, the man-eater: 'You need a
life companion, what is known as a normal man' (p. 20). (In the dialogue
between Serge and the worldly, sympathetic Maggie, the playwright goes
to great lengths to defend and to exonerate same-sex desire and at one
point nearly trips himself up when he has Maggie say: 'You're not the cheap
promiscuous sort like so many of your tribe, God help them, sure what
else can they do' (p. 22).)

Illustrating MacLiammoir's theory of homosexual attraction, Serge lives
out his sexual and emotional destiny. An American lover turns up, William
Vandam, a straight-identified man who falls in love with Serge primarily
because of his status as a great artist. Vandam is all agog, American and
star-struck by Serge's dancing, and he confesses to Serge that this is his
first homosexual affair. They stay together for six months. Then Serge gets
a bad review and attacks Vandam for not properly understanding his relation with his art, dance. At this crucial moment Vandam confesses that
a former (and hitherto unmentioned) girlfriend has returned and that
therefore he wishes to end his relationship with Serge and return to 'normality'. In returning to the safety of heterosexuality, Vandam is careful to
distance himself completely from any taint of sexual difference: 'I can see
only the tragic part of it because of the world's attitude towards him [Serge]
and his tribe' (p. 53). Furthermore, in retreat from his previous sexual identity, Vandam pretends to Maggie that he and Serge had not been lovers
and she takes this opportunity to admonish him: 'You shock me, Bill,
because you take the same attitude as the world that condemns him and
all the while you're taking an advantage you're ashamed to admit' (p. 53).
(This persona of the 'straight' American lover recurs again in *Enter a Goldfish*,
perhaps reflecting an episode in MacLiammoir's own life.)

With the failure of this affair, Serge resolves to devote himself completely
to his art and embraces solitude, but at the eleventh hour salvation is at
hand with the appearance of another suitor. This new admirer, an older
man and a widower, declares his passion, thus achieving the idealised sexual
conjunction. This 'normal' man, older and assuredly heterosexual, and
therefore beyond possible temptation and fickleness, provides Serge with
the required opposition of 'normal' and 'so'.

MacLiammoir, now too old to play the lead, appeared in the play as
Gonzales, the husband of Maggie (a role notable only for its being written

completely in Spanish). Nevertheless, Serge is MacLiammoir's alter ego, the cosmopolitan aesthete, the tragic diva in search of true love, all of this derived from his earlier memoirs, but transposed to a more contemporary setting. Much of MacLiammoir's final writing turns on this imaginative device, resurrecting the youthful experiences of the child actor and Twenties artist, but revitalising these experiences with a new frankness, a willingness to speak the name of forbidden love or loves.

Finally, a point needs to be made about the place of MacLiammoir's play in the context of gay representation on the modern Irish stage. It would seem that, even after the staging of *Prelude on Kasbeck Street*, the public domain was still considered a dangerous place wherein to depict sexual difference. Although Irish fiction explored the homoerotic more and more openly, with novels like Paul Smith's *Summer Sang in Me* (1975) and John Broderick's *The Trial of Father Dillingham* (1983), theatre still skirted around the edges.[20]

ENTER A GOLDFISH

MacLiammoir's final volume of memoirs, written in the year before his death, was published by Thames & Hudson in July 1977 and received a warm reception from the Irish and English press. However, some reviewers expressed puzzlement at the third-person narrative employed by MacLiammoir. Sheridan Morley in *The Times* wondered if it could be called a novel,

> partly, because some of the details have already been outlined in the rich, if confused, tapestry of MacLiammoir's other writings: more probably, I suspect because it details one or two homosexual and other encounters which even at this late stage the author is not prepared to document more fully.[21]

Another reviewer, the Gate Theatre's celebrated playwright Denis Johnston, also queried this form: 'This persistent vein of anonymity has the peculiar effect of encouraging the reader into a deeper suspicion of the facts than of the fiction.'[22] These questions about the veracity of MacLiammoir's last memoirs are difficult to understand when one considers MacLiammoir's lifelong habit of self-invention. *Enter a Goldfish* is simply the final act in this continual process of self-generated drama, a fictive rendering of a life already completely fictionalised. Ultimately, the new point of departure in this final version, in comparision with all the previous autobiographies, is a new willingness to focus on the homoerotic. MacLiammoir is remaking his life, but this time he is empowered by his encounters with Wilde. Here MacLiammoir uses art to imitate life, inventing a fictional counterpart and protagonist, Martin Weldon; and thus the novel focuses on Martin's artistic and emotional development. This novel, loosely based on MacLiammoir's own life, reveals itself to be more direct and less equivocal than any of his earlier 'confessional' memoirs and relates closely to the issues raised and explored in *Prelude on Kasbeck Street*.

Three vital new elements, all interconnected, are introduced in *Enter a Goldfish*, and each element forms part of the sexual subtext of the novel/memoir: a sexualised father-figure ('Daddy with the Hard Hat'), the exoticism of a Spanish setting, and, finally, openly homoerotic sex scenes. All of these images are gathered into the dream sequence that opens the novel, a sequence repeated again and again throughout the novel, of a father/lover:

> I'm going to bite you / I'm going to bite you / I'm going to bite you / all down here. And the powerful baritone whisper grew louder and softer, the smooth palm stroking the little boy's body under the sheet grew deeper and lighter, and slowly it faded and the child was asleep again. . . . It was Daddy with the Hard Hat. (*EAG*, p. 9)

MacLiammoir follows the childhood and adolescence of Martin Weldon, a child actor and only brother of four older sisters (like MacLiammoir himself); in doing so, he gathers a most revealing grouping of images around the sexualised 'Daddy with the Hard Hat', reflecting many of the sub-conscious fears of an outlawed sexuality. This dream of 'Daddy with the Hard Hat' pursues the protagonist throughout the novel, and this fantasy eroticisation of the patriarchal figure is always followed by the nightmare intervention of the forces of authority and repression, the troops of a police state arriving to punish the sexually different. 'Daddy with the Hard Hat' is, first, the source of erotic pleasure, and, then, the agent of repression.

Significantly, the various occurrences of this nightmare enable Martin to realise his homoerotic desires as the distress of this ordeal drives him into the arms of other men. This following scene, set in Spain, a place of threat and also of erotic promise, is of primary importance in terms of MacLiammoir's writings, as it is his first explicitly related homosexual love scene:

> What was this? Juan whispering in his ear words that he could not hear, was climbing into bed beside him. Ever since Oliver Twist and increasingly often after the opening of *Joseph and his Brethren* his life had been full of grown men who would ask him for his autograph at the stage door and often when left alone with him would kiss and embrace him. He had taken it all for granted and had even wondered, when such favours were neither offered or begged for, what was wrong with the poor gentleman. But never before had something like this occurred. Never

before had any of these admiring and affectionate gentlemen got into bed with him and they were all older and more authoritative than the sixteen-year-old Juan. Never before now had anyone burned his mouth with kiss after kiss until it hurt, or done what Juan was doing now. For Juan, already divested of his own shirt, was alternately stroking and kissing his face and body, and gently pulling off his pyjamas. Ah no, nobody in London had ever gone so far as this, and for a few moments Martin, in whose nature passion and prudery was so often at war together, put up a struggle. But his cousin was too old for him and too resolutely determined and at last the younger of the partners yielded. (*EAG*, p. 109)

Enter a Goldfish, otherwise a tiresome rendering down of MacLiammoir's early life into some sort of family sitcom, is invigorated by a latent frankness in sexual matters. The technique of normalising a damaged and dysfunctional childhood into a picturesque, endearing family saga is shared by other writers (for example, Durrell and Mitford), but his image of 'Daddy with the Hard Hat' tends to subvert the contrivances of this sitcom.

Likewise, his treatment of the adult sexuality of the hero, Martin, mirrors precisely the experiences of Serge in *Prelude on Kasbeck Street*. Martin's encounter with an American lover is paralleled by Serge's affair with Vandam. Here again, MacLiammoir replicates his theory of homosexual attraction between the 'normal' man and the 'so' man:

Since that night in the Calle San Fernando, when the bold brazen Juan Fuentes had forcibly made love to his 'cousin' Martin had been perfectly aware of his own prematurely awakened but undeniably inborn sexual nature. So it was no surprise to him to observe the unmistakable look in the American's eyes, the unmistakable deepening in his voice, when he added to his last words about making friends in French: 'because that is what we are doing, isn't it? Making friends, real friends.' (*EAG*, p. 204)

The American, Robert, proceeds to explain his same-sex desire for Martin in terms that sound suspiciously like ersatz Freudianism, and, in the course of this explanation, Robert seeks justification for his excursion into the world of homoerotic desire. Robert has been jilted by a two-timing girlfriend back home, a variation on the 'I-was-to-be-married-but-she-died' rationalisation of lack of interest in heterosexual desire, and, because of this trauma of erotic disempowerment, has been forced to 'turn' to men for sexual pleasure:

'And since that day, Martin, I've never looked at a woman — in that way, I mean. Couldn't, somehow. Oh, I don't mean because I'm a woman-hater: it was just that I could never trust myself — or any of them — in love. Even the physical urge for them faded away. I turned not with any real ease because I'm not a true born homo — but I turned towards my own sex. But, until today I've never met a single person I felt I could love. Oh, the occasional rather sordid sort of slap-happy affair with some reasonably attractive young effeminate. Then I saw you and you know the rest.' So all things worked out happily for them both and for the next five or six years they spent a lot of time together. (*EAG*, p. 205)

MacLiammoir closes *Enter a Goldfish* with the meeting between Martin Weldon and his future partner, Linden Evans (Hilton, thinly disguised), referring to them as 'the Couple' and prophesying complete personal and professional happiness for them both. More importantly, the ending of the novel indicated the fact that MacLiammoir had reached a point in his writings when public and private discourse could be accommodated within one text. It meant that the homoerotic, ironically that which characterised him most directly in terms of public perception in Ireland, could now be directly articulated in his writings. For MacLiammoir, the lifelong taboo on the love that dare not speak its name had eventually been broken, and the unspeakable was finally made to speak.

Abbreviations

AFH   *All for Hecuba*, London: Methuen, 1946
EAG   *Enter a Goldfish*, London: Thames & Hudson, 1977
IBO   *The Importance of Being Oscar*, Dublin: Dolmen, 1963
ONI   *An Oscar of No Importance*, London: Heinemann, 1968
PKS   *Prelude on Kasbeck Street*, unpublished script, 1973

Notes and References

1   *From Did You Know that the Gate* . . . Gate Theatre programme, 1940, p. 1.
2   Terence Brown, *Ireland: A Social and Cultural History*, London: Fontana, 1981 p. 137.
3   Christopher Fitzsimons, *The Boys*, Dublin: Gill & Macmillan, 1994, p. 41.
4   Alan Sinfield, *The Wilde Century*, London: Cassells, 1994, p. 11.
5   Victoria Glendinning, *Rebecca West: A Life*, New York: Alfred Knopf, 1987, p. 25.
6   Michael MacLiammoir, *Theatre in Ireland*, Dublin: Colm O'Lochlainn, 1950, p. 25.
7   Michael MacLiammoir and Eavan Boland, *W. B. Yeats and his World*, London: Thames and Hudson, 1977.
8   Brown, op. cit., p. 167.
9   Michael MacLiammoir, *Theatre in Ireland*, p. 43.
10 Ibid., p. 222.
11 E. M. Forster, *Maurice*, Harmondsworth: Penguin, 1972, p. 136.
12 Sinfield, op. cit., p. 176.
13 Jonathan Dollimore, *Sexual Dissidence*, Oxford University Press, 1991, p. 14.
14 Hilton Edwards, Introduction to *IBO*, p. 5.

15 Sinfield, op. cit., p. 130.
16 Fitzsimons, op. cit., p. 295.
17 Ibid, p. 295.
18 See Antonia Fraser, *The Warrior Queens*, New York: Knopf, 1989.
19 Quentin Crisp, *The Naked Civil Servant*, New York: Plume, 1983, p. 56.
20 Two such theatrical productions are revealingly analysed by Lance Pettit, 'Opposite Camps', *Graph*, no. 7, p. 12.
21 Fitzsimons, op. cit., p. 299.
22 Ibid., p. 299.

8 The Ear of the Other
Dissident Voices in Kate O'Brien's *As Music and Splendour* and Mary Dorcey's *A Noise from the Woodshed*

ANNE FOGARTY

> Act so that there is no use in a centre.
> GERTRUDE STEIN, *Tender Buttons*

Many recent discussions of lesbianism in literature depict it in terms not merely of an absence but of a ghostly void that resists all attempts to people it with living voices and bodies. No amount of 'outing' of writers and works, it is argued, can compensate for the censorship which has placed the emotional and erotic experiences of lesbianism far beyond the pale of representation or distorted them so that they became at best a coded and spectral language.[1] As a consequence of social interdictions, the portrayal of the lesbian subject in literature is muffled, opaque, and indirect. My concern in this essay is to treat two fictional works by the Irish writers Kate O'Brien and Mary Dorcey, which, by contrast, depict love relationships between women unabashedly and directly. Their texts, *As Music and Splendour* and *A Noise From the Woodshed*, I shall contend, fracture the laws of heterosexual love stories while exploiting and extending the conventions of lesbian erotic narratives.[2] They eschew the mitigations of indirection, the protective barriers of allusive symbolism, and the palliatives of romance plots borrowed from and directed at an always disapproving straight audience. Instead they create fictions which are grounded in presence, the quotidian, and what Mary Dorcey terms 'all the small . . . do all over again things' (p. 1). In addition, I shall argue that sexual liaisons in their texts are represented by means of conflating images of seeing and of hearing. In this way these writers find a way both of marking inter-personal relationships which are extra-ordinary and of indicating the manner in which these connections circumvent the problems of domina-tion and submission which frequently accompany heterosexual bonds.

By depicting lesbianism as an open secret, Kate O'Brien and Mary Dorcey defy the social conventions that surround it in taboos and prohibitions. The transgressiveness of their fictions lies in part in the fact that they flout transgression and seek to legitimise, or rather assume from the outset as natural, a way of life which traditional views of sexuality condemn as perverse and antisocial. Furthermore, by portraying love relations between women in terms of their reciprocity and normality, they rout those stereotypical and negative images which haunt the pages of literature and the popular imagination. In addition, through marrying fantasy and realism in their writing, they avoid the problem of simply swopping dystopian views of lesbians for Utopian ones. Both authors resist linearity and closure, and in so doing they create the possibility of a lesbian continuum which stretches beyond the pages of the text into an unformed but definite future. In this manner too they posit a women's time which is part of, and not outside, history.

Although pleasure is a central theme of these writers, and indeed is the primary dynamic force in their texts, I shall also argue that O'Brien and Dorcey are involved in the creation of what Deleuze and Guattari call in their pioneering reinterpretation of the work of Franz Kafka 'a minor literature'.[3] Thus their writings are of moment not just for their sexual dissidence but also because they utilise this potential subversiveness to explore the otherness of Irish society. By becoming strangers within their own culture, both these writers find themselves in a position to critique those aspects of modern Irish identity which they find confining and anti-democratic. They use the double self-estrangement that stems from their perspectives, as social outsiders because of their chosen sexual identity, and as writers situated in a supposedly post-colonial or anti-colonial Ireland. Thus they produce an alternative cultural politics which is at once challenging and problematic but above all else constructive.[4]

IS THERE A LESBIAN AESTHETIC?

> For if Chloe likes Olivia and Mary Carmichael knows how to express
> it she will light a torch in that vast chamber where nobody has yet been.
> VIRGINIA WOOLF, *A Room of One's Own*

The very attempt to engage with the theme of lesbianism in literature brings one face to face with a series of apparently irresolvable ontological problems. First, what does it mean to use the term lesbian? Secondly, is there a congruence, or at the very least a series of hidden but identifable affinities, between the sexual identity of writers and the works of art which they produce? In other words, of what value are the notions of a lesbian or gay authorship or of a lesbian or gay textuality in the study of literature?

Critical debate which has grappled with these questions thus far has concentrated on problems of definition. As in the case of feminist theory, the most vexed questions within gay and lesbian studies today centre around notions of identity and difference. Although the need to construct a new discourse free of the taint of heterosexual prejudice is a shared aim of all recent theorists of lesbian identity, opinions diverge as to how criticism might best explore the existence of alternative sexualities. The primary difficulty is that of inventing a vocabulary that avoids the essentialist and reductionist views of what Janice Raymond terms 'heteropatriarchy'.[5] As Michel Foucault has persuasively argued, twentieth-century notions of homosexuality are always coloured by the fact that they originate in the efforts of Victorian sexologists to codify and pathologise behaviour which they held to be deviant and unnatural.[6] Thus, paradoxically, any attempt to highlight and to celebrate gay and lesbian identities in a positive fashion is always overshadowed and even in part determined by the prejudices which were part and parcel of the modern endeavour to define sexual aberrancy in a scientific fashion. No matter what our allegiances may be, the resulting stigma has left seemingly ineradicable traces in the descriptive vocabularies which may be marshalled in order to describe ways of life which fall outside the socially accepted norm of reproductive heterosexuality. Furthermore, as Eve Kosofsky Sedgwick has pointed out, despite the growth of tolerance in European and Western societies in the last few years, we must still remain cognisant of the fact that for much of the twentieth century gay and lesbian realities have been underwritten by what she terms 'the epistemology of the closet'.[7] The silences and indirections dictated by social prejudice against gay and lesbian individuals and communities have given a peculiar cast to the self-appointed discourses and metaphors used to describe alternative sexual lifestyles. Although they apparently function as antitheses, the secrecy of the closet and the divulgences involved in 'coming out' remain inextricably linked.

Notwithstanding these obstacles, the primary achievement of gay and lesbian cultural inquiry in the past two decades has been to set in motion a critical debate which both challenges and countermands the censoring silences imposed by heterocentric points of view. Not surprisingly, much effort has been devoted to overhauling and redefining the discourses that promote what Foucault terms 'perverse implantation'.[8] While all commentators are in agreement that lesbianism should no longer be seen in terms of the negative otherness which it represents for heterosexual culture, opinions still differ as to how the positive revalorisation of marginalised sexual identities may be undertaken. Critics seem initially to divide into two groups, one which places emphasis on the metaphorical ambiguities of lesbian identity and the other which insists on a materialist but sometimes literal definition of this concept. In a pioneering but controversial essay, Adrienne Rich constructs an account of lesbianism which views it as the inverse of patriarchy. For her, to be a lesbian is not simply to have a particular kind of sexual preference, but to live in a gynocentric world which rejects the exploitative hierarchies of a male-dominated society. Famously, she posits the existence of what she terms the 'lesbian continuum', that is the enduring but hidden reality of 'woman-identified experience' throughout history.[9] Thus she defines the term lesbian as a metaphor for feminist solidarity and rebellion and as a portmanteau phrase for all those aspects of women's lives which fall outside the enforced androcentrism of heterosexual societies. In her view of things, the word covers both the particularity of same-sex passion and the more general phenomenon of female friendship. Several critics have, however, found Rich's postulates to be so all-embracing that they are well-nigh meaningless. Catherine Stimpson, by contrast, proposes a conservative and severely circumscribed definition of the lesbian in the interests of honouring the integrity of the life experiences of women who have been stigmatised as deviant on the basis of their sexual tendencies. To desexualise the notion of lesbianism is for Stimpson dangerously to purge it of the material import which it has had for countless individuals throughout history. Hence she holds the lesbian to be 'a woman who finds other women erotically attractive and gratifying'.[10]

Recent commentators, in turn, have pointed out that a third standpoint is possible which allows one to recognise the specificity and potential radicalism of lesbian identity without reducing it either to a universal, transhistorical essence (as in the case of Rich) or to a positivist, behavioural category (as in the case of Stimpson). Thus Monique Wittig, Judith Butler, Biddy Martin and Shane Phelan argue that any attempt to define lesbianism in terms of its uniformity and authenticity are limiting and undesirable.[11] They indicate that efforts to impose restricted confines on same-sex love as a mode of existence have always been at the service of maintaining the spurious coherence of heterosexuality. Wittig makes the case that lesbianism, because it exists outside the binary oppositions which structure heterosexual relationships, may be used as a fulcrum whereby to dislodge conventional notions of gender and femininity. Judith Butler likewise argues that lesbianism calls into question the unspoken assumption that biological sex precedes gender and thus determines our identity. She proposes instead a new understanding which views gender roles as performative, that is, as the projection and enactment of real but always mutable affects, identifications and desires.

In a similar fashion, Biddy Martin and Shane Phelan maintain that for lesbianism to remain a potent basis for social critique it is important for it to resist any attempt to fix or falsely universalise it. In addition, warning voices have been raised about the tendency, even within such openended political readings which have just been outlined, to see lesbian culture in Utopian terms only. As Katie King points out in a recent essay, it has been the fate of lesbianism to serve as a constantly shifting sign in the history of the women's movement and to be construed as the mystical wellspring of the subversive energy of gynocentric programmes for political change.[12] It is often over-invoked as a magical talisman which guarantees the incorruptibility and probity of feminist values and principles. Given the fragile and contested nature of homosocial identities, it seems advisable not to regard lesbianism as a fixed set of givens or as a register for particular forms of political belief or of cultural values. The term may variously be seen as a social construct, a mark of oppression, and a sign which describes the historically variable circumstances and interpretations of erotic and interpersonal relationships between women.[13] Even in acknowledging the fact that lesbianism refers to the material reality of women's sexual and emotional choices and the effects which these have on numerous other aspects of their lives, it should simultaneously be possible to view it not as the locus of a privileged epistemology but, in the words of Teresa de Lauretis, as 'a space of contradictions, in the here and now, that need to be affirmed but not resolved'.[14]

In the light of these realisations, literary criticism has set itself the task not of setting up cast-iron laws which insist upon an absolute congruence between the sexual status of authors and their works, but of uncovering the plurality of representations of the lesbian which exist in all aspects of cultural production. This process of reclamation has involved the construction of histories of lesbian literature, the examination of the narrative structures and tropes which typify such texts, and the analysis of the forms of reader response which they encourage.[15] Indeed, many critics argue that lesbianism should be seen not just as an aspect of the thematic content of a literary work or of the biography of its author, but rather as a crucial and irreducible facet of its aesthetics. In particular, it has been emphasised that the phenomenology of reading lesbian fiction follows particular patterns dictated by the peculiar themes and encrypted structures often assumed by this mode of writing.[16] In the interpretations of the fiction of Kate O'Brien and Mary Dorcey which follow, my concern is to look at lesbianism as a material context for their work, as a referential sign, and as a metaphor for the particular forms of writing practice which they have in common. My objective is to describe lesbian literature not as a fixed and ineluctable entity, but as a complex set of interactions between author, text and reader. Thus while I certainly hold that the writing of Kate O'Brien and Mary Dorcey depends upon what Bonnie Zimmerman calls a 'vision with a difference' which is in part rooted in their rejection of heterosexual modes of thinking, at the same time I shall make the case that the perverse reading strategies which may be applied as part of the process of interpreting their texts uncover not the timeless verities of lesbian love but its ambiguities and contradictions.[17] Their work produces a symbolic discourse of lesbianism not simply to displace prejudicial views of same-sex love with harmonious new understandings, but also in order to articulate the incoherence and complexity of all forms of erotic desire.

'FORBIDDEN INTERLUDES': KATE O'BRIEN'S *AS MUSIC AND SPLENDOUR*

> Some one who was living was almost always listening. Some one who was loving was almost always listening. That one who was loving was almost always listening. That one who was loving was telling about being one then listening.
>
> GERTRUDE STEIN, *Ada*

Nothing else in Kate O'Brien's literary career prepares us for the richly realised intensity and satisfying roundedness of her final novel, *As Music and Splendour*, published in 1958. All of its many elements were anticipated in her preceding work, including the themes of exile, romantic quest and sexual discovery, as well as her modernist insistence that individuation can be achieved only through the experience of dislocation and alienation. However, despite its evident self-reprise, this final novel succeeds in imbuing familiar themes and motifs with a new energy and momentum. Few of O'Brien's previous fictions succeeds in examining the development of the heroine at such close quarters and with such detailed concentration. Tellingly too, lesbian and homosexual love are not simply relegated in this last novel to a subplot, as is the case in *Mary Lavelle* and *The Land of Spices*.[18] Instead, for the first time in O'Brien's *oeuvre*, lesbian love is moved literally and metaphorically centre-stage as the author recounts the transformation and emotional growth of her heroines who are training to become opera singers. Hence this final fiction is compelling because it is a unique instance in Irish literature of the period of what Terry Castle calls the 'counterplot' of lesbian fiction.[19] Heterosexual romance here no longer displaces the story of lesbian love. In fact, as will later become evident, it is frequently depicted either as the negative counterpart to or as a metonym for female same-sex desire.

As Music and Splendour differs too from O'Brien's preceding work because it succeeds in overcoming that impasse faced by her heroines as they attempted to co-ordinate their *Bildung* or moral growth with their sense of vocation, and their desire for emotional and sexual freedom with their equally imperative need to achieve material independence and make their way in the world. Where hitherto her female protagonists appeared doomed owing to the limited economic choices and vocations open to them, Rose Lennane, Clare Halvey and Luisa Carriaga, the chief figures in this novel, are fortuitously saved from the traditional restrictions of women's domestic and social roles because of their talents as singers. Professional fulfilment, emotional independence and moral detachment and flexibility are within the compass of these heroines in a manner unthinkable for Agnes Mulqueen in *The Ante-Room* and for the protagonist of *Mary Lavelle*. However, despite these new-found possibilities of escape and freedom, the abiding mood of the novel is melancholic and valedictory. The lyric by Shelley from which O'Brien culls the title of her work explores the pain of love and treats of its inevitable demise:

> As music and splendour
> Survive not the lamp and the lute,
> The heart's echoes render
> No song when the spirit is mute —
> No song but sad dirges,
> Like the wind through a ruined cell,
> Or the mournful surges
> That ring the dead seaman's knell.[20]

O'Brien's epigraph fuses the second and third stanzas of Shelley's poem. Significantly, she isolates those lines which particularly associate the passions of love with the destruction of home or 'the well-built nest' which is the momentary result of the communion of lovers. Thus the elegiac mood of Shelley's poem frames, anticipates and underwrites O'Brien's text. Like him, she sees the waning of love as a correlative of the deracination felt by the exile.

The novel traces a trajectory from the voluble but inarticulate despondency of childhood to the eloquent but muted grief of adulthood. It plots a course between Clare's words of comfort to the sobbing and homesick Rose on the opening page to the parting description of the 'sad quiet' of Clare's heart as she leaves the convent school in Paris after a brief return visit now burdened with adult insight into the emotional life of Mère Marie

Brunel, the nun who had once been her mentor and teacher. Sadness and leave-taking are hence depicted as occasions but also as the signs of a female world of emotion, sexual passion and empathy. In the interpretation which follows, I shall argue that the plot of the novel invites us to become attuned to and to acquire this silent language of 'mournful surges' which expresses the painful emotional and intellectual progress of the principal characters. The act of reading *As Music and Splendour* requires a responsiveness to the Orphic language of departure and desire which is its mainstay.

In his analysis of the poetry of Charles Baudelaire, Walter Benjamin has described 'love at last sight' as the most characteristic form of erotic encounter in the modern metropolis.[21] In its restlessness and anonymity, modern life in Benjamin's eyes depends upon the excitement of haphazard and always transitory moments of pleasure. His comments thus suggest the possibility of a new ontology of desire which questions the rigid fixities of bourgeois norms of love with their emphasis on permanency, legality and conventionality. Kate O'Brien's final novel, I would suggest, may be viewed as a fictional meditation which bears out Benjamin's philosophical speculations. As in the encounters depicted in Baudelaire's poetry, lesbian love in her text is urban, fleeting and adventitious. It finds expression in stolen moments between the performance of an opera and the return of real life and in various transitional and passing phases in the lives of Luisa and Clare. It lives in a space in-between. Yet owing to its fluidity it is capable of disrupting the workings of heterosexual love and of challenging comforting romantic notions of constancy and fidelity.

O'Brien successfully uses the details of an opera singer's professional life, with its inevitable wanderings from one engagement to the next, its loneliness, and its devotion to artistic ambition, as metaphors for the questing, unforeclosed, but inherently satisfying nature of the new mode of desire which she describes. Her heroines, like the principal figures in Baudelaire's poetry, are roving and restless. They are *flâneuses* who wander the streets of the numerous cities, including Paris, Rome, Naples, Venice and Milan, which form a backdrop to their lives.[22] By adopting the street-walking existence which typifies the lives of characters in modernist novels such as Joyce's *Ulysses* or Woolf's *Mrs Dalloway*, they extend themselves, but also plumb the depths of those feelings of homelessness and destitution which dominate their consciousness from the beginning of the narrative.

However, despite this portrayal of love as thwarted, doomed and transgressive, O'Brien does not suggest that the experience of same-sex love is marked by a negative sense of difference. Nor does she depict it as distorted by social stigma or forced to become that self-destructive 'well of loneliness' which Radclyffe Hall describes as the lot of the sexual invert.[23] Rather, loss in her novel is transformed into a mode of recuperation and restitution. The absence of the beloved does not stem the ability of the female Orpheus to sing of her love. On the contrary, grief inspires her further and becomes the very basis of her operatic eloquence. Indeed, the tortured inner worlds of many of the principal characters, both male and female, provide evidence that they possess that capacity for reparation which Melanie Klein views as a fundamental aspect of psychic development.[24] Klein suggests that children interact in conflicting ways with the world around them and that in particular they are torn between feelings of love and hatred towards the primary object of their affections, the mother. She argues that those guilty emotions which inexorably pursue us into adulthood are not merely negative impediments but positive signs of the impetus to make good the damage which we have done to others because of the conflictual nature of this primal and founding relationship. Through feelings of guilt, we attempt to resolve ambivalences and negativities in ourselves. Similarly, for the characters in *As Music and Splendour*, a tormented conscience is depicted not so much as a sign of lack brought about by being an exile or social misfit, but as the very condition for emotional development and growth. At various junctures in the novel Clare and Rose acknowledge that they consider themselves to be sinners. They do so, however, not as an act of self-denunciation, but as a declaration of their belief that their feelings of pain and regret will extend rather than debilitate them. Thus, in the penultimate chapter, Clare decides that she is on the whole fortunate and concludes that 'life turns out to be an unceasing argument with conscience everywhere. So also here' (p. 321). In an earlier conversation with Iago Duarte in which she defiantly admits to her love for Luisa, she declares that 'none of us is innocent' (p. 289). She also confides to Thomas that she feels an affinity with Miriam, the tortured and guilt-ridden heroine of Nathaniel Hawthorne's *The Marble Faun*.[25] Rose is likewise convinced of the saving connection between guilt and reparation. In reflecting on the ultimately wrong-headed love affair with René which she herself had instigated, she decides that, although it is 'a sin', it still could be 'a blessed and irresistible sweetness, a true explanation of life, for better or worse' (p. 267).

Memorably, Kate O'Brien uses Gluck's opera, *Orfeo ed Euridice*, as the anthem of her female lovers, Clare and Luisa, in the novel. The choice is both judicious and telling. In the first instance, it allows the author to unite her two principals on stage, in the roles of Orfeo and Euridice, originally intended for a man and a woman, that is, a *castrato* and a soprano, are now frequently played by two women, one of whom of course cross-dresses in order to perform the male lead.[26] Thus O'Brien uses this opera as a symbolic occasion which paradoxically marries and also separates her chief characters. Within the protective domain of art their love is allowed to blossom. The sight of the cross-dressed Luisa is a sign which we can read as both conventional and subversive. The traditions of bourgeois theatre sanction the existence of so-called trouser parts and open up the possibility of a radical subtext of desire which the inveterately heterosexual focus of operatic plots denies.[27] The roles of Orfeo and Euridice provide Clare and Luisa with the language which expresses the joy and anguish of their love. Unlike Monteverdi's *L'Orfeo*, which at least pays lip-service to the received story to the extent that it allows the lovers to be reunited only in heaven, Gluck's opera rewrites the tragic outcome of the Greek myth. At the end of the latter's work Amor intervenes on behalf of Orpheus and allows Euridice to be restored to her lover in this world following his double loss of her.

The opera thus furnishes a fitting set of metaphors for the difficulties and pain of lesbian love in a world which, however Bohemian it may be, ultimately disapproves of such liaisons. Just as repeated performances of Gluck's opera bring Orpheus and Eurydice together only to separate them all over again, so too the changing circumstances of the lives of Clare and Luisa occasionally allow them to keep company but also inevitably drive them apart. However, the triumphant reworking of tradition carried out by Gluck and his librettist Ranieri de' Calzabigi, whereby one of the most best-known classical stories functions as an allegory of love and pleasure as well as of death and separation, opens up the possibility of a new story of desire which is founded both on loss and on fulilment. Within the parameters of tragedy, Gluck, and by extension Kate O'Brien, find the lineaments of a more hopeful view of human relationships in which seemingly fatal separations lead in the end to even more joyous reunions. Like Gluck, O'Brien eschews the consolations of a mythology of romantic love which culminates in a heavenly reunion in favour of an Orphic plot which allows the possibility of an enduring although beset union in this world. Enlightenment reason and utopianism are chosen in preference to classical idealism and apotheosis.

Moreover, by using the operatic myth of Orpheus and Eurydice as the primary vehicle for desire in the novel, O'Brien insistently blurs the dividing-lines between lesbian and heterosexual love. By doing so, she depicts sexual passion as a single spectrum rather than as a socially prescribed list of permissible or impermissible choices. The fateful Orphic nature of love is common to all of the passionate affairs in the text and not just to that of Clare and Luisa. There is scarcely a character in the novel who is not subtly linked with the painful pleasures and the

Shelleyean 'mournful surges' of desire. The singing teacher, Iago Duarte, is described as tragically marked by his youthful relationship with Mère Marie Brunel, the nun who initially coaches Clare, Luisa and Rose in Paris. She, we learn, enters a convent when she discovers that marriage to Duarte is impossible because he is a spoiled priest. Duarte, in imitation of the compulsive destructiveness of the operatic and Shakespearian tragic hero Iago, whose name he bears, repeats the mistakes of this abortive love by becoming enamoured of both Luisa and Clare during the course of the novel. Rose Lennane, Clare's constant companion and double throughout the narrative, falls fatefully in love with Antonio de Luca, a Tuscan aristocrat, who then betrays her by going ahead with a socially advantageous marriage which his family have arranged for him. Equally, Rose's first love affair with a young French opera singer, René Chaloux, is represented as destructive and riven by conflict. Signor Giacomo Buonatoli, the kindly but stern teacher and mentor who schools Clare and Rose in Rome and prepares them for their operatic careers, is locked in a tragicomic marriage to his despotic and alcoholic wife, a one-time soprano, who survives in a miasma of faded memories of her erstwhile success as a diva. Two of Clare's admirers and confidants, Thomas Evans, a Welsh composer and singer, and the Irishman Paddy Flynn, a lapsed clerical student, are also shown to be painfully, irredeemably and hopelessly in love with her. Hence all of the figures in the novel are marked by the otherness of desire either because they suffer from unrequited love, as in the case of Thomas, Paddy and Rose, or because the person upon whom they centre their affections is elusive, resistant or recalcitrant, as in the case of Clare, Iago Duarte and Signor Buonatoli.

By using Gluck's *Orfeo ed Euridice* as a leitmotiv which interlinks Clare and Luisa, O'Brien succeeds in creating a potent and expressive language for their love, avoiding any narrowly descriptive account of their relationship. The opera becomes emblematic of the amorous discourse which they share and which is intended solely for the ear of the other or lover. This lover's discourse is presented tantalisingly and allusively. Only a reader who becomes sympathetically attuned to its meaning can enjoy its resonance. Hence, when Clare and Luisa are reunited in Rome after several years of separation, they greet each other by singing fragments from the opera. Clare recognises Luisa before she sets eyes on her when she overhears her singing Orfeo's aria, 'Che puro ciel', which opens the final act of the opera and marks his passage into the underworld. She responds by singing Euridice's preceding aria, 'E quest' asilo ameno', which concludes Act II of Gluck's work.[28] Both arias express the joy which Orfeo and Euridice experience in the fields of Elysium because of the freedom which they afford from the pains of mortal life. Their mutual expressions of happiness also anticipate their forthcoming reunion. Thus Clare and Luisa use their knowledge of Gluck's opera to encode their emotions and to secrete their burgeoning love for each other in the libretto. Their singing is followed by an embrace; we are told that they 'fell into each other's arms' (p. 79). The narrator too is privy to this cryptic but expressive discourse. She describes Clare's reaction to this reunion with Luisa as follows: 'Clare stood quiet. The beauty of Luisa's singing shocked her' (p. 79). Such moments of attentive listening are frequent in the novel. They are naturally linked with the workaday aspects of the life of an opera singer, who always performs for an audience even when training, but they are also characteristic of the interpretative skills required by readers, friends and lovers because of the doubleness of most of the musical performances in the text.

Vocal music is staged in *As Music and Splendour* not only to display technical brilliance, but also to express the private emotions of the singer in question at that moment of her life. Above all, Kate O'Brien describes the ideal lover as someone who listens and who not only picks out the implicit meanings of musical works and the artistry of the performance, but also responds to what Roland Barthes calls 'the grain of the voice'. The latter describes the 'grain' as 'the body in the singing voice'.[29] He argues that in paying attention to the physicality of musical performance and to the materiality of language we enter into an erotic relation with the singer. Further, he maintains that vocal music is split into two spheres. Borrowing terms from Julia Kristeva, he calls these dual aspects the pheno-song and the geno-song. The pheno-song covers, in his view, all those features which derive from the structure of the sung language, ranging from the mode of expression chosen by the composer to the form of interpretation constructed by the singer. The geno-song, by contrast, is 'the volume of the speaking and singing voice, the space in which the significations germinate'.[30] It is in this latter conjoint space created by the co-operative interaction of singer and listener that the love relationships in Kate O'Brien's novel are enacted. Above all, the liaison between Clare and Luisa depends upon a semiotics of passion and friendship which they construe on the basis of their shared knowledge of, and love for, vocal music. As will later be seen, the growth of their feelings for each other is mapped out in the narrative as the movement between two key musical occasions in which they both take part: the first is their enactment of Gluck's *Orfeo ed Euridice*, and the second is their performance, under the direction of Iago Duarte, of Pergolesi's *Stabat Mater*.

In drawing thus subtly on the implicit as well as overt eroticism of operatic music, O'Brien is, of course, aligning herself with a time-honoured tradition within gay and lesbian subculture which has only in recent years been explored in any depth. Virginia Woolf and Willa Cather both make use of the mode of the *Künstlerroman* and of the metaphors of operatic performance in their fiction in order to establish queer moments or possibilities of cross-identification which do not adhere to the conventions of heterosexual desire.[31] In *The Queen's Throat* Wayne Koestenbaum considers the importance of opera for homosexual audiences. He argues that gay adulation of opera queens or divas may be attributed to the new horizons of identity and of erotic desire which they open up for the listener who is sensitive to its delights. Opera, he claims, makes him feel 'two-gendered'[32] because it allows the possibility of moments of cross-identification which exploit the passing scenario of straight love and yet fracture those social codes which insist that sexual desire is immutably heterosexual.[33] Through his pleasure in the music, the gay spectator imaginatively becomes one with the diva. As Koestenbaum explains, 'listening, your heart is in your throat: *your* throat, not the diva's.'[34] Like Barthes, he insists that the physical appeal of the operatic performance, and of the singing voice in particular, licenses the emergence of erotic feelings and of queer moments which are otherwise suppressed. In the heterosexual economy, gay and lesbian bodies are denied outlets of expression. But, in Koestenbaum's view, listening to an opera dislodges the power of straight censorship and 'restores queer embodiment'.[35] The overdetermination of operatic roles and emotions and the 'splendour' which it unleashes, both visually and aurally, allows them readily to function as vehicles for transgressive physical states and desires. Clare Halvey notes at the beginning of O'Brien's novel that their benefactors have chosen a peculiar career for both Rose and herself, as they will spend their lives 'singing and acting away as fallen women' (p. 32). The heroines in most of the works which they will be called upon to perform, with the exception of those of Mozart and Gluck, she notes, are either mad or bad. It is thus intimated that opera paradoxically enshrines stereotypical images of femininity while also sanctioning those aspects of female behaviour which society usually condemns, such as insanity and immorality. The confines of opera contain the possibility of its own subversion.

Above all, its ambiguities provide a haven within which what Terry Castle calls 'homovocality' can develop and be explored.[36] For Castle, diva-worship, the intense and libidinal relationship of the audience with a female singer, takes on particular import for the lesbian spectator. She expands on this phenomenon in the context of her own fascination with the mezzo-soprano, Brigitte Fassbaender. She concludes that the appeal of the woman-identified diva, whether she plays a trouser role or not, stems from her ability to communicate 'gynophilia' or exaltation in the presence of the feminine. Precisely because of her polymorphous ability to inhabit dual gender roles, the mezzo-soprano underlines the constancy of woman-centred affections. Both in male transvestite and female roles she sings of her love of women. At the same time, she is characterised by her difference, which stems in part from her ability to blur the boundaries between gender identities both physically and vocally.

O'Brien likewise endows her heroines, Clare and Luisa, with the disturbing but gratifying otherness of the mezzo-soprano. In contrast to the heterosexual Rose, who has a perfect soprano voice, Clare and Luisa are marked as different both in terms of their voices and of their sexuality. Luisa, we are told in chapter 1, has a voice which is, in the eyes of the nuns who are in charge of her training, a peculiar mixture of the mezzo-soprano and the operatic. Clare, similarly, although she is assigned soprano parts throughout, has a voice which is disconcertingly hybrid. Her friends and her audience find her at once passionate and distant. Giacomo in conversation with Thomas Evans comments cryptically that he has been concerned about the disturbing qualities of 'coldness' and 'sisterliness' (p. 175) in his two Irish protégées, Rose and Clare. Manuel Arrez, who takes part in a production of Bellini's *Norma* in Naples in which Clare stars, confides in chapter 12 to his friend Iago Duarte that she has the voice of a *castrato*. Although his remark is intended primarily as a disparaging assessment of her musical abilities, it acts further as a veiled comment on her ambiguous sexual status. Luisa and Clare are likewise coupled as oddities in that their vocal talents make them more fitting for the performance of German *Lieder* and church music than of opera. While Rose seems automatically destined for the public adulation of a successful prima donna, their careers follow a more torturous route. Clare has to struggle to mould herself for the operatic roles which she is called upon to play, but is ultimately, like Luisa, attracted to the *gravitas* of religious music. In this manner, the sexual otherness of O'Brien's romantic heroines finds an objective correlative in their musical capabilities.

Through such deft allusions, the author conveys the difference which has inscribed itself in the very being of her two lesbian principals. The vocabulary which describes the many facets of the training of an opera singer is thus given a double valency. Significantly, this discourse which stamps Clare and Luisa as different is ambiguous and indirect. Unlike Radclyffe Hall's Stephen Gordon, they are not branded with the mark of Cain. Instead their otherness is coded in terms of the specificity of their vocal talents and the musical pleasure which their performances afford their audiences and each other; it is shorn of any suggestion of perversion. The sexual proclivities of O'Brien's central female figures are as much part of them as their singing voices. Hence their desires are depicted as a result of the complex interaction of nature and culture. Furthermore, in utilising the trappings of opera as metaphors for the emotional development of her heroines, O'Brien harnesses the dual tendencies of this art form. It affords her the possibility of constructing a plot which depends alternately on the comfort of romantic illusion and on the disenchantment which may be effected by the mode of realism. Theodor Adorno argues that the opera is the bourgeois art form *par excellence*.[37] It depends, in his view, on that contradictory admixture of myth and enlightenment which forms the bedrock of bourgeois culture. All operatic productions, he notes, involve the use of magic and ostentation and demand a child-like belief in illusion on the part of their audience. Yet, at the same time, it must be recognised that opera first came to the fore under the auspices of composers such as Monteverdi and Cavalli in the republican city-states of seventeenth-century Italy. Hence it blossomed at the instigation of a burgeoning bourgeois class.[38] From its very beginnings, as Adorno explains, it was shaped by the warring forces of Christianity and rationality. Significantly too, the story of Orpheus is one of the arenas in which these opposing tensions of opera have been acted out. By assaying that most prototypical of all theatrical plots, Gluck attempted to reform and to restore balance to the musical tradition set in motion by Monteverdi with his pioneering version of the Orphic myth.[39] In particular, Gluck set out to curtail the emotional excesses of the singing styles which had by his day become the predominant characteristic of theatrical performances. The Gluckian reform of operatic conventions introduces a fresh sense of restraint and order into a medium which yet derives its strength from its ability to suspend our disbelief. Furthermore, Adorno holds that just as opera is torn between a mythic impulse on the one hand and a desire to demystify on the other, so too does it constantly pit the forces of culture and nature against each other. Despite its reliance on costume and an entire panoply of codified meanings, the passion expressed by operatic music shows that nature always prevails against all convention. The naked and apparently natural truth of human emotions constantly disturbs the orderliness of operatic artifice.

In *As Music and Splendour* O'Brien makes full use of these dual propensities of opera. On the one hand, the exotic world in which her heroines find themselves is used as a vehicle for the romance and otherness of their existence. Yet, on the other hand, the precise reckoning of their earnings and the constant description of their painful efforts to eke out their resources and to pay off their debts to their benefactors in Ireland and in Paris firmly reminds us of the commercial and material interests which feed off the mythic imaginings of opera. Thus, in the description of the aftermath of the climactic staging of *Orfeo ed Euridice* which signals the deepening of the bonds of love between Clare and Luisa, O'Brien skilfully interweaves fantasy and realism:

And as the lights went out and they turned and ran to their dressing-rooms, hand in hand, they went on singing.

The music they both loved had carried them far tonight, together and above themselves. Their descent was slow and reluctant, and their hands did not fall apart when they paused in Clare's doorway.

Still Orpheus and Eurydice, their brilliantly made-up eyes swept for each the other's face, as if to insist that this disguise of myth in which they stood was their mutual reality, their one true dress wherein they recognised each other, and were free of that full recognition and could sing it as if their very singing was a kind of Greek, immortal light, not singing at all. (p. 113)

The continuance of the performance of love after the footlights have been extinguished blurs the distinctions here between myth and reality. The fantastic passions of the stage fuse with the real desires of these two women. The return to the dressing-room becomes another perilous descent into the underworld of human relationships. Moreover, the description of their parallel joy in the presence of the other is couched in a language which avoids any unequal apportioning of roles. The emotional bond between Clare and Luisa is placed firmly outside the power play of scopic economies.[40] Their gaze is caressing and sustaining rather than objectifying and possessive: 'their brilliantly made-up eyes swept for each the other's face'. Each looks on behalf of the other as well as on her own account. Moreover, their shared vision is depicted as freeing and mobile. It tracks freely through the dimensions of light and sound. It does not seek to establish epistemological fixities or to pin its hopes on jointly reconnoitred truths. Yet the portrayal of this stolen moment of love as 'a kind of Greek, immortal light' suggests that Luisa and Clare achieve a new form of mythic transcendence which outstrips even the aesthetic possibilities of Gluck's opera. While the sensuality of their emotions is underscored, their relationship is represented as chaste and uncorrupted. It seems to exist in a fantasmatic space which assuages and cancels out all of the neediness and heartache of desire.

However, in the ensuing paragraphs reality reasserts itself. This portrayal of everyday concerns is as crucial to an understanding of the connection between Clare and Luisa as the remoulding of the Orphic legend. The narrator swiftly returns us to the mundane details of everyday life, thereby deliberately puncturing the mythic moment which she has just established. Orpheus and Eurydice kiss and become themselves again. They cold-cream their faces, banishing the final vestiges of the liberating but static disguises of art. In this anti-mythic reality, the needs of the body cannot be as easily appeased as in the protected realm of opera. Clare and Luisa are 'ravenous', we are informed, after their demanding exertions on the stage. They also end the night, not 'hand in hand' but separate and unfulfilled. The social exigencies of Rome render their needs ghostly and almost immaterial: 'So the gathering broke up dreamily, and melted, singing, calling, through the light and shadows; and some who had desired to take each other home got lost, lost the one they sought, and called and sang and vanished' (p. 120). The satisfying harmonies of Gluck's opera are dissipated by the dissonances and inevitable divisions of everyday reality. The quotidian appears to be a greater obstacle for O'Brien's lesbian Orpheus and Eurydice than the elemental forces of evil and death against which their operatic doubles battle.

Yet O'Brien does not suggest that myth and reality are somehow to be regarded as eternally warring opposites. Nor does she intimate that art provides compensations that everyday life cannot supply. Rather she posits a counterpoint between the two spheres which enables the meanings suppressed in one area to emerge in the other. The romance of art allows her characters to involve themselves in the 'experimental embrace' of love affairs which fly in the face of conventional morality (p. 182). It also permits the development of an intersubjective space in the form of the many sustaining listening relationships depicted in the novel which the alienation of modern living seems otherwise to forbid. Throughout the novel the pleasure of performance is described as dependent upon the silent attentiveness and unspoken empathy of the audience. Luisa describes the way in which the terrors of performing in La Scala are diminished by the comforting realisation that the theatre is full of 'absolutely, quiet people' who have come there 'to do nothing else but listen' (p. 91). Paradoxically, the production of silent wonder is the predominant effect of the operatic voice. The shared space of understanding and pleasure which is opened up by vocal performance seems to elude language. Thus Rose's wooing of the Roman audience is portrayed as follows: 'Always her voice surprised them, and sometimes it had the effect of tricking them into silence — so quietly it could move out over them, making them wonder sometimes, instead of assent, which was their habit' (p. 133). The homovocal and transgressive delight of listening in *As Music and Splendour* exists in a closeted domain which is shown, as on this occasion, to be at once hidden and readily available. This motif of a mode of communication, which is both elusive and silent (and also transcends the barriers of language), is established in the opening chapters. The training which Clare, Rose and Luisa undergo in the convent of Les Pieuses Filles de Sainte Hélène in Paris ensures that they first acquire the discipline of listening before they learn to sing. The young performers fret under the severity of these rules. Paradoxically, the acquisition of this ability to discern the hidden strains of a cloistered silence or otherness in the music which they hear becomes their first induction into 'the commonplace troubles' of love (p. 24).

Clare, who is described by René as 'a terribly good listener' (p. 158), is especially associated with the moments of queerness and cross-identification. These are the hallmarks of the other language of silence and desire which Kate O' Brien subtly articulates throughout the course of the novel.[41] This hidden dimension of meaning is often conjured up through the invocation of the two most frequent tropes used to represent same-sex desire, gender liminality and gender separatism.[42] The first of these notions of the lesbian assumes that she is, in fact, inverted and has a man's heart trapped in a woman's body. As such, she is stranded between male and female gender identities and is as a consequence liminal to both. The second trope, by contrast, views the lesbian in separatist terms as what Adrienne Rich calls a 'woman-identified woman'. While O'Brien's portrayal of Clare Halvey echoes such ideas, it also firmly readjusts them. Clare's listening relationships connect her severally with Rose, Luisa, Thomas Evans and Paddy Flynn. The ambiguity of her identity is thus mirrored by her cross-associations with companions of both sexes. This is particularly emphasised in her friendships with Rose and Thomas. Rose's fate is used throughout the novel as a register of Clare's own progress, while her intimate conversations with Thomas also provide a measure of her deepening insight into the emotional conflicts in which she finds herself embroiled. Chapter 10 makes the uncanny doubling of Clare and Thomas most explicit. When Clare mentions the similarity between her grandmother and herself, Thomas counters with the recognition that Clare and himself are so alike in appearance that they might even be considered 'twins' (p. 203). In his study of doubles in literature Karl Miller argues that tales of division and possession are fictions of escape.[43] In showing what it is for someone to be two inimical or incompatible things at the same time, such narratives, he contends, try to depict an impossible coincidence of meanings or identities which cannot obtain in reality. Thus, in endowing Clare with a protean identity, O'Brien tries to extricate her from the constrictions of a world which does not allow her the freedom openly to be herself. She is at once male-identified, woman-centred, and a guilt-ridden solitary and outsider. Her many-sidedness defies any facile attempt to categorise or define her.

Through her ability to associate with a range of contiguous selves of both sexes, the central character of *As Music and Splendour* enacts the alternative ethics of lesbian love. Unlike the philosophy of jealous possessiveness which is shown to be the basis of heterosexual relationships, female homosocial desire in the novel is rooted in tolerance and sisterliness. The uncovering of a 'disruptive space of sameness', which Marilyn Farwell identifies as one of the key ways in which lesbian narratives revise the hierarchising and discriminatory differences of heterosexism, is the primary means by which Kate O'Brien indicates the alterity of the love stories which she unfolds.[44] Clare is bemused by the male insistence that the knowledge of Luisa's infidelities should breach the bond between them. She explains the unconditional nature of their love to Thomas as follows: 'Men, as you call them, don't seem to be able to endure things. I don't know what sex you suppose me to belong to, but I can endure Luisa's life. I love, her, you see' (p. 211). When Iago Duarte similarly raises the problem of Luisa's promiscuity, her retort effectively dismisses his pettiness: 'And are we in charge of her?' (p. 295). She thus suggests that their love rejects the tyrannies and desire for mastery shown by the conventional, straight lovers of the novel such as Paddy and René. Paddy constantly tries to curb Clare and is angered by her refusal to countenance his Catholic prudishness, while René childishly declares that he wishes to master Rose.

Clare's relationship with Luisa, by contrast, is based on their tacit but unqualified understanding of each other. After her return from a concert tour of South America, Luisa realises that 'home-coming' for her meant that 'Clare would be singing again' (p. 243). In chapter 12 their separate interior musings on the difficulties which beset their relationship converge in that shared homovocal space which they have constructed for themselves: 'Luisa smiled and heard her own voice in clear memory — *Che farò* — and telepathically she found Clare's eyes and knew that Eurydice also heard her singing, far away' (p. 264). For all its pain, the Orphic language which links them negotiates and overrides any intervening obstacles.

This counterplot of lesbian love also redefines the heterosexual bonds in the novel. Eve Kosofsky Sedgwick has commented upon the way in which literary representations of the rivalries between two men for the affections of one woman are often used as a veiled means of expressing undercurrents of male homosocial desire which must otherwise be repressed.[45] Ultimately, heterosexual love, that is, the conquest of the woman by one of the men, becomes the means of keeping the spectre of homosexuality at bay. *As Music and Splendour* disturbs the symmetry of such heterosexual configurations of desire.[46] Rose, who is depicted as caught between the attentions and jealousies of René and Antonio, rejects the customary passivity attributed to the woman in the plot of male homosocial desire. Instead she turns the situation to her advantage and eventually casts aside both of her lovers despite the pain which this causes her. In the closing pages of the novel we learn that she has decided to move to America with Silas Rudd, a potential new patron who has been wooing her. Similarly, the story of the cross-relations of Clare, Luisa, and Iago Duarte inverts the pattern of desire described by Sedgwick, because it centres now not on 'homosexual panic' and male–female relationships but on lesbian love.

It is Iago who is forced to recognise that he plays a minor role with respect to the two women with whom he is fleetingly but obsessively in love. This displacement of heterosexuality by female homosocial desire is crystallised in one of the culminating performances of the novel. In chapter 13 the enactment of Pergolesi's *Stabat Mater* by Clare and Luisa is depicted as a source of humiliation rather than triumph for Iago Duarte. Although he had intended to use the occasion to exhibit his mastery of his two protégées, it becomes instead a proof of the unwieldiness and permanency of the links between the two singers. Fittingly, a choral work which dwells upon the pain of love unites them on stage.[47]

Yet, although *As Music and Splendour* unequivocally celebrates the enduring relationship between Clare and Luisa, it focuses far more upon the grief of separation than on the joy of physical and emotional union. This sense of a perdurable sadness which underlies all of the events of the novel stems for the main part from the fact that Rose and Clare are involuntary exiles from Ireland. O'Brien uses the double vantage-point of her heroines as a means of scrutinising Irish culture from afar. However, her principal characters, though transplanted to Italy, never succeed in relinquishing the values imparted to them as children. It seems no coincidence that the author's signature on the final page also describes a geographical transplantation from Roundstone to London. In a similar fashion, the narrative refuses a notion of centre. Ireland and Italy are represented as parallel and opposing spaces in the novel. Each country alternatively acts as the locus of otherness. On many occasions Rose and Clare realise that their lives would have been dull and restricted if they had remained in Ireland. In conversation with Clare, Rose comments that they have exchanged the 'rule-of-thumb' uniformity of Irish life for the constant excitement of their new existences (p. 189). In the same exchange, Clare muses that, if they had stayed at home, Rose might have become a shop assistant and she herself a nun. Through these juxtapositions, O'Brien constructs a pointed critique of the conservatism and narrowness of modern Ireland. Yet she does not suggest that her heroines have abandoned their original identities in their desire to embrace the liberating freedoms afforded their 'Italianated' selves (p. 135). Instead she depicts them as painfully poised between two cultures and as incessantly beset by a yearning to recoup the innocence and completion of their childhood past. Ireland, thus, is represented as a negative point of departure on the one hand, and as a place of paradisal happiness on the other. It both censors desire and is at the root of all the restless feelings of longing which impel and disturb O'Brien's heroines. Significantly, the homesickness which eternally bedevils them is triggered by their memories of an originary, gynocentric world. Rose constantly harks back to life in Lackanashee and to images of

Miss French, one of her benefactors, and of her mother and sister. Clare, likewise, derives strength not from her relationship with her father but from her cherished memories of her grandmother in Ballykerin. In this manner, the difference which marks these two characters is depicted as the dual result of their sexual unconventionality and of their national background. Although Ireland endows Rose and Clare with feelings of lack, at the same time the alterity of their identity as Irish women is seen as enhancing rather than disabling them. Above all, the Ireland from which they draw sustenance is rural, female and domestic. Clare, in particular, is haunted by the memory of the 'civilised, good voice' of her grandmother, who lives in the west of Ireland, telling her to come in out of the wind to her tea (p. 14).[48] The semiotic plenitude and innocence of this lost childhood world appear to be the inverse of the moral conflicts and confusions of their adult life in Italy. Yet, as the novel indicates, the secret but insistent language of homovocality links these two opposing places. Through such daring and suggestive metaphorical entwinings, O'Brien succeeds not just in mounting a subtle but firm critique of the small-mindedness of Catholic morality, but also in suggesting that the values of the lesbian mode of being which her novel describes are of a piece with the ideals of Irish cultural nationalism. *As Music and Splendour* radically interweaves a discourse which insists on the racial purity and primal innocence of the Irish with a discourse of sexual dissidence. Thus the novel constantly underlines the chastity and moral fastidiousness of Clare and Rose as well as their Bohemianism and liberalism. However, O'Brien's final fiction shows that Ireland is still not ready to accept the radical presence of dissident voices, even though it has given birth to and shaped them. When Clare returns home to attend her dying grandmother at the end of the novel, she is shocked by the 'primitive life of her own people' and recognises that she could never lead the 'uncomforted' existence which is their lot (p. 343). She is faced with a stark choice between Ballykerin and a 'return to the world' (p. 344). Perforce, she chooses the latter. We are told that, with her departure, 'Ballykerin ended' (p. 344). O'Brien finally dashes the myth of a pure and romantic Ireland to pieces because it is not capacious enough to accommodate the queer appropriations to which she has subjected it in the novel. Instead we are left on the final page with Clare's resigned declaration that sin 'was the word of all' (p. 346). The attentive reader will pick up on the implication that the sin which *As Music and Splendour* has explored without any compunction is, in fact, as the ending of Joyce's 'The Dead' states, 'general all over Ireland'. But, for the period in which O'Brien was writing, only a fiction of hopeful exile and Orphic sadness is capable of relaying this radical insight.

'LISTENING WITHOUT DIRECTING': MARY DORCEY'S
A NOISE FROM THE WOODSHED

Was not writing . . . a secret transaction, a voice answering a voice?
                                                    VIRGINIA WOOLF, *Orlando*

To move from the melancholy of O'Brien's fiction to the celebratory vigour
of Mary Dorcey's short stories is to perform a quantum leap in terms of
the directness with which the emotional worlds of lesbian women are portrayed. This immediacy is evident in the different scenarios and time-frames
chosen by these two writers. Where O'Brien situates her novel in late
nineteenth-century Italy, Mary Dorcey sets her stories in contemporary
Ireland. Thus the theme of exile no longer acts as a metaphor for the
otherness of lesbian experience in the latter's work. Instead, as my interpretation will propose, her stories initiate a process of 'transculturation'
which forces us to look at the many facets of modern Irish life from marginal
points of view.[49] Dorcey dislocates the homogenising perspectives of
heterocentrism not by denouncing or banishing them, but by setting up
an interplay between normative and eccentric visions of the world. Her
stories both explore the conflicts and divisions between straight and lesbian communities and also show how they are inextricably entangled. We
are made aware of the distance between these two cultures on the one
hand and their adjacency on the other. In thus foregrounding but refusing to countenance the differences between margin and centre, Dorcey
unleashes what Deleuze and Guattari call the revolutionary potential of
literature. They argue that revolutionary writing has a threefold set of
characteristics: it deterritorialises language; it connects the individual to
a political immediacy; and it emphasises the collective assemblage of enunciation.[50] The following discussion will show how Mary Dorcey's fictions
deterritorialise and refashion the Irish short story in the manner suggested
by these two critics. In her hands, this mode of writing is no longer the
domain of 'the lonely voice', as Frank O'Connor contends in his exploration of modern Irish practitioners of this form of fiction.[51] Instead her
stories set up zones of contact between self and other which break down
false divisions. They also map out constant lines of flight from the con-
finement of normative and heterocentric values.

The title story of Dorcey's collection *A Noise from the Woodshed*
immediately immerses us in the world of gyn-affection. This text both
introduces us to the overall themes of the collection and initiates us in
the reading relations which are an indivisible aspect of the meanings being uncovered. While the opening story presents itself as an *apologia* for
lesbian love, it also crucially enacts the processes of female desire through

its structures and rhythms. In this manner the subject and mode of enunciation become one. The very grammar of the narrative becomes an embodiment of its theme. This story, which gives an account of the way in which her love for another woman completely alters the narrator's way of looking at the world, sets in motion what Kevin Kopelson terms an 'ontoerotic' vocabulary which allows the construction not only of a female beloved but of one who is both individual and multiple.[52] Conventional systems of reference are transformed as the speaker describes the exhilarating dislocations of love. Thus the voice which narrates the story eschews the pronoun 'I'. Instead she refers to herself as 'you'. In so doing, Dorcey exploits the fruitful ambiguities of deictic reference. Her female narrator, instead of being tied to a narrowly defined subjectivity, is simultaneously engaged in a self-address, a conversation with her lover, and a dialogue with the reader. All three perspectives intersect and coalesce in the pronoun 'you'. Dorcey uses this overlapping of subject positions to create an atmosphere of playful intimacy. The narrator tells her story in the form of a polylogue. She forestalls, anticipates and answers objections or questions which might be raised by her threefold audience:

> But this cannot be normal surely? This impromptu lying about in strange places, this loss of purpose and perpendicular, this reckless wastage of time and crockery, this surrender of sense to the senses, this wallowing in all flat surfaces: carpets and floorboards and baths and riverbanks and beds of pine needles — oh yes, even up there in the woods — nowhere spared; the groanings of boughs over your flesh — no it cannot be all like this, surely?
>
> Well it isn't at all, all like this, you might tell them, if you could put yourself in the mood long enough to tell them. There is so much else going on and failing to go on. There is work, and the lack of it, money and the getting of it, love and the losing of it. There is all this death and dying, this destruction and hunger and torment. (p. 7)

The solipsistic intensity of the lesbian love affair at the heart of the story is thus woven into an endless litany of events. In this manner too Dorcey questions the way in which traditional narratives have falsely eclipsed women's wishes and needs: 'Oh yes, one of you says, it's all been going on before, going on for millennia before, except that it wasn't going on for themselves' (p. 11). By contrast, her account of love is more expansive; it invites the reader to collaborate with the narrator as she rewrites the universe in terms of female homoeroticism. The headlong, run-on periods which give the story its peculiar rhythms mimetically reflect this notion of an all-embracing desire which laps up and dissolves differences.

Above all, the revolutionary potential of lesbian love realises itself through the emergence of new modes of apprehension which circumvent the limitations of language. As in the case of Kate O'Brien's novel, this alternative awareness is the result of the listening relations around which this title story is constructed. In a discussion of her work, Mary Dorcey is careful to distinguish between Joycean stream of consciousness and the forms of narration which constitute the typical scaffolding of her narratives. Unlike the self-enclosed voices in Joyce's work which are usually depicted as thinking in an isolated space removed from the world, she argues that the voice in her stories is always a 'person talking, addressing itself aloud to a listener'.[53] In addition, she holds that the primary aim of her fiction is to allow the reader to hear better. 'A Noise from the Woodshed' succeeds in attuning us to other modes of apprehension through its seductive rhythms and its use of a plot which toys with but eventually abandons the conventions of realist description. The noise from the woodshed which momentarily troubles the narrator and her lover seems to belong initially to a world of Gothic hauntings and Freudian repressions. It is described as a 'startling and disturbing noise that might have been many things or one' (p. 15). Yet, surprisingly, these sounds turn out to be both literal and metaphorical. In one explanation which is proffered to us, we are told that they are caused by two American women who are camping out in the shed:

> We heard the noise, she said. Yes, that was us, they said. We should have known, she said, I mean recognised it, knowing you were coming back. And of course you should have too and now that she said it you did — recognise the sound. It wasn't, after all, for the want of hearing it. But then other people are different, especially if you haven't even heard them speaking or weeping or singing, and anyone can make a mistake about these things, and you had. (p. 17)

The process of getting to know the meaning of this unfamiliar noise is presented as a necessary aspect of the narrator's initiation into the values of this woman-centred world. She has to acquire, like the reader, a new attentiveness to things and people that are other and different and seem therefore to fall outside the pale of conventional discourse. Thus the story urges us to abandon the view that unfamiliar noises might be ghostly and unsettling. Dorcey wittily inverts the Gothic associations of unearthly and inexplicable sounds. We are asked to recognise the commonplace nature of lesbian desire rather than its disquieting otherness. The noise from the woodshed becomes a metaphor for the joyous nature of female love and for its unquestioning embrace of the familiar and the unfamiliar alike.

The succeeding stories in the collection continue this revisionary process. However, none of the ensuing texts achieves the lyrical and sensual abandon of the opening tale. Instead we return seemingly to the safe and recognisable confines of the realist narrative and leave the discomfiting woodshed apparently far behind. However, Dorcey strays back to the lonely-voiced domain of the Irish short story tradition in order to remake and redefine its conventions. All of the narratives in *A Noise from the Woodshed* experiment with the conventional themes, plots and structures of short stories. Yet, paradoxically, in her postmodern refashioning of this mode of writing, Dorcey succeeds in restoring some of the time-honoured functions of the storyteller as expounded by Walter Benjamin.[54] The latter explains that true storytelling is a social activity which is predicated on the communicability of experience. He contends that the novel, by contrast, displays 'the profound perplexity of the living' (p. 87) and depends upon the solitary reader for its reception. Although many of the protagonists in Mary Dorcey's short stories suffer from this profound perplexity, they generally find a means of escape from their predicament. This escape is depicted both on a thematic and a formal level. Moments of liberation are achieved through the actions of the characters and the poetics of the texts themselves.

Thus in 'A Sense of Humour' Kate escapes from the vulgarity of the pub in which she works and the unconscious cruelty of a would-be lover to a space which lies beyond the confines of the oppressive familial world in which she lives. Her sudden insight into the narrowness of her existence acts simultaneously as a commentary on the restrictiveness of the narratives used in order to portray the lives of women like herself:

> A wave of exultation rose in her, a burst of consciousness so swift and sudden that she almost jumped from the ground where she stood and heard herself in the same instant cry aloud for joy. She opened her eyes and gazed about her, marvelling. What a little thing had held her captive — what a small, insignificant, scarcely visible thing had kept her prisoner! She had believed in place. She had believed in circumstance, she had allowed herself to be bound by the trappings of situation: this sky, these patched stony fields she could hardly now discern, a circle of hills, a house, a voice, a face, a pair of hands. The trivia of place — furniture, that could be found anywhere. (p. 42)

The wave of exultation experienced by the protagonist here is both unexpected and liberating. Up to this point the story has depicted, with chilling insight, the tawdriness of modern Irish rural existence. The pivotal anecdote about a pornographic, inflatable doll told by Robbie, the man who is attempting to woo her, sums up the debasement of this environment. Kate's sudden onrush of joy in the concluding moments of the story reads like a *non sequitur*. Yet this transition into a postmodern indeterminacy is executed with conviction. Kate is rescued not by the comforting possibility of exile, but by her recognition that places no longer matter.

Her joyousness shatters the conspiracy of silence which she had earlier felt to be the reason for the emotional deadlock of those around her. It likewise undermines the very basis on which the narrative of her life has been founded thus far. This alternative perspective replaces her modernist sense of alienation with a postmodern suspension of belief in metaphysical fixities. In particular, it questions the validity of traditional pieties about family and place. Dorcey shows that the otherness associated with the nameless, gynocentric and defiantly radical space of the initial story exists too at the heart of this seemingly irredeemable Irish rural community. The double-voiced discourse of her narrative allows her to construct a narrative which at once depicts with painful realism the oppressive nature of Kate's existence and portrays the beginnings of her rebellion against those conditions which constrain her.[55] Even though she is still alone at the end of the tale, she has been freed from the loneliness of her fate and has entered the sustaining and 'sheltering' space of the woodshed (p. 42).

Several of the other stories in the collection likewise enact a double plot. In this way they both undertake a critique of contemporary Irish society and insist that the sexual otherness and dissidence which it shuns and pillories is an indivisible part of its fabric. Thus 'A Country Dance' intertwines the tale of a lesbian erotic encounter with a portrayal of the homophobia of a rural community. The two female characters find themselves ruthlessly exposed and under scrutiny when they take the floor together at a country dance:

> I open my eyes. The music has stopped. Behind you I see a man standing: his eyes riveted to our bodies, his jaw dropped wide as though it had been punched. In his maddened stare I see reflected what I have refused to recognise through all these weeks. Comfort, sympathy, a protective sister — who have I been deceiving? I see it now in his eyes. Familiar at once in its stark simplicity. Making one movement of past and future. I yield myself to it; humbled, self-mocking. Quick as a struck match. (p. 54)

In conflating the self-critical gaze of the first-person narrator here with the threatening and denigrating gaze of the anonymous male observer, Dorcey indicates the coincidence of, as well as opposition between, gay and straight perspectives. However, the menace of the dance-hall is ultimately cancelled out by the desire felt by the two women. Although the Irish social world represents a constant threat to the well-being of Dorcey's protagonists, her narratives always open up new spaces of pleasure and fulfilment which coexist with the old, impossible, trivialising places. 'A Country Dance' ends, therefore, with the two lovers in bed. A noise disturbs them but it belongs simply to the enabling space of love and intimacy and not to the violent menace of the dance-hall:

> 'I thought I heard a noise downstairs,' you say.
> 'Yes, but it was nothing,' I kiss your eyes shut. 'Only the cat with a bird,' I answer as you move into sleep, your cheek at my shoulder. 'Nothing.'
> Far out to sea, a gull cries against the coming of light. For a little longer night holds us beyond the grasp of speech. I lean and blow the candle out. (p. 63)

In a similar fashion, the heroine of 'The Husband' remains beyond the grasp of speech. Her bid for freedom and abandonment of her marriage in favour of a lesbian relationship is described from the viewpoint of her husband. His uncomprehending account of her final actions on the morning on which she leaves him provides us paradoxically with the impetus to imagine her unvoiced version of events. The absence of her story underlines both its coherence and its inaccessibility. Only the reader capable of seeing through the skewed narrative of the husband will hear that other story whose noise can be heard but which remains obdurately elusive.

The narrator in 'Introducing Nessa' tells us that 'people only see what they have heard of' (p. 148). This story tries to pry apart the subterfuges forced on lesbians by a censorious straight society from the positive reality of love and desire which these pretences mask. Dorcey constructs this narrative in such a way that we expect the tragic irony of an O. Henry ending. The central crisis of the story is caused by Anna's denial of her female lover, Nessa, when in the company of her straight friends. The dénouement, however, cancels out the gloom of the 'sweet, practised endings' which we have been anticipating. Even though the lovers are now estranged, they end the story linked by mutual understanding. Once again, it is a noise, this time of laughter, which leads the way into this other liberating dimension:

> And then Anna heard the last thing in the world she had expected. A sudden explosion of sound came through the phone so that she had to hold it out from her ear. It was a second before she realised that Nessa was laughing. And not in derision or scorn but a giddy whooping and bubbling mirth.
> 'Men,' Nessa said again, the single word struggling to be engulfed once again by a wave of laughter, so that after a moment Anna found she was laughing too. And so there they were, no more than five miles apart, in the early hours of the city; tight to their receivers and carried over

the distance; bouncing, gushing like water, unstoppable, laughter ran along the wires that joined them. (p. 159)

In this manner the double-voiced discourse of the story sets up a counterpoint between two intertwined but opposing plots. On the one hand, it shows how heterosexual prejudice stealthily undermines the relationship between Nessa and Anna, while on the other it celebrates the defiant continuance of gyn-affection. The joyous excess of female desire cuts across the negations of heterosexual meaning.

Thus the melancholy but hopeful Orphic departures of Kate O'Brien's novel become transformed into the open and joyful spaces of Mary Dorcey's fiction. The Ireland which the latter represents is still taken to task for the sexual repressiveness and homophobia which it promotes. However, it has shed the confining fixity which characterises it in the stories of Frank O'Connor, Mary Lavin and Seán O'Faoláin. Instead, despite itself, Dorcey's Ireland has acquired a postmodern openness and flexibility. Its landscapes now are capable of accommodating the noisy indeterminacy of alternative loves. Lesbianism is no longer the silent cry of an exile on the Place de la Concorde but the familiar sounds from the woodshed just outside our door.

Notes and References

1   Bonnie Zimmerman describes the coded language to which many writers resort to depict non-heterosexual relationships as a 'zero degree deviancy' because it uses symbols not so much to express as to blot out lesbianism. Elizabeth Meese thinks of the lesbian as 'a shadow with/in woman, with/in writing', and Terry Castle declares that the lesbian is a 'ghost effect' or spectral presence in modern culture. See Catherine Stimpson, 'Zero Degree Deviancy: The Lesbian Novel in English' in Elizabeth Abel (ed.), *Writing and Sexual Difference*, Brighton: Harvester, 1982, pp 243-59; Elizabeth Meese, *(Sem) erotics: Theorizing Lesbian Writing*, New York University Press, 1992, pp 1-21; Terry Castle, *The Apparitional Lesbian: Female Homosexuality and Modern Culture*, New York: Columbia University Press, 1993, pp 28-65.

2   Kate O'Brien, *As Music and Splendour*, London: Heinemann, 1958; Mary Dorcey, *A Noise From the Woodshed*, London: Onlywomen Press, 1989. All further references to these texts will be noted in parentheses.

3   Gilles Deleuze and Félix Guattari, *Kafka: Toward A Minor Literature*, trans. Dana Polan, Minneapolis: University of Minnesota Press, 1986.

4   For a suggestive linking of the radicalism of the gay and lesbian liberation movement with the potentially liberal values which stem from the anti-colonial ethos of the modern Irish state, see Kieran Rose, *Diverse Communities: The Evolution of Lesbian and Gay Politics in Ireland*, Cork University Press, 1994.

5   Janice Raymond opposes the positive effects of 'gyn/affection', that is, of loving relationships between women, to the constrictions and oppressions of 'hetero-reality' which is under the control of men (see *A Passion For Friends: Toward a Philosophy of Female Affection*, London: Women's Press, 1986).

6   Foucault makes the case that late ninteenth-century society, far from repressing
     peripheral sexualitities, actively encouraged their investigation and proliferation
     in order to control them more fully (see *The History of Sexuality*, vol. 1: *An In-
     troduction*, London: Penguin, 1979). However, as many critics have pointed out,
     Foucault's history entirely omits any reference to lesbianism. It also fails to in-
     clude the points of view of those ostracised as perverts by the linguistic
     mechanisms of control which he describes.

7   Eve Kosofsky Sedgwick, *Epistemology of the Closet*, Brighton: Harvester Wheat-
     sheaf, 1991.

8   Foucault, op. cit., pp 36-49.

9   Adrienne Rich, 'Compulsory Heterosexuality and Lesbian Existence' in *Blood Bread
     and Poetry: Selected Prose, 1979-1985*, London: Virago, 1987, p. 51

10   Catherine Stimpson, 'Zero Degree Deviancy', pp 243-4.

11   See Judith Butler, 'Imitation and Gender Insubordination', in Diana Fuss (ed.),
     inside/out: Lesbian Theories, Gay Theories, London: Routledge, 1991, pp 13-31; Biddy
     Martin, 'Sexual Practice and Changing Lesbian Identities' in Michèle Barrett and
     Anne Phillips (eds.), *Destabilizing Theory: Contemporary Feminist Debates*, Oxford:
     Polity Press, 1992, pp 93-119; Shane Phelan, '(Be) coming Out: Lesbian Identity
     and Politics', *Signs*, xviii (1993), pp 765-90; Monique Wittig, 'One is Not Born
     a Woman' in *The Straight Mind and other essays*, trans. Marlene Wildeman, Brighton:
     Harvester, 1992, pp 9-20.

12   Katie King, 'The Situation of Lesbianism as Feminism's Magical Sign: Contests
     for Meaning and the US Women's Movement, 1968-1972', *Communication*, ix (1986),
     pp 65-91.

13   For a history of the various social forms in which female friendship expressed
     itself see Lillian Faderman, *Surpassing the Love of Men*, London: The Women's
     Press, 1991.

14   Teresa de Lauretis, 'Eccentric Subjects: Feminist Theory and Historical Con-
     sciousness', *Feminist Studies*, xvi (1990), p. 144. For a similar argument which pro-
     poses that it is possible to see lesbian subculture as a possible site of resistance
     without at the same time assuming that it is coherent or unified, see Ann Ferguson,
     'Is There a Lesbian Culture?', in Jeffner Allen (ed.), *Lesbian Philosophies and Cultures*,
     State University of New York Press, 1990, pp 63-84.

15   See, for example, Gabriele Griffin, *Heavenly Love?: Lesbian Images in Twentieth-
     Century Women's Writing*, Manchester University Press, 1993; Karla Jay and Joanne
     Glasgow (eds.), *Lesbian Texts and Contexts: Radical Revisions*, London: Onlywomen
     Press, 1992; Paulina Palmer, *Contemporary Lesbian Writing: Dreams, Desire Dif-
     ference*, Buckingham: Open University Press, 1993; Bonnie Zimmerman, *The Safe
     Sea of Women: Lesbian Fiction, 1969-1989*, London: Onlywomen Press, 1992.

16   The divergences between the horizon of expectations of straight and gay readers
     still remain a matter of contention. Susan J. Wolfe and Julia Penelope argue, for
     example, that there is a crucial difference between these two audiences. They claim
     that 'a Lesbian may choose *not* to write as a Lesbian; that is, she may refuse to
     reveal the reality of her experience as a Lesbian in her writing. A non-Lesbian
     cannot choose to write or read as a Lesbian' (Sexual Identity / Textual Politics:
     Lesbian (Decom) positions' in Susan J. Wolfe and Julia and Penelope (eds.), *Sex-
     ual Practice, Textual Theory: Lesbian Cultural Criticism*, Oxford: Blackwell, 1993, p. 10.

17 By contrast, Bonnie Zimmermann assumes that the perverse strategies of inter-
    pretation adopted by lesbian readers lead to the resolution of textual ambiguities
    (see 'Perverse Reading: The Lesbian Appropriation of Literature', in Wolfe and
    Penelope, op. cit., pp. 135-49).

18 For a discussion of the way in which the theme of lesbian and homoerotic love
    is often hidden in subplots in O'Brien's novels see Emma Donoghue, 'Out of Order':
    Kate O'Brien's Lesbian Fictions' in Éibhear Walshe (ed.) *Ordinary People Dancing:
    Essays on Kate O'Brien*, Cork University Press, 1993.

19 Castle, op. cit., pp 66-91.

20 Percy Bysshe Shelley, 'Lines: When the Lamp is Shattered' in *Shelley's Poetry and
    Prose*, eds. Donald H. Reiman and Sharon B. Powers, New York: Norton, 1977,
    pp 637-8. I am grateful to Éibhear Walshe for this reference.

21 Walter Benjamin, *Charles Baudelaire: A Lyric Poet in the Era of High Capitalism*,
    trans. Harry Zohn, London: Verso, 1976, p. 125.

22 Benjamin examines the roving perspective of the *flâneur* in Baudelaire's poetry
    (see *Charles Baudelaire*, pp. 126-31). For a consideration of the extent to which
    women were excluded from this public activity and relegated to the part of the
    invisible stroller see Janet Wolff, 'The Invisible *Flâneuse*: Women and the Literature
    of Modernity' in *Feminine Sentences: Essays on Women and Culture*, Oxford: Polity
    Press, 1990, pp 34-50.

23 Radclyffe Hall, *The Well of Loneliness*, London: Virago Press, 1982.

24 Klein argues that the omnipresence of guilt in adults 'has very valuable aspects
    because it implies the never fully exhausted wish to make reparation and to create
    in whatever way we can' ('Our Adult World and its Roots in Infancy' in *Envy and
    Gratitude and other works, 1946-1963*, London: Virago, 1988, p. 259).

25 Hawthorne's *The Marble Faun*, London: Penguin, 1990, is a fable of guilt. Miriam's
    complicity in the murder of the Model, a mysterious figure who haunted her,
    acts as an allegory of the links between civilisation and transgression. This crime
    marks her but also lends force to the paintings which she produces. O'Brien sug-
    gests a similar link between creativity and sinfulness.

26 The *castrato* Gaetano Guadagni sang the role of Orfeo at the first performance
    of the opera in Vienna on 5 October 1762. It was Hector Berlioz who initiated
    the tradition of assigning the part to a woman. In his adaptation of Gluck's work
    for the Parisian stage in November 1859 the contralto Pauline Viardot-Garcia took
    over the role of Orfeo. The use of a female lead remains, however, controversial.
    Purists argue that, in the absence of a *castrato*, Orfeo is most approriately played
    by a male counter-tenor. For a discussion of the performance history of this opera,
    see Cristoph Willibald von Gluck: *Orfeo*, ed. Patricia Howard, Cambridge University
    Press, 1981.

27 For a critical account of the misogynist underpinnings of opera see Catherine
    Clément, *Opera or the Undoing of Woman*, trans. Betsy Wing, London: Virago, 1989.

28 Gluck added this aria to the second version of the opera destined for a Parisian
    audience. The original score of the opera more fittingly imposes silence on Euridice
    in Act II, as she is literally dead.

29 Roland Barthes, 'The Grain of the Voice', *The Responsibility of Forms: Critical Essays
    on Music, Art and Representation*, trans. Richard Howard, Oxford: Blackwell, 1985,
    p. 276.

30 Ibid., p. 270.

31 For a discussion of the way in which Virginia Woolf retells the story of Mozart's *The Magic Flute* from a female point of view in *Night and Day* see Jane Marcus, *Virginia Woolf and the Languages of Patriarchy*, Bloomington: Indiana University Press, 1987, pp 18-35. Willa Cather in *The Song of the Lark*, London: Virago, 1982, tells the tale of the rise to success of Thea Kronenberg as an exponent of Wagnerian opera. As in her other fictions, Cather uses this plot in order to suggest undercurrents of queer emotion which cannot otherwise be expressed. Thea explains that her passionate involvement with Wagner's heroines is due to the fact that they appear in works which are 'full of the thing every plain creature finds out for himself, but that never gets written down' (p. 540). Like O'Brien, Cather values opera because of the way in which it licenses transgressive emotions. Tellingly in her prefatory comments she announces that her novel is the inverse of Oscar Wilde's *The Picture of Dorian Gray*.

32 Wayne Koestenbaum, *The Queen's Throat: Opera, Homosexuality and the Mystery of Desire*, London, GNP Publishers, 1993, p. 40.

33 Deborah E. McDowell discusses Nella Larsen's use of the strategy of 'passing', that is, the concealment of black and homosocial themes in plots which 'pass' as stories that focus on white or heterosexual perspectives (see '"It's Not Safe, Not Safe at All": Sexuality in Nella Larsen's *Passing*' in *The Lesbian and Gay Studies Reader*, eds. Henry Abelove, Michèle Aina Barale, and David M. Halperin, London: Routledge, 1993, pp 616-25).

34 Koestenbaum, op. cit., p. 42.

35 Ibid.

36 Castle, op. cit., p. 227.

37 Theodor W. Adorno, 'Bourgeois Opera' in David J. Levin (ed.), *Opera through Other Eyes*, Stanford University Press, 1994, pp 25-43.

38 See F. W. Sternfeld, *The Birth of Opera*, Oxford: Clarendon Press, 1993.

39 Claudio Monteverdi's *L'Orfeo* is frequently accredited with being the first opera ever composed.

40 For a discussion of the way in which patriarchal signifying practices use the gaze as an instrument of domination see Laura Mulvey, 'Visual Pleasure and Narrative Cinema' in *Visual and Other Pleasures*, Bloomington: Indiana University Press, 1989.

41 For an account of the usefulness of a notion of the 'queer' in breaking down conventional definitions of gender boundaries see Eve Kosofsky Sedgwick, 'Queer and Now' in *Tendencies*, London: Routledge, 1994, pp 1-20.

42 Eve Kosofsky Sedgwick identifies these two patterns in the work of Willa Cather (see 'Willa Cather and Others' in *Tendencies*, pp 167-76.

43 Karl Miller, *Doubles: Studies in Literary History*, Oxford University Press, 1985, pp 1-38.

44 Marilyn Farwell, 'Heterosexual Plots and Lesbian Subtexts: Toward a Theory of Lesbian Narrative Space' in Karla Jay and Joanne Glasgow (eds.), *Lesbian Texts and Contexts*, p. 93.

45 Eve Kosofsky Sedgwick, *Between Men: English Literature and Male Homosocial Desire*, New York: Columbia University Press, 1985.

46 For an examination of the counterplot of lesbian love in the novels of Sylvia Townsend Warner see Terry Castle, 'Sylvia Townsend Warner and the Counterplot of Lesbian Fiction' in *The Apparitional Lesbian*, pp 66-91.

47 It is, of course, of note that, for the second important musical occasion linking her lesbian characters, O'Brien chooses Pergolesi's *Stabat Mater.* Like Gluck's opera, this work is occasionally performed by two female voices. Musical historians, however, argue that the parts are intended for a male alto and a female soprano.

48 For further discussion of the significance of Clare's reminiscences of her grandmother see Adele Dalsimer, *Kate O'Brien: A Critical Study,* Dublin: Gill & Macmillan, 1990, pp 120-3.

49 Mary Louise Pratt uses the term 'transculturation' to describe the way in which the cultural representations of marginal groups frequently appropriate materials and themes from dominant or metropolitan societies (see *Imperial Eyes: Travel Writing and Transculturation,* London: Routledge, 1992).

50 Deleuze and Guettari, op. cit., p. 18.

51 See Frank O'Connor, *The Lonely Voice: A Study of the Short Story,* London: Macmillan, 1963.

52 Kevin Kopelson coins the term 'ontoeroticism' in order to explore the binary pairing of self and other in lesbian narratives by Virginia Woolf and Gertrude Stein (see *Love's Litany: The Writing of Modern Homoerotics,* Stanford University Press, 1994, pp 74-103).

53 'The Spaces Between the Words: Mary Dorcey Talks to Nuala Archer', *The Women's Review of Books,* viii (1990), p. 24.

54 Walter Benjamin, 'The Storyteller: Reflections on the Works of Nikolai Leskov', in *Illuminations,* trans. Harry Zohn, London: Fontana, 1970, pp 81-109.

55 For an account of the doubleness that characterises women's writing see Elaine Showalter, 'Feminist Criticism in the Wilderness' in *The New Feminist Criticism,* London: Virago, 1986, pp 125-43.

9 Piggies and Spoilers of Girls
The Representation of Sexuality
in the Novels of Molly Keane

MARY BREEN

I

When the Irish novel *Good Behaviour* was short-listed for the Booker Prize in 1981, few people had ever heard of its seventy-seven-year-old author, Molly Keane. Such a polished and sophisticated novel excited interest among a wide range of readers. Research found Molly Keane, a widow with two daughters, living quietly in the small, secluded village of Ardmore, in Co. Waterford. Keane had had a previous literary career, between 1926 and 1961, when her work had been published under the pseudonym of M. J. Farrell. During this period she had written eleven novels and six plays, of which two 'were big successes, three . . . weren't and one . . . was a staggering failure'.[1] The sophisticated and black literary imagination displayed in *Good Behaviour* is clearly evident in all of the eleven early novels. This essay examines some of the main preoccupations of all of these novels, concentrating on two of the early ones, *Taking Chances* (1929) and *Devoted Ladies* (1934), and on her later masterpiece *Good Behaviour* (1981). Primarily I am interested in Keane's representation of sexuality. As a preface to this, because of the paucity of critical and biographical work available on her, I shall give a short introduction to her life and work.

Molly Keane was born Molly Skrine in Co. Kildare in 1904 and died in April 1996 (during the completion of this essay). Her family belonged to the privileged Anglo-Irish Ascendancy; she describes them herself as 'a rather serious hunting and fishing, church-going family'.[2] Her mother, Moira O'Neill, was a poet known as 'the poetess of the Glens', and she also did literary reviews for *Blackwoods* magazine;[3] her best-known work *Songs of the Glens of Antrim* was published in 1900. According to her daughter, she took very little interest in her children's lives, devoting her energies to writing; Keane remembered her childhood as one of neglect and isolation. In an interview with Polly Devlin she explained how she 'was always disliked as a child. My mother didn't really like me and the aunts were ghastly to me and my father had absolutely nothing to do with me.'[4] Until she was fourteen years old she received no formal education, but suffered at the hands of a succession of governesses. At fourteen she was sent to 'a prim, suburban boarding school' in Bray, Co. Wicklow. She was desperately unhappy here and claimed that:

> I might never have become a writer had it not been for the isolation in which I suffered as an unpopular schoolgirl. My unpopularity, that went to the edge of dislike, drove me into myself. I was walking among stars that had a different birth and I certainly learned the meaning of the black word 'Alone'.

Keane tended to present herself as a philistine, describing her interests as a young woman as 'hunting and horses and having a good time'. She wrote her early novels under the pseudonym M. J. Farrell in order 'to hide my literary side from my sporting friends'. We may note that the neutral initials M. J. also hid the gender of the author. Although her family lived the elegant life of the Ascendancy, there was very little ready money, and Keane says that she began writing as a way of supplementing her dress allowance. It seems likely, however, that she used this rather frivolous reason as a blind to protect herself and her early writing from serious critical attention. A young woman who completes her first novel at seventeen and who goes on to write prolifically over the following years, and who was still writing novels in her eighties, is a serious novelist. In her interviews Keane presents a kind of depreciating self-parody, which reveals very little about her serious attitudes to her writing. Because of her unhappy childhood, she left home at the earliest opportunity and went to live with family friends, the Perry family of Woodruff House, Co. Tipperary. Here she met Bobby Keane, whom she later married, having first lived with him for six years, and John Perry, who worked with her on several of her successful stage plays in London. These details of Molly Keane's social and family background are important because the decaying Anglo-Irish Big House and its daily routine form the setting for all of her novels. Her experiences as a child and a young woman, in particular her relationship with her mother, and her isolated life as an unpopular schoolgirl clearly inform the imagination of the novelist. The settings of the novels are confined and detailed; her intimate knowledge of the way of life of the

Anglo-Irish in their Big Houses in the early part of this century is deployed
in minute detail. Selfish and emotionally manipulative mothers occur frequently in Keane's novels, as do isolated and unhappy daughter-figures.
There is a concentrated focus on unattractive women who stand 'alone'.
The settings of all of Keane's novels are very similar, and so too are the
families who lounge elegantly in these exclusive settings. The decadence
that Showalter[5] associates with cultural decline is everywhere in Keane's
representation of this social world. Voracious, cruel and power-hungry
mother-figures dominate many of these households unchecked by indolent,
foxhunting, uninterested fathers. Like Charlotte Brontë's Mr Rochester, these
men 'are skilled in the petty dissipations of the rich and worthless'. But,
unlike Rochester, these characters are without critical self-awareness: they
are presented as complacent and self-satisfied. Children struggle to maturity
in this debilitating environment where the primary concern is 'good
behaviour', in the drawing-room and in the hunting-field. Unattractive,
very often overweight, unmarried daughters flounder about in search of
husbands, and when that fails, they fill their days with endless small tasks,
like washing dogs and arranging flowers, and in futilely giving their love
to those who don't want it.

Keane wrote her first novel, *The Knight of Cheerful Countenance*, when
she was seventeen. The was published in 1926 by Mills & Boon, then not
exclusively the publishers of romances, who paid her £70 for it. This was
followed by *Young Entry* (1928), *Taking Chances* (1929), *Mad Puppetstown*
(1931), *Conversation Piece,* (1932), *Devoted Ladies* (1934), *Full House* (1935),
The Rising Tide (1937), *Two Days in Aragon* (1941), *Loving Without Tears*
(1951) and *Treasure Hunt* (1952). All of these have been reissued by Virago
Press in recent years. During this period she also wrote the plays *Spring
Meeting* (1938), *Ducks and Drakes* (1942), *Treasure Hunt* (1949) and *Dazzling
Prospect* (1961). Many of these plays were written in collaboration with
John Perry and directed by John Gielgud. As Russell Harty recalled, 'She
was a fashionable dramatist of the late fifties, where she was a licensed
darling'. Keane's husband Bobby died suddenly in 1938. After the failure
of her play, the unfortunately named *Dazzling Prospect*, in 1961 Keane gave
up her writing career as M. J. Farrell, and returned to Ireland to raise her
two daughters. In 1981, after two decades of silence, *Good Behaviour* was
published, her first novel written under her own name. This was followed
by *Time after Time* in 1983 and *Loving and Giving* in 1988. (She also published a cookery book, *Nursery Cooking*, in 1985, probably as a satiric tribute
to what she describes as the poisonous food she was fed in the nursery
as a child.)

Very little critical work has been done to date on Keane. In Ann Owens
Weekes's 'Seeking a Tradition: Irish Women's Fiction' Weekes mainly

discusses *Good Behaviour*, a novel she sees as 'a needed corrective, or widening, of Bowen's picture' and 'a satirical glance down fifty years to the last September of Anglo-Ireland'.[6] In *The Irish Novel* James Cahalan is much more dismissive of her work: 'At worst, her fiction seems a lighter rehash of the fading Ascendancy world explored by Bowen'.[7] My argument will be that Cahalan's criticism fails to observe the critical difference between Bowen's Irish novels and Keane's: although both deal with the Ascendancy world, Bowen's novels are realist, while Keane's are satire or black farce. Rather than seeking to produce a 'rehash' of Bowen, Keane approaches her subject from a totally different imaginative perspective, and her writing can more successfully be compared to certain elements in the work of Maria Edgeworth, particularly to *Castle Rackrent*, than to Bowen's *The Last September*, which Cahalan seems to have in mind. Cahalan does concede, however, that 'at her best Keane explores the sexual conflicts of Ascendancy women with a boldness not found in Bowen'. It is this 'boldness', which Cahalan does not further define, that marks Molly Keane's work and may, as I shall suggest, draw readers nurtured on the absurd or the 'Theatre of Cruelty'. There are also some interesting essays on Keane in collected works on women novelists.

Tasmin Hargreaves, in 'Women's Consciousness and Identity in Four Irish Women Novelists', observes that 'no one in Keane's fictional world is capable of love'. For Hargreaves, 'Keane offers a deeply ironic, witty and painful critique of alienated being'.[8] The Virago editions of the M. J. Farrell novels all have substantial introductions, which supply some informaton about Keane's background but not much discussion of the novels themselves. Keane herself wrote the introduction to her first novel, *The Knight of Cheerful Countenance*, in 1993, almost seventy years after its first publication. In this she sketched in the lifestyle of the Ascendancy, in a situation where 'the world of my youth has vanished'. *Conversation Piece*, which was reissued in 1991, has an interview with the author by Polly Devlin, who also wrote introductions to five of the other novels. *Taking Chances*, one of the novels focused on in this essay, has an introduction by Clare Boylan. *Treasure Hunt*, which is dedicated to John Perry, is introduced by Dirk Bogarde, who remembers seeing the successful play of the same name which preceded the novel and which ran successfully for a year in 1949. The tired post-war British audience 'welcomed it with roars of delight'. The cast included Sybil Thorndike, Irene Brown, Alan Webb and Milo O'Shea. In 1987 Russell Harty wrote a brief and self-deprecating introduction to *Loving Without Tears*, which contains one of Keane's most bitter satires on motherhood. Harty's introduction is not concerned with the novel itself, but with his friendship with Keane; this forms the major subject of the preface. He does, however, give warning, however inadequately, of 'a certain bitterness. Indeed, a certain cynicism' in the novel. Caroline Blackwood, in her perceptive 1986 afterword to *Full House*, points out the profoundly philistine nature of Keane's Anglo-Irish society, where books and reading are looked on with contempt. She notes too Keane's representation of a stagnant world where love affairs are like games that are played to break the monotony, cruel games where nobody wins, and the 'unkind' mothers who create emotional devastation.

The most difficult task when discussing Keane is to find a genre into which she can fit comfortably; in fact it is easier to decide the genres to which she does not belong. Although her novels have been described as Big House novels, in my view, they refuse to be so classified. The settings are those of the Big House, but her concerns, as I shall show, are not those of the conventional Big House novel of Anglo-Irish literary tradition. Although there is a wealth of realistic detail, the fictional form she adopts is not exactly realist: there is no moral critique in Keane, no controlling irony. Neither are her novels romances, although a superficial reading might presume them to be so, and Keane herself certainly thought about her early novels in this way. Keane does not romanticise her world or treat it nostalgically, she ruthlessly satirises it; her Big Houses are not the centres of dignity that Yeats presents in *Ancestral Houses*. Her novels belong, I believe, to the Irish comic tradition, the tradition of Swift and Maria Edgeworth of *Castle Rackrent*. In Vivian Mercier's definition, Keane would appear to belong amont these satirists: Mercier defines satire in the context of Irish tradition as employing 'wit, humour, parody, and even wordplay besides the irony which is often regarded as its most characteristic device'.[9] Mercier also discusses the motives for satire, of which in his view the most spurious are those whose 'ultimate aim is to inflate their authors rather than to deflate the foolish and the evil'. The more laudable motives are those which, 'though mixed, include selfless indignation and a desire for abstract justice'. Keane's childhood experiences of Anglo-Irish life — the lack of emotional and imaginative nourishment, the total philistinism of her world — gave her every reason to feel 'indignation' and every right to seek 'abstract justice'. Keane chose her subject and her form well; as Mercier points out, 'Satire demands a spice of danger; it cannot be achieved by denouncing the weak and impoverished'.[10] Keane satirises the world of the privileged Anglo-Irish, her own world. The idle, pleasure-seeking lifestyles of the decadent Anglo-Irish were a worthy subject. Like Swift and Edgeworth in their time, Keane belonged to this world herself and, except for her childhood, seems in real life to have been a contented member of it. Nevertheless, satire does not condone or accept, it condemns what it represents. Presumably in order to protect herself and her life in her milieu, Keane wisely used a pseudonym, not simply because her 'set' frowned on literary pretensions, including even reading, but also because all her characters and settings, as she admits, are drawn from life.

In all of her novels, with the exception of *Good Behaviour* which has a first-person narrator, Keane uses omniscient narrators. The action is frequently focalised through a central character, whose view seems to closely mirror that of the narrator. Her narrators appear more voyeurs than as the judging, ironic narrators of classic realism. Classic examples of unreliable narration, they are intensely interested and usually deeply implicated in the ugly but compelling sexual power-struggles that are enacted between the characters. There are no good or sympathetic characters in Keane, no idealised figures for the reader to identify with. Neither is there a central ground of moral rightness; indeed, there are no generalising or explicit judgements, and the narrators do not direct or guide us. Keane might even be seen as parodying realist fictional form, for although she often ends her novels with marriage, these are never happy endings. These challenges to realism and moralising satire make Keane an intensely interesting and disconcerting novelist, and they also complicate and qualify any interpretation of her representation of sexuality.

II

The rest of this discussion explores her satiric depiction of heterosexual, gay and lesbian relationships and her recurrent unsympathetic representation of sexually undesirable women. Her novels are concerned with two groups of people: those who are involved in sexual relationships and those who remain outside. The central relationship in *Devoted Ladies* is a lesbian one; in *Good Behaviour* the narrative focus is on the homosexual relationship between two young men; and in *Taking Chances*, the novel is dominated by the heterosexual attraction between a young man and woman. In all three novels there are unwanted women who are marginalised by the central sexual relationship, which excludes them. Keane is unusual in presenting gay and lesbian desire as an integral part of a complex range of sexual possibilities. This might be seen as an advance on Victorian and Edwardian repression of the very existence of such desire. But although Keane makes alternative sexualities visible, she also circumscribes them very decisively. In her influential essay 'Compulsory Heterosexuality and Lesbian Existence' Adrienne Rich argues:

> Any theory or cultural/political creation that treats lesbian existence
> as a marginal or less 'natural' phenomena, as mere 'sexual preference',
> or as the mirror image of heterosexual or male homosexual relations
> is profoundly weakened thereby, whatever its other contributions.[11]

Keane does not marginalise lesbian existence; in fact in *Devoted Ladies* she centralises it. But she does present it as a 'mirror image' of heterosexual relationships. Rich goes on to argue in the same essay that it is not enough merely to tolerate lesbianism:

> Feminist theory can no longer afford merely to voice a toleration of 'lesbianism' as an 'alternative life-style', or make token allusion to lesbians. A feminist critique of compulsory heterosexual orientation for women is long overdue.[12]

Keane does not, of course, construct the kind of critique that Rich has in mind here, but she does, however negatively, treat lesbian existence as a legitimate subject. In this study I have grouped heterosexual, gay and lesbian relationships together because Keane does not present gay and lesbian relationships as marginal or apart. They are, in fact, an interwoven part of a complex series of interpersonal relationships depicted against a background of decaying Ascendancy life. This is not to suggest that gay and lesbian relationships are presented as enabling in Keane's novels; they are seen as imprisoning and debilitating, but no more so than the heterosexual relationships her characters are involved in. I shall argue that these heterosexual, gay and lesbian relationships are strikingly similar because the same heterosexual trope of desire is used throughout. In accordance with this, masculine desire is presented as strong and active, and feminine desire as passive and submissive; in all her same-sex relationships, traditional masculine and feminine roles are adopted. E. A. Kaplan argues that:

> As long as the structures of sexual attraction are locked into defining the masculine as dominance — cold, driving, ambitious and manipulating — and the female as the submissive — kindness, humaness, motherliness — the fact that some women are allowed to step into the masculine role leaves the structure intact: the gaze is not male but masculine and phallocentrism remains.[13]

Paradoxically, in Keane's representation of heterosexual desire in *Taking Chances* she constructs her female subject, ironically called Mary, as sexually active and desiring, thus questioning the traditional active / passive dichotomy between the male and the female. On the other hand, her homosexual and lesbian protagonists seem to remain imprisoned in a predetermined heterosexual trope of desire.

Keane's novels concentrate intensely on sexual desire, which is presented as the cornerstone of identity, and on its consequences. Desire is represented as a destructive force in the lives of her characters, dividing those characters into two distinct groups: 'they who have power to hurt', and those who, lacking this power, are hurt. If identity is dominated by sexuality, then those who are not considered sexually attractive, to either sex, have no recognisable value. In Keane's novels it is significant that only women are sexually unattractive; her male characters never fall into this category. Sexually unattractive women must search elsewhere for status and power in a society whose value system is so narrowly constructed. Unattached women abound in Keane's fiction; they are the marginal others in a society obsessed with sexuality and sexual gratification. This focus on the ability to marry (or mate) is not, of course, new or peculiar to Keane. The characters in Jane Austen's novels display a kind of spinster-baiting, similar to that in Keane, and Austen's marriage-obsessed society views unmarried women as an aberration and a horror to be avoided; a typical example is Miss Bates in *Emma*. In Austen's novel, however, Emma is criticised by Mr Knightley, the perfect gentleman and the voice of correct behaviour, for her treatment of Miss Bates, while in Keane the novels themselves cruelly lampoon these women and no corrective or consolatory moment is ever staged.

It is worth noting that while, as I have said, same-sex desire is presented in Keane's novels as frequently, or almost as frequently, as heterosexual desire, the undesirable single woman is perceived as the true aberration, the freak of nature. In Keane it is sexual desirability which is essential for the successful formation of identity. The society that Austen critiques in her novels sees marital status as the chief source of female identity, whereas Austen presents marriage as a prize awarded for moral self-knowledge, rationality and self-control. This draws a clear distinction between Austen and the world whose values she critiques. This distinction, as I have suggested, is not so clear in Keane. Without the moral guidance of the narrator, it is the implied reader who judges.

Good Behaviour traces the decline of an Anglo-Irish family, the St Charleses of Temple Alice. The novel has a first-person narrator, the only daughter of the house, Aroon St Charles. Aroon is obese, unattractive and desperately willing to please; she is naïve and sexually ignorant, and constantly presents facts in order to show herself in a favourable light. By constructing Aroon as an unreliable narrator, Keane ruthlessly exposes her lies and pretensions and the ridiculous façade behind which she hides her manipulative and jealous nature. Aroon's fake exterior is a paradigm of her world, where every economic and political reality is ignored or manipulated to buttress a decadent and diseased way of life. One of the great ironies of this novel is that this sexually naïve narrator presents a story which is dominated by the sexual exploits of its other central characters. Aroon's father, a major in the British army, conducts affairs with almost all the female characters in the novel, and several others whom we never meet, while remaining securely married to Aroon's mother.

Major St Charles's sexual desire is presented as active and demanding, although it is hidden by a deceptively helpless charm, while the women he seduces are passive and accepting, some to the point of self-annihilation. Mrs Brock, the children's governess, commits suicide when she discovers that she is pregnant and the Major ends their affair. Nod and Blink Crowherst have to leave their home and go to England when Nod too becomes pregnant by the Major. She desperately, but unsuccessfully, attempts abortion by means of hot baths and bottles of gin. But the Major's sexual exploits merely form the backdrop for the central sexual relationship in the novel: the homosexual relationship between Aroon's brother Hubert and his sophisticated friend from Oxford, Richard Massingham. *Good Behaviour* is a retrospective novel in which Aroon, in an attempt to understand her life, looks back from her bleak middle-aged spinsterhood to her childhood and adolescence. Her story is one of loneliness and isolation, except for the middle section of the novel which deals with the glorious few weeks that Hubert and Richard spend in Temple Alice. Aroon describes lovingly and with minute attention to detail, but little understanding, the relationship that develops between her brother Hubert, his friend Richard and herself. The young men are physically beautiful and seemingly totally at ease with their sexuality, although unwilling to disclose it in public, being well aware of the punishment meted out to those who step outside accepted male homosocial behaviour:

> There was a quick, hard grace about their movements, in the way they put links quickly into the cuffs of evening shirts, such a different tempo from a girl's considered gesture. They wore narrow red braces and their black trousers were taut round waist and bottoms. (*GB*, p. 90)

The gaze here is female; although Aroon presents herself as naïve, passages like this reveal her consciousness of active sexual desire or longing. The boys bring an extra glamour to Temple Alice; their days are idle, they drink gin and lemon in their room before dinner, and dance languidly with Aroon in the drawing-room in the evening. Their relationship is exciting, even dangerous; there is a constant power struggle between them, and a threat of infidelity. Despite the homoerotic nature of their relationship, however, their roles are allotted in a conventional way. Richard is aggressive and predatory in his desire — 'masculine' — while Hubert is passive and malleable — 'feminine'. As a representation of gay desire, this limits the relationship, trapping it in a set of predetermined oppositons which are the traditional hallmarks of heterosexual relationships.

An air of exclusiveness surrounds Hubert and Richard even when they are doing something as prosaic as taking fleas from a dog:

Hubert was sitting, a dog on his knees, below the negro's shaded lamp.
The light on his bent head shone his hair to blue-black, and the forward turn of his neck, between hair and white shirt collar, was as dark
a brown as his hands on the white dog. Richard standing behind the
tall wing chair, stooped his extraordinary height over Hubert and the
little dog. His eyes, when he raised his head towards us, held a look of
anger and loss as if he suffered some unkind deprivation — something
quite serious, like getting left in a hunt. (*GB*, p. 97)

But even this subtly lit cameo of the two young men groups them in a
standard Edwardian pose of the happily married couple. The 'wife' sits
passively on a chair, head bent, while the 'husband' leans devotedly and
possesively over her.

The mystery and glamour that surrounds them even affects the old house.
Temple Alice, although large and imposing, is a cold comfortless house,
full of ugly furniture; it has a leaking roof, hard beds and soft, cold bath
water. But when Richard and Hubert come to stay, the old house is
transformed by their presence and the excitement that surrounds them:

But in this eternal August the place took on a sumptuous quality. Every
day the lean deprived face of the house blazed out in the sunlight. Sun
poured onto the damp-stained wallpaper, through the long windows. It
shone on us from when we woke until we changed for dinner. (*GB*, p. 89)

Despite their careless and arrogant attitude to life, the boys are vulnerable
to the social threat of homophobia. As Eve Kosofsky Sedgwick says, 'For
a man to be a man's man is separated only by an invisible, carefully blurred always already-crossed line from being interested in men.'[14] In order
to protect themselves from being thought 'interested' in each other, Hubert
and Richard involve Aroon in their cruel games of deception. Aroon is
a willing accomplice, but this does not excuse the arrogance of the boys'
behaviour.

In those last days the boys kept me with them continually. Each day
of early September was more perfect than the last. Grapes were ripe in
the battered vinery — those muscatels Mummie knew how to thin and
prune. Butterflies — fritillaries, peacocks — spread their wings on
scabious, sedum, and buddelia, waiting heavily, happily for death to come.
We sat among them, eating grapes, the sun on our backs. (*GB*, p. 99)

In this passage Aroon captures imaginatively the fleeting nature of the boys'
relationship: for a short but glorious time, like the butterflies, they are
happy, but the inevitable conclusion of this intensity must be death. Driving
back through England on the way to Cambridge, Hubert is killed in a car
crash. Keane here makes the direct connection between same-sex desire

and death — the standard ideological response to 'perversion'.[15] In Keane this fate awaits not only the 'pervert', but many of her female heterosexual characters who love too much. Mrs Brock is an example of this, as is the central female character, Maeve, in *Loving and Giving*.

Because of her marginality as one of Keane's unwanted women, Aroon finds in her relationship with Richard and Hubert an opportunity to develop a sense of herself as a sexually desirable being. From this she forges a sense of identity which is as false as Richard's pretended desire for her, upon which it is based, and which lasts throughout her life despite the fact that Richard never returns to Temple Alice. As Aroon tells us, she 'knows how to construct this truth'. But this meagre proof of herself is not enough to sustain her, for despite her ability to transform in fantasy the smallest display of interest shown in her by Richard into a consuming desire, Aroon still has to find an expression for her own sexuality. In the event, she displaces her own sexual desire into an obsession with food and its consumption. Food becomes a source of power and control. As we learn in the opening chapter, she eventually uses it to kill her mother and then asks for the same dish to be kept warm for her own luncheon. Keane suggests that those who never find a way to express their sexual desire end up as cruel and destructive self-deceivers. As a large and sex-ually unattractive girl, totally lacking in self-confidence, Aroon strives to attract attention to herself by other means. When she first meets Hubert's friend Richard, the only way she can think of to make the boys take notice of her is to eat enormous quantities of food at dinner. The boys do notice, and are amused by her. These gastronomic feats earn her the nickname Pig. Aroon's relationship to food is a complex one; it at once empowers and enslaves her. It provides solace in an otherwise lonely life, but it is also fraught with anxiety. When Aroon's father dies and she thinks that her mother will inherit everything, she is agonised by the fear that her mother will ration her food. By the end of the novel Aroon is a lonely and isolated figure possessed by a strong desire to justify herself, but she is also free and independent. That desire to speak about her life which motivates the narrative is a product of this newly found independence. Aroon is not liberated by weight loss, or by suddenly becoming sexually attractive, or by an offer of marriage or of love, but by the fact that her father has left the estate to her. From being the undesirable daughter, she becomes the head of the family. She directs their affairs and takes charge of her now elderly mother and at last attains what she always wanted: the power to exercise complete control over other people's lives. She gets what Sara Sceats calls 'revenge-by-looking-after'.[16] All of Keane's unwanted women seek continually to be included, to be part of a relationship; but all experience moments of dreadful clarity when their isolated and unwanted state is brought home to them with appalling finality. Aroon, who has thought of Hubert, Richard and herself as a 'trinity', is brought to the full realisation of the exclusiveness of the boys' relationship and her own marginality when she overhears them laughing at her:

> I stood outside the door with the dreadful glass in my hand. Inside the room I heard them begin to laugh, relieved giggling laughter, and when they supposed I had gone, shouts of laughter followed me — laughter that expressed their relief from some tension and left me an outsider. Puzzled and anxious I sat in my bedroom, sipping at the disgustingly powerful gin without gaining from it any lift or exuberance. I waited for the minutes to pass, minutes that I had so carelessly expected to spend in their company. Soon the gin overcame the pain, but not my misturst, or certainty in happiness. (*GB*, p. 96)

The moment of clarity when Aroon, the unwanted single woman, vividly sees her exclusion is a recurrent motif in Keane. In *Devoted Ladies* and *Taking Chances* the unwanted women, Piggy and Maeve, have similar epiphanies.

Devoted Ladies was published in 1934. In the opening chapters the action takes place in London, in a world of chic parties, beautiful flats, Bohemian lifestyles and talk of literature and art. But the action very soon returns to the familiar setting of an elegant but decaying Big House in rural Ireland, where life centres on horses and hounds, fishing and shooting. The central relationship in this novel is a lesbian one. Keane has explained why she chose this as a subject:

> I suppose I was rather curious and shocked by coming upon all that. Before then no one thought anything of two elderly ladies setting up house together. I'd certainly never heard a murmur. I was excited by finding out about lesbians and homosexuals. It was new. It made a subject. My interest went in spasms, there would be a sudden arousal of interest that took over, something new — like this — that would be the start of a new book.[17]

From this rather innocent statement it would seem that Keane did not have a particular agenda when she began to write *Devoted Ladies*; lesbianism was simply a new subject. Belying this casualness, however, the narrative itself displays an intense, almost voyeuristic, interest in the relationship between the two women. Although the novel has an omniscient narrator, its action is frequently focalised through Sylvester, an Anglo-Irishman who has a successful career as a writer. He lives mainly in London, but retreats to Ireland to write. There he stays with his two unmarried cousins Piggy and Hester. The action of the novel traces the complicated relationships that develop between a group of ill-assorted people who come to stay with them. We see much of the action through Sylvester's eyes; he is observant, distant, and at times intensely cruel and manipulative. His main interest is in Jessica and Jane, the lesbian couple. He is fascinated by the cruelty of their relationship; when Jane falls in love with a friend of his, George Playfair, he abandons his status as an observer and strives to help Jane escape from Jessica.

In this discussion I will draw on Adrienne Rich's analysis of the use of the word 'lesbian':

> I have chosen to use the term lesbian existence and lesbian continuum because the word lesbian has a clinical and limiting ring. Lesbian existence suggests both the fact of the historical existence of lesbians and our continuing creation of the meaning of that existence. I mean the term lesbian continuum to include a range — through each woman's life and throughout history — of woman-identified experience: not simply the fact that a woman has had a consciously desired genital sexual experience with another woman.[18]

Considering Keane's representation of woman-identified experience and using Rich's concept of a 'lesbian continuum', we find in this novel two relationships between women which could occupy positions almost at either end of such a range: one between Jessica and Jane, which is genital/sexual, and the other between Piggy and Joan, which is apparently non-sexual. I shall argue that these two, seemingly very different, relationships have startlingly similar elements. Jessica and Jane's lesbian existence and Joan and Piggy's female friendship parallel each other throughout the second half of the novel. Keane satirises the butch/femme roles that Jessica and Jane adopt by exaggerating them into grotesque figures of fun. Jessica is strong and assertive, and she has a violent temper which she relieves by chewing on the side of the bath until her teeth bleed or by deliberately cutting herself. Her physical appearance is a ridiculous contradiction between her feminine body shape and her desire to appear 'masculine':

> Jessica's dark hair was cut with charming severity. If her dark face had been less heavy and turbulent in expression Jessica would almost have succeeded in looking as hard and boyish as she hoped she looked. But this plan of hers had been spoilt by God in the beginning, for he had given her a positive bosom and massive thighs. She was a heavy-minded woman too, without much gaiety of spirit. It was typical of her to break chains and bite baths in moments of stress, so did she grind her teeth into life and with as little satisfaction to herself. (*DL*, p. 42)

Jane, by contrast, is slight, fair and pretty, except for the scar of her hare-lip, and exaggeratedly feminine and helpless. From the beginning of the novel their relationship is described in sado-masochistic terms. Jane, alcoholic and helpless, is in constant fear that Jessica will kill her. This is not simply a pose, although Jane adopts many poses. When at a party at Sylvester's Jessica sees Jane lying on a sofa talking to George Playfair, she is consumed with rage:

> 'I can't bear to see her like that', Jessica went on, 'half asleep — half drunk. It disgusts me. Why, I'd rather see her dead, I think.' And with this she picked up a bottle of tonic water and made menacing gestures with it across the room at Jane.
>
> Jane had just time to scream: 'Now, Jessica, don't throw that bottle at me' — when Sylvester saw the crash of broken glass and heard Jane scream: 'Oh — you're horrible to me', as she bowed her bleeding head upon his divan. (*DL*, pp 16-17)

This is followed by a reconciliation between the women that makes Sylvester feel:

> slightly sick, partly from the sight of Jane's nasty blood and partly from his understanding of that fierce instinct to cherish that Jessica — drunken, pallid and tender — displayed now as she sponged Jane's head with his favourite sponge; dreadfully protective where five minutes ago she had been to all intents and purposes a murderess. Jane . . . her crooked mouth a little open and her whole attitude as drained of emotion as that of any woman at the conclusion of a blood quarrel with her mate. It was unbearable. (*DL*, p. 18)

Frank O'Connor, lamenting the lack of a good modern Irish satirist, complained: 'None of us could ever fashion a story or play into a stiletto to run into the vitals of some pompous ass.'[19] Keane seems to have mastered the technique; in this passage she manages to satirise not only the two women but her narcissistic camp observer Sylvester as well. But she does not reserve her ironic presentation for her lesbian and camp characters; her straight characters receive similar treatment. Although Jane protests, with good reason, that she is afraid of Jessica, she is also intensely aware that Jessica's strength gives her a sense of vitality: 'Now Jessica — although she is horrible to me — she's a real live woman' (*DL*, p. 19).

The appropriately named George Playfair, a charming but boring man, is to be Jane's rescuer. The relationship between Jane, Jessica and George develops into a bitter contest. Jane sees George as a means of escape from the exciting but deadly grip of Jessica. The narrator constantly reminds us that it is Jane's weakness that ties her to Jessica: 'Jane was easily defeated in any emotional contest. All her opponent's points of view became instantly and agonisingly her own' (*DL*, p. 200). This relationship which is held together by Jessica's strength and Jane's weakness is mirrored in the other important woman-centred relationship in the novel: the friendship between Joan and Piggy. Piggy is totally subservient to Joan; she allows herself to be abused and used and still remains devoted and loyal. Piggy, as her name suggests, is fat and unlovable, while Joan is beautiful and happily married. Throughout most of the novel we see Piggy through Sylvester's eyes. He despises her and searches constantly for ways to humiliate her, as do most of the characters in the novel. Jessica describes her as a 'fidgety, over-sexed woman'.

As her relationship with George develops, Jane becomes obsessed with escape. She learns very quickly that the life she and Jessica and their gay valet Albert live in London will not be acceptable in Ireland. When Albert begins to behave secretively, Jane is appalled:

> He can't have an affair here. His affairs belong to another life where they were faintly amusing and anyhow did not matter. . . . Here she would not have such rudeness. No, she would deny it all, all. This life and that were a world apart; one could escape, surely one could escape. (*DL*, p. 257)

In Keane it would seem that Ireland is represented as narrower and more prescriptive than England. Yet, ironically, Jane wants to escape from England to Ireland. The ambiguity in Keane's writing is evident here, as it is extremely difficult to decide which place the novel approves of; again, the lack of a moral judgement leaves the reader puzzled.

The two woman-centred relationships in *Devoted Ladies* are destroyed in order for the heterosexual relationship between George and Jane to survive. But this 'happy' ending is weakened by the way in which Keane represents the love between George and Jane:

> The stupidity and tenderness of such love as George's encompassed Jane entirely. . . . She was enthralled and held away from herself. She was the Jane he thought her to be. She would forever protect him from the Jane she was. (*DL*, p. 264)

This extremely cynical statement, which for once is unfocalised through character and seems to be the voice of the narrator, is another good example of the radical denial of moral statement in Keane.

Devoted Ladies ends with a resounding climax, suitably at the end of a bloody and successful day's foxhunting. Piggy and Jessica, the two unwanted women, are excluded from the hunt: when they arrive, the others want nothing to do with them:

> Jane, George and Joan and Sylvester, all so quiet and aloof after their morning's endeavour, belong to the moment and to each other, not to any outsiders. Certainly not to Piggy and Jessica. With Piggy and Jessica they were in no accord. (*DL*, p. 279)

Jessica, the outsider, comes 'Obviously screaming for her lovely' (p. 280). She is consumed with a desire to punish: 'She would require no more of Jane after she had destroyed her. She only required her destruction' (p. 281). The scene that takes place between the two women shows Jessica's power and cruelty and Jane's helplessness. Jane knows that George will not want her if Jessica tells him about her past. In order to love George and be loved by him Jane cannot be herself. As Jessica remarks,

> I just can't stand aside and see you make such an absurd sentimental mess of your life. Of course, if this man should have enough vision to want you when he has some idea of the real you, then I have nothing to say. (*DL*, p. 291)

This disturbs the seemingly happy resolution of the novel. If Jane can only truly be herself with Jessica, then that, no matter how difficult, must be preferable to playing a part. (This is an implied reader's comment, because the narrator makes no judgements about the matter.) Yet this is complicated by the fact that Keane constantly shows Jane as playing at life; she is presented as a woman without ideas, as a hollow shell that must be defined by a stronger character. In her relationship with Jessica she found a way to think; Jessica's ideas 'fitted well into the hollow place in her mind where her opinion might, had she owned such a thing, have belonged' (*DL*, pp 200-1).

The motif of exclusion used in *Good Behaviour* is even more frequently used in *Devoted Ladies*. Piggy is constantly aware of her own marginality:

> And Piggy stood beside them. Alone, burningly alone, terribly apart and unwanted. This was typical of so many moments in Piggy's life, sickening, frightening moments in which she was impotent and alone. (*DL*, p. 193)

— and again:

> Piggy endured one of those terrible poisoning moments when she knew herself to be outside love forever. Blindly aware that this thing was never for her. (*DL*, p. 170)

In Keane exclusion from love is the only marginality to be feared. To be in a relationship, no matter how cruel, is to be whole; to be outside is to be 'impotent' and 'terribly apart and unwanted'. When Joan insults Piggy, beyond even her capacity to forgive, she turns to George and finds in his kindness a new location for her loving and giving: 'Every desire that Piggy had was sublimated into a single wish to serve.' It is this desire to serve George that drives Piggy to kill Jessica:

> Piggy did not think. She only felt and knew. Her blind gift of serving where she loved cast out all fear. She put her foot down on the accelerator and the car leapt forward and dropped. (*DL*, p. 303)

In one violent impulse Piggy kills Jessica and herself. This emphasises the capacity for destruction which characterises Keane's unwanted women, Piggy and Aroon.

In *Taking Chances* (1929) Keane's focus is on heterosexual love and its all-consuming power. She uses a familiar plot structure and setting. Sir Ralph, Maeve and Ger live in their elegant Big House, Sorristown. Maeve is engaged to Rowley, the handsomest man in the county. Her beautiful friend Mary arrives from London to be her bridesmaid, and the quiet contented lives of these young Irish people are shattered. Popular understanding of sexual relationships between men and women has been largely informed by Freud and Lacan, who have not essentially dispelled the time-honoured notion that women are 'naturally' passive and men 'naturally' active in sex. Women are seen as having no sexual autonomy. In almost all her novels Keane too fails to challenge this essentialist view of women's sexual desire as passive. We have seen in *Devoted Ladies* how Jane the 'feminine' partner in the lesbian relationship is without sexual autonomy. Even in her new relationship with George she remains passive; her escape from Jessica is orchestrated by others. In *Good Behaviour*, where the homosexual lovers replicate the conventional heterosexual pattern, Hubert, in his relationship with Richard, is weak and submissive. In *Taking Chances*, however, Keane constructs a woman, ironically called Mary, with an active sexual will. She is charming and selfish, cruel and destructive, and almost all the men in the novel are in love with her. Instantly attracted to Rowley, she actively pursues him, and very shortly after Rowley's marriage to Maeve they run away together. Maeve is virtuous and honest but sexually naïve. Keane, as Boylan points out in her introduction to the novel, 'manages to make virginity seem a kind of short-sightedness which turns marriage into Blind Man's Buff' (*TC*, p. xiii):

> Soon — in a few hours — they would be together for always, and each day would be a day to love each other more. And the nights. But Maeve's nice thoughts stopped short there in a mysterious, hallowed glow. (*TC*, pp 122-3)

Keane has no patience with sexual naïveté or passivity. She pillories Aroon and Maeve for their blindness to sex and power. The relationship between Rowley and Maeve is presented using the conventional binary opposition of masculine and feminine. Rowley, thinking of Maeve, 'was not too disturbed by the most negative acquiescence which was all he knew of her love for him' (p. 16). Maeve loses Rowley because of her passivity, and Mary wins because of her clearly displayed active sexual will. The virtuous Maeve, who should be the heroine, but whose suffering is dismissed in the novel (she has only 'the vitriolic, futile importance of a slighted woman'), voices her opinion and condemnation of Mary:

> Girls who have no respect for their slack, lustful bodies, who love and demand and take other women's dear mates; who never stop for fear or for favour; for whom ostracism is not punishment, but an amusement which they faintly deride. (*TC*, p. 235)

This may be Maeve's opinion of Mary, but how does the narrator view her? As always in Keane, any judgement of her characters is omitted or, as in this case, judgement is pronounced by the other, equally unreliable, characters. Above we have Maeve's judgement of Mary, but counterbalancing this is Ger's opinion. At many of the important moments in the novel the narrative is focalised through Ger; in love with Mary himself, he judges her with kindness and tolerance. But Ger, while morally more creditable, has proved himself unreliable as a reader of character many times in the novel. We are left, therefore, oscillating between many different moral perspectives, several of which seem to be irreconcilable.

Keane's novels are concerned with sex and power and with how the intimate connection between them influences the lives of her characters. For the purposes of her novels, she is evidently not interested in creating regulatory sexual categories, central or marginal. She is interested in how sexual attraction between people of opposite or the same sex works. Nevertheless, her representation of same-sex desire, although glamorous and exciting, is problematic. Both the lesbian relationship in *Devoted Ladies* and the gay relationship in *Good Behaviour* end in death. The only relationship which is based on mutual subjectivities is the illicit heterosexual one between Rowley and Mary in *Taking Chances*. As I have stressed throughout this essay, there are no clear moral judgements in her novels, which makes it difficult to come to any clear conclusions about her representation of sexuality. She is, however, an important figure in any consideration of the homoerotic in Irish writing, because in her fictional world lesbian and gay characters learn to suffer equally with their straight counterparts under the tyranny of love.

Abbreviations

DL   *Devoted Ladies* (1934), London: Virago, 1984
GB   *Good Behaviour* (1981), London: Abacus, 1982
TC   *Taking Chances* (1929), London: Virago, 1987

Notes and References

1   Taken from an interview with Polly Devlin which forms the introduction to *Conversation Piece,* London: Virago, 1991.

2   Ibid.

3   See John Quinn, *A Portrait of the Artist as a Young Girl,* London: Methuen, 1986. This collection of interviews with Irish women writers contains an interesting piece by Keane, pp 65-78.

4   This and the following reminiscences are taken from Polly Devlin's interview with Keane cited above.

5   Elaine Showalter, *Sexual Anarchy, Gender and Culture at the Fin de Siècle,* London: Bloomsbury, 1991.

6   Ann Owens Weekes, *Irish Women Writers: An Uncharted Tradition,* Lexington: University of Kentucky Press, 1990.

7   James M. Cahalan, *The Irish Novel,* Dublin: Gill & Macmillan, 1988, pp 207-8.

8   Tasmin Hargreaves, 'Women's Consciousness and Identity in Four Irish Women Novelists' in Michael Kenneally (ed.), *Cultural Contexts and Literary Idioms in Contemporary Irish Literature,* Totowa, NJ: Barnes & Noble, 1988, p. 279. See also Katherine Lilly Gibbs, *An Introduction to the Fiction of Molly Keane,* Ann Arbor: Dissertation-Abstracts-International, 1993; Clare Boylan, 'Sex, Snobbery and the Strategies of Molly Keane' in Robert E. Hosmer (ed.), *Contemporary British Women Writers: Narrative Strategies,* New York: St Martin's, 1993; Rudiger Imhof, 'Molly Keane, Good Behaviour, Time after Time and Loving and Giving: A Collection of Interpretations' in Otto Rauchbauer (ed.), *Ancestral Voices: The Big House in Anglo-Irish Literature,* Hildesheim: Olms, 1992; Bridget O'Toole 'Three Writers of the Big House: Elizabeth Bowen, Molly Keane and Jennifer Johnston: Essays in Honour of John Hewitt' in Gerald Dawe and Edna Longley (eds.), *Across a Roaring Hill: The Protestant Imagination in Modern Ireland,* Belfast: Blackstaff, 1985.

9   Vivian Mercier, *The Irish Comic Tradition,* Oxford University Press, 1962, p. 184.

10 Ibid.

11 Adrienne Rich, 'Compulsory Heterosexuality and Lesbian Existence' in Catherine Stimpson and Ethel Spector Person (eds.), *Women, Sex and Sexuality,* University of Chicago Press, 1980, p. 63.

12 Ibid.

13 Quoted in Marja Makinen, 'Embodying the Negated: Contemporary Images of the Female Erotic' in Sarah Skeats and Gail Cunningham (eds.), *Image and Power,* New York: Longman, 1996, p. 42.

14 Eve Kosofsky Sedgwick, *Between Men: English Literature and Male Homosocial Desire,* New York: Columbia University Press, 1985, p. 89.

15 For a discussion of this topic see Jonathan Dollimore, *Sexual Dissidence: Augustine to Wilde, Freud to Foucault,* Oxford University Press, 1991.

16 Sarah Skeats, 'Eating the Evidence: Women, Power and Food' in Sarah Skeats and Gail Cunningham (eds.), *Image and Power,* New York: Longman, 1996, p. 121.

17 Quoted in Devlin interview cited in note 1 above.

18 Rich, op. cit., p. 80.

19 Mercier, op. cit., p. 182.

10 Dearg Dobhogtha Cháin/The Indelible Mark of Cain
Sexual Dissidence in the Poetry of Cathal Ó Searcaigh

LILLIS Ó LAOIRE

With the publication of *An Bealach 'na Bhaile/Homecoming* (1993), the poetry of Cathal Ó Searcaigh became available to a wider readership, one without the fluency required to read his poetry in the original Irish. However, critical analysis of his work has been mainly confined to short reviews and articles in literary journals. It is timely, then, that his work should receive more attention, particularly in the context of the theme of sexual dissidence. In a sense, Ó Searcaigh's poetry has been critically interpreted in terms of its bright, celebratory lyricism. This tendency can obscure the disruptive and complex poetic forces beneath the shining planes of the surface. His poetry often deals with the tensions which occur between the individual and the immediate community or large powerful institutions. He uses a disparate set of literary references within his poetry and attempts to establish connections between his formative experiences in a rural Irish-speaking region and subsequent influences, stemming from later experience and from his wide reading, and to forge these into a coherent voice. Much of his work has a public dimension, while being at the same time intensely personal. He deals openly with homosexual love in his poetry, contributing greatly to its distinct perspective. Homosexual love has until very recently been taboo in Ireland, although decriminalisation has created more openness in this area. Opinions and attitudes are complex and varied. In an interview with *Innti* 1988, the poet Pearse Hutchinson, in answer to a question about the fear of excommunication of homosexual people, comments:

221

Well, even in the fifties, in Dublin at any rate, the civilisation of the blind
eye always existed, even more so than in London, regarding gay people.
But since everyone knows now that such people exist, in ways it is easier
to attack it. . . . I must say that I believe that a lot of people are more
genuinely open in this country, more truly open in ways than in
England for example. But the other people are always there. And that
kind of love is against the law in this country still, something which
is not true of England.[1]

The puritanical atmosphere which prevailed in Ireland after independence
compounded this situation. Hutchinson again neatly summarises:

Once I discovered sex I began to chafe at the almost incessant killjoy
barrage that came at me from all sides: school, pulpit, confession box,
home. . . . Puritanism seemed to me the worst thing ever invented, it
was my enemy, and with it I identified (not unnaturally, given that prevailing late Forties atmosphere) Ireland itself. So I rejected Ireland . . .[2]

There was an added difficulty within a state which attempted to control
and censor the traditions of Irish poetry. Hutchinson adds:

We were not yet blest with Barry [Hutchinson's English teacher] when
whichever Brother it was told us to open *Filíocht na nGael* (the standard
school-anthology). He went through it with us page by page, instructing
us to write, above certain poems, 'Ná léigh'. This means: 'Don't read'.
Needless to say those of us who were at all interested in reading couldn't
wait to get home to see what forbidden joys were in store. Nothing out-
of-the-way to be sure.[3]

Ó Searcaigh, then, both because of his openness and his medium, strikes
at the heart of post-independence puritanism, his homoerotic perspective providing much of the force behind his onslaught. In this essay I propose
to examine Ó Searcaigh's poetry in the light of this perspective. I will argue
that, regardless of his imaginative perspectives, his homoerotic perspective underpins his position and informs his viewpoint. In discussing the
love poetry, I shall attempt to demonstrate some of its other underlying
themes, which are also manifest in his non-erotic poetry. Many of the points
made in this essay are a development of ideas already touched upon in
my introduction to Ó Searcaigh's collection *An Bealach 'na Bhaile/
Homecoming*, and in that respect the two essays are complementary.

The lack of willingness to approach difficult areas, and the unease aris-
ing from it, are widespread within Irish culture. It is all the more important, then, to acknowledge writers when they explore such subjects in their
work and to attempt to interpret this directness. Ó Searcaigh's openly gay
stance and his world's ambivalence to it create a certain tension in his

poetry. This manifests itself in his decision to locate himself in his native place, his (off-) centre, and in his relationship with its people, whether as individuals or as a community. He also inhabits a wider literary world and is a skilled and enthusiastic interpreter of many different literary traditions. This other existence gives him a dimension which allows him to be a part of the community and apart from it at the same time. He always chooses the margins, never being fully inside or out. This manifests itself in his portrayals of other marginalised members of the community. To him these are not sociological or anthropological specimens, but flesh-and-blood characters who form an important part of his memory, and thus of his creative reference. The poems which commemorate men and women from the area pay homage to people who influenced him as a child (*BB*, pp 112-39). In these the public and private voices are apparent. He is at once marking the passing of a particular era and also fondly remembering the death of his mentors and friends. These poems have been dismissed as sentimental nostalgia by some. There is nostalgia, as there must certainly be when a whole way of life has ended with the passing of such people, but he does also bear independent and sympathetic witness to the bleak, attenuated existences lived by some of them. In the poem 'Caoradóir/Shepherd' (*BB*, pp 122-5), he lets us see the effects upon one man of 'constant struggle with the tyranny of the mountain'. He is exploring rural decay in his own region, an issue that has recently begun to exercise others in the public domain. Greagóir Ó Dúill writes of this poem: 'This is a level of sympathy which is out of the ordinary — and the conversational language is a masterful display of poetic ability, it is unconstrained, stately, incremental and piles up insights in order to tell the agonising story properly.'[4] In 'Bean a'tSléibhe / Mountain Woman' (*BB*, pp 116-19) he gives a succinct picture of his subject in a few words:

> She inclined to flesh but also to fun
> And though she was fond of swearing and gap-toothed
> She was never gruff or gloomy with us
> When we visited her on Sundays
> And she made us a drop of tea
> While she hotly 'dashed' this and 'dratted' that.

This character is in some ways an archetype, derived from a number of women in similar situations, and it seems to me, therefore, that because of his perspective, the poet identifies with those who are liminal. Tree images and symbols abound in his work, and here the tree is held to represent this woman's resilience, her spiritual beauty and closeness to the recurring natural cycle, 'growing and withering according to the season'. Neidí Eoin, a local storyteller, is evoked in similarly affectionate terms,

through an accumulation of fire imagery over the course of the poem
'Oícheanta Geimhridh/Winter Nights' (*BB*, pp 112-15):

> While he crackled with stories there in his corner
> we'd explore the fire-place of his mind
> stirring the embers of his memory . . .

These old people provided a learning environment for the poet's imagination, which he was not completely aware of at that time.

Children's books in Irish in those days were almost non-existent, and indeed Ó Searcaigh recalls that his first encounter with written literature was hearing his father read Burns aloud when he was so young he could hardly understand a word of it. In orally based communities the older people are the repositories of information, the libraries. Often they are also the only ones who have the leisure to instruct the young. Ó Searcaigh is simply acknowledging that fact. Neidí Eoin again is at the centre of the poem 'Cré/Creed' (*BB*, pp 128-9), dispensing valuable advice:

> preaching to us [. . .]
> hearty lessons
> from the living book of his life
> reminding us [. . .]
> not to become trapped by our opinions.

The imagery in this poem as the title suggests is overtly religious, and the tone is one of contemplative peace. The old man is called *diaganta*/godly, which affirms him as a human manifestation of the divinity. The skilful use of such imagery heightens the effect of the opposition to monolithic dogma, the poem's central idea. Moreover, it could be argued that it presents an alternative to that dogma by using exactly the atmosphere of the Church, in which such unbending rules have often been presented. The phrase 'go ndeirim rudaí nach bhfuil sa Phaidir' (that I say things which are not in the Lord's Prayer) is a disapproving one, usually used in the third person. By changing it here to the first person, the poet refashions an authoritarian rhetoric and transforms it into a strong assertion of his right to freedom of speech in his poetry and his refusal to be circumscribed. This same idea is present in 'Bean a' tSléibhe/Mountain Woman', and there the controlling forces are clearly identified as 'na sagairt agus na TDs', Church and state. In the postscript to *Suibhne* Ó Searcaigh confirms that such ideas underpin his poetic philosophy: 'Sometimes we are cut off from the great sea of wonder and then we are only a lagoon; often a stagnant pool of filth, we possess neither an entrance nor an exit. . . . In the words of Krisnamurti "Be entirely free from beliefs so that one meets life anew each minute."'[5]

The lessons that he learned in his childhood were reinforced when he encountered the writings of Walt Whitman and the 'Beat poets', particularly Jack Kerouac and Allen Ginsberg. These writers placed a high premium on freedom and self-expression, and their lack of a specific and limiting location and their sexual frankness and openness also appealed to him. He pays tribute to this influence in the prose poem 'Do Jack Kerouac'. Significantly, he prefaces it with a quotation from *On the Road*: 'The only people for me are the mad ones, the ones who are mad to live, mad to talk, mad to be saved, desirous of everything at the same time, the ones who never yawn or say a commonplace thing but burn, burn like fabulous yellow roman candles' (*BB*, pp 188-91). In this poem he achieves a synthesis of what in Irish-language terms are known as *iasacht* (the foreign) and *dúchas* (the native), a process that first began with the arrival of Christianity in the fifth century. America, so important to Ireland as both an imaginative and real destination, has come home to roost on his own doorstep. He no longer wishes physically to encounter the wide open spaces of America, since he has acquired them imaginatively, in his own interior life. He has grafted them on to his own tree. Crucially, this mixture of American and Irish literary styles attempts to broaden and to deepen a celebration of the homoerotic in his poetry. He juxtaposes these two very different traditions and connects their similarities, achieving a remarkable synthesis that is characteristic of much of his work. The fact that he is comforable within his own cultural and literary heritage enables him to do this successfully. The overtly sexual 'Rinne muid Oirféas as gach orifice/Orpheus emerged from every orifice' only rephrases what he has already stated in 'Fothrach Tí i Mín na Craoibhe/Ruin of House in Mín na Craoibhe' (*BB*, pp 98-9): 'gach foscailt ina feadóg fhiáin ag gabháil fhoinn/every wound is a tin-whistle making wild music'.[6]

This short poem is a key statement on Ó Searcaigh's part. In this case the old deserted house is presented as a free entity welcoming the wild inspiration of the storm. The ruin is contrasted with 'teach téagartha teaghlaigh/a comfortable domestic place' which, of course, devotes all its efforts to keeping out the wind. The theme of this poem is, I believe, a metaphor for the poet's own existential identity. He is alone and open without the stout barriers which domesticity can erect against subversive creativity.

Subversion of normative assumptions is also an element in his love poetry. The fact that the poems deal with homosexual love renders this so, and instances occur from the outset of his literary career, in his first collection *Súile Shuibhne*.[7] Many people have, predictably and unimaginatively, read these as if they had been written from a woman's point of view. Here is one example of such a reading: 'I thought that these [poems] represented no amendment to the originals but took particular notice of how passionately the poet spoke on behalf of the girl. I was blind to the [proper] sense until I read the introduction by Lillis Ó Laoire.'[8] This is another manifestation of Pearse Hutchinson's 'civilisation of the blind eye'.

In many of the love poems Ó Searcaigh draws upon the song poetry of the eighteenth and nineteenth centuries, which has come to be regarded as one of the great accomplishments of Irish literature. (This was achieved, of course, only after it had been validated by publication and translation.) Love in the songs is usually unrequited or beset by material difficulties. The formulaic language is intense and passionate, and the intricate assonant metres serve to heighten the emotional atmosphere. In the realm of oral poetry, it is only when the songs are sung in traditional style that they become fully realised. This is particularly true nowadays when our dependence on the literary makes us impatient with the similarities between the seemingly interminable reworkings of the formulae. In this matter it is necessary to adopt the aesthetic judgements of the people who maintain this tradition.[9] Songs in Irish tend to be lyrical, with no specific narrative to thread the verses together in a particular order. The narrative, known as *údar* or *brí*, was always recounted before the song was sung and, although less common nowadays, is still regarded as the proper way to begin. This serves to clarify the events to which the verses allude and to fix their order. The oral nature of the tradition means that sometimes the songs become detached from their stories, which caused one collector to complain: 'It is a pity that these songs are so little self-explanatory. How much more interesting many of them would be if we knew all the circumstances.'[10]

Commenting on this observation, Hugh Shields says: 'Ambiguity, after all, invites intelligent listeners to interpret what they can of a text.'[11] Of course, interpretations vary according to the perspective of the singer, and it is a time-honoured practice for songs to be used in different contexts according to the feeling of the singer. Women sing men's songs, and the reverse is also true. Hugh Shields also states that the beginnings of the songs often 'evoke a previous undefined context of intimacy.'[12] Indeed, some songs are concerned with subjects which were almost impossible to discuss openly in a society bound on all sides by tradition. Love of any kind, and specifically the homoerotic, could be a difficult matter within this culture, and song provided a release from that silence and allowed expression of pent-up emotions. Those who could not themselves compose used the compositions of others. Thus these songs lent themselves to covert or encoded erotic messages. The corpus is full of strong direct statements from various points of view:

> Beloved most beloved to whom I gave all my love
> Don't you remember how you charmed me and betrayed me
> afterwards

> Now I am empty and my mind is full of sorrow
> As I watch my lover being coaxed by another man.[13]

Here is another example:

> Mary and King of Sunday
> Is there no help in store for me
> Will I never live
> In one lodging with him
>
> My destruction and sore grief
> That we are not tonight being married
> My man under the sod
> And you at your woman's wake.[14]

Hugh Shields again gives a valuable insight:

> These beginnings imply a change of situation: by tenses of past and future,
> by a demonstrative, by contrast and comparison. . . . Narrative 'signals'
> also occur, the clearest of which in love songs are the pronouns of first
> and second person, but used without clearly defined reference in a way
> that modern pop song may have imitated. . . . As the text develops, one
> 'identity' may readily give way to another, which has an interesting effect
> on love poetry when male and female identity are thereby confused. A
> situation with perspective may unfold, or just a few 'narrative glimpses',
> perhaps without any narrative resolution, or perhaps with more than
> one. A whole song indeed may picture a 'reality' which is as much of
> the mind as it is accomplished fact.[15]

Cathal Ó Searcaigh is the conscious heir of this tradition and is acutely
aware of its possibilities for his poetry. That the songs may often not be
gender-bound or even gender-specific has allowed him to exploit the ambiguity within the tradition and to create his own reality from it. The lack
of self-explanation in the songs provides opportunities for creating a 'reality
of the mind' — in his case, a reality imbued with a homoerotic sensibility.
He does this in a number of ways: by reworking and adapting old songs,
by alluding to them, by incorporating lines from them into his poems,
and by composing new poems which attempt to reproduce the metrical,
linguistic and emotional style of the old songs. Greagóir Ó Dúill has
commented on the number of Ó Searcaigh's poems which contain the
pronoun *tú* and states that 'The number of his poems which speak directly
to the *you* of the poet or the beloved, is . . . remarkable, but according
to the inescapable grammar of the writer's two-hand reel with the reader,
the *you* must stand for the reader, enticing him into the dialogue of the
poem.'[16] This is another way of seeing Shields's 'previous undefined
context of intimacy'.

All this is necessarily quite difficult to convey in translation, and readers of *An Bealach 'na Bhaile/Homecoming* will notice different styles being used by different translators. Some stay closer to the original text, while others are freer with it. This stanza by Gabriel Fitzmaurice stays close to the original while conveying its spirit:

> Chiap tú mé is chráigh tú mé is d'fhág tú mar seo mé
> gan romham is gan i mo dhiaidh ach seachrán agus sliabh,
> gan amach i ndán domh as duibheagán seo an dorchadais,
> óir ba tusa an ball bán a bhí riamh ar an oíche i mo chliabh.

> You tormented me and distressed me and left me in the lurch,
> Nought before me and nought behind me but mountain and
>   my search
> Nothing before me now or ever but night's abyss, this dark
> For you were the one bright spot in the midnight of my heart.
>   (*BB*, pp 142-3)

It must be said that the metre of the translation is more regular than that of the Irish. This rhythmic irregularity, which occasionally occurs in the old songs also, conveys a sense of the emotional turbulence which underlies the poem. This is also apparent in other poems; for example:

> Inniu is mé ag siúl mar a dtéimis i gcónaí Dé Domhnaigh
> Suas Malaidh na Míne is amach droim Loch an Ghainimh
> Bhí cuma bheag chaillte ar sheanbhailte bánaithe na gcnoc
> Is ach oiread leo siúd, ó d'imigh tú uaim, níl gnaoi ar mo shaol.

Gabriel Rosenstock is freer in his translation, which makes impressive imaginative leaps serving to highlight certain points in the poem. His metre is, however, strict and regular:

> Today like all Sundays I'm out taking the air,
> Up by Malaidh na Míne, way beyond Sandy Lake,
> The villages are all empty, windswept and bare
> As though they had died in their sleep for your sake.
>   (*BB*, pp 144-5)

It is perhaps in the poem Laoi Cumainn/Hound of Ulster (*BB*, p. 166) that Ó Searcaigh achieves the greatest synthesis of the layers of tradition which he uses in his love poetry. It is a rich and joyful celebration of physical love. The text in the original contains many echoes and allusions for the skilled reader of Irish literature. In this respect it is strongly reminiscent of the poetry of Nuala Ní Dhomhnaill, particularly 'Mo Mhíle Stór'. In this poem she juxtaposes some of the most memorable phrases from the corpus of women's poetry in Irish, but her achievement goes far beyond well-crafted pastiche. The associations set off by such allusions in the reader's mind acquire added significance at the poem's end. Her recalling of the Gaelic voice reappropriates an eroticising of male beauty. The traditional material deals with love which is full of youthful passion, something which is quite normal in heroic poetry. She extends and redefines this in terms of the straight grey hair of middle age, thereby giving love a contemporary post-heroic continuation which is never found in the old poetry. In Ó Searcaigh's poem, the title is the first important signal for us to sit and take notice. *Laoidh cumainn*, literally 'lay of friendship / affection', was the term occasionally used by the professional poets of the medieval bardic schools for a praise poem for their chief and patron. The poet's relationship with his chief was often defined in terms of physical affection, and there are numerous references to the poet and his patron sharing the same bed. Until recently it has always been accepted by scholars that this was no more than a literary conceit, but this was to overlook the referential claim of the conceit: often poet and patron did in fact share the same bed, and public demonstrativeness of the lord's affection was proof of the poet's privileged position. Furthermore, physical affection between males was validated in a homosocial ordering of relations, within which the eroticisation of male relations was naturalised.[17] Ó Searcaigh reminds us of that tradition with his title and firmly places himself within it. His poem is, of course, not addressed to his lord but to his lover, whom he compares to 'Cú na gCleas / the Hound of the Feats' (i.e. Cú Chulainn). The slaughtering hero of the Ulster Cycle might seem unlikely material for a love poem. Ó Searcaigh, however, is deliberately recalling the tenderness expressed by Cú Chulainn in his lament for his foster brother Ferdia after he had killed him at the ford. Ferocity and tenderness are two sides of the same coin:

> When we were away with Scáthach
> learning victory overseas
> it seems our friendship would remain
> unbroken till the day of doom.
>
> I loved the noble way you blushed,
> and loved your fine perfect form.
> I loved your blue clear eye,
> your way of speech, your skillfulness.[18]

Moreover, he inserts half-lines from the most famous love songs in Irish, which trigger a whole set of associations. These are 'na dealraitheacha deasa ó do ghrua / those darting rays from your cheek', from 'The Red-haired Man's Wife', and 'ag síorthabhairt grá duit / forever giving you love', from 'Dónall

Óg'. The former is a love song composed by a man who had been cheated by another and who had thereby lost the woman he loved; the latter is the passionate outcry of a young girl deserted by Dónall. Ó Searcaigh, then, is exploiting the ambiguities of the love-song tradition and connecting them to the older literature, thereby establishing a position of authentic continuity for himself within Gaelic tradition. Again, this quite public function is inextricably linked with a deeply private expression of love. In treating his theme in this manner, he expands the boundaries of that tradition and extends his own possibilities within it.

As in the poem 'Cré / Creed', he also appropriates religious symbols and uses them for his own purposes in the love poetry. 'Searmanas / Ceremony' (*BB*, pp 156-7) is typical of such appropriation. One critic has described this poem as insufferable,[19] referring to its opening lines. Yet it seems to me that the evocation of physical love as a sacred rite sustains the highly charged emotional atmosphere of the poem. Its portrayal of the love which 'reopens Christ's wounds' (*BB*, pp 140-1) as the central celebration of Catholicism also challenges that Church's institutional intransigence with regard to it. The fact that such a portrayal might cause some readers to cringe is precisely the point which underpins all of his poetry — conventions are there to be challenged and altered. Poems such as 'Dhéanfainn an Ní Dodhéanta'[20] and 'Lá de na Laethanta / On Such a Day' (*BB*, pp 48-51) reaffrim this sense of purpose, while 'Sneachta/Snow' (*BB*, pp 58-9) is another powerful example of it. Lyricism and celebration can be as iconoclastic as angst and self-doubt, and perhaps it is in this respect that he most closely approaches what Jonathan Dollimore calls a transgressive aesthetic,[21] where transgression in a sexual sense can form the basis of a new vision and ordering of an individual's world. Dollimore discusses André Gide's important meeting with Oscar Wilde in Algeria in 1895, where initially Gide had erased his name from the hotel register and left the hotel in order to avoid meeting Wilde. Subsequently he changed his mind, returned and met Wilde. It was during this time that Gide fully acknowledged his homosexuality for the first time, a fact which was crucial to his development as a writer. Dollimore comments that

> For Gide, transgression is embraced with that same stubborn integrity which was to become the basis of his transgressive aesthetic, an aesthetic obviously indebted to, yet also formed in reaction against, Wilde's own. Thus liberation from the self into desire is also to realize a new and deeper self, belief in which supports an oppositional stand not just on the question of deviant sexual desire, but on a whole range of other issues as well, cultural and political. Integrity here becomes an ethical sense inextricably bound up with and also binding up the integrated self, with the result that this self becomes a powerful source of oppositional strength at once psychic, ethical, and political.[22]

Ó Searcaigh writes in 'Transubstaintiú/Transubstantiation' (*BB*, pp 184-5):

> Between the thought and the word
> are regions of ice and fog;
>
> but all my life I'll be
> shattering the frost, scattering the fog
>
> stirring and sunning
> with my heart's fiery rays
>
> so that you'll flower one day
> you that are only a shadow.

Although brightness is uppermost in his poetry, occasionally a darker side manifests itself. In the untranslated poem 'An Díbeartach',[23] which was not included in *An Bealach 'na Bhaile / Homecoming*, we get the reverse picture. *Díbeartach* means outcast or exile. This outsideness is seen in poetic as well as in social terms. It is prefaced by a line from 'Úirchill an Chreagáin', one of the great Ulster *aisling* poems of the eighteenth century.[24] In this poem a vision woman from the otherworld attempts to entice him away and points out to the poet that 'an tír seo bheith ag fonóid faoi gach rabhán dá ndéan tú de cheol / the countryside [is] mocking every spasm that you create in song'. Poets in Gaelic society often saw themselves and were seen by their communities as outside the bounds of accepted patterns. This marginality, of course, gave them freedom, but it carried a price. Ó Searcaigh identifies with Art Mac Cumhaigh, again establishing his credentials as he did in 'Laoi Cumainn / Hound of Ulster'. It is worth quoting the poem in full, in both Irish and English, as it has not previously been translated:

AN DÍBEARTACH

'An tír seo bheith ag fonóid, faoi gach rabhán dá ndéan tú de cheol'

(i)
> Ní thuigeann siad an buachaill seanchríonna
> a bhíonn ag cumadh ar feadh na hoíche
> thuas i gcnoic Bharr an Ghleanna.
> Tá a bhfuil ar siúl aige amaideach
> a deir siad thíos i dtigh an leanna —
> macasamhail an mhadaidh bháin
> a bhíonn ag cnaí chnámh na gealaí
> i bpolláin uisce ar an bhealach.
>
> > Ach fós beidh a chuid amhrán
> > ina n-oileáin dóchais agus dídine
> > i bhfarraigí a ndorchadais.

(ii)   Ní duitse faraor
            dea-fhód a dhéanamh den domasach
            ná an Domhnach a chomóradh mar chách
            ná grá na gcomharsan lá na cinniúna
            ná muirniú mná faoi scáth an phósta
            ná dea-chuideachta an tí ósta.

    Duitse faraor
        dearg dobhogtha Cháin
        a bheith smeartha ar chlár d'éadain.

THE OUTCAST

'This country to be mocking every spasm you create in song.'

(i)   They don't understand the ageing boy
            who composes all night long
            above in the hills of Barr an Ghleanna.
            All he does is foolish
            they say below in the pub —
            resembling the white dog[25]
            who gnaws the bone of the moon
            in the small water pools on the road.

        But his songs will yet be
        islands of hope and shelter
        in the seas of their darkness

(ii)   Not for you sadly
                to turn the peaty earth into good land
                nor the celebration of Sunday like the rest
                nor the love of neighbours on the day of tragedy
                nor the cherishing of woman in the protection of
                                                        marriage
            nor the good company of the inn.

        For you sadly
            the indelible mark of Cain
            smeared on your forehead.

Although the tone of isolation is unusual for Ó Searcaigh, he still trusts his poetic instinct. Indeed, the voice in the poem is very much that of a conscious artist who has made his choice but who fully realises the consequences of it. He accepts the mark of Cain and its attendant gains, while fully realising what he has irretrievably exchanged for it. It seems that this resolution has strengthened his poetry and allowed him to explore the new avenues which have opened up for him. He is at present working on a series of translations and adaptations of the Alexandrian Greek poet, C. P. Cavafy. The homoerotic sensiblity is the most obvious point of reference between the two poets, yet there are others. It is well known that Cavafy was immersed in the history and mythology of Greece and had the ability to discuss its characters as if he had known them personally. The same principle operates within oral culture in Ireland, and consequently such subjectivity is immediately appealing to an Irish poet immersed in Gaelic tradition. These adaptations are another attempt to continue the synthesis with which Ó Searcaigh has been so successful up to now and to explore further his poetic landscape where 'every enclosed field is like a verse/in the great poem of land reclamation' (*BB*, pp 94-5).

Abbreviations

BB   *An Bealach 'na Bhaile/Homecoming*, ed. Gabriel Fitz-
        maurice, Conamara: Cló Iar-Chonnachta, 1993

Notes and References

1   '"Rus in Urbe"': Comhrá le Pearse Hutchinson', *Innti*, xi (1988), pp 55-68. The question and full quotation in Irish (p. 61) read as follows: '*I gcás na homaighnéasach anois, nach bhfuil dul chun cinn mór déanta sa* [sic] *mhéid nach bhfuil eagla ar dhaoine go gcuirfear coinnealbháthadh orthu má deireann siad gur homaighnéasaigh iad?* Bhuel, fiú sna caogadaí, i mBÁC ar aon nós, bhí sibhialtacht na daille i gcónaí ann, níos mó ná i Londain fiú, ó thaobh na hataí bána de. Ach ón uair go bhfuil fhios ag gach éinne anois go bhfuil a leithéid ann, ar bhealach tá sé níos éasca a ionsaí. Agus athróidh Aids, ní saol na homaighnéasach amháin, ach saol gach éinne. Caithfidh mé a rá go gcreidim go bhfuil a lán daoine níos oscailte dairíre sa tír seo, níos fíoroscailte ar bhealaí ná i Sasana, mar shampla. Ach tá na daoine eile ann i gcónaí. Ach tá an saghas san grá i gcoinne an dlí sa tír seo fós rud nach bhfuil i Sasana. Ní féidir reifreann faoi sin a shamhlú go mórmhór tar éis na reifrinn eile.'

2   Pearse Hutchinson, *The Soul that Kissed the Body: New and Selected Poems in Irish with Translations into English and an Introduction by the Author*, Dublin: Gallery Books, 1990, p. 14.

3   Ibid., p. 15.

4   Greagóir Ó Dúill, 'An File is Dual: Filíocht Chathail Uí Shearcaigh: I dtreo anailís théamúil', *Comhar*, lii, 12 (Nollaig 1993), pp. 35-41. The Irish text reads (p. 41): 'Is leibhéal comhbhá é seo atá os cionn an ghnáith — agus is léiriú ar ardchumas filíochta an friotal atá ar nós comhrá, scaoilte, malltriallach, incrimintiúil a charnann tátail ar bharr a chéile leis an scéal a insint ceart coscarthach.'

5   Cathal Ó Searcaigh, *Suibhne* (*Selected Poems*), Dublin: Coiscéim, 1987. The Irish text reads (p. 150): 'Amantaí gearrtar an [sic] shiúl muid ar fad ó mhuir mhór an iontais agus ansin cha bhíonn ionainn ach murlach; linn mharbh an

mhiodamais go minic, gan isteach ionainn ná amach. . . . In the words of Krisnamurti etc. . . .'

6   The word *wound* which is used in the translation is not strictly accurate. (*F*)*oscailt* means simply an opening.

7   Cathal Ó Searcaigh, *Súile Shuibhne* (*Selected Poems*), Dublin: Coiscéim, 1983.

8   Dúghlas Sealy, review of *An Bealach 'na Bhaile/Homecoming, Comhar*, lii, 6 (Meitheamh 1993), pp. 21-2. Sealy comments on discovering that the love poems were homosexual (p. 22): 'Shíl mé nárbh aon leasú ar na bunleaganacha iad ach sna dánta seo agus sna dánta grá eile shonraigh mé cé chomh paiseanta agus a labhair an file thar ceann an chailín. . . . Bhí mé dall ar an gciall nó léigh mé réamhrá Lillis Ó Laoire.'

9   See Ruth Finnegan, *Oral Poetry: Its Nature, Significance and Social Context*, Cambridge University Press, 1977, for a discussion of the dynamics of song poetry.

10   Énrí Ó Muirgheasa, *Céad de Cheoltaibh Uladh*, Dublin, 1915, p. 255, quoted in Hugh Shields, *Narrative Singing in Ireland: Lays Ballads, Come-All-Yes and Other Songs*, Dublin: Irish Academic Press, 1993, p. 71.

11   Shields, op. cit., p. 71.

12   Ibid., p. 72.

13   Cathal Goan, *Róise na nAmhrán: Songs of a Donegal Woman*, Dublin: RTÉ Commercial Enterprises, 1994 (CD/Cassette, with accompanying booklet).

14   Énrí Ó Muirgheasa, *Dhá Chéad de Cheoltaibh Uladh*, Dublin, 1934, p. 145 (my own translation).

15   Shields, op. cit., pp 73, 74.

16   Ó Dúill, op. cit., p. 40.

17   I am indebted to Dr Máirín Ní Dhonnchadha, School of Celtic Studies, Dublin Institute for Advanced Studies, for kindly allowing me to read her work in progress on the subject of sexuality in bardic verse, and for her subsequent discussion and clarification of it.

18   Thomas Kinsella, *The Táin; translated from the Irish Epic Táin Bó Cuailgne*, Dublin: Dolmen Press; Oxford University Press, 1969, p. 200.

19   Sealy, op. cit., p. 22. 'Léigh mé na dánta grá arís, ach cé acu heitrighnéasach nó homaighnéasach é, ní fhulaingeoinn leithéid "Ar altóir . . . etc". Agus leanann sé ar aghaidh mar sin ar feadh seacht líne is fiche eile. Meascán masamasach de dhúil is de mhaoithneachas. ('I read the love poems again, but whether it is heterosexual or homosexual, I would not suffer the likes of "On the altar . . . etc". And it continues in that fashion for another twenty-seven lines. A nauseating mixture of desire and sentimentality.')

20   Ó Searcaigh, *Suibhne*, p. 101.

21   Jonathan Dollimore, *Sexual Dissidence: Augustine to Wilde, Freud to Foucault*, Oxford University Press, 1991.

22   Ibid., p. 17.

23   Ó Searcaigh, *Suibhne*, p. 119.

24   Seán Ó Tuama and Thomas Kinsella, *An Duanaire, 1600-1900: Poems of the Dispossessed*, Dublin: Dolmen Press, 1981, pp 176-81.

25   The phrase 'saol an mhadaidh bháin' ('the life of the white dog') corresponds to the English 'the life of Reilly'. Its use here contains an implied insult that the poet is a parasite, making no useful contribution to the life of the community.

11 'Tangles'
Addressing an Unusual Audience

DAVID GRANT

BACKGROUND

Throughout my career I have been concerned with the question of widening the audience for theatre. To begin with, in the time I spent as Publicity Manager for the Belfast Festival, this was the main focus of my work. It was obvious from attending events that the audience tended to be middle-aged and middle class. While this was hardly surprising, it was particularly frustrating at a time when I myself formed part of the age-range that was underrepresented.

Part of the solution clearly lay in a different form of marketing but even then it was evident that the nature of the artistic product itself needed to be more responsive to the interests and tastes of a younger audience if it was to be successful in attracting them. When I moved to the Dublin Theatre Festival as Programme Director in 1988, I became fascinated by the work of Wet Paint Arts. I had first encountered this specialist Young People's Theatre company when I had been guest editor of the special 'Youth and Community' issue of *Theatre Ireland* magazine in 1987. (Young People's Theatre is a term which I would reserve for professional theatre for young audiences, as distinct from 'youth theatre', which is participatory in nature.) I was impressed then by their systematic approach to building a new audience through a network of youth club contacts. I was also aware of their track record in developing plays specifically with that audience in mind.

The first Theatre Festival which I programmed (1989) included Wet Paint

Arts' production of Dermot Bolger's *The Lament for Arthur Cleary*. This proved to be one of the great successes of the whole programme and went on to win many prestigious awards, including the Samuel Beckett Award and an Edinburgh Fringe First. It also marked the end of the association between Wet Paint's founding Artistic Director, David Byrne, and the company and the beginning of a period of reorganisation which meant that no new theatre work was undertaken for a year.

During this period, in a chance meeting with members of the company, I suggested that a future play might address the issue of homosexuality. This suggestion took root, and a few months later I was unexpectedly invited to read a number of English plays on this theme with a view to directing one of them. While each had merit, all strongly reflected their English origins and all centred mainly on the issue of AIDS. While I fully understood the importance and urgency of this subject, it seemed to me to be quite separate from the broader issue of the treatment of homosexuals. It is strange to look back now on how attitudes in Ireland seem to have evolved, even since 1990 when these discussions were taking place. But I remember feeling a passionate concern to address broad issues of prejudice, rather than specific health issues which seemed to me to be of narrower concern. This is in no way to underestimate the importance of such health education, but it was hard not to feel that gay issues were becoming publicly more acceptable only because of the related health issues.

The other preliminary consideration was the social context in which Wet Paint performed. They tended (and have continued) to work mainly in disadvantaged areas. Given the prevailing extent of unemployment, to call them 'working class' would be something of a misnomer, but the term is convenient shorthand. This, then, was the very audience that in my earlier work I had been eager to reach. The additional challenge of addressing a difficult theme of considerable personal importance to me was irresistible. It was the coincidence of context and theme that was most attractive. Homosexuality can hardly be said to be an uncommon feature of Irish drama. One has only to think of professionally produced plays in recent years to come up with an impressive list.[1] Mostly, however, sexuality has been a secondary theme or has had mainly metaphorical significance. It has rarely been referred to in reviews. This reticence can, of course, be ascribed to the maturity of Irish theatre audiences and criticism.

There has been some debate about this critical reluctance to deal with the subject of homosexuality on the Irish stage, and it would be useful here to establish a context for *Tangles*. Lance Pettitt commented, in 1990: 'Within the last two years, Ireland's National Theatre has staged two productions which deal centrally with the subject of homosexuality in Ireland: Friel's *The Gentle Island* and Kilroy's *The Death and Resurrection of Mr Roche*. Most reviews of the plays made only a cursory reference to their gay context. Two plays on at the Abbey is not enough to counter ignorance or increase popular understanding.'[2] Further to this, Frank Thackaberry, founder of the Irish lesbian and gay theatre group, Muted Cupid, makes the following observation:

> We are not marginalising ourselves by forming such a theatre company and the great reaction from the mixed audience proved this. Yes, it is true that gay themes are dealt with in mainstream theatre but, just think, what exactly are the kinds of images presented? Plays like *The Normal Heart*, *Sea-Urchins*, *Bent*, all centre on the idea of Gay-As-Victim, be it from AIDS, queer-bashing or persecution. Don't get me wrong, *Bent*, for example, is a great play, but why is it performed so much here in Ireland. We set up Muted Cupid to explore a wider range of lesbian and gay issues. Nearer to the issues or day-to-day living than the issues of life and death.[3]

By now, one would hope that homosexuality has been so accepted by Irish society as not to deserve specific comment. However true this may be, it cannot be said of Wet Paint's target audience, where extreme homophobic prejudice is the rule rather than the exception. There was clearly a need to identify a script that was capable of meeting the issues head-on.

SOURCES FOR *TANGLES*

Having rejected the existing manuscripts, I had to come up with an alternative quickly. Wet Paint had a tradition of devising scripts through a workshop process with actors, a system I had previous experience of; but, although at that time I had not seen any of Wet Paint's devised work, I had reservations about this approach, as it seemed to me that it had often led to shapeless and unbalanced end-products. At the same time, I had come to place great faith in the instinct of actors in the development of character and dialogue. There remained, however, the residual task of creating a framework that could provide a structure for the actors to work within and which would also allow the chosen theme to be addressed.

The subliminal processes that underlay the eventual solution are hard to assess. But I would certainly acknowledge the effect of an interview I had conducted for *Theatre Ireland* with the actor Ian McKellen when he was touring his one-man Shakespeare show in support of AIDS charities. McKellen described a Shakespearian production which had impressed him:

> Last week, I saw Renaissance's *As You Like It*. A very clearly spoken production. With my mind full of problems of sexuality, when Rosalind and

Celia come on, I knew they were lesbian. They weren't played as lesbian. That didn't matter. I knew these two were lesbian so when one
of them declared her love for a man, I felt very strongly for the other,
particularly as I knew that in Shakespeare's time they would have both
been played by boys. And when they went off into the forest, and they
were exiled, and the one who had just fallen in love with a man decided
to dress up as a man, and off they went — the familiar lesbian couple,
one feminine, the other masculine — my awareness of Shakespeare's grasp
on sexuality was . . . well, my jaw was dropping.

And then the young man meeting his girlfriend in the wood and not
recognising her agrees verbally to make love to her . . . and poor Celia
has to sit through all this lovemaking, and never says a word. And I've
often wondered why. And I know why now — because I've brought my
own awareness of life to Shakespeare.[4]

This insight, together with Jan Kott's suggestion, in his essay 'Shakespeare's
Bitter Arcadia',[5] that sophisticated pre-Freudian psychology is at the heart
of Shakespeare's comedies of confusion, may have pointed the way towards
my use of the plot of *Twelfth Night* to provide a framework for *Tangles*.
In practice, this happened almost intuitively. One sleepless night I sat down
at a table and sketched out the basic storyline, went back to bed, and
discovered the notes almost to my surprise the next morning. These provided the basis of the final play.

The main plot of *Twelfth Night* involves the love of Duke Orsino for Olivia
and his decision to use Viola (a woman disguised as a man) as a go-between.
Olivia falls in love with the messenger, while the messenger falls in love
with Orsino, leaving Viola to conclude:

> O time! thou must untangle this, not I;
> It is too hard a knot for me to untie![6]

Hence the notion of emotional 'tangles' arose. By substituting a gay man
for Viola, a fascinating range of psycho-sexual possibilities were opened
up. Viola thus became Kevin, Orsino became his best mate Lorcan, Olivia
became Lorcan's 'ex', Oonagh, while Sebastian (Viola's twin brother) became
Stephen (Kevin's heterosexual twin visiting from the USA, having been
separated from his sibling at an early age). The scenario (based on the
Shakespearian plot) involved Lorcan, jilted by Oonagh, prevailing upon
his friend Kevin to go to her to plead his cause. Oonagh, however, is much
more interested in Kevin, who agrees to meet her with Lorcan in the hope
of engineering a reconciliation. Enter Stephen, who adds to the confusion by leading Oonagh to think that Kevin fancies her. The resulting chaos
pressures Kevin into telling his friends that he is gay. The second half of
the play then explores the fallout from this revelation.

The Shakespearian subplots found their parallel in the need to set these relationships in some sort of context. The benign Feste gave rise to the idea of an openly gay man called Fergus, and the characters of Sir Toby Belch and Malvolio between them gave rise to the eponymous Tangles — a lovable homophobic thug. This oxymoronic concept was central to the strategy of the play. It was felt essential that the vehicle for homophobia should be attractive to the most resistant element in the audience. This strategy created the danger that Tangles would come to dominate the play, and it was the tension between this risk and the overriding educational intentions that governed the way in which the final script emerged.

In the event, the relationships between all five characters became of importance to the development of the script, with only Lorcan and Fergus and Oonagh and Tangles never meeting. This arose not from some systematic plan, but more from the fact that in improvisation those pairs of characters never had much to say to one another.

STYLISTIC CONSIDERATIONS

The style of presentation was just as important as the content of the play. We needed an end-product that would be specific to Dublin, specific to the 1990s, and relevant not only to the audience but also to the cast. I needed a structure that was flexible enough to accommodate the flow of ideas in rehearsal, but robust enough to meet the demands of youth club touring. The answer lay not in theories about the future development of theatre in a video-dominated world, but in theatre history. It was, above all, the early theatre that had to cope with audience inattention. The medieval theatre recognised no class barriers. Shakespeare's theatre catered for a broad social spectrum.

The *commedia dell'arte*, with its tradition of free improvisation within a framework provided by a detailed scenario and well-defined characters, offered a particularly rewarding approach. *Commedia dell'arte*, of course, presupposes a cast steeped for a lifetime in its traditional techniques. For us, therefore, it provided a model for rehearsal, not performance. It gave us the means to create our script, which in the later stages of rehearsal became fixed.

Two other aspects of *commedia* became crucial to the production. One was the bold performance style which accentuated the non-naturalistic, symbolical qualities of the characters. The other was the staging method. Inspired by the carts on which much medieval and Renaissance theatre was performed, our brief to Ned McLoughlin, the designer, was for a simple raised platform with a get-round. Psychologically this would serve to

reinforce the stylised nature of the production, since the actors were raised above the audience, making them at the same time detached from and
dominant over them.

POLITICAL SENSITIVITIES

Between the drafting of the scenario and the rehearsal process Wet Paint
received the disappointing news that the expected support of Dublin County
Council for community touring in Dublin's outlying estates would not be
forthcoming. Whether anxiety over the theme was the governing factor
in their decision, as seemed initially to be the case, or whether, as was
subsequently claimed, the timing of the formal application was late is
of no real significance now. The political reality was that the County
Council was on the point of approving substantially increased arts funding
for Dublin's year as European City of Culture. To support a potentially
controversial play in this critical period might well have jeopardised this
development.

What was important was that Wet Paint was not deterred by the decision
and managed, with the help of the Project Arts Centre and many private
benefactors, to reshape the show and present it for three weeks at that
attractive central venue. The strategy then became to bring the young target
audience into the centre, rather than taking the show out to them. From
my point of view, the decision had the practical advantage of allowing
us a more elaborate set and technical facilities that would have been im-
practical on the road. Ned McLoughlin was able to let his imagination
run riot with a fun-filled structure of brightly painted, second-hand
furniture (including a few closets!). Inevitably, however, the pressure on
director and actors increased. The show had to work not only for our young,
theatrically unsophisticated audience, but also for a general theatre-going
audience. It was just as natural that the artistic demands of the show would
now be greater.

THE DEVISING PROCESS

The complexity of the scenario meant that the dialogue chiefly served
narrative development at first. But bit by bit a strong sense of character
emerged for each actor, and this fed into the detail of the script. In particular, it became clear that the relationship between Oonagh and Lorcan
was just as important as the attitudes of the gay characters. The tendency
of gay men to conceal their sexuality emerged as a broader metaphor for

that tendency in all of us, whatever our sexual orientation, to lack honesty in our personal relationships. Thus the play's conclusion became (in Oonagh's words):

> How can you say that Lorcan, after all that's happened. Think what it's been like for Kevin all these years. Never being able to tell us what was on his mind. And there we were always goin' onto him about our problems. There's things we try and hide from ourselves because we're frightened of them. We never find out who we really are 'cause we're too busy trying to be what other people think we are. And that can't be right.

What impressed me above all about the writing process was that it was precisely that. There was little indulgent free improvisation. Instead the objective of each scene was clearly set, the attitudes of the characters defined, and the material prepared by the actors was incorporated. Each actor contributed in this way, but it soon became apparent that Anthony Brophy, who played Tangles, was a natural writer of comedy. The breakthrough came early on, however, when Larry Lowry (Lorcan) arrived one morning with a speech describing his reaction to the discovery that his best mate was gay:

> Don't say it! Say nothing! I know what you're thinking. What? What? Don't look at me. I can't believe it. How do you think I feel? I know. I know. Imagine. Fifteen years. Fifteen years. I can't think about it. It's unthinkaboutable. Fifteen years. When I think about it. Jaysus, why I even held his hand in high babies. I hope Jenny D'Arcy doesn't bring that one up. And the soccer club. I won't be able to show my face — or anything else in the showers there again. Don't look at me! I know. His best friend. All those years. Oh, yeah! Very funny. I know what you're thinking. Fifteen years. And I never knew. He never told me. I never even had a notion. I didn't. I didn't know. How could he do this to me? How could I know? I'll never live it down. I'm just after thinking of it. Nine! We were nine. In the cubs, right. And he asked me to sleep over. Yeah, I know. I should have suspected. Sleep over, How are ye! I was nine. 'Let's sleep over.' Out in his back yard. In his oul fella's oul tent. Just the two of us. Oh, yeah. Very cosy. No wonder he got on with Oonagh so well — so much in common. Maybe she knew all along. Oh no! Maybe she thought I was. Come to think of it, that's how she broke it off. It must be. Stands to reason. Doesn't it?

The fragility of male sexuality, whatever its orientation came into focus in a number of scenes. This was particularly evident when it came to the dénouement. Our concern to make Tangles a point of contact for those most resistant to the play's message of toleration of diversity made it

difficult to undermine him without alienating the very section of the audience we were keenest to speak to. In this context, Wet Paint's policy of
bringing groups of youth leaders to workshop previews proved especially
valuable. This helped us refine the script, and the dénouement under-
went a number of changes in the final week of rehearsal. It would be truer
to say that it grew, as the following extracts will illustrate. Having discovered
that his mate Kevin is gay, Tangles is conciliatory and even appears to be
reconciled to the openly gay Fergus. Originally this was the end of the
play, but it was felt in workshops to be too sudden a transformation. We
therefore allowed Fergus to answer back:

TANGLES: Are you comin', Fergus?

FERGUS: No!

TANGLES: Why not?

OONAGH: Yeah, why not, Fergus?

FERGUS: What's this? Live and let live time?

TANGLES: Well, fuck off so.

OONAGH: Ah, hang on. Tangles.

TANGLES: For wha'?

OONAGH: Go on, Fergus. He's making the effort.

FERGUS: 'Cause he's giving his mate the benefit of the doubt?

TANGLES: Hey, hey, you're queer, right. So you're bent, you're bent. What
I'm now saying is, I'm accepting it. So there's no problem. We'll leave
it at that.

FERGUS: I'm not asking you to accept me. I didn't need your approval
up to today. Why should I need it now?

TANGLES: Listen. I don't know what we're arguing about. OK, you've had
a rough time, right. People bouncing you around the shop. But if you
listen, what I'm saying is — you're alright. If you wanna stick around,
stick around. I can't say fairer than that, can I?

FERGUS: I'm glad that you're seeing things so differently all of a sudden.
But it's not enough for you just to turn a blind eye to me and Kevin,
if the rest of us are still invisible.

Tangles moves to go.

No, let me finish. Do you know how many of us they think there are?
One person in ten, Tangles. One in ten. That's five people on every
bus. Three in every classroom. One on every football team.

LORCAN: Not on our team there isn't!

KEVIN: Oh yeah?

FERGUS: So next time you're in a pub, a shop, a crowded DART, just
remember, Tangles — we're everywhere! You can pretend we don't exist.
But you're fooling no one. No one but yourself. (*To Kevin*) Let's go find
that brother of yours. Are you coming Tangles?

The initiative was therefore passed to Fergus, but it was argued in the next
workshop that Tangles's credibility was undermined.

TANGLES: (*Crosses the stage as if to exit. Then pauses. Looks at Kevin and Oonagh and Mandy. Then at the audience.*) I'm thinking about it. (*He crosses to Fergus*). You're a cheeky little bollix, aren't you?
FERGUS: I bet you say that to all the boys.

We hoped that this would redress the balance. But at the following workshop it was suggested that there was still some way to go. The final version ended as follows:

> All except Tangles freeze while he addresses the audience. Lorcan and Mandy come out of the freeze only for their interjection.

TANGLES: I know what you're thinking. Why doesn't Tangles lay him fucking out? He has. Many times. And for wha'? It achieved nothing. We're both still here. We're both still different. I mean, it didn't solve any problems, you know. And hard as it may be to believe, I do have problems. Genuine. I mean, there are days when women haven't clawed each other's eyes out this body.
MANDY: Oh yeah?
TANGLES: I mean, we all hit rough patches . . .
LORCAN: Yeah!
TANGLES: I know he bleedin' does. (*At Fergus*) So it isn't just weirdos like you who have all the worries. I suppose we do have that much in common. Life's a tough game, whatever way you play it.

The character of Mandy was introduced in the revised version of the play that was toured to Scotland and the Royal National Theatre in 1992 and reflected the inadequacy of seeking to accommodate all female attitudes towards male homosexuality in one character. She began as Oonagh's best friend and developed into Tangles's girlfriend. In the spectrum of attitudes that the six characters of the final version represented, Mandy sits beyond Tangles in her raw homophobia. She is never reconciled.

THE GAY MESSAGE

From the outset the underlying intention of the play was modest. It did not seek to articulate the deeper complexities of gay relationships. Instead it set out to demonstrate the mundane cruelty that most homosexuals suffer at some time in their lives. The play also challenges the superficial liberality to which many people today pay lip-service. In this regard, the relationship between Oonagh and Fergus was the most expressive as the following scene illustrates.

OONAGH: You know Fergus, you're a terrible waste. Are you sure you're
queer?

FERGUS: No, it's just a joke between me and Tangles.

  Fergus moves as if to kiss her.

OONAGH: Come on. Be serious. How do you know that you are?

FERGUS: I never said I was.

MANDY: Everyone knows you are.

FERGUS: So what are youse asking me for?

OONAGH: I was just wondrin' . . .

MANDY: . . . did you never want to try it with a girl?

FERGUS (*to Mandy*): Are you offrin'?

MANDY: No!

FERGUS: Did you?

MANDY: What?

FERGUS: Ever want to try it with a girl?

MANDY: Fuck off!

OONAGH: Fergus!

FERGUS: Women can be gay too you know.

OONAGH: But it's not exactly natural, is it?

FERGUS: It's natural for me.

OONAGH: Does it hurt?

  Mandy sniggers.

FERGUS: Does what hurt?

MANDY: What you do.

FERGUS: How do you know what I do?

OONAGH: Ah, you know what I say.

FERGUS: If I asked youse a question like tha', I'd get a slap in the mouth.
  I'm gay. Not an exhibit in a Freak Show!

MANDY: D'you wanna bet!

OONAGH: It's OK, Fergus. I understand.

FERGUS: No youse don't understand. I mean, how could you? You don't
  know what it's like growing up frightened by how you feel. Hidin' from
  yourself. And all round you there's people saying that what you feel
  is wrong. That it's against the church. That it's against the law.

MANDY: Bleedin' right it is!

FERGUS: And because you're not lettin' on, you never meet anyone else.
  And they never meet you, cause they're too busy hidin' too. Then one
  day you do meet someone — someone special. Maybe you phone Gay
  Switchboard . . .

OONAGH: I've never heard of that.

FERGUS: . . . maybe you go to a gay club . . .

OONAGH: Oh, I've heard about them.

FERGUS: . . . worried you'll meet someone who'll give the game away.
  And then you work it out that they're just as scared . . .

MANDY: Dead right!

FERGUS: . . . scared you'll give the game away on them. And so bit by
bit, you meet a lot more people who feel the same way you do, and
you get to realise that it's not so awful after all. And then, maybe you
fall in love . . .

OONAGH: Did you ever fall in love, Fergus?

MANDY: D'you call that love?

FERGUS: . . . and suddenly it all seems so natural, and you realise what
all your straight friends have been goin' on about all the time.

MANDY: Gives you the creeps just to think about it.

FERGUS: You're not scared anymore. You're proud to be yourself. To
stand up and be counted.

In what was generally a very bright and funny script these moments of
introspection often achieved a telling silence in the audience which was
very satisfying. They were followed by a stylised section in which Fergus's
parents were represented by faceless puppets. The substance of the text
was based on a list of common reactions of parents given to us by a self-
help group for parents whose children are gay.

    Puppets are brought on representing Fergus's parents.

FERGUS: Look Ma. Look Da. I've somethin' to tell you . . .
    Da looks at Ma. The mother looks at Fergus.
No ma I've not got anyone pregnant . . .
    Ma looks at Da.
No, Da. I'm not in any trouble. I just want to tell you I'm gay . . .
    Da draws back.
What's that Da? No son of yours' a sissy? . . .
    Ma looks at Da.
Maybe it's just a phase? . . .
    Ma looks back at Fergus.
No. I don't want to see the priest . . .
    Ma advances.
Why, would I want to see a shrink? There's nothing wrong wi' me . . .
    Da puts hands on thighs.
Well, it's not my fault, if it's like flamin' *Dynasty* in this house . . .
    Ma's head drops.
It's not your fault either. For God's sake, it's no one's fault! There's
nothing to feel guilty about. It wasn't anything you did or didn't do.
It's just the way I am . . .
    Ma lifts her head.
Am I happy this way? Yeah. I am. Or at least I would be if you didn't
keep goin' on about it . . .
    Da advances. Arms drop.

> I don't want to talk to my mother like that, Da, but she doesn't give
> me much chance to do anything else . . .
>   *Ma moves forward.*
> I know you're only worried for me. But what is there to be worried
> about? . . .
>   *Parents look at each other.*
> No, I won't catch AIDS . . .
>   *Both look at Fergus.*
> Because I know what to do to stay safe . . .
>   *Da draws back.*
> No Da, I don't think that there's any fear of my friends comin' round
> and fancying you' . . .

The last line of this speech usually got one of the biggest laughs of the night.

Another important part of the process was a workshop with a Dublin
gay youth group. Interestingly, their main reservation about our first draft
was that they perceived it as showing Fergus, the openly gay man, as a
victim. This, they felt, conformed to stereotypes which the gay community were seeking to challenge. Out of this discussion arose a new scene
in which Fergus confronts Tangles' bullying head-on.

> TANGLES: Y'know, there's nothing worse than freaks, who try to shove
> it down your throat that they belong to an orderly, happy society. I
> mean, they stand out like bleedin' sore thumbs. Dykes, blacks, chinks,
> knackers,[7] queers — you name it, they're only put here to fuck things
> up. And I've never shied away from my task of making the streets clean
> for decent, hard-workin' folk who don't want their city littered with
> these hideous eyesores. I mean, blacks should never have been allow-
> ed here. They belong in bleedin' Africa. Chinks should take their
> noodles and their prawn crackers and ship back to bleedin' Tokyo. And
> as for queers, don't ask me where they bleedin' come from. Outer fuckin'
> space if you ask me. We should shove them all in a space rocket, and
> blast them off to bleedin' Mars. (*To Mandy*) It'd make our bleedin' job
> a lot easier. I'll tell ya that for nothin'.
> FERGUS: Just who do you like?
> TANGLES: Wha'?
> FERGUS: OK, what do you like?
> TANGLES: I like lotsa things.
> FERGUS: Name one.
> TANGLES: Me Ma.
> FERGUS: Your oul' one did a runner two years ago.
> TANGLES: How do you know?
> FERGUS: Everyone knows. (*Pause.*) Who?
> TANGLES: I've loadsa mates.
> FERGUS: Like who?

Tangles is uncomfortable. He looks for support from Mandy, who teases him by pretending not to notice.

TANGLES: Bubbles.

FERGUS: The Ping Pong Champion of Mountjoy?

TANGLES: Donkey.

FERGUS: You're dreaming. No one's seen Donkey since the school burnt down.

TANGLES: Will you stop. I see him every Friday in Zippy's.

FERGUS: Tangles, you're barred from Zippy's. And Dwyers. And Charlies. And McGraths. And . . .

TANGLES: Sure they were all kips. I hang around the chippy now.

FERGUS: You wrote off Luigi's Lambourghini. You're brown bread if you go within a mile of the place. You know, you remind me of a Beatles song.

TANGLES: Eight Days a Week?

FERGUS: Nowhere man. I think this is yours.

Fergus presses the banana skin into Tangles's hand and exits.

TANGLES: Did the Beatles sing tha'?

This tended to create an almost tangible tension in the audience, and on one memorable night resulted in a round of applause on Fergus's exit.

MUSIC

The essential final ingredient was the music and in this we were fortunate in happening upon the services of Nico Brown. He not only wrote a set of very catchy tunes, but also wrote the lyrics. Significantly, it was in the songs rather than the dialogue that we were able to get much more specific about the issues. Two lyrics come most to mind. Fergus's song at the end of the first act allowed us to simulate the venom that can characterise homophobia:

FERGUS:

Nice work Kevin. Magic evening.

It certainly went with a bang.
Did you notice the way
When you mention you're gay
How it makes you feel
One of the gang?

So, you want to be one of the crowd, eh?
Nobody likes being alone.
Is that why you spent
A whole lifetime pretending
That you were Sylvester Stallone?

> Oh, hats off to you Kevin, fair play mate.
> You did it. You said it. You're gay.
> But we boys and girls
> Who have come out to play —
> We don't get it all our own way.

CHORUS:

> Nancy boy, fancy boy, beef bandit, fairy cake
> Shirt-lifter, limp-wrister,
> Ain't you got what it takes?
> Bender, dirt-track rider, homo, queen,
> Where's your handbag, you fag,
> Where's your rude magazine?
>
> Mary, Fairy, Julian Clary,
> Bull dykes, dick-lickers, lesbos, queers,
> Bum-boys, bumrubbers, fruitcakes, faggots,
> Get you, one of them.
> Come on, camp it up, dears.

FERGUS:

> It's amazing what people will call you.
> The attack in the back is the worst.
> At the end of the day, the best way to play
> Is make sure it's you telling them first.
> If you're gay and don't say,
> At the end of the day,
> When you do say it's true,
> They all knew anyway.

Another highlight of the production was Tangles' rap which managed to encapsulate every imaginable cliché about male homosexuality:

LORCAN: It's not as if he ever gave me a clue.
TANGLES: It's the smell.
LORCAN: Jaysus, tell me this whole thing isn't true.
MANDY: That's how you tell.
LORCAN: So what the fuck am I supposed to do?
MANDY: Well, if he's bent.
LORCAN: Against the church.
TANGLES: He wears scent.
LORCAN: Against the law.
TANGLES: Bent.
MANDY: Scent.
TANGLES: ⎫
MANDY: ⎬ It's elementary.

LORCAN: What, the fuck's he done to me?

LORCAN:
MANDY: } Fuckingenderbendershagbagfagbag.

TANGLES:
MANDY: } If there's one thing I hate . . .

MANDY: Did he ever give you flowers?

LORCAN: All those hours in the showers!

TANGLES: Did he ever touch your . . .?

LORCAN: No!

MANDY: Or your . . .?

LORCAN: No!!

TANGLES: Or your . . .?

LORCAN: No!!!

LORCAN: Fifteen years.

TANGLES: They're very patient, these queers.

MANDY: And now the whole estate is going to think
'cause you're his mate you operate the same way.

TANGLES: How to spot the gay. Identification of the bent population is me specialisation. Pay attention while I mention the essential referentials: *Pink Pyjamas.*

LORCAN: Wha'?

MANDY: Expression like a llamas, Low-alcohol beer, bursting into tears;

TANGLES: — characteristic of queers, that —

MANDY: smoking Marlboro Light;

TANGLES: wearing trousers too tight;

MANDY: getting jobs packing peaches;

TANGLES: idolising all their teachers;

MANDY: being scared of getting fat;

TANGLES: and going like that,

MANDY: Yeah. Wearing Paisley cravats

LORCAN: Are they all hairdressers?

TANGLES:
MANDY: } Not necessarily!

ALL: Mincing down the street, poncy sandals on their feet, wearing poloneck sweaters, writing dirty letters, staying at home to wash their hair, exotic underwear, Boy George CDs, putting Immac on their knees, popping panties in their purses, (*breath*) and wanting to be nurses, fucking fagbag ragbag, shagbag, fruit, he's a fuckin' gender bender, he's a rooty-toot-toot, he's a queer up to here, he's a poof on the hoof, and if there's one thing we hate . . .

LORCAN: It's the fact he's my mate! (*Spoken*) Here, at least I'll get me *Playboy* back.

At the end of the rap all three disappeared into a wardrobe, usually to a round of applause which Fergus then interrupted with this variant on Shylock's *cri de coeur* from *The Merchant of Venice*:

> A joke's a joke, a laugh's a laugh, but a person's a person, and you can't keep taking' the piss! I'm as real as he is. If I break a leg it hurts, if I cut myself I bleed, if I'm shot in the head, I fuckin' die. There's no difference between him and me.

The mood of this speech was taken up in the finale which ended in a kind of miniature céilidh, asserting the essentially celebratory nature of the production.

KEVIN:

> It's a matter of chance
> Whether you dance
> With the opposite sex or not.
> It isn't as though
> We all of us know
> What king of a body we got.
>
> It's a little known fact
> But when you're attracted
> To others of opposite kind
> There's bits of yourself
> Are left on the shelf
> For they're of a different mind.

ALL:

> Oh, your knees are heterosexuals,
> But bits of you are gay,
> One of your legs is a lesbian,
> The other's either way.
> The ears are queer, you're bent up here,
> Likewise in one of your eyes, but Jayz,
> Your poor oul' feet they can't compete
> And they change from day to day.

AUDIENCE REACTION

We were able to gauge audience response in a number of ways. We considered the attentiveness and reaction during the performances themselves. This was almost invariably good, with the Tangles character able to interact with the audience in a way that tended to defuse potential disruption. We also sought feedback from youth leaders, and many groups held discussions after seeing the performance; all reported that the performance had stimulated debate. There were also workshops held by the Family Planning Association after the second run of the production. These set out to assess the extent to which the play had caused those who saw it to question existing prejudices. They reported a significant amount of questioning of pre-existing attitudes.

These indicatons should be taken in conjunction with an anecdote told to me by one of the youth leaders about a previous Wet Paint performance. He recalled how attempts to initiate a discussion a few nights after the theatre visit had come to nothing. Some months after the event, however, the same group were away on a residential course, and late at night a spontaneous discussion of the play occurred. He was struck by the amount of detail the young people remembered.

Notes and References

1   Brian Friel's *The Gentle Island*; Thomas Kilroy's *The Death and Resurrection of Mr Roche*; Frank McGuinness's *Carthaginians, Innocence* and *Observe the Sons of Ulster . . .*; Jim Nolan's *Moonshine*; Aodhan Madden's *Sea Urchins*; Ken Bourke's *Wild Harvest*.

2   *Graph*, no. 7 (1989).

3   *Theatre Ireland*, no. 27.

4   Ian McKellen in an interview for *Theatre Ireland*, no. 16.

5   Jan Kott, 'Shakespeare's Bitter Arcadia' in *Shakespeare, Our Contemporary*, London: Routledge, 1988.

6   *Twelfth Night*, Act II, Scene 2.

7   The reference to 'Knackers' triggered one of the most interesting workshop discussions. A representative of a Travellers' group accepted that this was a way of associating different forms of prejudice together, but felt that the reference might alienate the young people she hoped to bring to the show from the play's broader message.

12 Pigs and Provos, Prostitutes and Prejudice
Gay Representation in Irish Film, 1984–1995

LANCE PETTITT

The more homosexuality emerges as culturally central, the less sure become the majority as to what exactly it is.

JONATHAN DOLLIMORE[1]

If this Bill is passed, I am concerned about the possible effects on Irish society. Will we now see exhibitions in public by homosexuals holding hands, kissing, cuddling, etc.?

PAUL MCGRATH, TD[2]

My overall aim is to establish Ireland as a film space, in the broadest sense . . . so what all this is doing is creating jobs in a definite way and at a lower cost than industrial jobs. For far too long that reductive view of the cultural space has held us back from developing its full potential in terms of job creation. This is an area which is job-rich and has the added benefit of being personally enriching.

MICHAEL D. HIGGINS[3]

INTRODUCTION

This essay examines a set of interrelations between the recent history of film activity in Ireland and the development of gay cultural politics. It would be tempting to see the coincidence of decriminalisation and equality legislation on homosexuality (1993) and the current high profile of film making in Ireland as self-evident indicators of Ireland's growing maturity, independence and liberalism. Instead, I want to show how both elements

252

of this paralleled historical context are problematic, and that they do not represent an unqualified, progressive social development in contemporary Ireland. It seems to me that both 'film activity' and homosexuality have shared a fractious, officially suspect existence in Ireland since before the state's formal inception in 1922. The Irish state's history of support for an indigenous film industry is chequered: it retrospectively claims a national cinema based largely on foreign finance and exiled talent, but has until recently abused many of its home-based film-makers. The state and churches have denied or decried homosexuality rather than acknowledge the material existence and moral soundness of homosexual activity in Ireland.

Within this broad context, I will focus on comparatively recent films (between 1984 and 1995) which represent gay male desire, narratives featuring men who choose men. Irish film images of lesbians in the same period can be counted on one hand. I do discuss them in course of my analysis, but my main concern is gay representaion. The term 'gay representation' is used in two related senses. Firstly, I use it to imply the experience of being *subjected to* a process of image-making in a society where, to misquote Jarman, 'heterosexuality is just common, not normal.'[4] Secondly, I use it in the sense of gay men being *active, productive agents*, reading and making films in Irish society. Even within the limited historical scope of this essay, the state has supported the making of film in Ireland in an ambiguous fashion. It set up Bord Scannán na Éireann (the Irish Film Board) in 1980, signalling an official recognition of the need for state funding of indigenous film production, but after seven years suddenly dismantled it, leaving would-be film-makers in the desert for a further six years. The Film Board 'Mark II' was officially relaunched under the twin influences of Albert Reynolds and the newly appointed Minister for Arts, Culture and the Gaeltacht, Michael D. Higgins, in March 1993, the night after an 'Oscar party' had been held at the Irish Film Centre building.[5] The film that had won all the awards was Neil Jordan's *The Crying Game*, the same film that had been showing six months previously when the IFC was officially opened by Reynolds. The irony of these coincidences will be explored more fully in the fourth section of this essay. If the state has been indifferent or ambiguous about the role of film in national life until recently, its attitude to homosexuality has been unequivocal. Until July 1993 homosexuality was criminalised in Ireland, its laws being based on British legislation dating back to 1885. Rulings or pronouncements made by the judiciary and the predominance of Roman Catholicism as an institutional form of religion with a controlling influence on the state education system meant that homosexuality was assigned a deviant or aberrant condition. Although the state's law has now changed, current formal dogma maintains the reasonable position that 'homosexual activity' is sinful, whereas homosexuality *per se* is merely an 'objective disorder'.

This essay does not seek to claim that there has been an unproblematic liberalisation of social attitudes to different expressions of sexual orientation over the past decade in Ireland. Nor does it claim that there is a gay film movement in Ireland. However, nearly all of the films discussed may be described as indigenously written, directed and produced. This has to be seen in the context of two material factors. Firstly, despite the current buoyant mood about film production in Ireland, the industry remains relatively small, dependent and fragmented. Secondly, despite the palpable impact of the political lobbying group, Gay and Lesbian Equality Now (GLEN), in pressuring for the 'sexual orientation' clause to be inserted into the Incitement to Hatred Act (1989) and in the form of decriminalisation and equal age of consent laws (1993), the comparatively recent phenomenon of an organised, 'out' gay consciousness in Ireland has yet to work its way fully through the culture of Ireland.[6]

The aim of this essay, therefore, is to explore a parallel history of both film and an emergent gay movement by giving analyses of individual films produced at different moments. These analyses will examine how homosexuality is represented through the character, narrative and genre of the films in question. As the title of my essay suggests, the words 'gay and Irish' have largely been assumed by the dominant and official discourse as mutually repellent, resulting in a series of film representations which conceptualise 'gay' as a highly problematic form of identity: socially, politically and morally marginalised within Irish culture and society. The analysis provided by this essay shows that the category 'gay' still largely functions within film to signify a range of aberrant, negative types, but that it is becoming increasingly apparent that definitions of straightness are, and always have been, dependent on a 'queer' element. This overall tendency is evidenced in the available films, which will be subjected to critique by three different but related strategies.

Firstly, we need to recognise that such forms of representation are not inescapably negative by reading the images and narrative 'otherwise'. Such a strategy is premised by the notion that film stereotypes are not 'fixed', natural forms but culturally constructed and therefore subject to history.[7] Accordingly, 'negative' images of gays and so-called 'straight' images are rendered susceptible to reinterpretation and can be appropriated and subverted by gay viewers. What this strategy reveals is that straight versions of gay people are tendentious, that the conceptualisation of homosexuality is implicitly linked to expressions of their own heterosexual identity. It is disturbing to straights that homosexuality is so closely related to them, as Dollimore has pointed out:

> A terror of the other may be premised on a terror of the proximate; not
> only does the excluded remain adjacent, but the adjacent becomes
> threatening in a way that the excluded never quite does.[8]

A corollary of this strategy is that we can inhabit their 'hetero' images and
bring out the homoerotic potential in their heroes. This has implications
for reading a whole host of cultural imagery, not least film. As Mark Simpson
has pointed out, images of men intended to connote heterosexual
masculinity are displayed so that 'their bodies are placed in such a way
as to passively invite a gaze that is *undifferentiated*: it might be a female
or male, hetero *or* homo.'[9] The pressure generated by such representations
results in a shift whereby the boundaries between straight and gay are
challenged, and the existence of the culturally enforced difference on which
homophobia is based is thus effectively threatened.

The emphasis of the second strategy of critique is different in that it
seeks to demonstrate that there are examples of gay representation in and
through the medium of film in Ireland that offer positive images, contra-
dicting the commonly viewed negative stereotypes. We can instance films
which are made by openly gay film-makers in a conscious effort to offer
a direct, overt counter to hetero images for gays in Ireland, *Chaero* (1988)
being a 'first' of its kind. This kind of critique has been carried through
in some of the most recent films such as Eve Morrison and Michael Ennis's
Summertime (1995). There are also examples of attempts at collaborative
work between film-makers, theatre group and gay support groups to produce videos for use within the gay community in Ireland, like Adam Keogh's
Don't Fight It, Feel It with Muted Cupid Theatre Company (unfinished,
1991). These kind of films emerge from the historical and political context of campaigns for 'Equal Rights' for lesbians and gays, based on what
has been termed 'identity politics'. In the 1990s the longer-term results
of the pragmatic step of asserting an 'essential' homosexual identity to
justify legislative equality post-Stonewall have been challenged by various
activist groups and in theoretical debates. The urgency of working for *a
politics of difference within equality* is stressed, rather than mistakenly seeing legislative equality as a guarantor of liberation.[10]

A third strategy develops the interrogation of the gay/straight categories
of sexual orientation suggested by the first strategy and receives impetus
from the outcome of the second. It logically posits that 'gay' and 'straight'
should themselves be brought into question as 'norms'. *The Crying Game*
(1992) and *Boys for Rent* (1993) are films that sustain readings which attempt
to examine or move beyond the paradigm of 'identity' politics. They are
films which flirt with a libertarian and a more radical 'queer' agenda which
seeks to deconstruct normative categories. In different ways such films
can be seen to address and combat a host of straight prejudices in

different generic and iconographic forms, but these films are doubly significant for the 'internal' debate that they have created within a gay culture in Ireland, a debate that is also taking place in Britain and America. What are the boundaries of what has so far been a broadly liberalising agenda regarding, for example, lesbianism, transsexualism? Emergent Irish lesbian film makers remind us of their marginalised position within Irish culture; films like *The Crying Game* continue to manifest male anxieties about women as well as offering fun to gay men, *Boys for Rent* raises awkward questions about male sexual desires and the criminalisation of sex-workers; Ger Philpott's *Change* (1995) addresses the response to HIV and AIDS in Irish society, and *Bent out of Shape* (1995) looks at violent homophobia.

NEGATIVE IMAGES / COUNTER-READINGS: *PIGS* TO *THE COURIER*

It remains a popular, liberal response to condemn film stereotypes out of hand as a flawed way of representing social types in fiction. As Richard Dyer has pointed out, however, such condemnation is rarely accompanied by an explanation of how stereotypes doggedly persist in cultural representation.[11] The key to understanding what characterises their effectiveness is that they are *apparently* static forms; the fixed nature of types is produced as the result of a continuous and strenuous representational activity which takes place within socio-cultural history. Being the product of culture and history, not nature and timelessness, stereotypes are in fact susceptible to change and reappropriation.

The two films discussed in this section, *Pigs* (1984) and *The Courier* (1988), both feature characters who are marked out by a series of narrative and iconographic conventions to be 'gay' in ways that (it is assumed) will be recognised by a largely heterosexual audience. *The Courier* was made and publicised as an attempt to engage film with life in contemporary Ireland: its attempt at 'realism' was a feature recognised if not praised by its critics. Frank Deasy and Joe Lee intended the film to buck what they perceived as the rural, past-bound clichés of Irish film. They offered instead representations of the marginal, unfavourable aspects of contemporary Irish experience, like urban housing estates, crime, drugs — and homosexuality. Cathal Black's *Pigs*, although an altogether more subtle, better-made and more admirable film, presented a *mise-en-scène* which managed artfully to combine Georgian decay, urban squalor and homosexuality. The film is set in a squat, and the central gay character, Jimmy, is linked by association to familial disruption and moral corruption. He inhabits the same world of drugs, filth and organised criminality, and his sexuality is seen in the same light. It might be concluded that both these films present 'negative' images and narratives in which gay characters are criminals or victims. Within the dominant cultural discourse, this world is held at a distance; it is seedy and yet 'exotic'. *Pigs* confirms many of the views of heterosexual Irish society.

Yet in other ways the film offers a liberal, sympathetic and non-condemnatory view of gay life. It points at the hazards of being gay-bashed and of being susceptible to blackmail ('they take advantage of people like you', advises one Garda). The attitudes of the Gardaí harassing Jimmy have to be contextualised within its narrative. To them Jimmy is feminised, an incomplete man ('why can't you be a man for once?'), and they taunt him for not living with his wife (though it is never established that he actually has one). Indeed, Jimmy is shown as a kind 'housewife' by cooking for the others, being tidy in the squat, and wearing a towel like a skirt. While these traits act within the film to mark him out as gay, they are far from being negative; in fact they are represented as positive attributes. He gathers around him all sorts of marginalised individuals in his squat, uncomplainingly showing acceptance and compassion for all their faults and the trouble they cause him. The pimp, prostitute, mental patient, failed businessman, the petty criminal and small-time drugs dealer are a surrogate family to him and he is the homemaker of the squat. To the state (the Gardaí and the social worker) and the gang who beat him up, he constitutes a problem and deserves to be victimised. Sadly, he ends up confessing to a criminal fraud of which he is not guilty. This conclusion to the narrative limits the scope for a progressive reading, restricting it to evoking sympathy with Jimmy for his predicament, and questioning of treatment by police. To a liberal viewer, the 'pigs' of the title refers to the behaviour of the Gardaí (pigs = police?), not the conditions in which Jimmy's squat-mates live. It is difficult but not impossible to resist the view that Jimmy remains a criminal and a victim.

The film could be said to reflect the popular consensus in Ireland about homosexuality at the time: at worst, an evil, sub-human or pathologically criminal condition; at best, an unfortunate failing deserving sympathy and compassion. There are two kinds of progressive recognition operating in *Pigs*. Firstly, homosexuality is visibly present in the frame; it is being represented, not inferred. This is a form of acknowledgement in itself. *Pigs*, perhaps for the first time, provides Irish cinema with a scene actually portraying a gay bar. Secondly, there is also a scene where two guys among the group of squatters and their friends are faced with a predicament over Jimmy's sexuality. One of the younger members of the gang comes downstairs to invite Jimmy up to join an impromtu party. Music is playing, drink is being taken, and dope is being smoked. In a quick sequence of point-of-view shots, Jimmy looks at the young man, who is aware of the attention but averts his gaze; then Jimmy catches another man looking at him too. It is the glance of recognition between two men, each of whom knows that the other is gay. Another character jeers that the second man is going to get off with Jimmy, repeatedly taunting 'Who's dominant tonight?' To cover up, the second man gets violent and verbally homophobic towards Jimmy, who is roughly thrown out. It is a brief but significant moment in the film, and is most poignant for gay viewers familiar with disavowal or violence in repressed homosexual desire.

The Courier is an attempt to make a Hollywood-style urban thriller set in contemporary Dublin, using a young cast and production team, with an original rock music score by Irish bands. It attempts to deal with problems of inner-city crime based on the drug trade. It was poorly scripted and directed by an inexperienced team of people, and its overall finish is unconvincing. It is a formula movie and provides an example of how an often incredible plot and weak characterisation can be coupled with generally poor acting performances. It is symptomatic of one strand of film production in Ireland from this period which saw value in making films with a contemporary, realistic and commercial appeal. Val (Gabriel Byrne), outwardly a local businessman but really a cruel gangster and drug dealer, manipulates young people in Dublin's city areas through extortion. Towards the latter half of the film its young hero, a motor-cycle courier (Padraic Ó Loinsigh), tracks down Val to his lair, and we learn that Val is leading a double-life in more senses than one. Gabriel Byrne's performance was notably better than the rest of the cast and was 'effortlessly villainous in all sorts of obvious ways (the white suit, the vulpine smile, *the penchant for rent-boys)*' (my emphasis).[12] The 'bent' businessman is seen out cruising for rent-boys to take back to his private sauna club. This night-time activity is synonymous with the shadowy criminal underworld which he inhabits. As such, it is difficult to resist the claim that Val and *The Courier* represent gayness in a negative fashion.

Yet *The Courier* can yield positive, gay pleasures, but only by reading against the grain of the narrative organisation and presentation of character. The film is unremittingly addressed to a heterosexual audience in that it goes through the formula of boy meets old school girlfriend (she works in a bank where he delivers packages). The film is centred on how they get together, form a relationship, how he triumphs over evil (Val), and they end up leaving Dublin together. It is a fairly unproblematic treatment of the theme of Ireland in the 1980s, and in terms of its sexual politics it seems very straight (forward). For a gay viewer, however, the film provides the vicarious pleasure spectacle of Ó Loinsigh's semi-naked body displayed

in a number of the obligatory bedroom scenes (loin sigh!). With stun-
ning blue eyes and model looks, the star-hero is a focus of attention for
a gay viewer, who is treated to a series of shots which project the actor
as a 'to-be-looked-at' image. Ó Loinsigh's character is the quintessence
of sensitive, boy-next-door type which has a positive currency within both
youth and gay cultural iconography. The potency of same-sex desire
presented in the photography of the male lead is actively policed and suppressed by the film's narrative conventions. I am claiming nothing more
for *The Courier* than the fact that within the same film there are not only
the more obvious 'negative' stereotypes of gays but also the potential for
straight characters to be appropriated by gay viewers. This type of viewing strategy is produced out of the material circumstances within which
gay people find themselves. If a society, through legislation and cultural
mores, criminalises certain forms of sexual pleasure and the expression
of them, then the discriminated group is forced to raid the oppressor's
representational territory, transforming images and codes, subverting the
cultural boundaries that they effectively patrol. As one film critic has
pointed out, there is:

> always a tension, a divergence of interests, between the film traditions
> and the deviant positions of the sub-cultures, a tension now smoothed
> over (as in many of the films of gay/lesbian 'affirmation'), now exploited
> or heightened.[13]

Such dissident viewing activity is symptomatic of an oppressive, illiberal
culture. It is one form of gay viewing which deals with the onslaught of
heterosexist imagery that provides pleasurable fantasy, one that is perhaps
necessary given the conditions, but ultimately unsatisfactory because covert,
compromised and proxy. But it is not the only means available for gay
representation in the senses outlined at the beginning of this essay. We
shall see more open challenges and alternatives offered in the films
discussed in the next section

FROM CRIMINALITY TO ASSERTION: *REEFER AND THE MODEL* AND *CHAERO*

> I do hope that some time in the future we get to see a gay film in this
> country.[14]

The reviewer's complaint is specifically about the censorship of sex scenes
between two men in a (non-Irish) film called *Fun Down There*, shown during
the Dublin Film Festival in 1990. If a gay film is defined as one in which

characters and action represent gay men as having legitimate sexual desires and allows gay viewers to take pleasure in overt, direct ways, then the reviewer's hopes had already been fulfilled in 1990. The period between 1988 and 1992 is probably the most significant four years in recent history for both film production and the campaign for homosexual legislative rights. Historically, it is a moment of conjunctural shift. In response to the closure of the Irish Film Board (IFB), film-makers organised a campaign lobbying government for reinstatement of finance and proper support structures for a film industry. In 1988 the European Court ruled in favour of David Norris's appeal that the legislation criminalising homosexuals should be changed, and Gay and Lesbian Equality Now (GLEN) was formed to lobby for equal rights legislation.

In March 1988, Joe Comerford's *Reefer and the Model* (*Reefer* in this essay) won Best Feature Award at the Celtic Film Festival and the Europa Prize in Barcelona in June. During the spring and summer of that same year a short, sixteen-minute film was in production by a Dún Laoghaire College of Art and Design (DLCAD) film student, Matt Hayes. *Chaero* was exhibited that autumn and won a design award. Although in many ways very different kinds of film, both attracted critical attention and, moreover, exemplify a different kind of gay representation to that of *Pigs* and *The Courier* discussed above.

Comerford's film is significant because it got made, finally, despite the collapse of the IFB, and because he portrays a gay character in a different way to previous attempts. He has commented that he is not entirely happy with the overall result of the film, which, he feels, could be improved by either shortening or lengthening the final edited version (which runs 105 minutes).[15] The *Irish Times* agreed with this, commenting that it was a 'brave but faltering attempt by director Comerford to grab the nettles of contemporary Ireland: politics, prostitution and homosexuality'.[16] In Britain, Derek Malcolm agreed that even if it was somewhat flawed, the version screened remains a challenge to 'conventional thinking about the Provos, the Ascendancy, religion, prostitution and homosexuality'.[17] Set and filmed on location in Galway, the plot brings together a group of outsiders in Irish society: a women (the 'model'), a former drug addict, returned from London, where she was involved in prostitution; an IRA man on the run; a gay character called Badger; and Reefer, a ne'er-do-well boat-owner with an Anglo-Irish Ascendancy background. In similar fashion to *Pigs*, the film features a makeshift, unorthodox Irish family, where all the members derive support and comfort from being bonded together in their shared estrangement. Also like *Pigs*, this film — by the juxtaposition of marginal individuals — attempts to question their status as sick, deviant or 'problems' within the eyes of the state.

Leading Irish film academics have commented on formal aspects of
Reefer. Kevin Rockett and his co-authors praise its 'aesthetic experiment
and political questioning,'[18] and, similarly, Martin McLoone observes the
juxtaposition of European non-narrative with Hollywood continuity narrative at different points in the film.[19] *Cinema and Ireland* notes that the
closing moments of the film are tantalisingly ambiguous. Is the Model
giving birth or aborting the baby she has conceived with Reefer? The would-
be father is left floundering in the sea, Badger is in prison, and Spider
has been killed. If the end is deliberately inconclusive, both sets of critics
are in agreement about the most subversive aspect of the film:

> the scene in the pub on the Aran Island ('The American Bar') in which
> Badger dances with, gently fondles, and then kisses his male lover
> during the céilidh.[20]

There is nothing in the film to suggest they are 'lovers': rather, it is more
likely that the two men are taking the opportunity to follow up a chance
cruise, Badger and the Irish soldier having already been caught 'cottaging'
by the army sergeant. Their participation in the céilidh defies 'mainland'
codes, and their kiss is a moment of remarkable tenderness between two
men that provides for a poignant screen moment: showing a northern
Presbyterian man coupling with a soldier from the Irish Republic suggests
a vision of sexual and political daring.[21]

Commenting on this particular scene, Comerford makes two things
clear about its significance which other commentators have not expanded
upon.[22] Firstly, the scene takes place on Inis Mór, a Gaeltacht area, where
the locals are seen to tolerate the two men dancing among them. Secondly, Comerford points out that it is the intolerance of an outsider, and a
representative of the state, the army sergeant, that provokes the violence.
Metaphorically, there is a link between state repression of what it sees
as sexually and politically deviant behaviour. The Irish soldiers are on
leave from border patrol where they stop incursion, which is comparable
to the activities of the Gardaí in *Pigs*, policing deviance from within. Comerford's films all tend to combine politics and aesthetics in ways that are
not always straightforward. For this he attracts adverse criticism and can
alienate sections of his audience. Within the context of this essay, *Reefer*
has been seen as an important watershed film: its gay representation is
challenging and allied to other kinds of socio-political struggle in the film.
As an ironic footnote to the film, Martin McLoone noted wryly that the
Haughey Fianna Fáil government which unceremoniously cut the Irish
Film Board in late 1988 had helped to fund *Reefer*. Its non-commercial
'message' was clear, but was not appreciated by official culture.[23]

Produced and shown later in 1988, *Chaero*, the first film made by an openly gay Irish film-maker, marks a distinct break and exemplifies the moment of conjuncture that was mentioned at the beginning of this section. The film provides a narrative which directly and exclusively features issues relating to gay men in an Irish setting. Hayes's film was conceived as a final-year student project film at Dún Laoghaire College of Art and Design, but he had other motives and expectations for the film. Specifically, he wanted to make a film on gay teenagers in Ireland, to show how adolescence for them is doubly difficult because of the way their sexuality is formed within a particular kind of heterosexual culture.

> I wanted to talk about that situation to a wider public. . . . Everybody sees it [homosexuality] as a threat — but they never see it from the point of view of the young people in the situation.[24]

The film cost IR£2,000, with about half that money being recovered from a television transmission on RTÉ. It was shot in Dublin using actors from the Dublin Youth Theatre and took some six months to make. *Chaero* is a short film, with a small cast and shot in colour, using a similar kind of setting to *Pigs*. Once again, that which is gay is associated with the urban decay of inner-city Dublin. The film won a design award for the use and photography of the wasteland, derelict factories and surrounding streets through which the action of the film is played. Hayes's selection of the urban setting was forced largely by the economic constraints of the small budget, but, basing the film's setting on personal experience, he associated Dublin with offering the possibility of a gay social life not available in a rural, small-town situation in Ireland (Hayes is originally from Kilkenny). If city life can offer a degree of anonymity and opportunity, it can also bring an increased chance of discrimination and threat, which is essentially what the film's narrative deals with. The story presents Ritchie and Chaero as ordinary, working-class Dublin teenage boys whose friendship and homosexuality develop naturally. The expression of that sexuality is tentative, confusing and scary, as is the case for most adolescents. In a scene crucial to the plot and to the wider issue of representing gay sexuality, the boys realise the nature of their desires. Playful wrestling in a disused warehouse becomes a first sexual embrace and almost a kiss, but this is interrupted by the arrival of Doyle. A couple of days later Ritchie summons up the will-power to tell Chaero about his feelings: 'That day . . . I don't know what happened. I just thought . . . I just thought you were beautiful.'

The emotional difficulties of being open about their feelings to themselves as much as to each other is further compounded by the fact that Doyle, who spotted them together, begins blackmailing them to keep their 'secret'.

The film clearly delineates the problem for the boys as being not their own feelings, which are 'normal', but the social prejudice and fear represented by Doyle. Hayes himself points out the difference between his own film and previous images of gays in Irish culture: 'all the other images were negative, awful'. In contrast, he 'wanted to show something positive, celebratory. . . . I wanted to show that teenagers can be ingenious in dealing with the problems they face'.[25] Ritchie and Chaero turn the tables on Doyle by getting him drunk and taking Polaroids of him being 'kissed' by Chaero. Armed with this counter-blackmail threat, the boys walk away from Doyle, and the closing sequence/dialogue recalls that of the opening. In this sense, within the space of sixteen minutes, the order of their lives has been restored after being threatened, and the narrative follows a conventional situation-comedy structure. The important thing here is that their gay relationship is taken as the starting-point, the 'norm'; the device of blackmailing Doyle represents a subversion that counters the real fear which many gay people experience in their school and work lives. The script of *Chaero* is realistic and witty; the confidence which the boys gain from this episode is shared with the gay viewer in a particularly sharp exchange between Ritchie and the defeated Doyle, Ritchie taking a term of abuse and using it in self-mocking triumph:

> DOYLE: Where's me fags?
> RITCHIE: We're the only fags around here, Doyle.
> *Chaero blows Doyle a kiss. They walk away.*

Chaero was shown at several festivals in Ireland, broadcast on national television (although on the 'First View' 11 p.m. slot) and internationally, so it has reached a wide audience. Remarking on his film being shown in a lesbian and gay film festival in San Francisco, Hayes observed:

> A lot of the gay films were very arty — some looked like rock videos. What made *Chaero* different from the rest was that it had a basic story line and was a black comedy.[26]

This description by the writer/director summarises what are both the strengths and limitations of the film. It is a simple, realistic and largely conventional film, but its narrative contains deeply subversive elements within an Irish context. The critical response to *Chaero* in Ireland was generally favourable among the middle-class and liberal newspapers, even if some of them were coy about the exact nature of the subject-matter. The *Irish Times* talked about a 'tale of teenage friendship', but Michael Dwyer in the *Sunday Press* was more outspoken in outlining the plot: 'a pair of young gay Dubliners are discovered and blackmailed by a local thug'. *Film Base News* (before it became *Film Ireland*) commented that the film 'handles with honesty rarely seen themes about sexuality'. Surprisingly, it took two years for *Gay Community News* to offer a review of the film, accompanying a showing at a National Gay Federation fund-raising event in May 1990. The historical significance of the film is clearly recognised, as are its direct, psychologically beneficial effects for a gay audience: 'As a contribution to gay culture, *Chaero* is an important film and should be seen by gay people'.[27]

The comment indicates that this representation is specifically of and for a gay people: 'educating' the heterosexuals of Ireland is a secondary feature. It is different again from *Pigs, The Courier* and *Reefer* in that the image and narrative is positive and distinct from other forms of socially ostracised groups; gay characters are represented not as unfortunate victims, but doing something for themselves as active, 'heroic' buddies. Generally, the film was indicative of a growing sense of confidence and self-assertion among gay people in Ireland. This spirit is informed by the idea that 'the perception of oppression makes us want to become who we are, not who we are made out to be'.[28]

LESBIAN *UNDERCURRENTS* TO *THE CRYING GAME'S* 'HOMO PROVO'

That spirit was further boosted with the passing of the European Court's decision against Ireland in the Norris case in 1988. However, assessing the impact of this historic judgment is a difficult task, since it produced contradictory reactions within different elements of Irish society. To the Catholic lay right it was a defeat provoking alarm: 'We [*sic*] are faced with homosexuality as a politicised cause, we are challenged by the demands of the homosexual movement in Ireland'.[29] To the gay community it acted as a spur for activity and further organisation, largely with the formation of GLEN as a direct, parliamentary lobbying body for lesbians and gay men.[30] Crucially, social and cultural organisation within the gay community moved up a gear. From this point on there was a definite potential for more people to feel good about being gay in Ireland than perhaps ever before. 'Tel-a-Friend' (the gay telephone line) organised a fund-raising showing of *Donna Herlinda and her Son* at the Academy Cinema; *Gay Community News* had been founded in February and began to articulate a 'gay voice'; and in August Aodhan Madden's *Sea Urchins* played at the Project Arts Theatre. The Fianna Fáil government, however, felt *inaction* was the appropriate response to the Norris case, and it would take the prodding of their coalition partners to force them to respond responsibly. Eventually the official response took five years to enact full decriminalisation, and the process of providing just and fair laws continues to take place. In this section I will consider images of homosexuality created from three distinct production backgrounds: first, an independent company for RTÉ (the national broadcasting corporation); secondly, some of the student projects and 'shorts' which came out of DLCAD's film school in the early 1990s; and finally, a major feature-length film made outside Ireland by a maverick Irish director that focused on the issues of sexuality and national identity.

Within this period when differing ideas of homosexuality were being contested in Ireland, the decision in 1990 of RTÉ to co-produce a half-hour drama about a failed lesbian relationship, entitled *Undercurrents*, demands some consideration. Stephen Rooke and Reg Renwick's screenplay (produced by Emdee Productions) was effectively endorsed as the broadcasting establishment's cultural response to the ongoing debate about homosexuality. Firstly, it is revealing that expensive, 'quality' television production values should be deployed for such a moribund treatment of lesbianism. Secondly, given that the homosexual equality lobby was arguably at that time a gay male-led initiative, and popularly perceived as such through figures like Senator Norris, the selection of lesbianism as a film drama project seems a skewed attempt by official culture to address homosexuality in Ireland. Unintentionally, *Undercurrents* makes the 'absence' of Irish lesbianism all the more pertinent to mainstream *and* subcultural audiences alike, articulating as it does a male-centred and a profoundly ignorant view of female homosexuality. One is tempted to argue that, in the face of an increasingly 'loud and proud' and politically shrewd 'Equality Now' movement, this production attempted to regain cultural hegemony with its particular version of a lesser known aspect of homosexuality which was more 'vulnerable' to misrepresentation.

Helen is a beautiful, artistically talented concert organist who, at the opening of the film, returns to Ireland as a success. The film works through a series of extended flashbacks which recall her schoolgirl and early adult friendship with Lisa. Helen's feelings were evidently stronger and more insistent than Lisa's and were not fully reciprocated. As they grow up Lisa inevitably chooses a man (John), excludes Helen, breaks the intimacy once shared, and has a baby with John. Helen's alternative as a rejected dyke is left to pursue her ambitions and develop a career, leaving Lisa in fulfilled, heterosexual bliss. The narrative comes (almost) full circle with Lisa and Helen getting back together (Lisa: 'I need you as a friend'), but towards the end of the film a recurring flashback sequence of Helen's childhood depicts her being sexually abused by her father. The film unequivocally offers this as an 'explanation' of Helen's sexual orientation. While Lisa is fulfilled by a good man (who provides her with children), Helen's achievement in her career is supposed to be seen as a kind of compensation or product of a fatal distraction caused by her abusing father. Her lesbianism, the mystery which the film cannot or will not confront, is accounted for by her lack of a good man. Despite being 'tastefully' shot and supported with incidental passages of classical music, the film is a tawdry effort. Its major flaw was that the script was unconvincing (which was not surprising, having been written by two men), and there has yet to emerge a lesbian film-maker from Ireland to do justice to this kind of material, despite some promising short films made by Collette Cullen at the London College of Printing. It would be difficult to construe the representation of Helen as positive in any sense. My point here is to question RTÉ's decision to back a production which clearly supports such a damning version of homosexuality in the face of the increasing confidence of gay men. At the time lesbianism provided an easier target because of its lack of cultural visibility, though this has altered somewhat since Emma Donoghue's recent outspokenness.

The graduates of the DLCAD's film school made a series of film shorts between 1991 and 1992 which offer, albeit from a different kind of production base, a small but significant set of gay film representations leading up to decriminalisation. A number of students realised interesting, if incomplete, short film projects. Adam Keogh (now living in London)[31] produced a clutch of unfinished films and video projects in 1991 which directly relate to the shift in political and social attitudes on gay-related issues which took place in the years before 1993. *Appearances* (1991) was devised as a thirty-minute mainstream broadcast programme, concerned with people's deceptive exterior appearances, but also addressing the invisibility of sexual orientation. *Pink* (8 minutes, unfinished) and *Don't Fight It, Feel It* (also unfinished) were aimed at more specific youth audiences. The latter video, set to Primal Scream's record of the same name, was planned for production with the Dublin-based, Muted Cupid Theatre Company.[32] It was envisaged that this video would be used by befriending and counselling groups like 'Icebreakers' or the Youth Group in Dublin as a way of broaching the difficulties of coming out. Keogh's attempts point to a more proactive and direct interrelation between film-maker and gay community than could be offered by late-night television broadcasts on national television. His joint initiative, though unrealised, typified the growing confidence of individuals and groups at this time. In his final-year project, *Sexy Revolution* (1992, 18 minutes, but never finally edited), Keogh made a documentary which tried to 'capture the mood of change' before the decriminalisation vote actually took place. Keogh set sequences of the lesbian and gay float of the St Patrick's Day parade in Dublin and images of naked men dancing against interviewees (gay and straight) giving their views about changes in sexual attitudes in Ireland in general. Keogh was clear about his aim: 'not to make a complaint, let's make it a celebration'; yet he was cautious about the extent of the liberation of attitudes which would follow decrimalisation. He maintains that it is still easier to be out gay in London than in Ireland.

Other short films of interest to come out of these two years at DLCAD include Conor Flemming's *The Visit* (c. 1991), Cilian Halpin's *What's Your Problem?* (1991, 12 minutes) about a gay couple who find out that one of them is HIV, and Rachel Smith's *The Pearl* (1991, 16 minutes).[33] This latter film deals with a couple living in a bedsit, one of whom gets 'queer-bashed'. The shock and after-effect is too much for him to bear: 'I didn't think this could happen. . . . I want to go away.' The film concludes with a surreal, dreamy escape to a kitsch beach peopled with male hunks (played by Action Man dolls) and is a comment on the necessity of exile, a reality that many gay men and lesbians have faced in the past because of intolerance within Ireland. Some of the better produced and finished work of graduates has been broadcast on national television, albeit in a late-night slot (*Chaero* and *The Pearl* for instance), but DLCAD film school acts primarily as a training ground for the production and technical skills of the film and television industry. Like the other major art college in Dublin, the National College of Art and Design,[34] Dún Laoghaire does provide a liberal, if predominately middle-class, atmosphere which is conducive to the exploration of aesthetic, sexual and political alternatives. However, owing to the small scale of production and the college's primary commitment to learning and experimentation, its overall effect has remained marginal.

Many of these better expressions on film and video fed into the growing number of festival and independent cinema venues in Ireland and abroad. In Ireland the Dublin, Cork and Foyle Film Festivals were established venues that had been programming films with gay interest since the late 1980s, but in October 1991 Donal Sheehan launched the first Lesbian and Gay Film Festival in Cork with a Saturday-morning seminar entitled 'Into Celluloid'. The central aim of the seminar, and by extension the Festival, was to 'examine the potential for lesbian and gay film in Ireland'.[35] In Dublin the Lesbian and Gay Film Society began monthly film showings (of mostly mainstream American and European origin), starting in March and running through to the summer (but showing *Chaero* in May). The gay community's organisation of films has always tended to have been on a sporadic and largely voluntary basis, coming and going depending on individual or small-group enthusiasm and financial resources. But between the larger festivals and smaller groups, a gay film viewing culture was nurtured. The Dublin 'straight' film festival continued to show a lot of non-indigenous gay films, even if in censored form (as the reviewer of *Fun Down There* had complained in 1990). Niall O'Leary could claim proudly in a 1993 review in *Gay Community News* that 'Queer cinema represented itself glowingly at this year's Dublin Film Festival, rating amongst the funniest or the most beautiful to be seen.'[36] Clearly there was a potential for lesbian and gay film exhibition in Ireland in both commercial and political senses. From a brief survey it is obvious that the contribution of Irish-produced film images in the early 1990s is small in terms of screen minutes. But this has to be put in perspective: many were made by independent or student film-makers, and their impact has to be judged in the context of being restricted to late-night television slots or cinema festival screenings. The growth of 'gay' programming within established festivals and the foundation of the Cork Lesbian and Gay Film Festival are testament to a consolidation of exhibition space for gay images which itself is part of an international phenomenon in film and video distribution.[37] Film-makers in Ireland who were gay were becoming more open about putting their ideas and concerns on film. Despite this, gay audiences were still watching themselves being represented in an economic and cultural process dominated by heterosexuals.

It is with a sense of proportion that this section concludes with an examination of what became the major film event of the 1992–3 season, the release and reception of Neil Jordan's *The Crying Game*. As a major feature film by an Irish screenwriter and director which portrayed a transsexual and a gay IRA man, its carefully orchestrated release could simply be seen as an example of astute straight film distributors cashing in on the 'queer' potential that Sheehan had anticipated. In the context of this essay, the two most significant things about *The Crying Game* (1992) were that it was not funded and produced by Irish money and that it was written by a straight male. Mark Simpson was unequivocal in his judgements about the film's 'national' origins and sexual politics:

> *The Crying Game* is neither a 'progressive' nor even a 'British' film. Instead it is a thoroughly American film which women, gays, blacks and transsexuals should be deeply mistrustful of. But most especially women.[38]

Competing claims made about the 'nationality' of *The Crying Game* are instructive. To some, the film was British, being funded and produced by Palace Pictures and Channel Four Films, but others like Simpson and Sarah Edge have placed the film within an American movie genre, pointing out its deep-seated misogyny, and Simpson has in addition criticised the negative portrayal of transsexuals.[39] My aims here are, firstly, to stake a claim for the film's Irish origins; secondly, to consider the consequences of this for debates within Irish culture; and thirdly, to argue that, for all its limitations and faults, it retains positive aspects for gay viewers.

As has been noted earlier, *The Crying Game* happened to be programmed for the opening week of the new Irish Film Centre building in September 1992, and the government minister responsible for the promotion of the arts and culture, Michael D. Higgins, was able to announce the reactivation of the Film Board in the immediate post-Oscar success of the film in March 1993. Clearly, the leading national film institution, the film 'industry' and the state department responsible for film promotion was keen that the success of Jordan's film should somehow signify a connection with, and a justification for, the minister's initiatives. Liam O'Neill has acerbically pointed out that the Irish state's late interest in the film business derives in part from the July 1992 publication of the Coopers & Lybrand *Report on Indigenous Audio-Visual Production Industry*, 'a report which served to significantly enhance the legitimacy of the film industry within Ireland's politico-business establishment'.[40] The claiming of *The Crying Game* as 'Irish' by, and in the terms of, the political establishment was dependent upon notions of identity which were deeply troublesome to contradictory positions on homosexuality/nationality at that time. Reconsidering the film in an Irish context, Simpson's playing down of the gay element ('the film's latent homosexuality is a red herring') is made at the expense of his case about the film's misogyny. He continues that 'an awareness of the film's 'homosexuality' has the added effect of dispelling any remaining notions of the film's 'examination of nationalism'.[41] On the contrary, it is precisely in accepting the representation of a 'homo Provo' which for me makes it a most provocative Irish film. Rightly, I think, Julie Wheelwright has claimed that the film 'brilliantly fuses anxieties about sexual identity with questions of nationalism'. The fact that the idea for the story came out of a period of Jordan's own experience of living out of Ireland perhaps explains both his ambivalence towards Ireland and its political establishment, and his attempt to 'think otherwise' about the representation of sexuality.

In an interview for the London-based *What's On* magazine, Jordan recalled the difficulties in which the British film industry found itself as production of *The Crying Game* neared completion. He has the eye of an outsider who distances himself with the self-deprecating observation:

> [The end of Palace Pictures] felt like the end of the British film industry. But I'm not English, I'm Irish, so I can't speak with authority on the subject, just as an outsider it seemed extraordinary to me.[42]

However, Jordan has also criticised the lack of opportunity, funding and obfuscation in Ireland regarding film-making: 'There's no alternative [to emigrating]. There is nothing for me here.'[43] In Ireland The *Evening Press*, delightedly claiming the film as Irish, also suggested that Jordan had deliberately not sought finance from within Ireland in order to maintain editorial independence about the film's content,[44] while Jordan himself commented: 'There was no Irish money in the film at all. Like most Irish movies it was financed from England.'[45] While source cash is a vital factor in determining the 'nationality' attached to a film, Jordan clearly sees other elements as contributory. He has said that 'The attempt to imagine another state of living, another way of being, is I believe very Irish.'[46] This statement carries a political charge regarding both national and sexual identities. One commentator succinctly articulated the fear within dominant formations of political power by presenting the imaginary dilemma: 'What's worse — finding out your lover's an IRA killer or your girlfriend's a man?'[47]

The record of the Irish state's repression and marginalisation of Irish republicanism is implicitly questioned by Jordan and Rae's sympathetic characterisation of Fergus. If the republican movement represents a repressed 'other' within the political establishment's official version of Irish history and culture, then gay republicanism offers an image of a double oppression. The Irish *Sunday World* published an article in which a republican prisoner, Brendi McClenaghan, serving a sentence in Long Kesh, was 'outed' by the paper in an attempt to create negative publicity for Sinn Féin.[48] Similarly, in Britain there are instances of official and populist homophobia being conflated with a virulently anti-Irish and anti-republican sentiment. The figure of Roger Casement would provide an historical example, but contemporary examples also occur. The *Sun* ran a story entitled 'Homo Provo' which drew parallels between *The Crying Game* and the arrest of Patrick Kelly. To score propaganda points, the article quoted a 'senior London detective' who said:

> The IRA are normally very conservative about sexual matters and pre-
> judiced against homosexuals . . . but they still recruited Kelly who was
> a practising homosexual for more than 20 years. That's a measure of how
> desperate the IRA are becoming. They are now resorting to using a man
> of Kelly's sexual orientation whom they would not normally touch with
> a barge pole.[49]

The intent is clearly to discredit the Provisional IRA through an appeal to the *Sun*'s homophobic readership. Both Irish and British tabloids latched on to an important point about the attitude of Sinn Féin to homosexuality. McClenaghan has himself written on the difficulties of being gay within the republican movement, indicating that Irish republicanism has effectively repressed homosexuality within its own ranks:

With comments like 'It will harm the Movement/struggle', gays and lesbians are forced into invisibility within both the community and the Republican Movement, and consequently within the struggle.[50]

Jordan's film challenges both British and Irish state versions of republicanism in a limited way by constructing the film's point of view as Fergus's. In the first third of the film Fergus's republicanism is given a greater sense of purpose than the British soldier's. Jody's rationale is simply: 'I was sent . . . it was a job'. Dara MacNeill's review of the film in *An Phoblacht/Republican News* picks up that Fergus is portrayed sympathetically, but it rather cryptically avoids the issue of Fergus's sexuality to concentrate on the 'positive' portrayal of him as an IRA volunteer:

> By focusing in on him, what we see is one man attempting to work out a life out of the cards he has been dealt. We get inside his head, thus we see a human being.[51]

Since it is a well-established film cliché in many British films to present IRA men renouncing violence, giving up the gun, etc., the film is more subversive in the fact that Fergus wants physically to love his enemy as part of his understanding of himself. In this the film transgresses a traditional and residual version of Sinn Féin republicanism which has only supported decriminalisation since *circa* 1986 and recently amended its policy to make a positive statement of support for lesbian and gay comrades.[52]

The 'enemy' for Fergus is both the reluctant representative of the British state (Jody) but also the more intimate enemy of homosexual desire within himself, a force that he struggles to overcome. It is a significant weakness of the film that Jordan fudges this central difficulty because it avoids representing at this stage in the narrative the quintessential self-hatred of a repressed gay identity. In the early 'hostage' section of the film Fergus volunteers for the task of executing Jody. He fails to do so, and Jody is accidentally killed instead, thus refusing the Wildeian paradox of 'killing the thing we love most'. In the introduction to the published screenplay of *The Crying Game* Jordan observed that:

> Underlying this friendship lay an erotic possibility, a sense of mutual need and identification that could have provided salvation for their protagonists.[53]

He clearly cites of examples within Irish literature and drama which deal with the subject of male relationships between Irish and English combatants, specifically in Behan's *An Giall/The Hostage* and Frank O'Connor's short story *Guests of the Nation*. Such work constitutes part of a 'tradition' containing a submerged taboo about which Jordan is

refreshingly open: 'There's always homoerotic feeling between men in conflict.'[54] By mapping questions of sexual identity on to national
antagonism, Jordan attempts to construct a metaphor applicable to contemporary times but which

> lies in the broader history of Anglo-Irish relationships: two cultures in
> need of each other, yet at war with each other. The fact that such a theme
> can be relevant . . . in the nineties, for me, says more than I want to
> ponder about the current state of things.[55]

We come back to the point that many people have not taken seriously
the fact that Fergus is a closeted gay or comes to realise that he has a
more open sexual orientation than he thought he had. Even Simpson,
caught up in his eager polemic to condemn the misogynist elements of
the film, says that 'the film's latent homosexuality is a sub-textual red herring
to cover the film's tracks of heterosexual misogyny'. He further points out
that the film presents a male heterosexual view of homosexuality, and on
this point I think Simpson is understandably wary of rave reviews of a
film made by a straight film-maker about such contentious issues. He correctly identifies a number of characteristics of popular response to the
film which are corroborated by my own experience of discussion with
students. One such student, from the small republican area of Portadown,
found it hard to accept that Fergus was a 'homo Provo'. I was told that
Fergus only fancied Dil because he was drunk and mistook him for a
woman, and that he threw up at the revelation of his male anatomy. Such
readings are partial in two particular ways. Firstly, the disavowal of one's
fantasy of same-sex in repressed gay men can produce the kind of violent,
visceral self-revulsion that Fergus exhibits when the fleshy reality presents
itself. Secondly, it is hard to refute the fact that, fifty-five minutes into
the film, while Dil is expertly giving Fergus a blow-job, he sexually fan-
tasises about Jody. This is signified by the soft-focus, slow-motion 'dreamy'
sequence that is subsequently repeated five minutes later, even though
he has just vomited at the sight of Dil's penis. The published screenplay
confirms the object of Fergus's sexual desire: 'Jody [dressed in cricket
whites] releases the ball; we see Fergus in bed, breathing heavily.'[56] Later
in the film Fergus 'disguises' Dil by making him wear Jody's cricket whites.
Fergus's suppressed homosexual interest in Jody develops from the hostage
situation. Eighteen minutes into the film, just after Jody has shown his
captor a picture of his 'girlfriend', Fergus repels Jody's anti-Irish racism
by revealing his own name ('It's Fergus, not Paddy'). This leads to further
(physical) intimacy when Fergus is persuaded to handle Jody's penis and
is skilfully 'reassured' that 'it's only a piece of meat'. Moments later, under
cover of a joke, Fergus can say that 'the pleasure was all mine'.

There are enough moments in *The Crying Game* to support Fergus's
realisation of his own — if not wholly gay, at least more open — sexual
orientation. Furthermore, I cannot accept Simpson's blanket negative critique and dismissal of the film. As we have already seen, to pick up Dyer
again, it is not a new situation for gay viewers to find themselves in, having to work against a film's heterosexual assumptions. One could say it
is a condition of gay viewing for most of the time. Dil's travesty of femininity
is not to be taken seriously ('Details, baby, details'), and the dialogue is
of a stylised kind which resists straightforward appeals to realism. The
adoption of disguises, the deceptiveness of appearances, the denial of
repressed emotions which make up the substance of the script are recognised and its levels of ironies are enjoyed particularly, but not exclusively,
by a gay audience. The key to the film is that

> En route to becoming himself, Fergus finds that supposedly inherent
> identity is not all; a provisional invented one is a real alternative.[57]

The film has been accused of propagating misogyny, of trivialising
transsexuals, and of racial prejudice. These shortcomings or potentials are
not confined to heterosexual versions of the world; they can originate from
within gay viewers' groups too. It seems to me that the achievement of
the film is to throw up these kind of troubling questions. In the context
of this essay, it is important to avoid seeing *The Crying Game* as in some
sense a 'culmination' film. It is not. It is a debatable film that should not
be accepted as a beacon of gay liberation, nor, however, dismissed merely
as a product of a heterosexual reaction. I am not suggesting that a 'balanced'
response is either possible or desirable. The film's contrariness expresses
a moment of ideological contest between the dominant political/cultural
blocs and subordinate groupings which have a specific location within
an Irish context as well as relevance to the broader debates about 'queer'
film theory. Furthermore, it is important to recognise how Jordan's film
provoked an 'internal' debate within the subordinate groupings themselves,
indicating the difficulties of the transitional moment, from 'gay' to 'queer',
which occurred in the early 1990s.[58]

EQUALITY AND BEYOND . . .? *BOYS FOR RENT, SILENCES, THE HAPPY GORDONS, CHANGE, BENT OUT OF SHAPE* AND *SUMMERTIME*

In this final section we will briefly consider films produced between 1993
and 1995. One of them exemplifies the difficulties of making a film about
male prostitutes in Dublin and raises questions about the nature of male

sexual identity. The other films show that, despite the changes in the Irish law, younger Irish lesbians and gays — and teenagers especially — still have to face various kinds of social and institutionalised forms of homophobia in schools, within the churches, and in everyday domestic family situations. The latest clutch of films do show gays making a fight and continuing to live in hope. Nevertheless, for many the homosexual rite of passage — coming out — still remains a difficult journey to make whether it be from abroad or nearer home.

Debate accompanying the momentous change that is plainly taking place in Ireland is reflected in discussions within its film culture. Many social and cinematic issues remain unresolved, and new challenges have emerged in this 'new age'. Decriminalisation and equality laws have to be recognised as a watershed in Irish legal history, but lesbians and gays are only too aware that the everyday situation for them remains difficult. In terms of cinema, since about 1992 'queer' is suddenly fashionable: distributors realise that independent films can make money if carefully niche-marketed, and broadcasters know that a lesbian storyline will boost ratings.[59] Dominant cultural institutions such as mainstream cinema and the national broadcasting service relinquish their power reluctantly and have an inordinate capacity to appopriate the power of subcultural movements, reducing them to an interesting fad or an example of the exotic.[60] For film-makers creating representations of lesbians and gays, this presents a dilemma: to go mainstream, to remain close to their constituent audiences, or attempt to bridge the gap? In Ireland, as elsewhere in the 1990s, debates about the differences between 'gay' and 'queer', transgressive sex and being 'out' have been most intensive within the subordinate groupings themselves.

An example of this in an Irish context occurred following the showing of *For a Lost Soldier* (1993, Holland, Kerbosch) at the Lesbian and Gay Film Festival in Cork in October 1993. Set during 1944, *Lost Soldier* tells the story of a twelve-year-old Dutch boy's relationship with a Canadian soldier which develops at an emotional and physically sexual level. The 'Munster Diary Supplement' of *Gay Community News* reported that a walk-out occurred during the screening at the festival.[61] The protester condemned the decision to include the film in the programme, saying that 'This film is a highly manipulative and thinly disguised apologia for paedophilia and as such has no place in the [Cork] festival.' He agreed with the sentiments of a straight but gay-friendly ally who had sent a written complaint to *GCN*. Against such remonstrations, the festival organiser, Donal Sheehan, put the case for the showing of controversial films in an open society. He asked rhetorically if 'we should act as paternal censors to protect our audiences from films that might "corrupt" them?' He pointed out the irony of the situation where gays proposed to censor themselves to comply with the feelings of straights and because the film's subject-matter was unsettling for gay men. The rest of Sheehan's argument can be usefully compared with the statement made two years previously about the aim of the Cork Festival. Taken together, his comments suggest a marked advance in position:

> I do not see that the festival's role should be simply to entertain or present 'positive images' of lesbians and gays. I believe we ought to be screening challenging, difficult and transgressive material.[62]

This signifies a distinct break in attitudes concerning the politics of contemporary gay representation in Ireland and elsewhere. The debate has moved on from the promotion of images of affirmation and equal rights, to tackling all sorts of transgressive differences not confined to sexual orientation and which bring heterosexual, normative values into question. 'Queerness' explodes the centrality and assumed certainty of straight versions of behaviour by showing that there has always been a transgressive element within, and as an essential component of, straight culture. What is particularly challenging about Sheehan's thesis in this article is that he exposes the fears within 'straight gays' as well as heterosexuals by observing that paedophilia 'is an extremely sensitive subject and gay men are particularly nervous of the issue'.[63]

A film apposite to this topic is Liam McGrath's *Boys for Rent* (1993), which was an award-winning DLCAD final-year student film. *Boys for Rent* is a documentary in the investigative tradition which tries to contain the 'queer' elements that it reveals. Made by a straight director, it is ostensibly liberal in that it attempts to give a voice to Dublin's male prostitutes, a powerless and invisible group within Irish society, and in its attempt to combat the prejudice of commonly held social attitudes to the nature of male (homo)sexuality, male rape and paedophilia. To articulate such issues, McGrath skilfully employs firmly established documentary modes of address and iconography. Based on painstaking ethnographic research, the film was shot largely in monochrome, using authoritative, informative captions, a combination of filming techniques (including double-exposed sequences), grainy 'reconstruction' scenes shot in Super 8mm, 'talking head' interviews and the voice-overs of four prostitutes. The opening sequence and non-interview footage used actors, but all the words in the film were spoken by the rent-boys themselves. For the interview sequences McGrath used the convention of shadowing, partial framing or back-lit silhouettes to maintain anonymity.

It is a powerful, moving film which clarifies several points about male prostitution. Firstly, young boys and teenagers turn to it out of economic necessity, not choice. Many come from disrupted families and care homes, and some had already experienced sexual abuse. They were all aware of the health risks involved and of their exploited status: 'I'm not bent — as in bent — I'm a round boy as they say. The only reason I do it is for the money.'[64] This remark opens up a further point about the sexual identity of the teenagers. A caption informs the viewer that

> Not all the boy prostitutes would consider themselves to be homosexual. Some are bi-sexual, some are heterosexual, and others have little concrete notion of their sexual identity.

This is largely because that identity has not been allowed to develop outside of the confines of money exchange. Finally, all the prostitutes spoke about the sexual kick that the punters (most of whom identified themselves as 'straight') derived from the power to physically hurt and humiliate the rent-boys:

> Most of the guys are into violence. . . . In another episode I was tied to fucking banisters upside down and whipped with a hanger — a steel hanger. I didn't think that was one bit nice. . . . And when the money was gone — I thought, what have I to show for it — except the marks, y'know?

In a sequence from the near the opening of the film (and used again to close it) McGrath departs from the investigative-journalist imagery and introduces a startling kind of iconography which borrows from a gay film tradition of representation. The naked torso and head of a boy were photographed, the film rewound, and then a sequence of 'night-life' shots of Dublin city centre were shot at double-speed. The camera in close-up searches the boy's face and body which is positioned arms-by-side, head hung down and eyes downcast. McGrath's intentions were clear: he wanted to create an image of the boy as innocent victim, to show the initial 'purity' of the boy, and to juxtapose this with the corruption which prostitution brings.[65] Simultaneously the voice-over clearly infers that the punters are 'weirdos', but this creates a contradictory tension between voyeuristic visuals and the audio-track. While McGrath's purpose is clear, his use of imagery here is disturbing, deriving unconsciously from a repertoire of gay representation in books, film and art which has been termed by one critic as the 'sad young man' image.[66] McGrath was not consciously using the gay art film tradition of focusing on youths as objects of desire, one which features in various kinds of soft and hard gay pornography, but undoubtedly the sequence possesses an uncomfortable ambivalence. Such ambivalence lies at the heart of documentary films whose subject-matter is controversial or marginal. The film-maker encounters the dilemma of how to prevent the aestheticisation of those 'victims' whose lives are being documented. *Boys for Rent* struggles with this dilemma, ostensibly overcoming it, but does not fully grapple with the idea that 'the making of a representation of prostitution is an act of power itself'[67] with all the potential for reinscribing the taboos and exploitation. The film remains a challenging, if flawed document because it hammers home the points that so-called straight men are involved in under-age, sado-masochistic and homosexual sex. Secondly, it is clear that young men's emerging sexualities are being affected by a combination of economic circumstances and the transgressive practices of 'heterosexual' men. In these ways the film opens up a broader vista beyond the binary of gay/straight sexuality. But the film replicates the social anxieties about transgressive sex and the 'queering' of comforting, known boundaries based on gender and sexual-orientation that has accompanied attainment of limited legal equalities in Ireland.[68]

By way of concluding this essay, we can briefly discuss the work of other relatively inexperienced film-makers who have recently completed films. The work of Collette Cullen, Paula Crickard, Ger Philpott, Orla Walshe and Michael Ennis / Eve Morrison is by no means radically queer, but they have produced films which confront difficult areas of Irish lesbian and gay experience, including the continuing issues of comparative lesbian 'invisibility', living with prejudice about HIV and AIDS, homophobic violence and teenage gays.

Cullen is a Dublin-born graduate of the London College of Printing Film School and has made three short films. Her work attempts to address the almost complete lack of lesbian images in Irish film culture. *The Last Time . . .* (1993, 12 minutes) 'is a light hearted look at lesbian culture and explores lesbian sexual and erotic images'[69] by telling a short story of Mary's fantasies. She falls for a country-and-western carpenter who does some work at her flat, but the dream situation does not last. She ends up by ruefully promising herself not to fall for another woman — knowing full well that she will. The film was screened at the seventh London Lesbian and Gay Film Festival and internationally. *Home You Go* (1993, 12 minutes) involves a 'brief encounter which turns into a tale of obsession' and was the London College of Printing Fuji Scholarship entry. It was premièred at the Irish Focus festival in Boston and shown at the eighth London Lesbian and Gay Film Festival. At a train station a young woman accidentally finds the key dropped by the woman about whom she has been fantasising. The young woman lets herself into the other's flat and, in her absence, takes great pleasure in temporarily pretending to live with the object of her desire. In her most substantial piece of work, the aptly titled *Silences* (1995, 30 minutes), Cullen has produced a more complex narrative in what she describes as

an exploration of what is invisible, what is unsaid and the relationship
between self and other which is the core of all identity.

The story involves two London-based film-makers, Niamh and her English
girlfriend, Helen, going to Ireland to make a film. Although the two women
share a common sexual identity and a close working relationship, the trip
brings up issues for them which highlight cultural and personal differences
between them. They experience the stultifying, homophobic but at times
beautiful environment of Ireland quite differently. Niamh has a family,
an unhappy past, difficult relations with both her parents to whom she
is silent about her sexuality, and a limited kind of relationship with her
twin sister, Marion. Helen is an outsider experiencing another country,
different in social and cultural ways, and she is also on the edge of Niamh's
familial problems. The film shows the lovers filming at various seaside
locations, with scenes of this video footage being viewed by Niamh's parents,
and the two women socialising in a lesbian pub and a straight night-club
with Marion. The film gives a visible and affirmative image of a lesbian
relationship, including its moments of tension and a final lovemaking
scene. This comes about after Niamh and Helen have danced and kissed
together in the night-club, offending Marion's friends and revealing the
limits of her acceptance. The film ends with the couple returning to
London with the voice-over of the mother providing an ironic close: 'You
never know with Niamh, but I think they enjoyed themselves.' So while
Cullen's film present two lesbians dealing with the difficulties of their relationship, silences remain powerful and the outcome of Niamh's return visit
is problematic.

Paula Crickard's film *The Happy Gordons* (1995) is a half-hour documentary film that explores the dynamics of Irish emigration and
socio-political change in Ireland. Adopting the style and structure of
mainstream, broadcast documentary, the film features the stories of lesbians and gay men who have emigrated and who now reflect on their
reasons for leaving and the legal changes regarding homosexuality in
Ireland. In accordance with this approach, the actuality footage moves back
and forth from America to Ireland, from Dublin to Belfast, capturing the
atmosphere of celebration in 1993 and after. The articulation of a 'pink
wave' of emigrants in America produced a homophobic reaction among
the expatriate conservatives of the St Patrick's Day parade in New York.[70]
Scenes of protest are juxtaposed with the jubilant and liberating Gay Pride
marchers in Dublin and Belfast. With their own music providing the backing to the film, a relaxed and happy Carol Nelson and Maria Walshe, the
lesbian duo Zrazy, discuss the reasons why returning to Ireland is now
not just possible but productive:

> People who have to suffer just that little bit more to survive — not just to survive but thrive — end up having something really very powerful and valuable to contribute to the wider society that they come from.

Ger Philpott's brief but arresting and beautiful *Change* (1995, 12 minutes)[71] is more a filmed autobiographical presentation of dramatic episodes rather than a fully worked out narrative and none the less effective for this format. *Change* tells of the continuing pressures that taken-for-granted social and familial rituals exert on gay partnerships, particularly when one partner dies of AIDS. Through a tableaux of incidents, the film conveys the film-maker's sense of conviction and inner strength in the face of the deep-seated fears projected by straight Irish society. The relationship that he has had with his lover is not mourned, but remembered for its pleasures with quiet dignity.

Orla Walshe's *Bent Out of Shape* (1995, 25 minutes) employs a more mainstream screen social realism to present a narrative that shows how residual homophobia can still easily translate into verbal abuse and violent assaults on gay men. Danny, streetwise, in his twenties, takes a job in a suburban video shop that also sells under-the-counter hetero pornography to the housing-estate husbands of Northside Dublin. Danny befriends Stephen, a lonely boy who seeks refuge in hanging around the shop to avoid being bullied by a gang of his fellow-teenagers. In some deft and accurately observed sequences, Walshe establishes the rapport that builds up between the two. While they reshelve videos together, some fleeting point-of-view shots suggest Stephen's nascent gay sexuality, gazing at and brushing the muscles of Danny's arm. The gay man responsibly provides the shy boy, coming to terms with his adolescent needs, with friendship and support. However, one of the porno customers wrongly suspects that Danny is sexually preying on the boy. In a nearby pub a group of men decide one night that this suspicion is reason enough to beat up Danny. Stephen, strengthened by the support given to him, stands up to his own teenage tormentors, and the film ends with Stephen and the girl from the shop next door going to visit Danny in hospital.

A more explicit alliance between victims of male aggression is presented in Eve Morrison and Michael Ennis's film, *Summertime* (1995, 26 minutes). It captures the psychological nuances and outright violence of homophobic bullying experienced at school as well as the more subtle oppression of 'liberal' priests and parental ignorance. Different in that it is set in rural Ireland, the film presents Andrew as a rather ungainly, serious and introverted young man, on the point of doing his Leaving Certificate exams one summer. He is befriended by Victoria, whose London accent and cocky attitudes, belie the fact that she has an Irish mother and a violent English father, from whom both women have escaped back to Ireland. In an early version of the screenplay conceived as a feature-length film, Andrew and Victoria are expelled from school, go to London, and Andrew explores a gay relationship with an American before returning to come out to his parents. Financial and production limitations meant that this broader scope has been scaled down to a film for the RTÉ/BSE 'Short Cuts' scheme.[72] Even in its shortened version the film manages to convey the difficult and incomplete transition from passive victim to more open, assertive in-dividual. While he gains a degree of confidence from physically punching one of his bullies ('until he started punching me back'), the mental pro-cess of accepting himself is more difficult. Andrew makes a beginning by telling Victoria about falling in love with an American boy who taught him to swim one summer, but he cannot yet bring himself to confront his parents, although he knows they know he is gay. The film captures the emotional intricacies of coming out in Ireland but Ennis insists that

> It's not a polemic — but it is political . . . it brings up an awful lot of other things. Victoria's story is in many ways as important as Andrew's.[73]

What brings Victoria and Andrew together is a recognition of each other's emotional pain resulting from misogyny and homophobia. *Summertime* offers a critique of the spurious, conservative 'family values' that were pro-pagated so strongly in 1980s' Ireland by church and lay Catholic organisa-tions alike. Such values, which have conveniently overlooked marital breakdown, violence and sexual abuse within church and family, have been exposed in recent years. For gay teenagers these values represented a kind of mental oppression, especially in the rural Ireland like Ennis's home town, Prosperous, Co. Kildare. Yet Ennis does not crudely condemn all families: he presents Andrew's mother as loving and sympathetic, though ignorant of what her son is going through, and Victoria's mum is kind and capable as a single parent. Without being radically queer, *Summer-time* presents a confident, funny and, in the end, optimistic portrayal of a gay teenager in Ireland.

*   *   *

This survey of the most recent work in Irish gay and lesbian film in-itiatives suggests that the legislative changes of 1993 will provide the con-ditions for the 'release' of Ireland's inner exiles and maybe encourage some of its lesbian and gay emigrants to consider a return visit. But the limited opportunities of the Irish film industry, the socio-economic attractions of foreign capitals and a residual homophobic culture will ensure that gay and lesbian film-makers like Cullen, Keogh and Ennis may well continue to emigrate.

APPENDIX

Checklist of Films

The films discussed in the essay are listed chronologically and are based on creative Irish talent (screenplay, direction or production), though not necessarily with Irish financial backing.

DLCAD   Dún Laoghaire College of Art and Design Film School
LCP   London College of Printing
Muted Cupid are a gay and lesbian theatre group based in Dublin.

Screenwriter/ Director	Title	Date	Running Time	Company
Brennan/Black	*Pigs*	1984	78	Samson
McLaughlin	*She Must Be Seeing Things*	1987		
Deasy/Lee	*The Courier*	1988	86	City Vision
Comerford	*Reefer and the Model*	1988	105	Berber Films
Hayes	*Chaero*	1988	16	DLCAD
Rooke	*Undercurrents*	1990	28	Emdee/RTÉ
Keogh	*Appearances*	1991	unfinished	DLCAD
	Pink	1991	unfinished	DLCAD
	Don't Fight It, Feel It	1991	unfinished	DLCAD/Muted Cupid
Halpin	*What's Your Problem?*	1991	12	DLCAD
Smith	*The Pearl*	c. 1991	16	DLCAD
Flemming	*The Visit*	c. 1991	short	DLCAD
Keogh	*Sexy Revolution*	1992	18 unfinished	DLCAD
Jordan	*The Crying Game*	1992	120	Palace Pictures
McGrath	*Boys for Rent*	1993	16	DLCAD
Cullen	*Home You Go*	1993	12	LCP
	The Last Time	1993	12	LCP
	Silences	1995	30	LCP
Crickard	*The Happy Gordons*	1995	26	Lakmé Prods
Philpott	*Change*	1995	12	Caspar Films
Walshe	*Bent Out of Shape*	1995	28	Róisín Rua
Ennis/ Morrison	*Summertime*	1995	26	Storm Prods

Abbreviation

GCN   *Gay Community News*

Notes and References

1   Jonathan Dollimore, *Sexual Dissidence: Augustine to Wilde, Freud to Foucault*, Oxford University Press, 1991, p. 30.
2   Paul McGrath, Dáil debate on equality legislation, as quoted in *GCN*, July 1994.
3   Michael D. Higgins, 'The Work Aesthetic', interview in *Hot Press*, 8 Sept. 1993, p. 23.
4   *At Your Own Risk*, London: Vintage, 1993, p. 19.
5   Kevin Rockett, 'Culture, Industry and Irish Cinema' in John Hill and Martin McLoone (eds.), *Border Crossings*, Belfast: Institute of Irish Studies / British Film Institute, 1994, p. 130.
6   For a comparison of political and cultural developments in Ireland and Britain see my 'A Wilde Prophecy', *Sunday Tribune*, 19 Feb. 1995. Íde O'Carroll and Eoin Collins (eds.), *Lesbian and Gay Visions of Ireland: Towards the Twenty-first Century*, London: Cassell, 1995, presents a diverse and comprehensive range of documents, essays and interviews about developments in Ireland.
7   Richard Dyer, *The Matter af Images*, London: Routledge, 1993, p. 2.
8   Dollimore, op. cit., p. 52.
9   Mark Simpson, *Male Impersonators*, London: Cassell, 1994, p. 4. See also the kind of 'queer' readings of the Hollywood film product by Paul Burston, e.g. 'Cruising the Vampire' in *What are You Looking At? Queer Sex, Style and Cinema*, London: Cassell, 1995.
10 See the essays in Joseph Bristow and A. R. Wilson (eds.), *Activating Theory: Lesbian, Gay and Bisexual Politics*, London: Lawrence & Wishart, 1993.
11 Richard Dyer, *Gays on Film*, London: British Film Institute, 1977, p. 27.
12 P. Strick in a review of *The Courier* from unidentified photocopy source held at Irish Film Institute Library.
13 Richard Dyer, *Now You See It: Studies on Lesbian and Gay Film*, London: Routledge, 1990, p. 2.
14 *GCN*, Mar. 1990, p. 12.
15 Interview with author, March 1994.
16 *Irish Times*, 8 July 1988, n.p.
17 *Guardian*, 23 Nov. 1989.
18 Kevin Rockett, John Hill and Luke Gibbons, *Cinema and Ireland*, London: Routledge, 1988, p. 273.
19 Hill and McLoone, op. cit., p. 163.
20 Ibid., p. 163.
21 Comerford's original treatment contains details of Badger's Northern Irish, Presbyterian background which may not have fully emerged in the final script; see BFI Library Michrofiche holdings.
22 Interview with author, Mar. 1994.
23 *Film Ireland*, July/Aug. 1992, p. 13.
24 Interview with author, Mar. 1994.
25 Ibid.
26 As quoted in *GCN*, July 1990, p. 15.

27 D. Sherry, ibid.

28 Joseph Bristow, 'Being Gay: Politics, Identity, Pleasure', *New Formations*, no. 9 (winter 1989), p. 66.

29 *The Homosexual Challenge*, Dublin: Family Solidarity, 1990, p. 4. This is probably the best-informed, most carefully researched and cogently argued case against law reform of the period.

30 See Kieran Rose, *Diverse Communities: The Evolution of Lesbian and Gay Politics in Ireland*, Cork University Press, 1994.

31 Interview with author, Apr. 1994. Subsequent quotes are taken from interview notes.

32 This is a community-based group comprised predominantly, but by no means exclusively, of gay men and lesbians. The group has been established since 1991, presenting plays with special relevance to the Irish gay and lesbian community.

33 The author was unable to view either Halpin's or Flemming's films, but would like to acknowledge the help given by Ann O'Leary and Philip Davidson at DLCAD for the use of viewing facilities.

34 Michael Wilson, a graduate of NCAD, has produced a short video film dealing with male sexual abuse which has been shown in Berlin but the author has not been able to view this.

35 Quoted from the film festival programme listed in *GCN*, Oct. 1991.

36 'Sell Your Soul To See This', *GCN*, Apr. 1993, p. 16.

37 See *Sight and Sound*, Aug. 1992 (Special Supplement), pp 30-5, with articles by Ruby Rich and Derek Jarman discussing the origins and definitions of 'New Queer cinema' in America and Britain.

38 See Mark Simpson, 'A Crying Shame' in *Male Impersonators*, p. 165.

39 Sarah Edge, 'Representations of Women in *The Crying Game* (paper given at the 'Imagining Irelands' Conference, Dublin, Irish Film Institute, 30 Oct. 1993).

40 *Film Ireland*, no. 31 (Sept./Oct. 1992), p. 19.

41 Simpson, op. cit., pp 171-2. He is quoting part of Julie Wheelwright's review of the film *Opening the Borders* in *New Statesman and Society*, 30 Oct. 1992, p. 35.

42 *What's On*, 28 Oct. 1992, p. 18.

43 *Daily Telegraph*, 19 Feb. 1993, p. 13.

44 *Evening Press*, 30 Oct. 1992.

45 *Film Ireland*, no. 34 (Apr./May 1993), p. 20.

46 As quoted in Richard Kearney, 'Migrant Minds', in *idem* (ed.), *Across the Frontiers*, Dublin: Wolfhound, 1988, p. 199.

47 Wheelwright, op. cit., p. 35.

48 Letter to the author, 8 Apr. 1994.

49 *The Sun*, 20 Oct. 1993, pp 8-9.

50 'Invisible Comrades: Gays and Lesbians in the Struggle', *An Glór Gafa / The Captive Voice*, iii, no. 3 (winter 1991), pp 21-2.

51 Dara MacNeill, 'A Rea of Hope?', *An Phoblacht / Republican News*, 5 Nov. 1992.

52 The motion passed at the 1994 Ard-Fheis was 'That Sinn Féin give support to gay/lesbian comrades in their decision to 'come out', Sinn Féin *Political Report*, Dublin, 1994, p. 7. My thanks to Mícheál Mac Donncha for supplying the information.

53 *The Crying Game*, London: Vintage, 1993, p. viii.

54 *Film Ireland*, no. 32 (Apr./May 1993), p. 20.

55   *The Crying Game*, p. viii.
56   Ibid., p. 29.
57   J. Romney, in *Sight and Sound*, Nov. 1992, p. 40.
58   See 'The Politics of Queer', *Gay Times* (London: Millivres), May 1992, pp 20-9; Cherry Smyth, *Lesbians Talk Queer Notions*, London, Scarlet Press, 1992, and the essays in Bristow and Wilson, op. cit.
59   Followers of British TV soaps will have noted the lesbian plots of Brookside, Eastenders and Emmerdale Farm in 1995. In comparison, see Deborah Ballard, 'Mediawatch', *GCN*, Feb. 1995, p. 11, on Eoghan's coming out in RTÉ's *Fair City*.
60   Suri Krishnamma's film of Barry Devlin's screenplay *A Man of No Importance* (100 minutes, 1994) perhaps exemplifies this tendency. Set in Dublin in 1963, it concerns a middle-aged gay bus conductor (Alfie) who believes that he is Oscar Wilde. As Geoffrey McNab points out 'rather than acknowledge that Alfie is a victim of a prejudiced, repressive society, it persists in portraying its little corner of 60s' Dublin as a picture-postcard community, full of loveable eccentrics' (*Sight and Sound*, May 1995, p. 50).
61   *GCN*, Nov. 1993.
62   'Right to Reply', *GCN*, Dec. 1993/Jan. 1994, p. 3.
63   Ibid.
64   Viewing copy held at IFI Dublin. All quotes transcribed from this VHS copy.
65   Interview with author, London, Apr. 1994.
66   Richard Dyer, 'Coming Out as Going In: The Image of the Homosexual as a Sad Young Man', *The Matter of Images*, London: Routledge, 1993, pp 73-91.
67   Mick Wilson, *Film Ireland*, no. 40 (Apr./May 1994) p. 27.
68   Liam McGrath has followed up *Boys* with a documentary on the subject of male rape, *Things in My Head* (40 minutes, 1995), which was released after this essay was completed.
69   Thanks to Collette Cullen for supplying videos, synopses and review material of her work.
70   See Anne Maguire 'The Accidental Immigrant' in O'Carroll and Collins, op. cit., pp 199-211.
71   See also Philpott's book, *Deep End* (Dublin: Poolbeg, 1995).
72   Telephone interview with Hilary McLoughlin, January 1996. Original typescript of screenplay supplied by Michael Ennis.
73   Interviews with Ennis, November 1993 and April 1994.

Acknowledgements

I would like to thank all those people who gave me their time in the research for this essay, but in particualr the director/screenwriter interviewees, those who provided stills, Liam and Sunniva at the Irish Film Archive, the staff of the *Gay Community News* archive, and Éibhear Walshe for his helpful editorial comments.

Index